Flying Model Collectibles and Accessories

James C. Johnson

Schiffer Publishing Ltd®

4880 Lower Valley Road, Atglen, PA 19310 USA

Dedication

To Bill Darkow, the greatest friend and mentor a modeler could ever have.

Cover: Created by Harold Stevenson for the cover of *Flying Models*, April 1955. The engines on the cover are TWA.40 RC and a 1945 OK Furin 1.12. The engine on the spine is the 1947 Leja .994.

Library of Congress Card Number: 2003113375

Designed by Mark David Bowyer
Type set in Benguait Bk BT/Souvenir Lt BT

ISBN: 0-7643-1979-5
Printed in China
1 2 3 4

Published by Schiffer Publishing Ltd.
4880 Lower Valley Road
Atglen, PA 19310
Phone: (610) 593-1777; Fax: (610) 593-2002
E-mail: Info@schifferbooks.com

For the largest selection of fine reference books on this and related subjects, please visit our web site at
www.schifferbooks.com
We are always looking for people to write books on new and related subjects. If you have an idea for a book please contact us at the above address.

This book may be purchased from the publisher.
Include $3.95 for shipping.
Please try your bookstore first.
You may write for a free catalog.

In Europe, Schiffer books are distributed by
Bushwood Books
6 Marksbury Ave.
Kew Gardens
Surrey TW9 4JF England
Phone: 44 (0) 20 8392-8585; Fax: 44 (0) 20 8392-9876
E-mail: info@bushwoodbooks.co.uk
Free postage in the U.K., Europe; air mail at cost.

Contents

In Appreciation

A heartfelt thank you to all who helped and contributed to this journey. To my wife Janet Blair: for love, support, editing, and typing, and most of all letting me be myself. To Bill and Caroline Darkow: for friendship, support, contributions, editing, and use of your shop to photograph over 600 pictures. To Mike Hazel: for sharing your marvelous collection of control line speed kits and your friendship. To Bob and Peggy Parker: for your valued friendship and making me part of your family while shooting pictures of your fantastic collection of aeromodeling memorabilia. To Injae Chung Ph.D. for sending pictures of your collection all the way from South Korea. To Herman Chairez: for your friendship, encouragement, and sharing part of your growing collection. To John Brown: for sending a copy of eighteen years of your life, *Model Aviation Books*. To Mike Baker: who had the task of listing his father's lifetime accumulation of model airplane items on eBay. He shared a little history of the items belonging to the Robert Baker estate; some are included in this book. To Bob Maschi: for sharing the Ralph Costlow scrapbook with the rest of the world; you probably thought you would never get it back. To Delores Nelson: for proof reading the text. To Jim Alaback, Gil Coughlin, Tim Dannels, Perry Eichor, John Hall, David Lloyd-Jones, Rich LaGrange, Tom Lay, Morris Leventhal, Curtiss Mattikow, Bill Schmidt, Bob Watts and Michael Smith, curator of the National Model Aviation Museum: for all your collective information and support. To DeAnna Lee: for saving Red Costlow's papers, letters, photographs, and information on his life from the trash. To Dellora "Birdie" Burdorf: for sharing the memories of her fifty-five year relationship with Red Costlow. To Bob Christ: for tracking down information on Red Costlow all over Phoniex, Arizona. To Gary Oakins for tracking down Red Costlow's flying buddies from the 1947 Minneapolis Model Aero Club. To Jack Hudspeth, Fred Roberts and Jack Ritner for sharing their memories of the 1950 International Model Plane Contest. To Don's Camera, Olympia, Washington: for supplies, processing, and advice. To all the Control Line Stunt fliers in British Columbia, the Pacific Northwest, and PAMPA: for providing the joy that makes model aviation a meaningful, enjoyable, and worthwhile hobby and sport. To my mother and father Arnold and Janet Johnson: for their love and support of my modeling activities when I was growing up. To Peter Schiffer and his staff for giving me the opportunity to bring my love of model aviation to the world through this book. This book is the fruit of all those who have cared about model airplanes in one-way or another; I couldn't have done it without you.

Disclaimer and Trademarks

Foreword
What is a Flying Model Collectible?

In the course of this journey, what to include in this group of collectibles grew quickly. Soon it became apparent several books could be written on the subject, as well as general and detailed histories of individual manufacturers. "If it flies or is related to flying models" is the selection criteria and starting point for the items presented this book. Decisions were painfully made to omit entire categories of flying model collectibles in this first publication.

The items included in *Flying Model Collectibles* are but the proverbial "tip of the iceberg." In 1981, John Brown of Santa Ana, California, started to compile a list of books on model aviation in the English language. When he reached 250 titles, he thought he was close to finishing his research. Eighteen years later, his volume, *Model Aviation Books*, 2000 edition, was published, recording nearly 1,800 works. This text is a sample of the vastness encountered while examining model airplane collectibles. There are many collectors whose collections merit their own volumes. Bob Parker of Renton, Washington, has a collection of model airplane kits that is an amazing trip through history. Gil Coughlin of Tacoma, Washington, has displayed a small portion of his marvelous collection at the Northwest Model Expo in Puyallup, Washington and most recently at the International Modeler Show in Pasadena, California.

A few items not making it into this book are Ready to Fly (RTF) models, solid wood scale models, helicopters, Jetex™, rockets, and hovercraft, as well as Jimmie Allen items, Jack Armstrong, and paper gliders. History of these items dictates they are part of this vast category of collectibles. Especially the plastic RTFs made by Cox, Keilkraft, Comet, Aurora, Testors, Gilbert, and Wen-Mac. Stanzel's battery powered planes for kids deserve mention. It is only because of space considerations that these items are not featured in this book.

Jetex™ models and accessories were the wonderment of all boys from 1950s to the early 1960s and still have a following today. Davis Model Products has a new and greatly improved system currently on the market. Ready to fly models are being collected enthusiastically and are commanding higher prices than ever. It is only because of space considerations that these items are not featured in this book.

The desire to help collectors understand the current market was the most logical approach to this first volume. My aim is to direct both new collectors and those with growing collections to the multitude of items available in collecting field. *Flying Model Collectibles* is a guide to the directions in which collectors can go, and do so for a long time.

Flying model collectors will find engines, model kits, books, magazines, awards, AMA items, memorabilia, contest items, photos, and accessories in this volume. I have tried to not take away from other collectible books on the subject already on the market. Most notable is *Anderson's Blue Book. Flying Model Collectibles* brings us into the 21st century; the future regarding these collectibles is wide open. Many items are now finding their way into museums and will continue to be collected for the sake of history, value, and most of all, fun. ENJOY!

Model Aviation Bibliography, John J. Brown, 2000, 160 pages. *Courtesy of John Brown.*

Introduction

My intention for writing this book is to give an overview of the vast number of flying model collectibles being offered in today's market. I know of no other book available which features such a wide-range of objects produced and enjoyed by more than three generations of modelers. There have been so many collectibles produced over the past seventy-five years that it would be impossible to include them all in this volume.

Notes on Pricing

Pricing is the hardest part of putting together a collector book. I have only my own experience to go on, obtained through buying, selling, traveling to antique and collectible shows, and researching the subject over the past thirty-five years. No one can know everything. Pricing can resemble riding the stock market! Condition and rarity are crucial in determining value, but current desirability also plays a major role. Sotheby's auctioneers use nine guideposts for assessing value of fine art. *The Best of Everything: The Insider's Guide to Collecting—For Every Taste and Budget*, by John Marion with Christopher Andersen, highlights these guideposts. It is an excellent resource for anyone wanting to know how to assess value. One example of changing price trends occurred after the World Trade Center tragedy on September 11, 2001. Our nation demonstrated unity by rallying around the American flag, both figuratively and literally. In response, collectibles bearing patriotic themes or the American flag rose in value. A July, 1942 copy of *Aviation* magazine with the caption "United We Stand" and American flag on the cover sold on eBay for $960 in early 2003.

There are three types of prices used in this book. The first is a single price; this is the actual price paid. The second pricing method, using a range of prices, is for items where condition plays an important role in determining what an object is worth. The third pricing method is from actual eBay auctions, what was actually paid. The items in the section "Notable eBay Auctions" are the best examples listed of rare and hard to find collectibles from July 2002 to June 2003.

As with almost every antique and collectible book, the prices determined are a guide. The publisher and I are not responsible for price differences in this book and what occurs in the real world of collectibles. It is up to collectors to keep abreast of the current market prices and trends occurring in their favorite areas of collecting. Knowledge keeps the market reasonable, even when all the rules are swept out the door. There are always collectors willing to pay many times what something is worth. This will tip the balance, but once those collectors have that item prices seem to settle down. Another thing to remember, demand is stimulated by the items that are currently on the market. Rare and hard to find items only have value if some one wants them.

Flying Model Collectibles can be used as a reference in determining relative value. Current market value is determined in the real marketplace, antique shows, swap meets, collector sales, club meetings, estate sales, garage sales, and of course, auctions, both on- and off-line. Most of all, this book is meant to complement the fun and excitement that comes from building a collection.

Enjoying your collection is by far the most important goal to remember; it will reflect your unique personality and character. Your collection has grown through love, time, energy, and money. Some of the best moments in a collector's life are the joy of sharing their collection with other like-minded collectors.

The future of model airplanes is ever changing. The hobby has grown from models propelled by strands of rubber or spark and diesel engines to electric and turbine-powered planes. What was once made of balsa, tissue, and dope is now built with carbon fiber, foam, super glue, and plastics. Who knows what the future holds? Yet our collections will remain, as long as we are enjoying them. As the world changes, the yearning for our roots grows stronger, and what has fallen out of fashion once again becomes the trend. Thus, the collecting cycle begins again, by tucking that special engine or kit away for a future project that never seems to materialize. The most prized collectibles are those items that were of good quality, popular, and successful when they were marketed. The kits, engines, planes, and accessories that are desired today will be the best collectibles of the future.

The Collector and the Collection

For all modelers, the common justification is that our acquired engines, kits, and plans, will be used for **that next project.** Thirty years seems to pass quickly and one morning you wake up and realize you will probably not live long enough to build all the planes your ambitious mind has planned. Thus, the common justification steps in and creates a new role in your life, from active modeler to **collector**, meaning that we can now continue our buying, trading, sharing, and talking about the things we have rat-holed away, as long as the budget holds up! Modelers are notorious penny-pinchers but think nothing of buying that wanted engine or kit when the urge strikes.

Now that you are a "certified collector" (even your wife may think you are "certified"), what will you do with your accumulation? Some collectors use everything they buy to replicate history. Some become nostalgic collectors, surrounding themselves with memories of their youth; others go on to amass only engines, or model kits and memorabilia. There are super collectors and the value of their collections can grow into thousands, even hundreds of thousands of dollars. The last type of collector is really a collectibles dealer who most likely has a fine collection gleaned from the best of what he receives to sell.

Maintaining and displaying what you have collected can sometimes be overwhelming. I don't want to recommend any one way to clean engines, but for a long time I didn't really know how to do it properly. Forty years ago, Joe Wagner was asked how he cleaned his engines. He used rubber cement thinner, acetone, AeroGloss thinner, and paint remover; things have come a long way since then. Collector John Hall says he uses Castrol™ Super Clean Degreaser in the purple squirt bottle. I have used this and found it quite good. It removes varnish and built up gunk readily with the use of a stiff toothbrush. He recommends that this be washed off with warm water, then dry the engine with a heat gun. Do not spray this on and leave it for more than 30 minutes. If needed, repeat the process. **Do not use this product on painted surfaces or anodized metal**. Avoid using WD-40™ to lubricate your engines as it contains water and will cause rust over time on the internal parts of the engines.

Another collector, Bob Watts, related that he cleans his engines with an ultrasonic cleaner using a special non-ammoniated cleaner. He removes baked on carbon stains from the fins and head with a product called Aircraft Remover™, available at Auto Zone stores. **This product will also damage painted surfaces but not anodized surfaces.** Two other commercial products currently advertised in modeling magazines are Demon-Clean™ and Z-Best™. Z-Best™ should be used to clean a few engines at a time, as it seems to dry up once it has been opened. All of these products should be handled with rubber gloves and eye protection is necessary.

The ultimate in engine restoration information can be found at www.classicmodelengines/homestead.com. This site takes the potential restorer through the entire process required to bring an old engine back to life. Many engines are acquired in used condition yet remain great runners and collector items. An engine that has been cared for can last for years. The Johnson .35 Combat Special listed in the book is an engine I have owned for thirty-five years and is still a fine runner. The website shows how to lovingly restore a Fox .35 stunt engine, a great engine on which to do a first time restoration. Their cleaning method involves boiling the parts in a mixture of water and automatic dishwasher detergent for a half hour. Another method developed in the past couple of years uses a crock-pot and automobile anti-freeze to remove the heavy build up of baked on castor oil that occurs through normal engine use. An excellent book for just about every modeler and collector is *All About Engines*, by Harry Higley. It details the basics of maintenance and minor repair for many older engines. Most importantly, ask for help before risking damage to your collectibles. Many engines have been ruined for lack of knowledge.

Protecting your collectibles from the elements is of utmost importance. Keeping all your collectibles in a dry place is paramount to maintaining their condition. Bright sunlight will fade just about anything in just a couple of days, so keep your items away from it. Dust is another problem; many collectors use display cases with glass doors and this solves most of the dust problem. Old publications were often printed on cheap, highly acidic paper. They should be handled with care then stored in a dry cool place, preferably in acid-free clear protectors, then in archival storage boxes. The cost of these few items will be a small investment towards your peace of mind account. While you're ordering, treat yourself to a couple of pairs of white cotton gloves to use while handling photos, slides, plans, magazines, old books, all paper items, painted items and anything you want to be careful with. **You will be amazed at the difference they make.** Heat can be a problem, as it will dry items out, causing them to become brittle. Plastic covers for books and magazines are recommended for protection and storage. Collection conservation supplies may be bought on-line, through catalogs, and at larger antique shows. Bookstores can provide Mylar to protect books with nice dust jackets. Many flying model collectors may think this is overkill, but preventing damage is always easier than undoing it. Sometimes there *is* no undoing damage and the piece is ruined.

Insurance and appraisals are recommended for those whose collection has grown to over a couple thousand dollars. Use a digital camera and store images on a disk in another location (why not swap with a modeler buddy?). This is essential for insurance purposes or in case of fire, theft, and all those other things we would rather not think about. This issue is often not addressed until something terrible happens. If your treasures are stolen, seek help from your fellow collectors and use the Internet to spread the word among other collectors to recover items. Recently, noted modeler, collector, and manufacturer of BY&O props, Clarence Bull, passed away and his large collection of engines was stolen. Watchful modelers were responsible for the recovery of most of the engines and the arrest of the suspects. An *ongoing* inventory of your collection is one of the most important things you can do for your collection. Customized computer programs are now available to list item descriptions, prices, condition, and history of your purchases, or you can design your own database.

If you own a home or property and have not made a will, I recommend you do it now. You cannot take it with you and all that you do now will help your loved ones or friends keep order when the inevitable occurs. This book can be used as a guide to values, but prices fluctuate quickly. Providing written notes detailing your desires about the disposition of your collection will help everyone, and give you some peace of mind while you use and enjoy your collection. I have personally told my wife to get help from a couple of modeling friends. If you have something another collector wants, write it down and give them first chance to obtain it. Our fine friendships created though modeling and collecting can continue for years after our passing. Properly passing your collection on to those who will appreciate the time, money, and love invested, along with the love and enjoyment you received can be one of the greatest gifts of your life.

The August 2003 issue of *Model Aviation*, Dennis Norman wrote an excellent article titled "Our Stuff" dealing with the preparation for the inescapable fact of life. This article is the first I have read on disposing of the life-long accumulation of modeling supplies and mementos. It gives some good information for modelers, wives, friends, and family members. The best advice is to go slow and be careful if you are an executor or designated to handle the disposition. My dad, who has always given me good advice, once told me, "You will find out who your true friends are when someone dies." Most libraries carry *Model Aviation* or you can get this issue from any life-long member of the Academy of Model Aeronautics. (Dennis O. Norman, *Model Aviation*, August 2003, 83-86).

Collections seem to take on a life of their own. When Steve McQueen died of a rare form of lung cancer November 7, 1980, he had a great collection of over 130 antique motorcycles. This collection never made it into the museum he was planning.

Instead, it was split up and auctioned in Las Vegas, Nevada. New owners of the motorcycles are proud to say they own a bike once owned by Steve McQueen even though the museum plans were abandoned. Every collector has something that belonged to someone else that keeps the memory of the previous owner alive, sometimes for years to come.

Things to Remember

If you are just starting out, it is easy to get carried away! Collect the things you love, in the best possible quality, and you will never regret a purchase. It is also easy to begin collecting inexpensively. There are so many affordable collectibles, and the category of things related to flying models is so vast, it will not take long to accumulate a nice collection.

Select the direction you would like your collection to take. You may concentrate on just engines, and then decide to collect one of each from a specific manufacturer. Your collection will be a reflection of yourself.

Becoming a collector means you will be constantly searching for items, researching the subject, gaining knowledge from other collectors and dealers. Expanding your knowledge of the immense assortment of flying model collectibles will increase the enjoyment of collecting. As you come across unique collectible items, your interests may shift, taking your collection into new directions. If you see something you have been searching for, buy it. Do not let price determine the direction of your collection. Sometimes a few extra dollars on a much-desired item is well worth it. Bitter disappointment awaits the collector who hesitates on a special item, returning to a booth to find the item sold and the dealer gloating about the sale to boot! Many of you know what I mean, having passed on something you thought was over priced at the time and sorely regretting it down the road.

Enjoyment of your collection should be the primary force that drives you to be a collector. Investment buying can sometimes destroy the joy that got you started in the first place. Most of all, share your collection. After all, collecting is about people and history, not merely acquisition.

A Brief History of Model Aviation

"There is no such thing as progress if we don't know where we came from. Progress begins with that remembering and the rememberings of others gone, but not forgotten."
—*Bill Winter, 1998.*

The year 2003 marks the 100th Anniversary of the Wright Brothers' December 17, 1903, historic flight at Kitty Hawk, North Carolina. At that time, model aviation was still in its infancy, but closely followed the real world of aviation. Most early modeling efforts were done in the name of science. Without these early modeling efforts, it is doubtful the successes of full-scale airplanes would have been possible. Modeling has been the testing ground for all aircraft flying today.

Between 1799 and 1809 Sir George Cayley, father of British aeronautics, advanced "heavier than air" machines with the use of models. In 1809, his classic paper on Aerial Navigation became a foundation for all modern day aerodynamics. In 1848, William S. Henson and John Stringfellow achieved the first engine-powered flight with a small steam engine. The longest flight lasted a few seconds and went a distance of 120 feet. In 1871, Alphonse Penaud began selling rubber powered ready to fly models; in all, several hundred were sold. A similar toy airplane was the inspiration for the Wright brothers' further investigation of flight. For more than fifty years, rubber strands would become the primary power source for model airplanes. (Vic Smeed, *The Encyclopedia of Model Aircraft,* 9-12)

Model airplane clubs began forming around 1910; one of the first was the New York Model Aero Club. The club grew under the direction of Edward Durant. Many of its first members went on to distinguished careers in full-scale aviation. The first real book published in the United States on model aviation was *Boy's Book of Model Airplanes* in 1910 by Francis A. Collins. The Long Island Aero Model Club formed in 1911 along with the Bay Ridge Model Aero Club of Brooklyn. This was the beginning of friendly competitions. (Frank Anderson, *The Golden Age of Model Airplanes,* Vol. 1, 162-171).

On May 21, 1927, Charles Lindberg captured the hearts and minds of the whole world. This historic aviation milestone, a solo crossing of the Atlantic Ocean, changed model aviation and the world forever. Lindberg's remarkable epic flight sparked the imagination of almost every boy across the country. The model airplane became an extension of the dream of real flight. This single event gave rise to what was to become one of the most wholesome and engaging hobbies to envelop American youth. So great was its influence, many men of wealth and knowledge began to support this new pastime. It was even claimed that building and flying airplanes could end juvenile delinquency and crime.

Within a couple of years, hobby suppliers sprang up to fill the needs of over a million new modelers. Modeling supplies could be purchased in the bigger cities across America as larger department stores gave counter space to retailers. In 1929, magazines solely dedicated to model aviation began being published. Noteworthy were *Air Trails, Flying Aces,* and *Universal Model Airplane News. The American Boy* magazine published a model airplane designed by Merrill Hamburg called the "Baby R.O.G." in October 1927. The Airplane Model League of America (AMLA) was formed in September 1927, guided by founder William B. Stout. This would lead to the first National contest sponsored by the Playgrounds and Recreation Association for boys under the age of twenty-one. (Frank Anderson, *The Golden Age of Model Airplanes,* Vol. 1, 162-171) Frank Zaic has collected all the model material from *The American Boy* magazine from September 1928 to August 1934 and combined it in his book *Model Airplanes and The American Boy.* This collection of articles gives an excellent account of early model airplane history.

In just a few years, large clubs and contests with the support of business, civic, and youth organizations brought literally hundreds of thousands of people into this wonderful hobby. Hearst Corporation's Junior Birdman gained over 400,000 members in a short span of time. The Jimmie Allen Club and the Flying Aces Club became prominent among young model builders. This beginning became a rite of passage to equal that of baseball, lasting the next thirty-five years.

The industry took another huge leap with the introduction of the first mass-marketed model gas engine, the Brown Junior. William "Bill" Brown developed the Brown Junior in 1930 while he was attending high school! He passed away on January 8, 2003 at the age of 91. His close friend, Maxwell Bassett, designed a model plane named "The Miss Philadelphia III" and used one of the early Brown Junior engines for power. The plane was entered in the 1933 National Championship Model Plane Meet held on Long Island, New York. The model remained aloft for a record twenty-eight minutes. This model powered by Bill Brown's Brown Junior engine went on to sweep the entire field of competition. The domination of rubber powered model airplanes had come to an end. This single event in model aviation history revolutionized almost every aspect of the sport and hobby.

Soon after the miniature gas engine gained popularity, controversy would unite a nation of new modelers that had now grown to over two million. In 1937, Connecticut and Massachusetts became the first states to ban the flying of gas engine model airplanes. The threat of a nationwide ban by the U.S. Department of Commerce was the primary reason for the formation of a new modeling body that eventually developed into the Academy of Model Aeronautics. The national governing body for full-scale aviation, the National Aeronautics Association, stepped in and its influence would change the government's plans. The Junior Division of the NAA became the unifying body for modeling throughout the nation. New safety rules were proposed and presented to the Commerce Department and a statement was issued "which not only refused to ban gas model flying, but encouraged it." The new organization was called the NAA Academy of Model Aeronautics, Gas Model Section with Willis C. Brown serving as the first president. (George Wells, *Model Airplane News*, December 1963, 14-15, 34, 37-38).

Radio Controlled model aircraft debuted at the 1937 nationals when six models were entered. First place was awarded to Chester Lanzo. His aircraft was the only one to fly. Just two years later, at the 1939 nationals, twins Walt and Bill Good astounded the modeling world with a successful flight that included a figure eight and a landing at the feet of the controller. World War II began shortly thereafter and many of those who were involved in radio control were recruited to use their knowledge in the war effort. Hollywood movie star and early Radio Control pioneer, Reginald Denny, founded the Radioplane Company in 1939. Between 1941 and 1945, the company produced 14,891 target drones powered by thousands of engines made by Walter Righter and radio gear designed by Kenneth Case. In 1952, the company became the Radioplane Division of Northrop Aircraft, Inc. It would be ten years before a larger body of modelers would enjoy radio-controlled aircraft. (Hugh Maxwell, *Model Aviation,* July 1992, 33-36).

Naturally, during World War II, modeling took a back seat to the war effort. Modeling supplies were rationed – balsa, gas, rubber, and even paper (the lifeblood of the builder) were scarce and expensive. Innovative modelers found substitute materials, as did manufacturers. The national contest was cancelled in 1942 and would not resume until 1946. Two major events happened in modeling during this time. The "lowly" glider became a favorite modeling project and control line flying started to be enjoyed because of gas rationing. To obtain model fuel, flyers needed to obtain non-highway gas rationing coupons from the local rationing board. (Vic Smeed, *Model Flying - The first 50 Years*, 65).

Neville "Jim" Walker revolutionized model flying when he patented the "Ureely" and "U-Control" system in 1940. Joseph and Victor Stanzel gave Walker a run for his money by marketing the first control line kit, the "Tiger Shark" in January 1940. All were tenacious and tireless promoters of their products. Oba St. Clair, another true pioneer, also devised a control system similar to that of Walker's.

A lawsuit was filed in September 1953 by Jim Walker against L. M. Cox Manufacturing for patent infringement of his "Ureely" and "U-Control" system and went to trial in 1955. The trial settled once and for all the question of who was the first inventor of the bell-crank, the mechanism used in "U-Control." Based on testimony by Oba St. Clair that he created the bell-crank system, L.M. Cox Manufacturing won the lawsuit. This control mechanism is still used today. (Charles Mackey, *Pioneers of Control Line Flying,* 25-29).

The 1946 Nationals brought the spotlight back on model aviation. It started what is now called the "classic era of model aviation," and many older modelers still active today were part of this colorful revival. America's second largest paper, the *New York Daily Mirror*, Plymouth Dealers Association, Convair Aviation, Pan American World Airways and other organizations sponsored large meets, which drew crowds of over 100,000 people! Nearly every city in America had model airplane clubs. Control line and free flight models occupied every piece of land a boy thought he could fly.

Even though radio controlled planes had been around for several years, they entered mainstream modeling when the first commercially produced early radio sets hit the market around 1947. Before this, the modelers built their own radios and many new sets were offered in "kit" form. Vintage equipment was expensive and dependability was a far cry from what we enjoy today! Still, the dream of radio controlled model aviation made huge strides. Many wonderful designs were created and kitted to accommodate this growing market.

Around 1960, aeromodeling entered the modern era. For some of us, it is hard to believe more than 40 years have now passed. With the advent of reliable proportional radio controlled equipment, new engines and kit designs emerged rapidly. Equipment was still rather expensive and out of reach for most modelers. Competition from Japan in the electronics market would soon drop the costs, so all who wanted to enjoy the thrills of radio control could do so. By the early 1970s "full house" radios could be purchased for around $300. Radio control sets for today's modeler start at about $150 and are far superior, with servo reversing, memories, and longer user time. It is amazing what is offered on the current market.

Today, nostalgia abounds in the world of model aviation. With the creation of the Model Engine Collectors Association by Joe Wagner in 1959, engines have remained a very popular collectible. Steve Remington of Collect Air in Santa Barbara, California calls them "works of art and still a good value in today's collectible market." The Society of Antique Modelers (SAM) was founded about 1963 and enjoys a large following of dedicated builders and flyers. The preservation of early model airplane designs is strongly encouraged throughout the aeromodeling community. SAM hosts many local contests and an annual national contest. *Flying Models* magazine's long time writer, builder, flyer, and historian, Jim Alaback founded the organization called Kits and Plans Antiquitous (KAPA) in 1993. Kits remain a good value. Most modelers collect to build, but early kits in excellent condition are getting harder to come by. These are being saved and displayed in growing model airplane collections.

I believe the invention of the airplane is the single most important event to impact world history. It has changed every aspect of our lives. It has taken us into the world of space exploration, telecommunications, weather forecasting, mass transportation, national defense, food production and distribution, an aid in understanding our environment, medical transport, and search and rescue. Aviation has connected the world.

The advancement of general aviation coexists with model aviation. Even Colonel Charles Lindberg and Admiral Richard Byrd recognized in 1927 "that modelers of today would be the flyers and engineers of tomorrow." (Mathiews, *High Flight,* 16). It is hard to believe all this has happened to us in the course of one hundred years. Most amazing is the fact that it all started when Milton Wright bought a toy helicopter for his sons to play with, sparking the imagination of his two young boys, Wilbur and Orville Wright.

Chapter 1
Model Airplane Engines

Model airplane engines have long been the most favorite collector item of all flying model collectibles. Beginning in 1934, the first mass produced model airplane engine, the Brown Junior, was released to a nation of new modelers. During the next thirty years, more than four hundred U.S. model engine manufactures would create millions of these small engineering marvels. In the late 1940s, there is mention of "future collector engines" in *Model Airplane News.* The 1950s would see collectors begin to build collections in earnest. Ray Arden may have brought this about with the invention and introduction of the glow plug in 1946. The Drone Diesel was also successfully marketed in 1947-1948 by famed modeler Leon Shulman. The ignition engine quickly became outdated. Modelers have always wanted the latest equipment and glow engines eliminated many of the weak points associated with starting ignition engines.

Model airplane engines produced before the Brown Junior were heavy and not practical for modeling. The use of balsa wood for building hadn't yet been discovered. The British Stanger 3.7 cubic inch Vee-Twin of 1913 was used on a model in 1914 setting an endurance record that stood for eighteen years.

In 1932, William E. Atwood made a flight of over twenty-six minutes using a prototype of his famous "Baby Cyclone." This engine was almost half the size of the Brown engine and commercial manufacture began at the end of 1935. Between 1935-1939, it is estimated that one hundred thousand Browns and Cyclones were produced. Bill Brown and Bill Atwood's successes were the inspiration for all ignition engines produced in the 1930s. (Peter Chinn, *Model Airplane News,* August 1974, 14-16, 50). Noted engine designers are Mel Anderson, Dan Bunch, Walter Hurleman, Irwin Ohlsson, Dan Calkin, Francis Tlush, and Ben Shereshaw. The engines of the thirties are considered by many to be artistic engineering marvels although only a few manufactures would survive the war years.

During 1949, another advancement began that would bring millions of new modelers into the hobby, the small glow plug engine. The Anderson .045 Baby Spitfire, .049 Atwood Wasp, K & B Infant .020, McCoy "9," OK Cubs in .049, .074, and .099 configurations were the first small engines marketed and were aimed at the budding modeler wanting his first gas engine. These engines were revolutionary as they changed the hobby to one of affordability for every kid wanting to be a part of this great national pastime. Another result of small engine development was hundreds of new kits were designed, especially for miniature engines and aimed at youthful modelers.

The 1950s brought on a proliferation of glow engine designs. This was truly the golden age of model aviation. Modelers had much to choose from and competition among manufacturers became quite evident, particularly the names selected for these new engines. The highly competitive market would soon create several manufacturing giants that would introduce new flyers to their first venture into the wonderful world of model airplanes. Most notable were L. M. Cox, Fox, K & B, OK Cub, and McCoy. Of these, three remain today, L. M. Cox Manufacturing Company, Fox Manufacturing Company, and K & B. Fox is the only one remaining in the hands of its founders. These fine companies produced millions of engines for the next thirty years.

The Fox Manufacturing Company, led by Duke Fox, set the standard in stunt engines with the Fox 35 Stunt in 1948. This engine remains today, fifty-five years after its introduction, virtually unchanged from the 1948 original.

L. M. Cox started manufacturing engines for the tethered race cars craze in 1949. In 1952, Roy Cox entered the model airplane engine market with the Space Bug. Cox went on to become the king of small engine manufacturers with the Strato Bug .049 (1955) and other engines such as the Thermal Hopper (1953), Baby Bee (1955), Golden Bee (1958), Space Hopper (1959), Black Widow in the 1970s, along with their remarkable Tee Dee and Medallion engines. (Frank Anderson, *Anderson's Blue Book 2002*, section 2, 3-5). Their engines would introduce thousands of boys to the world of gas powered model aviation.

K & B introduced their infant .020 and .035 engines along with the Torpedo Green Head engines and these were remarkably successful.

McCoy engines of the late 1940s and early 1950s were high powered and used to set world records in Control Line Speed. They introduced their inexpensive "Red Head" line of engines in 1957-58; these engines became the first large engines many modelers would own. Herkimer Tool & Model Works, founded in 1938, produced OK engines. Their line of engines remained popular among modelers and this success led them into the small engine market in 1949. With an engine called the Cub produced in three displacements, .049, .074, and .099, thousands of kids flew their first airplanes using this engine. Millions were made over the next fifteen years. Sadly, they went out of business around 1964.

Today's model engine collectors are worldwide. Much has been written on engines produced in the United States, but not much on foreign engines. Importation of Japanese products in the mid-1950s affected every aspect of American consumerism. Model engines started to trickle into mainstream modeling during this period. Japanese engines became popular during the Korean and Viet Nam war years as returning servicemen's U.S. dollars could be stretched against the Japanese Yen. Ogawa Model Manufacturing, "O.S." is the oldest established producer of Japanese model engines, founded in 1936. (Peter G.F. Chinn, *Model Airplane News*, November 1956, 28-31). It was Bill Atwood who first imported O.S. model engines. The Max .29 and .35 engines first appeared on the market in late 1954. Japanese engines that gained prominence were Enya, O.S. Fuji, K.O, and Udea. These still have a large following today. Many of the smaller displacement engines were not exported and are hard to find in the United States. Engines produced in the mid 1960s are fine examples of craftsmanship and innovation. The Japanese manufacturers were tireless in their pursuit of excellence and made remarkable advancements, quickly grabbing a large share of the model engine market.

A European diesel model engine was first developed in 1942 by Klemenz Schenk Ing. of Switzerland. During the war, model engine electronics became impossible to obtain in Europe. This contributed to early diesel development. In fact, diesel engines were firmly established on the entire continent by the time the glow engine arrived. Popularity of the diesel model engine may have been purely economic as glow fuel was expensive and nitro-methane almost nonexistent in Europe. The use of glow engines in Europe did not gain popularity until they garnered wins at the World Championship contests. European designed and produced glow and diesel engines are fine examples of craftsmanship, innovation, and quality. Prominent European manufacturers are many: ETA, ED, Elfin, Frog, and Mills and Yulon are the most recognized British designs. Other nations produced engines and some made it to the United States. The Italian Super Tigre engines became popular imports. Iron Curtain countries built many engines but they mainly stayed in the countries where they were produced. The most recognized and still produced are the MVVS engines from Czechoslovakia and Moki engines from Hungry. Examples of foreign built engines for early American engine collectors were often acquired through trading at the World Championships.

"Global Engine Review" is a series of articles written by Peter Chinn beginning in 1963. These articles appeared in the *American Aircraft Modeler Annuals* 1963 to 1968. He documented 278 engines being produced throughout the world in 1963. These would include those being sold to modelers and limited production engines used for competition. One of a kind engines were omitted. The steady growth of engines available to modelers continued through 1968. That year, 377 model engines were listed from seventeen different countries. Peter Chinn wrote many articles on model airplane engines for virtually all model airplane magazines printed in English. He authored over two hundred "Engine Review" columns for *Model Airplane News* for more than twenty years. Other prominent engine men, including Clarence F. Lee and George M. Aldrich contributed their insight and expertise with regular columns and articles in *Radio Control Modeler, Model Airplane News,* and *Model Aviation* for more than thirty years. Articles by these three men are an important record for modelers and collectors researching history, data, and time lines for engines produced from 1950 to 1990.

Early ignition engines remain highly collectible, with dedicated organizations supporting modelers and collectors. The Model Engine Collectors Association (MECA) was founded in 1959 by famous modeler Joe Wagner. The Society for Antique Modelers (SAM) was founded around 1963 as John Pond and Lee Freeman made a road trip to the Stockton, California area for yet another free flight competition. The *Engine Collectors Journal* has been around for almost forty years, beginning in late 1963. Editor Tim Daniels continues his search for the history of model airplane engines and readily answers emails. If you are serious about collecting model airplane engines, I believe it is important to get involved and support the organizations that support your interest.

Frank Anderson's wonderful book *Anderson's Blue Book, 3rd Edition* is necessary for serious engine collectors. It is the most comprehensive work done on American model engines (1911-1965). The third edition includes 650 recent eBay sales. All collectors realize how important the world of Internet sales has become. Another book, when you can find it, is Mike Clanford's 1987, *A Pictorial A to Z Vintage and Classic Model Airplanes*, now out of print. This book has become highly desired and prices have ranged from $70 to $265 on eBay depending on who wants it badly enough that week.

Education is paramount in this area of flying model collectibles. The more you know about things you like, the more you will enjoy your collection. You will also avoid regrettable purchases. Deals can go in your favor when you know what you are looking for. Last year, I bought an early OS Max 35 stunt engine on eBay. The seller's picture showed a dirty, neglected engine I thought I would use for parts. My inspection found the engine had never been mounted or run. Sometimes half of the fun comes from getting a fifty-dollar item for ten bucks. It is also nice to find a "diamond in the rough" every once in awhile.

Vintage Engines

Brown Junior .60, c. 1939-41. *Courtesy of Bob Parker.* $150-250.

Brown Junior engine box, c. late 1930s, $25-60.

Baby Cyclone .359, model D, c. 1937. *Courtesy of Bob Parker.* New condition, $250-350.

Baby Cyclone .359, model F, c. 1938. *Courtesy of Bob Parker.* $250-300.

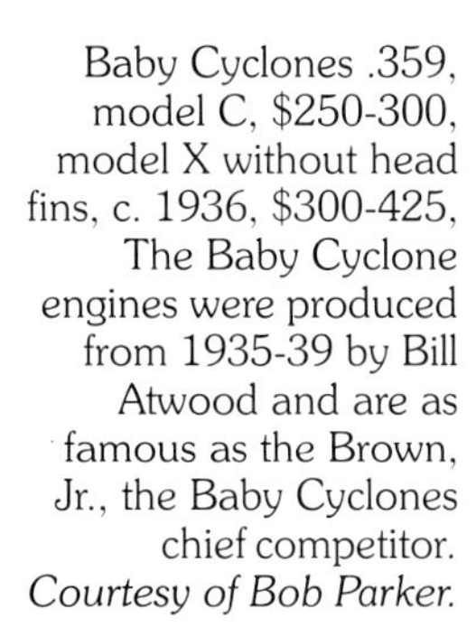

Baby Cyclones .359, model C, $250-300, model X without head fins, c. 1936, $300-425, The Baby Cyclone engines were produced from 1935-39 by Bill Atwood and are as famous as the Brown, Jr., the Baby Cyclones chief competitor. *Courtesy of Bob Parker.*

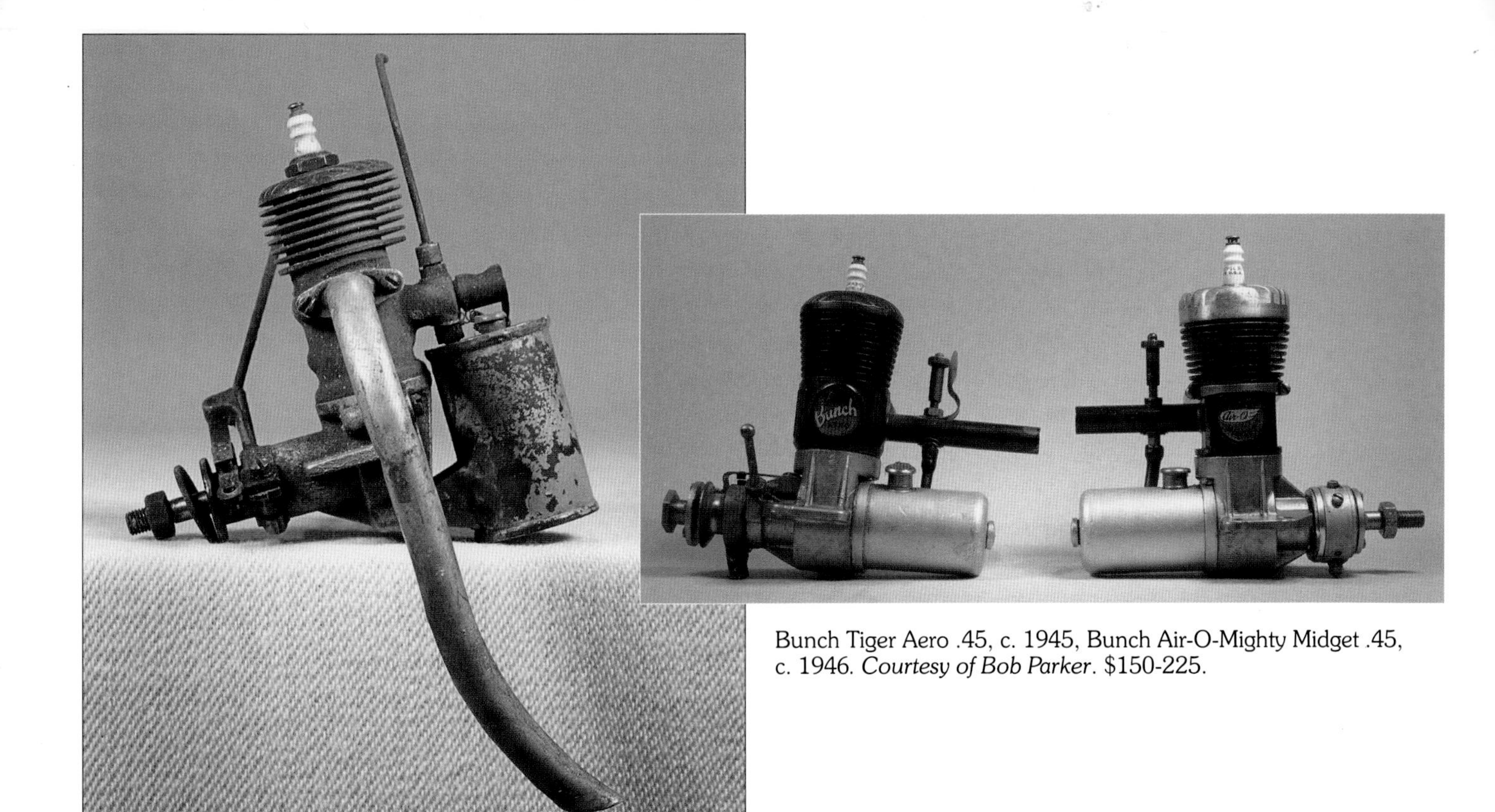

Bunch Tiger Aero .45, c. 1945, Bunch Air-O-Mighty Midget .45, c. 1946. *Courtesy of Bob Parker*. $150-225.

Dennymite Airstream Deluxe .573, c. 1938, produced by actor Reginald Denny. This engine is an example of how many engines are found, "a diamond in the rough." *Courtesy of Bob Parker.* $275-350.

Bunch Mighty Midget .45, c. 1940.
Courtesy of Bob Parker. $150-225.

Contestor D .60R, c. 1946, manufactured by Dan Bunch; this example is missing the rear tank.
Courtesy of Bob Parker. $165-225.

Ohlsson .56 Gold Seal, commemorative of the famous 1938 engine. Built by Herb Wahl in the early 1980s. *Courtesy of Bob Parker.* $400-450.

Ohlsson .23, c. 1938-40, this engine was very popular and was produced by Irwin Ohlsson. In 1940 Ohlsson Miniatures Company became Ohlsson & Rice. The O&R engines continued to be many modelers' first gas engine. *Courtesy of Bill Darkow*. $125-175.

O.K. Bantam .19, c. 1947. *Courtesy of Bob Parker.* $100-175.

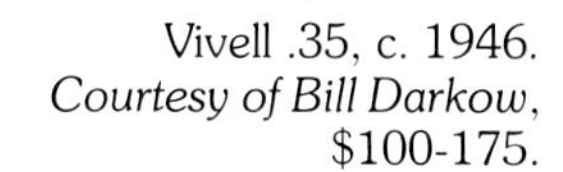

Vivell .35, c. 1946.
Courtesy of Bill Darkow,
$100-175.

Orwick .32, light blue anodized engine is a glow version from 1951. The green case is from 1948. They are shown together to highlight differences between the glow and ignition engines. Many engines started to convert to glow with the invention of the glow plug by Ray Arden in 1947. *Courtesy of Bob Parker.* $150-225.

Herkimer-O.K. Twin 1.2 ignition engine, c. 1940. This engine turned propellers from 16 to 20 inches, a real power horse. The cylinders are off set; after the war the engine was reintroduced with the cylinders opposed inline. *Courtesy of Bob Parker.* New, $450-800.

Delong .30, c. 1949. *Courtesy of Bob Parker.* N.I.B. $225-275.

O.K. Twin 1.12, c. 1945. *Courtesy of Bob Parker.* new condition $500-800.

Drone Diesel Gold Crown .29, c. 1947, produced by Leon Shulman. *Courtesy of Bob Parker,* used, $100-175.

Morton M-5 .922, c. 1945, front view; the condition of this engine is average, still highly sought after for their unique design. The Morton was also marketed by Burgess Battery in 1947. *Courtesy of Bob Parker.* $1100-1500, examples in new condition are double in price.

O&R .29 glow, c. 1950. *Courtesy of Bob Parker.* N.I.B. $175-225.

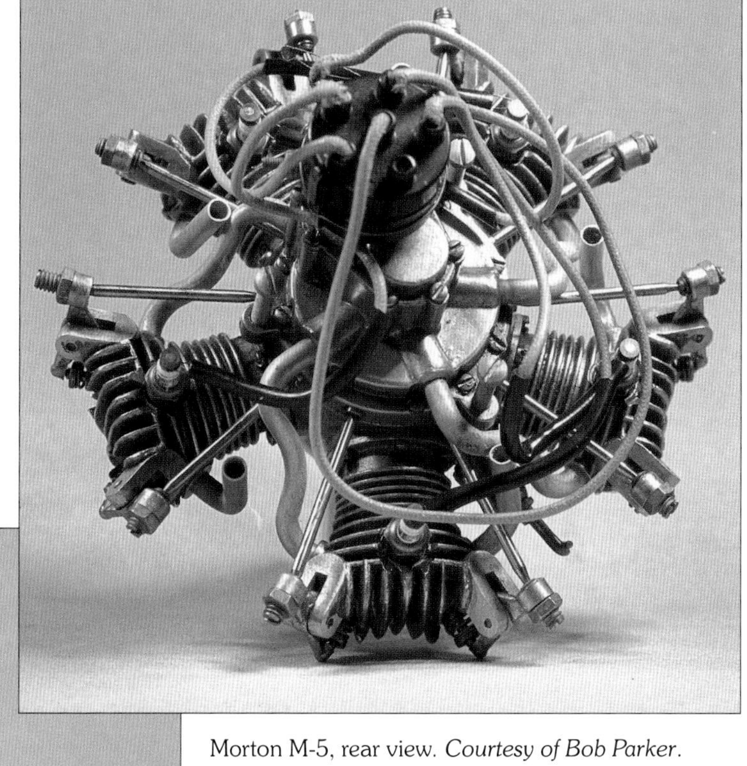

Morton M-5, rear view. *Courtesy of Bob Parker*.

O&R .29 marine glow, c. 1950.
Courtesy of Bob Parker, new $150-200.

Simplex Hornet .19, c. 1980, manufactured by John Morrill as a SAM legal engine. *Courtesy of Bob Parker.* $100-150.

Classic Engines

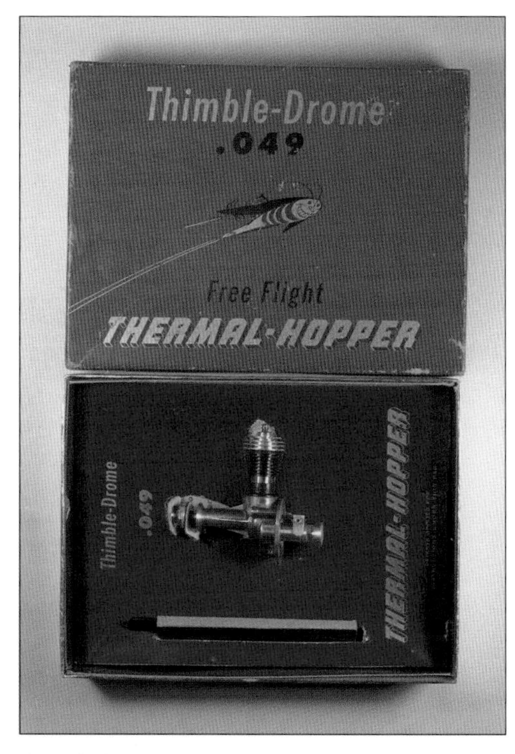

Cox. 049 Thermal Hopper, c. 1953, without box $35-80, with box $110-175.

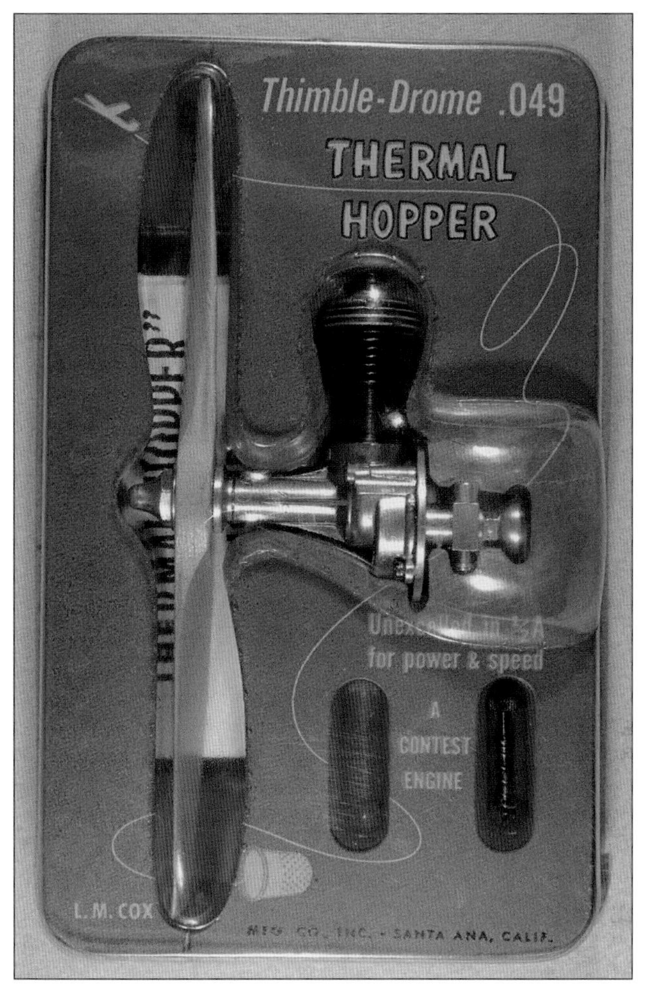

Cox. .049 Thermal Hopper in bubble pack, c. 1960. *Courtesy of Bob Parker.* $110-175.

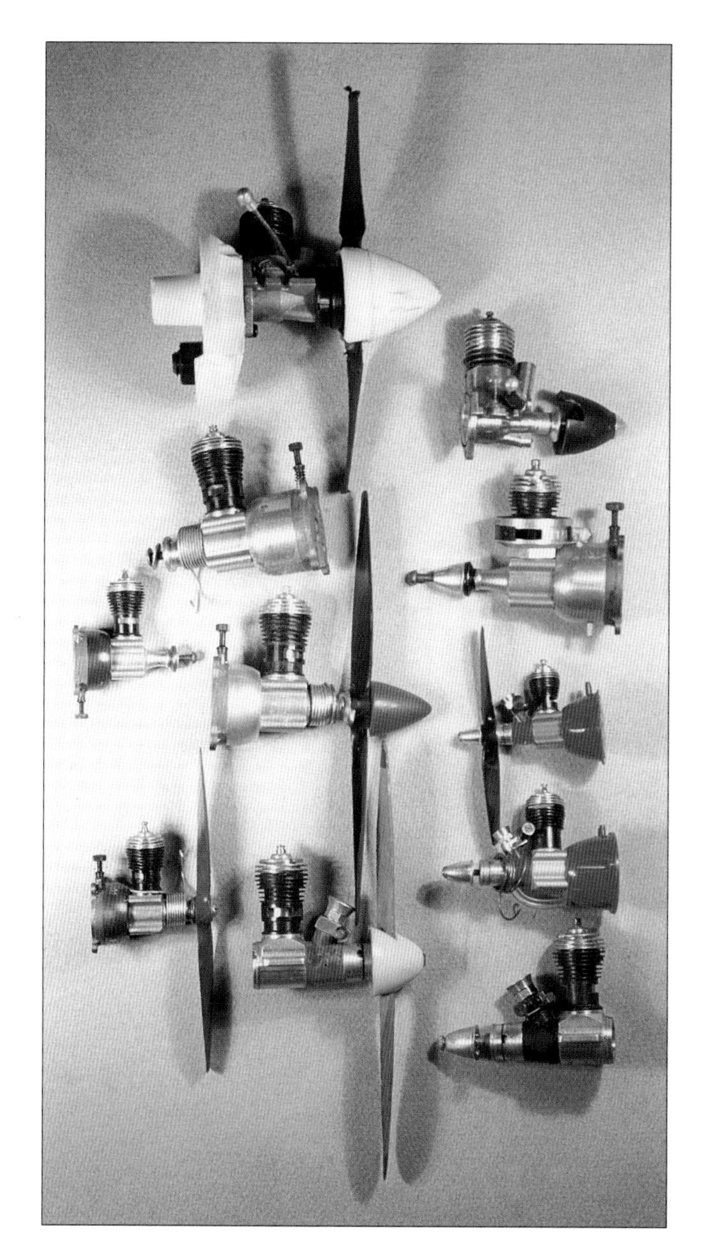

Common 1/2 A and 1/4 A engines, *top left:* Testors McCoy .049 from R.T.F plane, $7-15; Wen-Mac Mk II .049 c. 1960s, $5-10; Cox .049 Baby Bee with large tank, new $20; Cox .049 Golden Bee with muffler, new $20-30; Cox PeeWee .020, $10-20; Cox .049 Baby Bee with standard tank, new $20; Cox TD .010 $35-60; Cox TD .020, $30-60; Cox TD .049, (black) and .051, $15-35. The TD engines are susceptible to deterioration of the plastic parts. Prices for used engines are low, well cared for engines move toward the middle price range, and new engines with original packaging sell for the best prices. Early versions of the TD engines in their original boxes or packaging are the only ones being collected. Best to buy new engines, all others are runners.

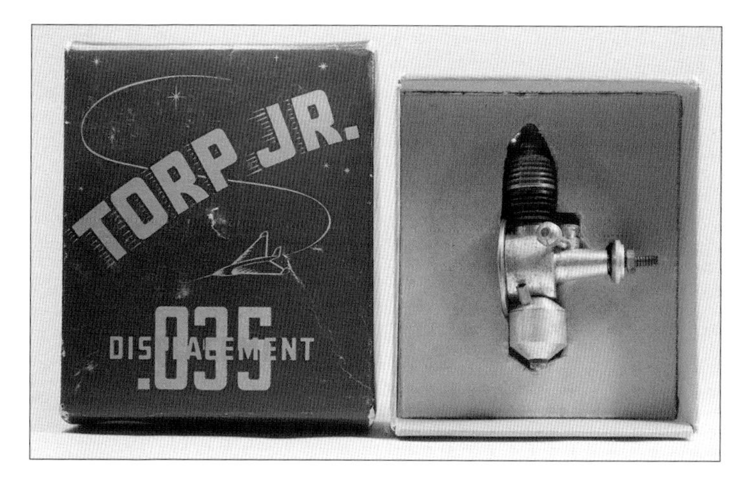

K&B Torpedo Jr. .035, c. 1950. *Courtesy of Bob Parker.* N.I.B. $90-150.

Cox PeeWee .020 new in bubble pack, c. 1960s. This engine came on a card of 12 engines and was torn off when the sale was made. *Courtesy of Bob Parker.* $30-50.

Cox TD .010, c. 1961, N.I.B. $60- 100.

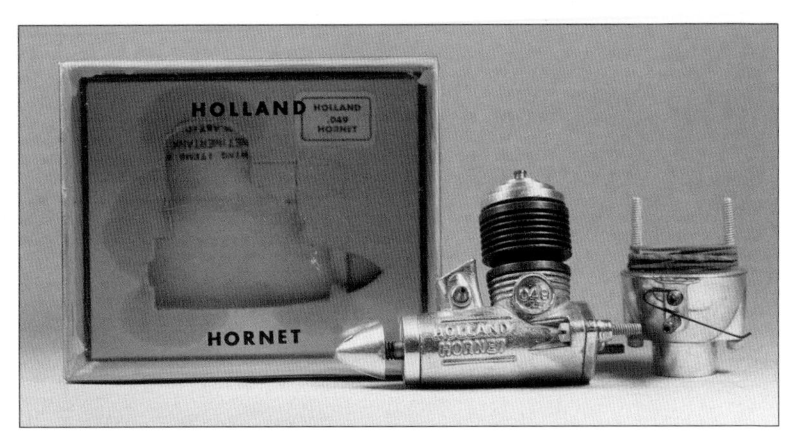

Holland Hornet Mk II .049, c. 1959.
Courtesy of Bob Parker. N.I.B. $75-140.

More 1/2 A engines, c. 1950s, *top left:* OK Cub .074, $15-25; *top center:* Royal Spitfire .065, no tank, $15-30; *top right:* OK Cub .049 AR, c. 1960 $10-25; *2nd row left to right:* Holland Wasp .049, has an H on the case, no tank, c. 1952, $35-65; OK Cub .049, $5-10; OK Cub .049A with red prop and plastic tank, new $20-25; *3rd row left to right:* Enya .049 used $35-65; OK Cub .049B with red anodized tank, new $20-30; *bottom left to right:* OK Cub .074, used $20-30; Anderson Baby Spitfire .045 short tank, c. 1949, $30-50; Anderson Baby Spitfire .045 with long tank, $30-50; OK Cub .049 with original OK Cub wooden prop, $15-25. These little engines are being added to collections out of fun. Needle valve at the top is an Austin Craft. $5-7. OK Cub made millions of small engines from .024 to .099 in over thirty-five versions.

Anderson Baby Spitfire .045 with short tank, c. 1949. This engine was Mel Anderson's first entry into small engine market. $30-50.

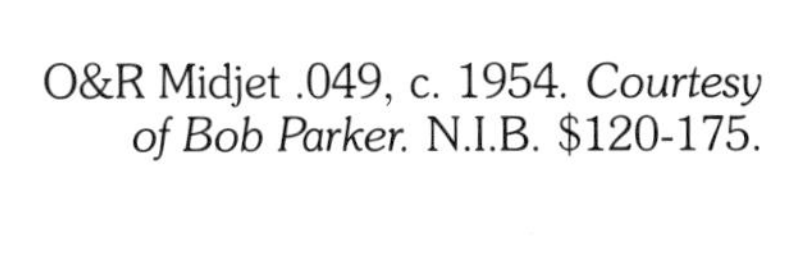

O&R Midjet .049, c. 1954. *Courtesy of Bob Parker.* N.I.B. $120-175.

OK Cub .049, c. late 1950s, in rare yellow box. *Courtesy of Bob Parker.* $50-75.

OK Cub .074 Diesel, c. 1953, N.I.B. $85- 125.

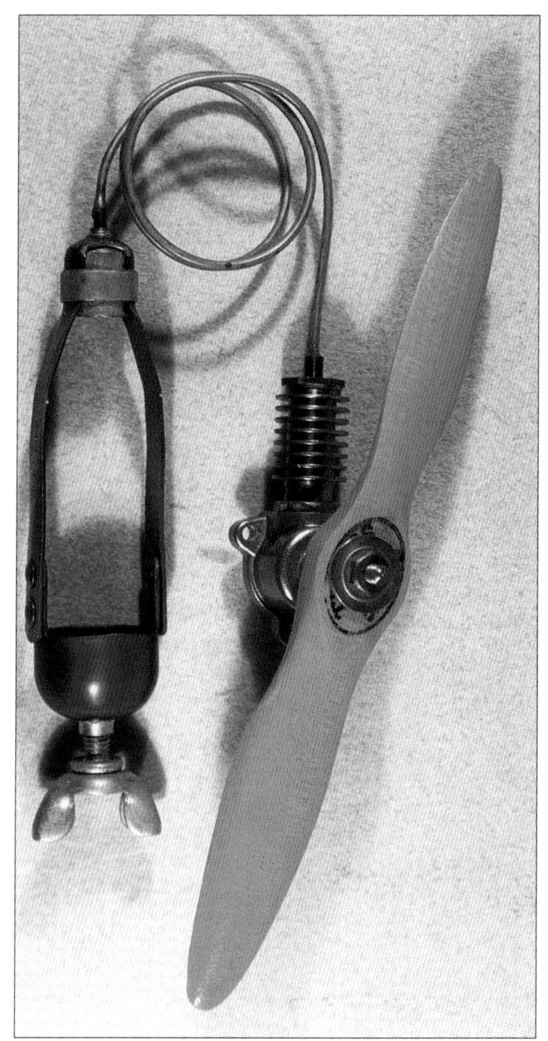

OK Cub CO2 engine, c. 1947-61, produced in three versions. *Courtesy of Bob Parker.* $30-60.

McCoy Red Heads .19, .29, .35, c. 1957-66. The McCoy RH engines were the first "large" engine for many modelers. They are plentiful and easy to find. They were sold inexpensively and many engines on the market have been abused because they were cheap. Used engines sell for $15-40, new engines go for $45-85, and if they come with original box, $85-120. The .40 is the most desired and hardest to find and in new condition can sell for $100-140. The lightning bolt engines appeared in 1966.

Forster .29 c. 1950-60s. In 1960 Forster-Appelt Manufacturing Company produced eight engines in the .29-.35 displacements. New, $75-100.

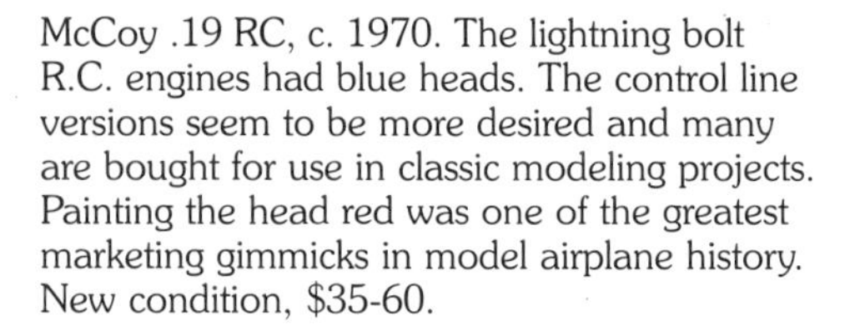

McCoy .19 RC, c. 1970. The lightning bolt R.C. engines had blue heads. The control line versions seem to be more desired and many are bought for use in classic modeling projects. Painting the head red was one of the greatest marketing gimmicks in model airplane history. New condition, $35-60.

K&B .35 standard intake and .35 RC, series 75 c. 1975. This engine was produced when K&B acquired Veco and had too many .35 sized engines. It didn't last too long on the market as the .40 sized engines were more desirable to R.C. modelers and control line dwindled in the 1970s. Stunt had moved up to larger engines. It is still a fine engine. Both of these are in new condition, $50-75.

K&B Green Head engines. The K&B GH engines have remained popular for over fifty years, first appearing in 1952, and are desired for their durability. Lud Kading and John Brodbeck founded K&B in 1946. Kading left the company in 1951. In 1955, the company merged with Allyn Sales. By 1960, K&B joined Aurora Plastics and dropped the Allyn name. No green head engines were produced on series 61 through 66 engines. Prices for N.I.B. engines will most likely continue to rise, .09, c. 1956, used $30-45; .45 RC, c. 1960, new $60-85; .45 Stunt, c. 1959, new $100-175; .19 c. 1951, used $30-50.

K&B Torpedo .40 RC, series 71, special gold-plated head and carburetor. The gold head Torp was not available to the public. It could only be won as a first place prize at the Spokane Internationals in 1971 and possibly 1972. The colonel at the Air Force base was good friends with John Brodbeck and had a special run of K&B 40's made just for the Internationals. The gold was a challenge to apply on aluminum. The Perry carb is also gold plated. Bob Parker (contributor of this item) won first place in scale using a BF-110 Messerschimt. *Courtesy of Bob Parker.* Rare, $200-250.

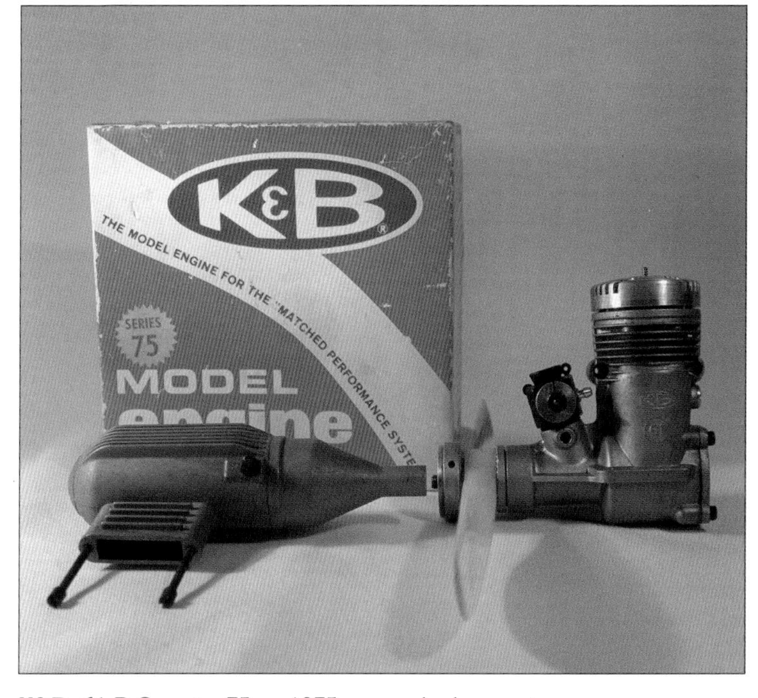

K&B .61 R.C. series 75, c. 1975, a popular low cost durable engine, engines equipped with Perry carburetor with pump are a little more, N.I.B. $55-75.

Fox Rocket .09, c. 1959, notice "missile age styling" on the box! This engine never gained popularity due to the Fox glow head. N.I.B. $30-40.

Fox Rocket .15, c. 1958, N.I.B. $35-55.

Fox .35, Arnold and Fox Manufacturing, c. 1950, with two bolt back plate and four bolt head, yellow box. *Courtesy of Bob Parker.* N.I.B. $135-175.

Fox .35, Arnold and Fox Manufacturing, c. 1950, red box. *Courtesy of Bob Parker.* N.I.B. $135-175.

Fox .19, Arnold and Fox Manufacturing, c. 1954, blue box, N.I.B. $80-125.

Fox .40 RC, c. 1961, short lived engine that came out in a rat race version in 1962. A ball bearing engine soon replaced it in 1964. Duke Fox was continually working to improve his product line of engines and new designs were regularly introduced, new $75-100.

Fox .29, this was one of a pair of engines bought in 1958 in Iceland for a twin engine scale project that was never finished by Ron Smith of Lacey, Washington. The plane sits in my rafters and one engine found a home in an old time stunter. N.I.B. $65-100.

Fox .35 Combat Special, c. 1956, N.I.B. $90-110.

Fox .40 Stunt engine, c. 1973-74, new in the box and should contain another venturi insert to be complete. This engine has the red, white, and blue worn box. Designed by George Aldrich, new $50-75.

Fox Engines, *left to right:* 1957 Fox .19, $20-35; Fox .15 RC, c. 1970s, N.I.B. $30-40; Fox .19, c. 1970s, new $30-40; Fox .15X, c. 1960s, $20-30; Fox .40, c. 1970s, $35-50; Fox .36X, matte case; other engines were produced with a shiny case, c. 1970s, $30-45.

The Fox 35 Stunt Engine

The venerable Fox 35 stunt engine was marketed in 1948. It was developed by Duke Fox and first manufactured in North Hollywood, California. In 1955, Duke Fox moved his entire operation to Arkansas. For fifty-five years, this engine has remained virtually unchanged. The engine has remained popular and, next to the Cox .049, has been used by more flyers than any other engine. The first real changes were switching to a three-bolt case from two bolts and changing the four-bolt head to six bolts. (Joe Wagner, *Model Aviation* Sept. 2001, 81-82). The second change occurred in the early 1970s when mufflers began to be used as flying fields started to disappear because of noise complaints. Muffler "ears" were added to the case so a muffler could be attached. There have been several special editions engines produced to celebrate the 10th to the 50th anniversaries of the production of this model. On the latest versions, modern technology has created an engine that is much better than the Fox 35 of 1948 and its predecessors. Fox Manufacturing Company also offers hemi-head kits and ABC piston liner sets for more power and smoother running. Over the years, folklore has emerged about the engine and the flyers that made it famous. The most well-known flyer was George Aldrich, designer of the "Nobler." Modelers have used the Fox .35 powered "Nobler" combination for fifty years. This arrangement has won more stunt contests than any other combination and continues to be a favorite within the stunt community today.

Fox .35 50th Anniversary Model, c. 1998. Only 500 were produced and come numbered with a signed letter of authenticity by Betty Fox. *Courtesy of Bob Parker.* $100-175.

Fox .36 rear exhaust control line stunt engine. c. 1975-1976. The 1976 version was advertised as "improved." The engine was well made but was a marketing disaster. Duke Fox was a great innovator and took many chances to bring affordable engines to the modeling community. *Courtesy of Bob Parker.* $75-125.

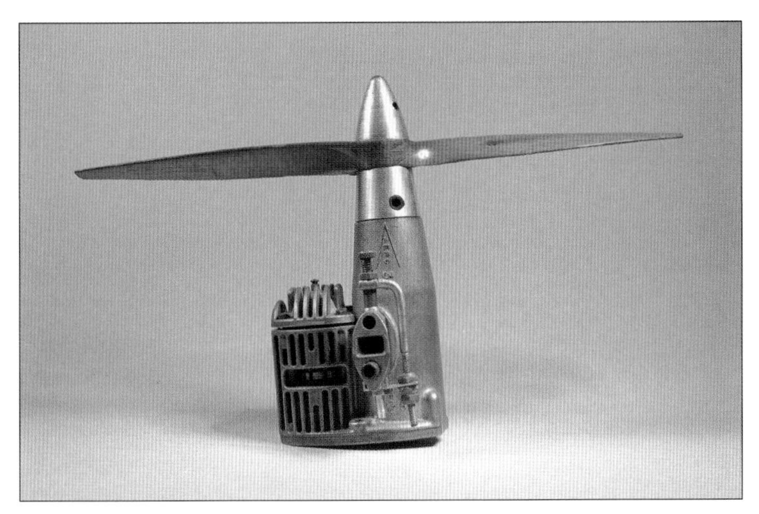

Aero .35, c. 1963, produced by Augie Savage and John Piston who invested over twenty years and twenty different versions before putting this engine on the market. This engine is worn out but still interesting because of its unique design. *Courtesy of Bob Parker.* $175-200, a new in the box engine may go as high as $400-500.

Johnson .35 Combat Special, c. 1960, manufactured by Dynamic Models, Inc, this engine is used and in good condition, $75-100.

Veco GP .35A stunt engine, c. 1959-65, with the increase in control line stunt activity during the 1990s, this engine has become highly desirable. They were well made and durable. Veco was bought by K&B in 1967. *Courtesy of Bob Parker.* N.I.B. $125-200.

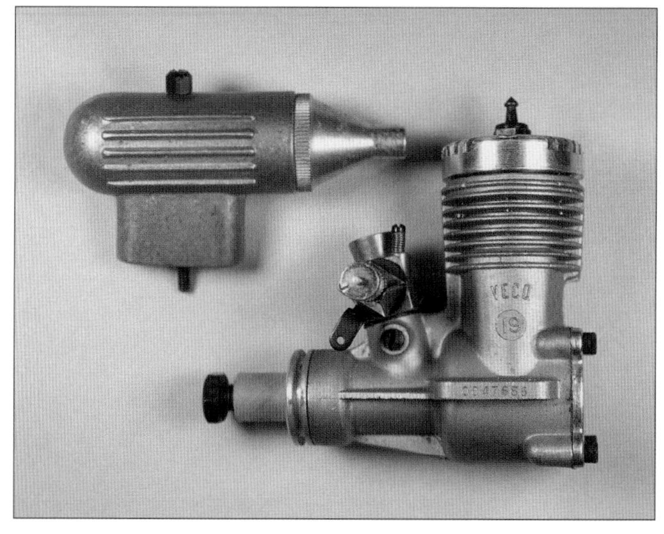

Veco .19 RC, series 1970, this great little engine came in a orange and white K&B box. The German HB .25 engine would use this muffler design, new, $50-70.

Veco engines, *left to right:* Veco 45 RC, c. 1962, new $75-85; Veco .29, c. 1953, this engine was reviewed in the April 1954 issue of M.A.N., new $70-90; Veco .19 RC, series 100 c. 1958-62, used $30-50; Veco .19 RC, series 1970, new $50-70; Veco .19 CL, series 100, c. 1956-59, new $40-60.

Foreign Engines

Webra 3.5 RC, Glo-star, c. 1966-70, made in Germany. N.I.B. $30-45.

Merco .61 RC, c. 1960s, featured with different carburetion on each engine, used $40-60.

Merco engines, *left to right:* c. 1960-70s, Merco .35 ball bearing, Merco .35 plain bushed, used $ 35-65; Merco .49 stunt engine, new $100; Merco .49 RC, used $50-75; Merco engines have been a mainstay in the U.K. for over forty years. Loyal Brits wouldn't think of using anything else.

Mills 1.3 diesel replica engine, manufactured in India. The first version of this engine appeared in August 1946 and was the first British diesel marketed. *Courtesy of Bill Darkow*, new condition $40-60.

Davies-Charlton 2.5 diesel replica engine, Aurora Manufacturing Company, the box in the photo is wrong but similar. *Courtesy of Bill Darkow*, $40-60.

Kometa .29 MD-5, c. 1965, made in the Soviet Union, complete with propeller, one look at this prop and you're glad to live in the "West;" not recommended for use. The engine looks like it will run ok, N.I.B. $35-45.

Super Tigre .46 RC, c. 1966-80s, used $ 75-120.

TWA .40 RC, c. 1970s, this engine was built by Theobald, Wisniewski, and Arnold (speed fliers from the 1960s and 1970s. *Courtesy of Bob Parker*. Rare, $175-250.

Super Tigre .35 stunt engine, c. 1970s, new $85.

Super Tigre G .60 BB RC, c. 1970s, a real brute, this is a large case version with a homemade needle extension. This was a popular engine and many still exist due to the quality of manufacturing. The ST .60 engine was produced in many versions. In good condition, $50-65.

Super Tigre Engines, c. 1960-70s, engine on top of the box is a .35 R.C. with a unique exhaust, like new. $80. Various sizes of .23, .35, .46, and .60 engines, the ST 60 with "Walt" on the motor mount is a Big Jim Greenaway stunt engine specially prepared for Walt Russel in the early 1980s, $150-250. Super Tigre engines are much desired not for collecting but use in modeling projects due to their power output and durability. The most desired are the .46 and small case .60 and in new condition can sell for $125-175.

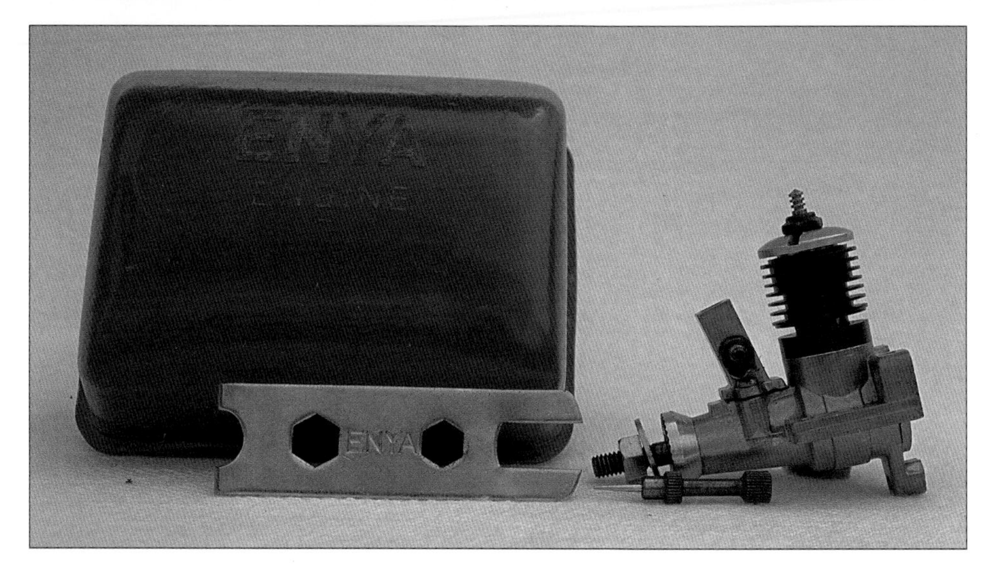

Enya .06 II, c. 1960s, N.I.B. $70-90.

NSU Wankel Rotary 4.9 ccm, (.30) engine, c. 1970-80s, made by O.S. for Graupner of Germany. The Wankel was reviewed in the September 1970 issue of *Model Airplane News*. N.I.B. $175-200.

O.S. Max Engines, this group comes from the 1970-80s and were some of the most popular engines during this time. They include a .15, .20, .25, .30, .35, early .40 H from 1966-69, .40H and the previous .49. In general, these engines look the same in appearance. Control line versions usually just have the carburetors removed and a venturi inserted. Prices are still under $100 for these engines. The engines from this group are selling in today's market for $25-75.

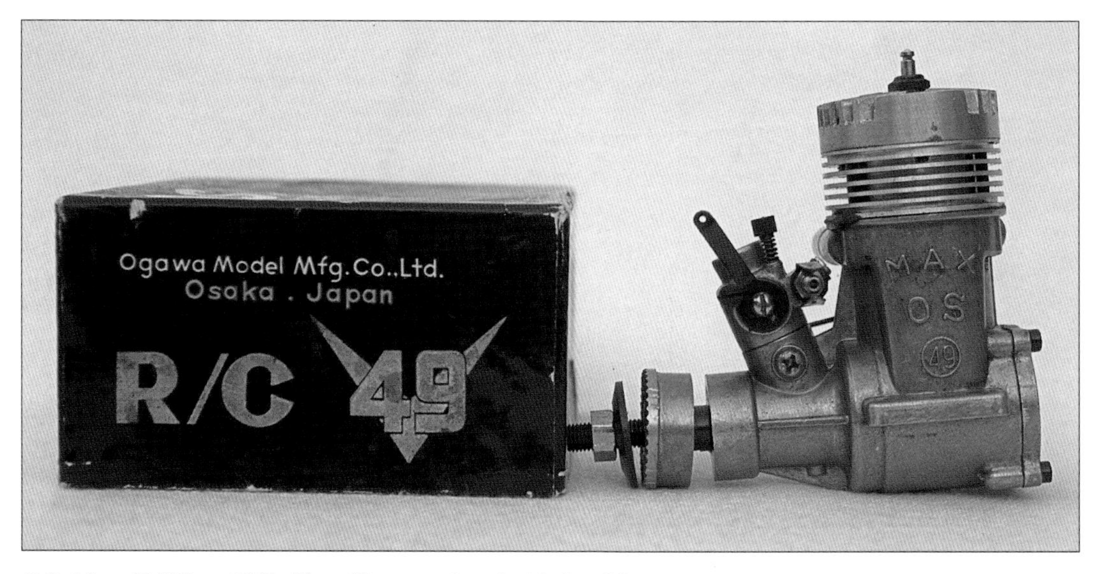

O.S. Max .49 RC, c. 1961. The .49 was replaced with the .50 in 1965. This engine is in above average condition, $65-90.

O.S. Max-S .35, c. 1970-80s, this engine is N.I.B. $60-100.

O.S. Max-S .35 stunt engines, left engine is from the early 1980s. The right engine is from about 1965 when the engine first came on the market. The 1965-66 engine has a noticeably shinier case and came with a rubber exhaust plug and no muffler. The Jetstream muffler was an optional item when mufflers were starting to be developed and used in world competition. The O.S. Max .35 is still a great engine; these engines are being bought for use and not collections. New condition, $50-100.

O.S. Max .40 H. These engines are set side by side so collectors and modelers can see the difference between the two engines. The engine was previewed in *Model Airplane News,* August 1965. The stunt version was examined in *Model Airplane News,* February 1971. The early version is a popular engine to convert to control line stunt. The engine on the left is the 1965 version, N.I.B. $108; the newer version, c. 1970-1980s, in used condition, $40-60, new condition, $75-85.

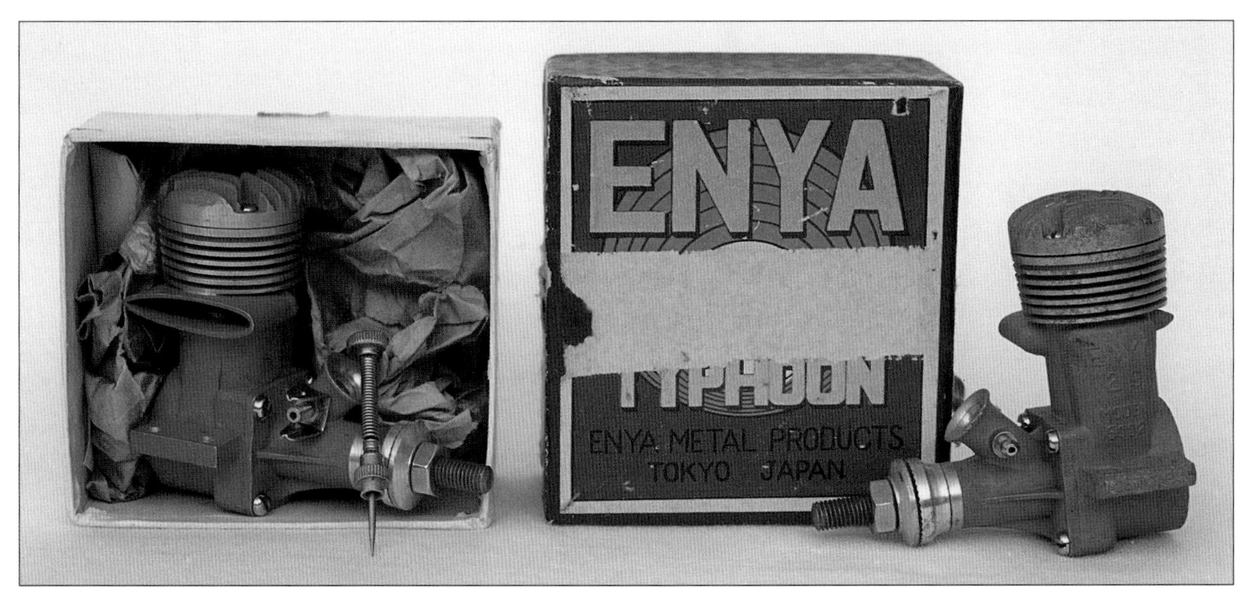

Enya .29 Typhoon, c. 1958, commonly known as the tear drop exhaust model, N.I.B. $100-125.

Enya .29 Tear Drop Exhaust, c. 1958. This pair of engines came from Ron Smith who flew Mustangs in England near the end of WW II.

Enya .29, no. 5224, c. 1960s. This is an early model with a matte case; it came with three different venturis and high compression head. This enabled the flyer to use the Enya in six possible configurations. Engines took awhile to break in. Runners are easy to come by and still excellent by today's standards. N.I.B. $65-80.

Enya .35, no. 5224, c. 1960s, in 1965 Enya MRC engines came in a plastic box packed in yellow foam starting with Enya .35 III. In the 1980s, the engine came in a red and black box. The name changed from Enya Metal Products to Model Rectifier Corporation around 1965. N.I.B. $65-80.

Flash .35, Taijet, c. 1970s, manufactured in Taiwan and imported by America's Hobby Center in New York. The engine came in control line and R.C. versions. Pictured is a stock muffler and a rare stunt muffler used with the engine set up for control line. The Flash .35 is often identified as an O.S. clone and some of the parts are interchangeable. N.I.B. $40-55; the stunt muffler in new condition, $20-35.

Enya .45, no. 6001, first engine on the left is a 1960s plain bushed matte case version in control line configuration with homemade venturi, new $85-125; the engine on the right is a ball bearing version with a stock venturi. The Enya .45TV control line engine was reviewed in *Model Airplane News*, March 1965. This engine was a very popular R.C. engine and easier to find in this configuration. New condition for both versions, $75-120.

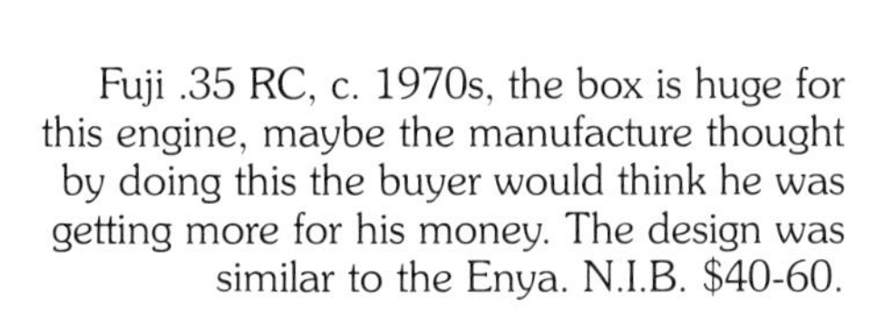
Fuji .35 RC, c. 1970s, the box is huge for this engine, maybe the manufacture thought by doing this the buyer would think he was getting more for his money. The design was similar to the Enya. N.I.B. $40-60.

Chapter 2
Model Airplane Kits

Model airplane kits have been a staple of the hobby for about a hundred years. The first real manufacturer was Ideal Aeroplane and Supply Company located in New York City. They were a main supplier of kits in 1911 and delighted boys for the next twenty years. By 1932, the company had grown to include over three dozen kits and every accessory needed to get a model airplane ready for its first flight. Ideal seemed to peak around 1928-1932, with the explosion of interest in aviation. After Lindberg's flight across the Atlantic, new companies grew to fill the needs of millions of boys wanting to experience the marvels of flight.

The Great Depression affected virtually every venue of commerce, but this would prove to be only a temporary setback to enthusiastic modelers. This history is wonderfully illustrated in Frank and Vickie Anderson's *An Encyclopedia of the Golden Age of Model Airplane, Volumes 1, 2, 3*. They have documented model aviation from 1907-1949, using first-hand accounts, vintage periodicals, books, and catalogs of the era. These three volumes come highly recommended by noted author Bill Hannan, who has also researched the early history of manufacturers, writing several publications on that subject.

Clearly, model airplane competitions and kit manufacturers went hand in hand. Being able to market contest winning models would boost sales and create more exposure for a company's line of other kits. This combination made heroes in the model world almost overnight. Most notable were Dick Korda, the Good brothers, Bill Dean, Don Still, Bill Winter, George Aldrich, Carl Goldberg, Hal deBolt, Chester Lanzo, Jim Walker, Frank Ehling, Jim Saftig, Lou Andrews, Davy Slagle, Bob Palmer, and Ed Southwick. As radio controlled modeling gained prominence, the names of Howard Bonner, Bob Dunham, Ken Willard, Don McGovern, Don Dewey, Maxey Hester, Cliff Weirick, Jim Kirkland, Walt Schroder and a host of other famous modelers endorsed products for the model industry. Their names would also be used to sell engines, kits, fuel, paint, propellers, and other accessories for a quickly expanding market. I could continue with this list of modeling giants, as there are many who deserve mention. If I have left someone out, I apologize!

Kits manufactured using the names of now famous modelers and their winning aircraft are still being modeled and produced today. Collectors seek out these winning designs. The most beloved and timeless designs command the highest prices, as do those that were of superior quality when they were manufactured. Kits from the 1930s through the 1950s mostly remain intact when collected. Later kits from the 1960s through the 1980s may still be built and flown. Kits are also used as patterns, not actually built from the kit, but to be built from scratch, using the kit parts as patterns.

Certain kits and their manufacturers have a strong following among builders and collectors. Ambroid, American Junior, Berkeley, Carl Goldberg, Cleveland, Comet, JASCO, Jetco, Megow, Scientific, Sterling, and Veco kits are highly sought after. Collectors also prize foreign model kits. Frog, Graupner, Kiel Kraft, Kyosho, Heron, Mercury, and Skyleader are some of the more desirable kits. Over the years, some companies have gone out of business or were bought out by other companies. Fox Manufacturing Co. purchased some of the remains of Berkeley and in fact, for a short time around 1960, Berkeley kits came out in orange and purple boxes under the Fox label. These kits command high prices on the open market. After that, Sig Manufacturing acquired some of the Fox kits; the "Super Sinbad" is the most recognized. Another design that has been through three manufactures is Ted Strader's little Nomad glider. Some designs are timeless and as long as a market exists, they will continue to be replicated.

Early 1960s to mid 1970s saw control line and free flight take a backseat to the now affordable and reliable world of radio control. The National Championships radio control event created instant heroes for the modeling community to ooh and ahh over. For most kids, radio control was out of reach financially and for the first time manufacturers began to shift marketing focus to more mature flyers. As teenagers, we realized radio control was beginning to dominate model aviation. I clearly recall in 1969 as we flipped through the latest issue of *Flying Models* magazine, my flying partner and best friend Pat Martinez remarked in dismay, "R.C. is taking *over.*"

Radio control kits are relatively new to kit collecting and have gained ground in the past five years. Notably, 1/2 A kits like the Goldberg Junior Falcon, Ecktronics, Nomad Glider, Scientific Miss America, Top Flite Schoolboy, Rascal, Sterling Minnie Mambo, and Jetco Navigator are being added to collections around the world. As a new generation of collectors recall the kits their youth, collecting kits of the 1960s is giving way to collecting those marketed in the 1970s. Most of these will be built and not saved as collector items. Some favorites of the seventies include the Airtronics Olympic 99, Dumas Mod Pod, Marks ModelsWindward glider, Goldberg Falcon 56, Top Flite Schoolmaster, and Midwest Das Little Stik. Hundreds of out-of-production kits bought for that "next" project are just now making it into the collectibles market.

Vintage kits are still an excellent buy when compared to prices of today's kits. Collector quality kits are becoming rare; I would estimate that only 10% of those on the market are of this high quality. Kits are kicked around and not stored correctly; over the years this causes deterioration of both the box and its contents. Decals deteriorate over time, becoming unusable. If you find that special kit, remember to store it in a dry place to preserve your treasure. The decals can be placed between wax paper and stored inside a book, just remember where you put them!

The future of model airplane kits and their desirability as collectibles is on the upswing. New in the box kits (NIB) will always command the best prices; scarce kits in this condition will only continue to rise in value. Buying kits at shows and from collectors is straightforward. In those cases, you can inspect the contents and bargain with the seller. Online buying can be a bit of a risk; new in the box sometimes means something different to the seller. Let it be known that if the parts are punched out, the kit is not NIB anymore. There are degrees of NIB, one being in the same condition as it was when it came from the hobby shop or manufacturer. Everything else is downgraded in price.

Common problems with kit boxes are tape, writing, stains, fading, and just plain deterioration that occur over time from being stored in the garage. A little wear and tear to the box is acceptable for scarce and rare vintage kits. If you want to build a model, you don't have to buy a kit; virtually all vintage kit plans are available to today's builders. Often a scratch built model will be a better flyer than a kit as manufacturers sometimes didn't care about the quality of the materials they used. Please see "Sources" at the end of this book for suppliers.

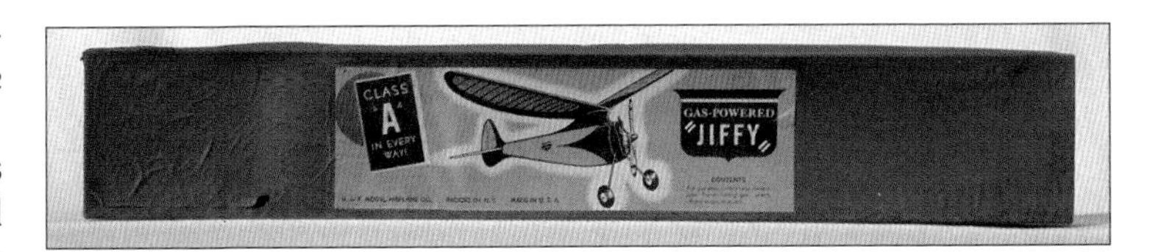

H & F Model Company, "Jiffy," free flight kit, c. 1941, designed by Sid Struhl. This model listed for $1.50 in the America's Hobby Center No. 12 catalog, (1942), eight years later it was still listed for the same price but under the Eagle label. *Courtesy of Bob Parker.* Near mint condition. $60-80.

Early Comet model airplane kit, c. 1930s. *Courtesy of Bob Parker.* $25-40.

Joe Ott Manufacturing Company

Joe Ott Manufacturing Company of Chicago, Illinois patented the Ott-O-Former building system. It was created to save time for the model builder. They advertised that it "saved" over half the construction time, was two-thirds lighter, and you could build better, sturdier models. An ad states, "No other designer or manufacturer is authorized to use this method, thus genuine Ott-O-Former kits are made only by Joe Ott Manufacturing Company." This company marketed model airplanes of fighters used in World War II with remarkable success. These were kits with models having wingspans ranging from 22 to 45 inches. Scale kits were quite popular during the war.

Joe Ott "...could be called the father of model aviation. At one time, Ott employed over 600 workers and turned out more than 50,000 kits a day." He is remembered for his series of plans appearing in *Popular Aviation* from 1929-1934. He became an instructor of Aeronautics at Texas A&M University. He was inducted into the AMA Hall of fame in 1982. "His vocation became his avocation, and he remained actively involved in those efforts up until he passed away in 1986." (John Pond, *Model Builder,* December 1986, 104, 106).

Joe Ott "Corsair," no. 3218, c. 1942, sold for fifty cents during the war, complete and in good condition, $25-45.

Scientific Model Kit, c. 1941, This box contained the "Wizard;" other designs that came in the same box were the Doodle Bug, Skipper, Little Rebel, Blue Phantom, and Air Raider, all had 25" wing spans. $15-25.

Falcon Model Airplane Company, "Doodle Bug" control line kit, c. late 1940s. Designed by Frank Greene. *Courtesy of Bob Parker.* N.I.B. $75-150.

Megow "Stardust" control line kit, c 1945-51, designed by Matt Kania. Before the outbreak of WW II, Fred Megow created the largest model company in the United States. After the war, Megow never regained the market they once commanded. *Courtesy of Bob Parker.* Mint condition, $110-175.

Cleveland "Playboy" free flight kit, c. late 1930s, this was and still is a popular design. The "Playboy" came is several sizes and was one of the best selling model kits of the entire Cleveland line. The "Playboy" was designed by Joe Elgin. *Courtesy of Bob Parker.* N.I.B. $80-120.

Cleveland "Superfortress," solid wood kit, c. 1940s. This was a large kit for being solid wood. It is getting harder to find kits in this condition. *Courtesy of Bob Parker.* Mint, $100-150.

Midwest "Jetstream" A-1 tow line glider, c. 1960s, designed by Warren Kurth, originally kitted by Ambroid in 1961. The design was a National Contest winner. N.I.B. $40-65.

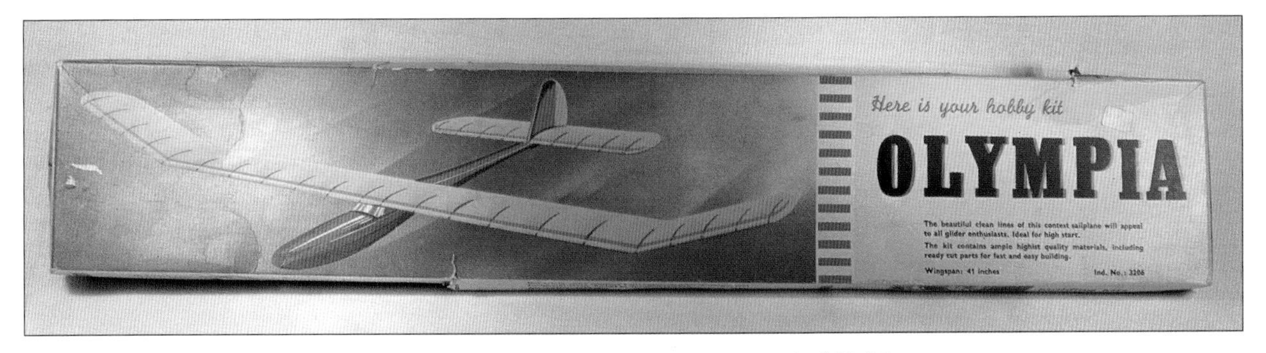

Greig Odense, "Olympia" tow line glider, c. 1950s, manufactured in Denmark, $30-50.

JASCO, "Spacemaster" 1/2 A free flight kit, c. 1950s, designed for the PAA event that was very popular with flyers in the 1950s, $25-35.

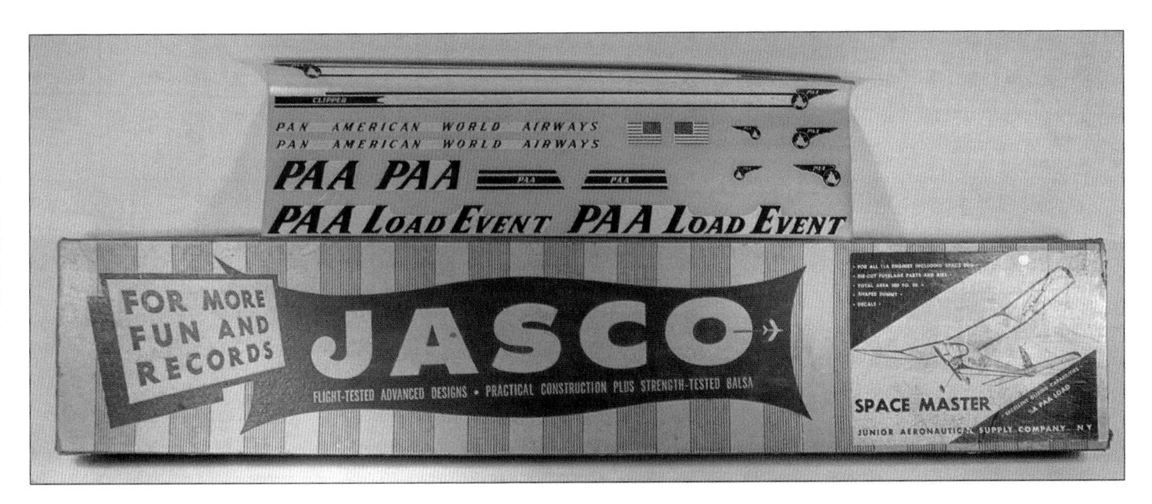

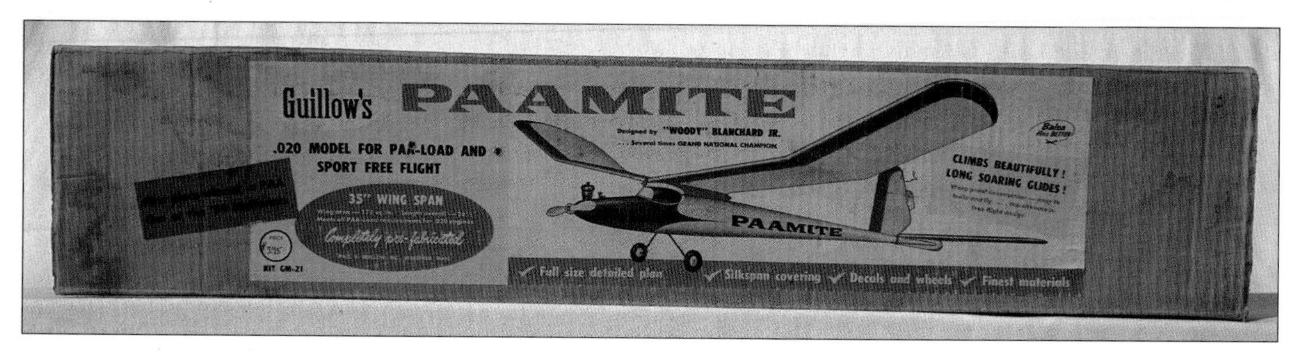

Guillow's "PAAMITE," c. 1960, free flight kit for .020 engines. Designed by four time Grand National Champion, Woody Blanchard Jr. Blanchard captured the National crown in 1954, 1955, 1956, and again in 1958. In 1958, he also captured the King Orange International crown for the third time. He competed in seventeen separate events at the 1958 Nationals. Woody Blanchard Jr. was elected into the AMA Hall of Fame in 1989. $25-40.

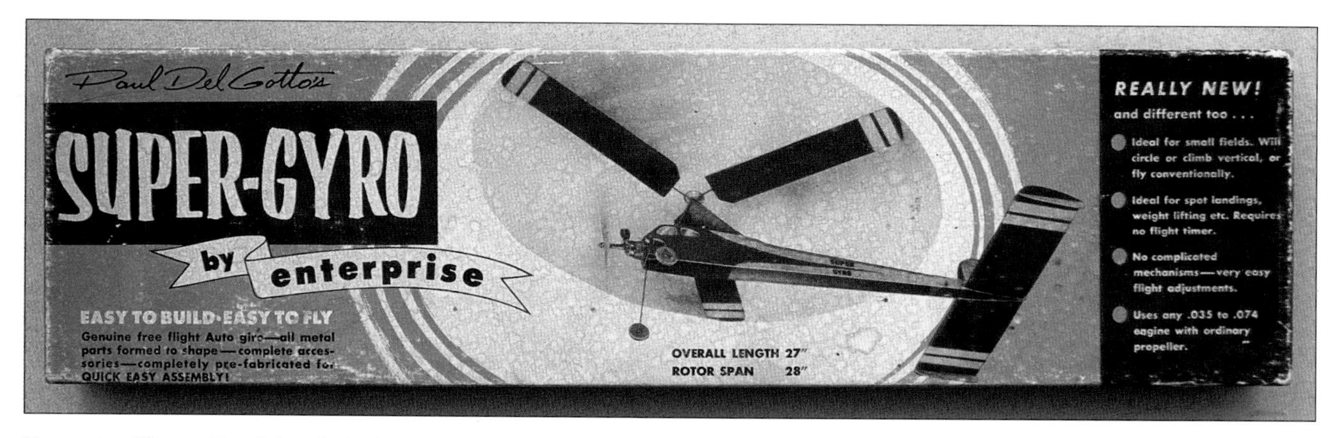

Enterprise "Super-Gyro" free flight helicopter, c. 1955, for .035- .074 engines, designed by Paul Del Gotto. *Courtesy of Bill Darkow*. $30-50.

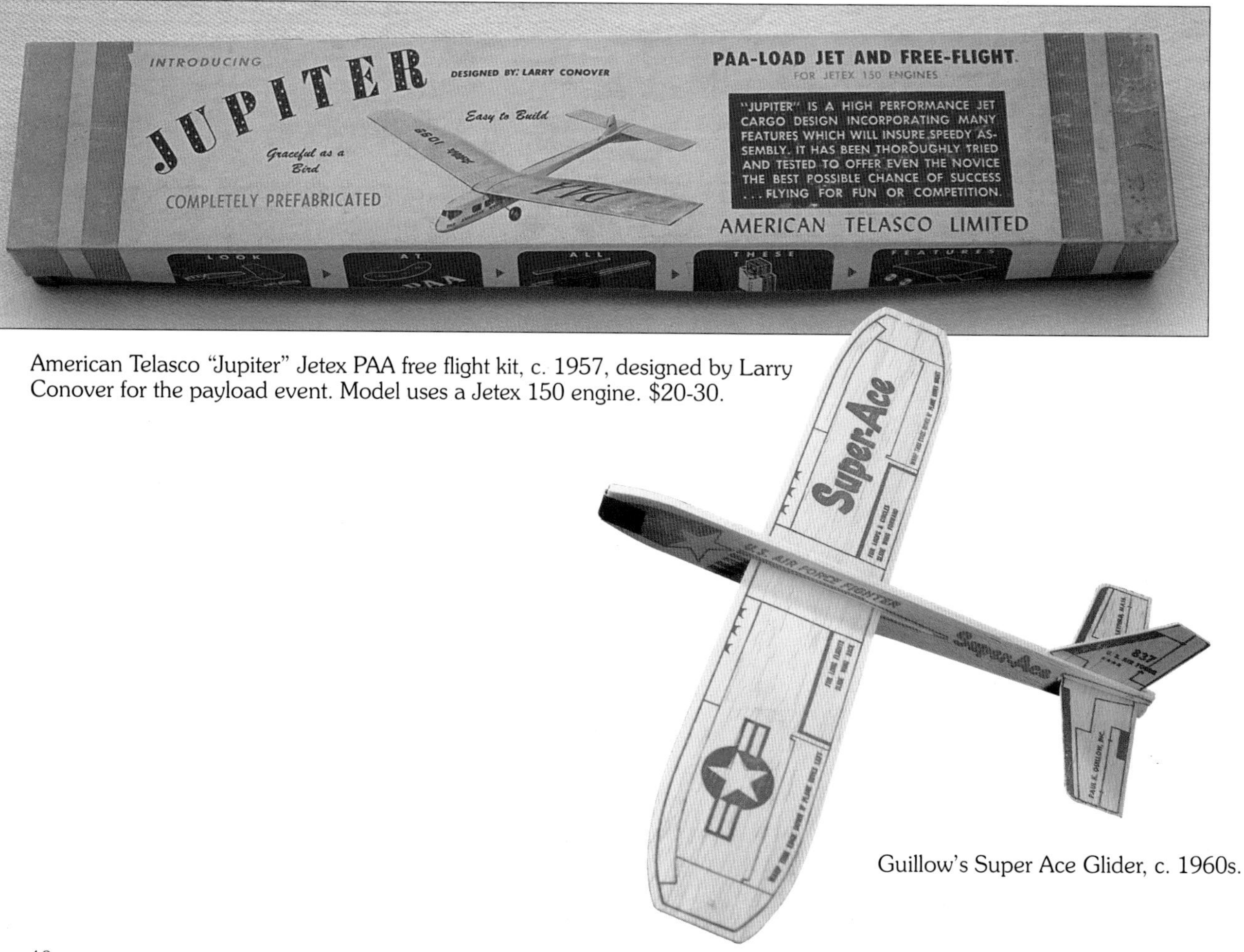

American Telasco "Jupiter" Jetex PAA free flight kit, c. 1957, designed by Larry Conover for the payload event. Model uses a Jetex 150 engine. $20-30.

Guillow's Super Ace Glider, c. 1960s.

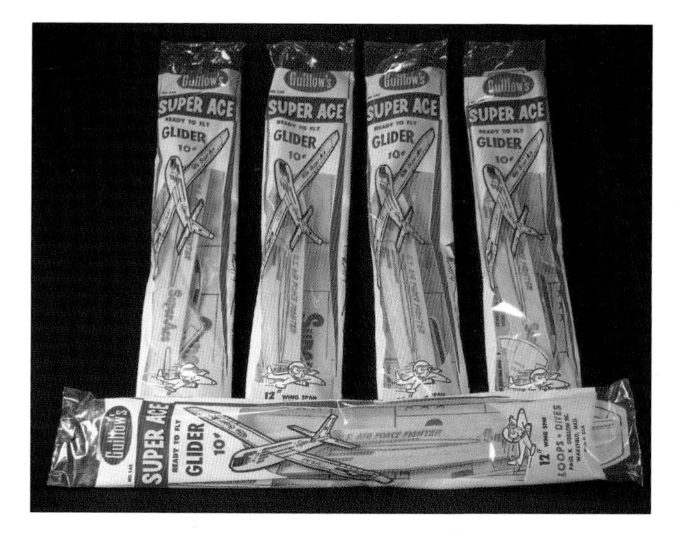

Guillow's Super Ace gliders in original packaging. Ten-cent gliders became a thing of the past about 1970. Every store in America carried ten-cent gliders made by several different companies and every boy had to have one. By trading in pop bottles at the local Speedy-Mart, my brothers and I were able to get them once in awhile. The rubber powered gliders increased to fifteen cents. $1-2.

Original 8x10 photo of a boy holding a speed model. The name on the plane says "Skipper." The various large trophies are from the 1950 Plymouth Internationals held in Detroit, Michigan. There is also one from the 1949 Plymouths. c. 1950-51. *Courtesy of Mike Hazel*, $10-15.

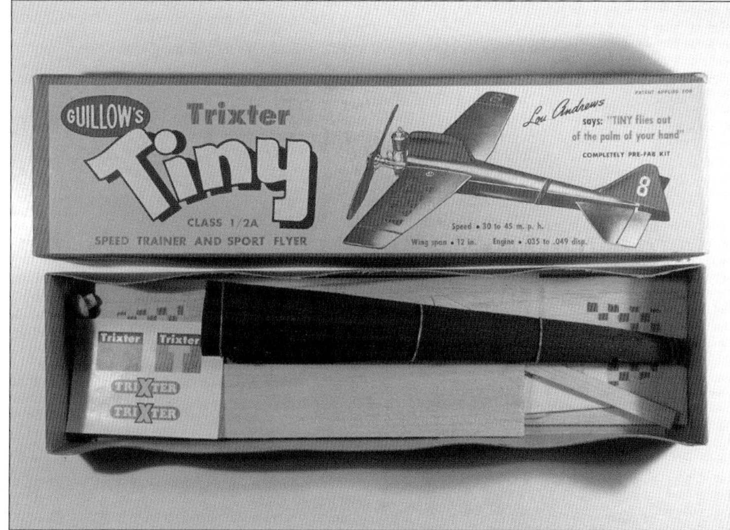

Guillow's "Tiny" 1/2 A speed trainer, c. 1952, unique construction, featuring sheet rolled and formed fuselage and sheeted flying surfaces, designed by Lou Andrews, mint condition. *Courtesy of Mike Hazel*, $65.

Megow "Perky," c. 1946, by Matt Kania, class A speed trainer typical of the period. *Courtesy of Mike Hazel*, mint condition, $60-80.

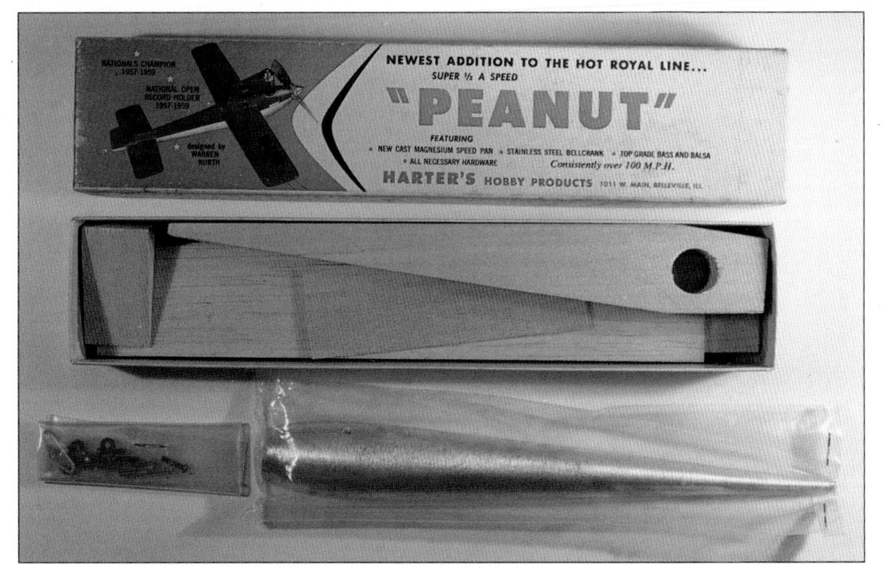

Harter's "Peanut" 1/2 A speed kit, c. 1960, designed by Warren Kurth. In a letter written by Warren to Mike Hazel, he said, "This kit box was actually a jewelry box. Several hobby shop dealers told me that because of the small size, they actually had more Peanuts stolen than they sold." Originally sold for $3.95, this one is in mint condition. *Courtesy of Mike Hazel.* $75-85.

AMECO "Scat," c. 1946, class B and C, 24 inch wing span, designed by Johnnie Casburn. *Courtesy of Mike Hazel*, excellent condition, $75-85.

Desert Model Company, "The Desert Streak," c. early 1950s, designed by Jim McElroy. The wings are made of sheet aluminum riveted on the trailing edge. An original designed speed pan is included in this rare kit. In Mike's notes he quotes Don McClave, "A really hot ship in 1952! I had one with a McCoy 29." *Courtesy of Mike Hazel*, excellent condition, $80-110.

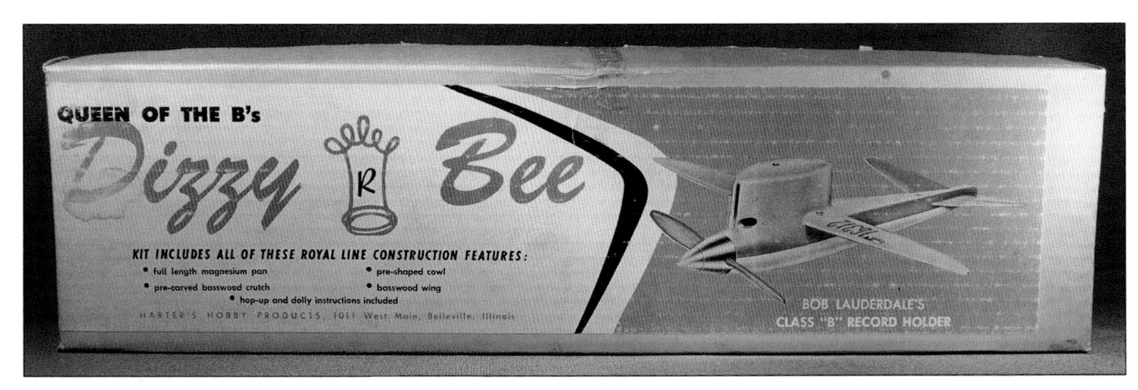

Harter's "Dizzy Bee" class B speed kit, c. 1960, published in *Model Airplane News*, August 1959. *Courtesy of Mike Hazel*, excellent condition, $65.

Cleveland "Topper II," c. 1947, box cover is incorrect, stating this model has a 20 inch wing span, it is actually 16 inches. Designed for class A and B engines, this kit's contents are still sealed in original cellophane wrap. *Courtesy of Mike Hazel*, near mint condition, $90-110.

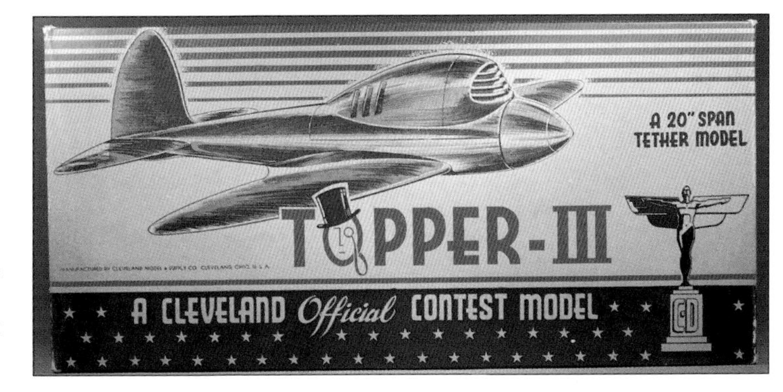

Cleveland "Topper III," c. 1947, this model has the 20 inch wing span. *Courtesy of Mike Hazel*, mint condition, $90-110.

Speedmaster Hobby Products, "Kansas Twister," class C speed kit, c. 1965-70. *Courtesy of Mike Hazel.* Excellent condition, $60-75.

Consolidated Model Company, "Hell Razor," c. 1949, designed by George Fong and used to win class D at the 3rd Plymouth International Model Plane contest in 1949 in the senior division. The design is featured in the December 1949 issue of *Model Airplane News* and went on to an AMA official speed record of 159 .23 mph. Consolidated was quick to market this kit as it came out in time for Christmas 1949. The two boxes contain the same model plane, Mike notes the yellow and red box contained enough wood to build two planes. *Courtesy of Mike Hazel.* Near mint condition, $75-85.

Consolidated Model Company, "1/2 A Hell Razor," c. 1950, designed by George Fong. This kit is exactly half the size of the class D version. Many companies that had a successful selling design would scale kits up and down retaining the original name. The planes didn't always fly as well as the original. Today's modelers are recreating past kits using modern building techniques and engines; some have been found to be excellent flyers when built with today's methods. The balsa wood used in kits sometimes determined their success in the hobby market. This little speed kit is in near mint condition. *Courtesy of Mike Hazel.* $35-45.

Berkeley Models, the "Bug," c. 1946, plans recommend using an ignition Arden .099 and Bantam .19 engines. Box cover proclaims new "Autotrol" control system, many manufactures didn't want to pay Jim Walker for the use of his patented control system. Kit includes Berkeley liquid cement that was still usable. *Courtesy of Mike Hazel.* Box in excellent condition and the contents are mint. $60-70.

Original printer's paste-up for advertising the "Hell Razor." c. 1950. Pricing of one of a kind, items like this depends almost entirely on the desirability of the content. *Courtesy of Mike Hazel.* $75-125.

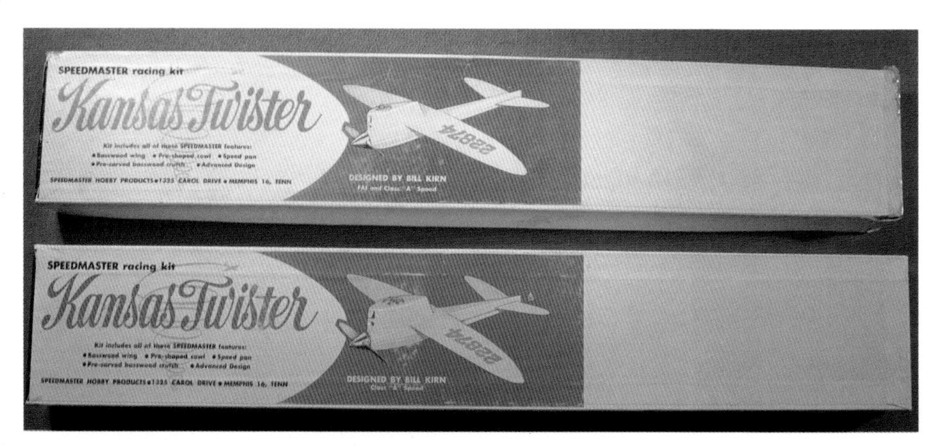

Speedmaster Hobby Products, "Kansas Twister," class A and B speed kits, c. 1965-70, designed by Bill Kirn. The class A kit is the easiest to find out of the three sizes. *Courtesy of Mike Hazel.* Excellent condition, $55-70.

Harter's "Dizzy Boy" class C speed kit, c. 1960, designed by Lauderdale with a 20 inch wingspan using a McCoy .60. *Courtesy of Mike Hazel.* Excellent condition, $70-80.

Modelcraft "Vee-Gee," c. 1942, designed by Granger Williams and Virgil Clark. Kit contains a can of dope and cement both are still liquid, excellent condition. *Courtesy of Mike Hazel.* $100-140.

Champion Model Research, "Hellhammer," c. 1946. This was another kit circumventing the Walker U-control patent, using a fixed line and a movable line actuating a spring-loaded elevator. *Courtesy of Mike Hazel.* Excellent condition, $70-80.

The deBolt Model Engineering Company, "Speedwagon 29B" c. early 1950s. Hal deBolt won fame at the 1946 New York Mirror Flying Fair and other east coast contests. He went on to pioneer radio control in the 1950s and produced a line of successful model airplane kits.

The deBolt Model Engineering Company, "Speedwagon" c. early 1950s, designed by Hal deBolt. *Courtesy of Mike Hazel.* Excellent condition, $65-85.

Wilport Models, "Go Jo," c. 1946, designed by Walt Wilson for "contest speed work," for .099 to .23 engines. *Courtesy of Mike Hazel.* Excellent condition, $65-75.

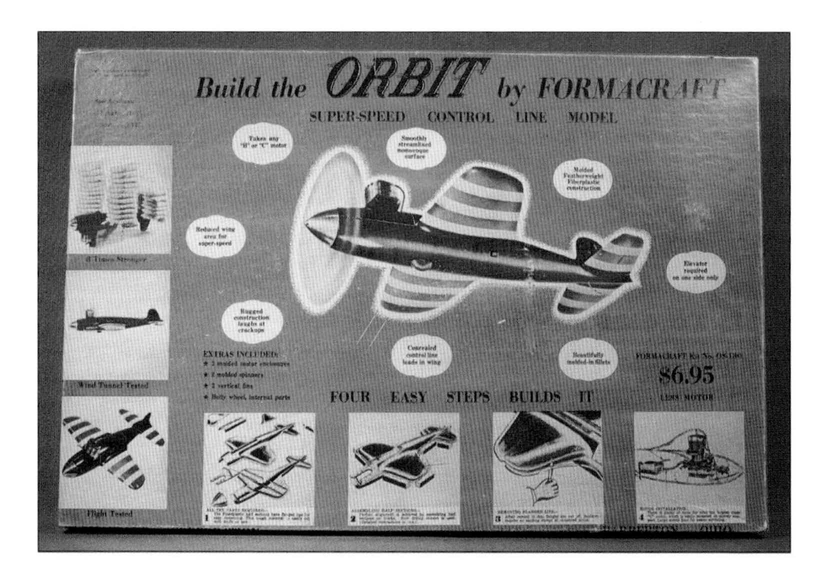

Formacraft Corporation, "Orbit," c. 1947, designed by Bill Harbaugh with well detailed plans and unique construction. Joe Wagner supplied this information about the kit, "The kit was made in the Cleveland area, and was heavily promoted locally. It went into production March or April of 1947, and was produced for 18 months or less. When the company ceased, they still had a large number of kits in stock. The main material was phenolic impregnated fiber." It was designed for the McCoy .49 and .60 engines. *Courtesy of Mike Hazel.* Mint condition, $100-120.

Berkeley Model and Supply Company

William L. Effinger founded Berkeley Model and Supply Company in a Brooklyn, New York garage in 1933. Berkeley produced America's first gas model, the famous "Buccaneer," in 1935. They were the first manufacturer of a kit for Dyna-jet speed models, "Squirt," in 1948 and 1/2 A powered helicopters. In 1957, it was reported that two-thirds of the over 150 model kits created were still carried in their current catalog and over two million had been produced. Scale kits were the foundation of the Berkeley line; the rubber powered Consolidated Fleester was the first in 1934. ("Berkeley, Where Those Kits Come From," *American Modeler,* January 1957, 20, 43). Effinger pioneered radio control with the DE Aerotrol in 1950 and Super Aerotrol radio kits around 1951-1952. Some of the most famous Berkeley kits are the Custom Cavalier, Powerhouse, Flying Cloud, Warhawk, Zilch, Sandy Hogan, Privateer, and Royal Rudderbug. In 1959 a four page ad appeared in the Air Trails Model Annual containing 102 model planes and 14 boats and ships. The ads for Berkeley models disappeared from the pages of model magazines by November 1959 ending its amazing history as one of America's premier modeling companies. Berkeley Models is considered by many modelers active in the 1940s and 1950s to be one of the finest model companies of the period. Bill Effinger was nominated into the AMA Hall of Fame in 1986.

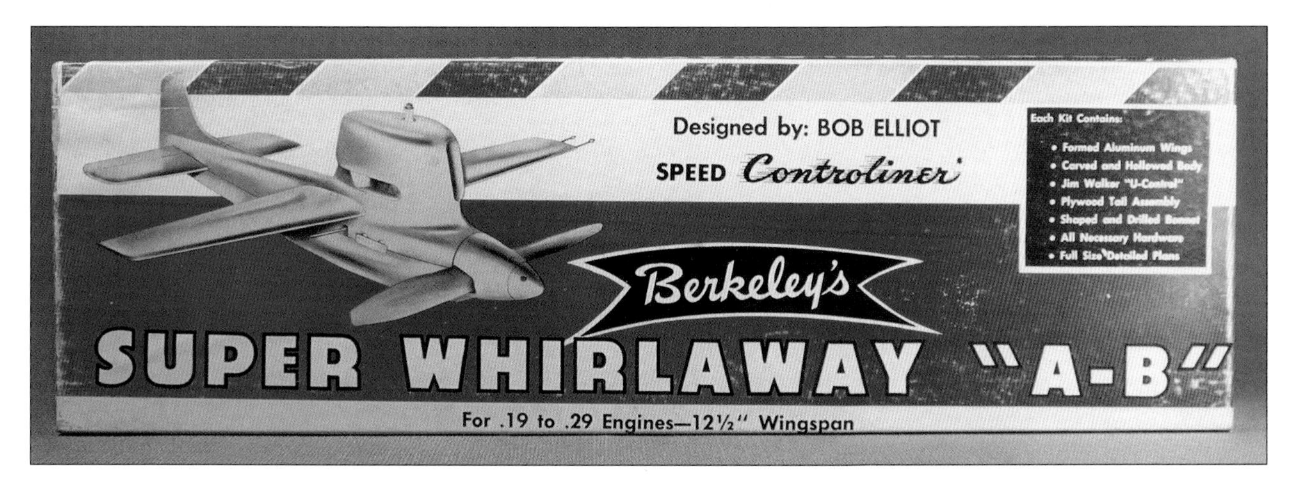

Berkeley Models, "Super Whirlaway A-B," c. 1954, designed by Bob Elliot for .19 to .29 sized engines, comes with preformed metal wings. *Courtesy of Mike Hazel.* Mint condition, $70-90.

Berkeley Models, "P-40 Warhawk," c. 1950, designed by Bob Elliot, one of the most famous old time stunters, winning the 1953 National stunt event in the Junior and open class. It is listed as one of the all-time Berkeley favorites. *Courtesy of Bob Parker.* $150-250.

Berkeley Models, "F4F Wildcat" c. 1950, for .09 to .35 engines with a 26" wingspan. *Courtesy of Bob Parker* $85-125.

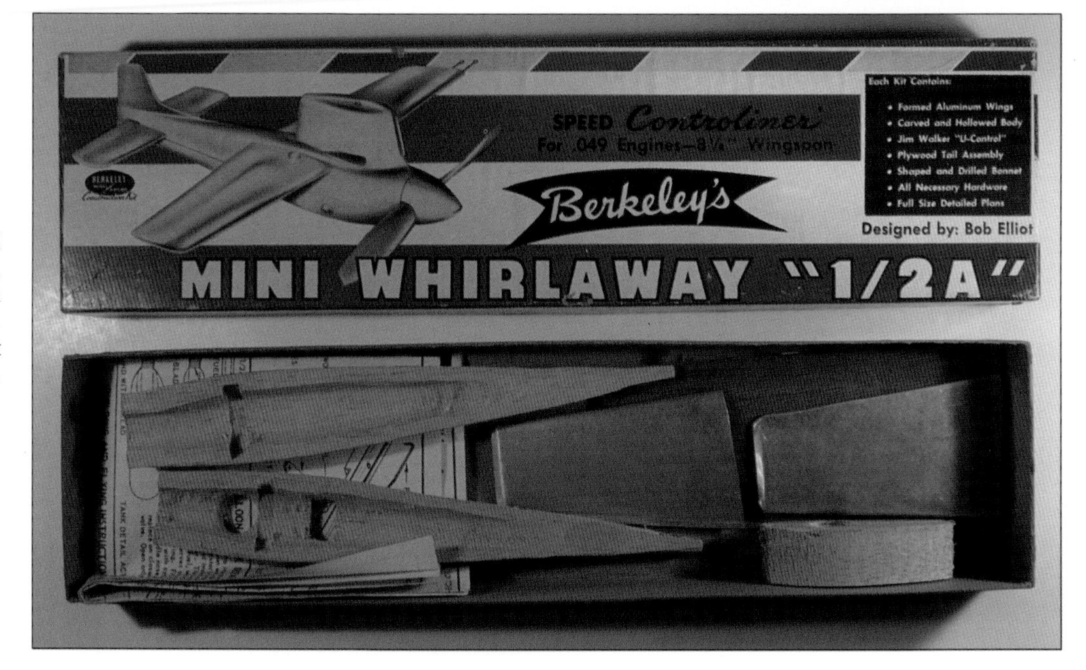

Berkeley Models, "Mini Whirlaway 1/2 A," c. 1954, designed by Bob Elliot with a small wing span of 8.25". *Courtesy of Mike Hazel.* Mint condition, $60-70.

Berkeley Models, "AJ-1 Savage," c. 1953, designed for two Jetex 100, 150, or 200 engines, two .045 to .099, another of the all-time favorites. *Courtesy of Bob Parker.* $90-150.

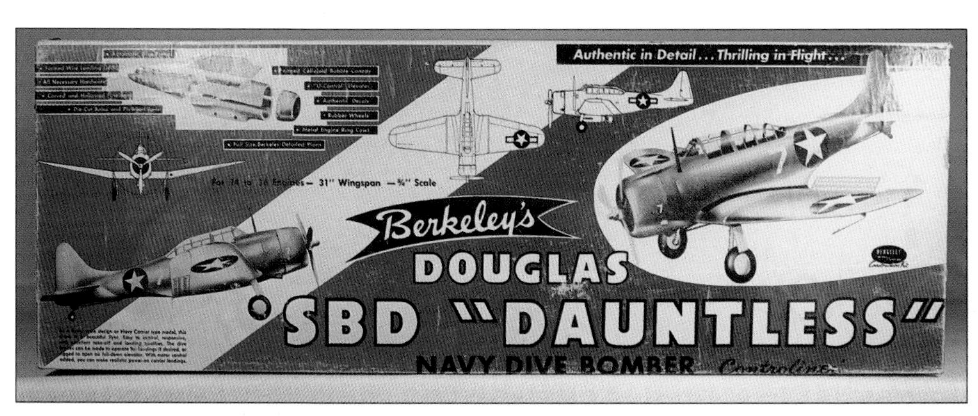

Berkeley Models, "SBD Dauntless," c. 1950s. *Courtesy of Bob Parker.* $80-150.

Berkeley Models, "F8F Bearcat" c. 1947-50s. This kit was popular and was one of their long running designs. *Courtesy of Bob Parker.* $100-175.

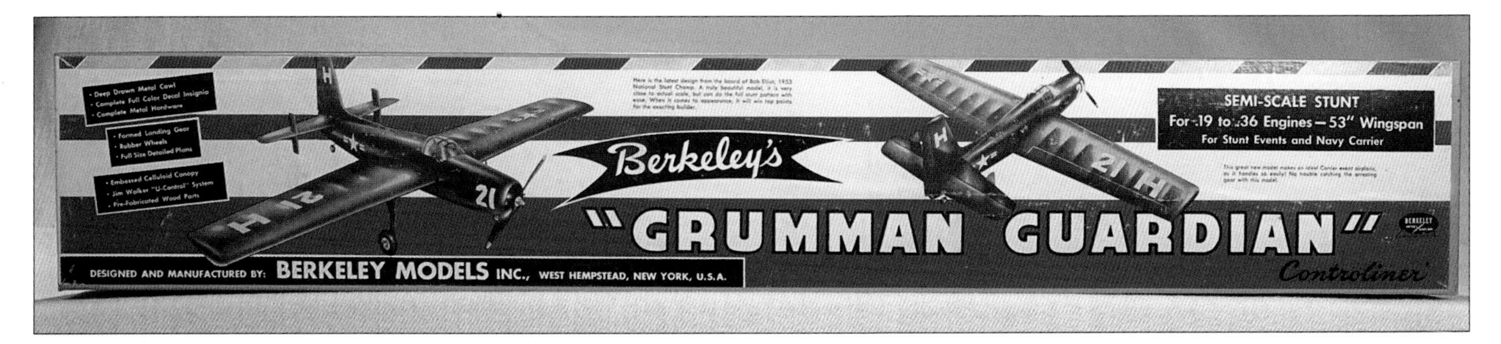

Berkeley Models, "Grumman Guardian" c. 1950s, designed by Bob Elliot. This kit was an all-time favorite. *Courtesy of Bob Parker.* $80-150.

Berkeley Models, "Aero Commander" c. 1957, designed after President Eisenhower's private plane. *Courtesy of Bob Parker.* $75-125.

company has sent engineers to Highline to lecture. It also has supplied a text it uses to teach new draftsmen and donated scrap airplane parts and sample drawings for the boys to study.

"Airplane drawing is more precise than mechanical drawing," Bitzan said. "Mechanical drawing, as taught in high school, is done to a 32nd of an inch. Airplane drawing requires draw-

BOB PARKER, a member of the drawing class, held a model plane which he made. Bob wants to be an aeronautical engineer.—Times photos, Roy Scully.

Bob Parker was fourteen when this picture appeared in the *Seattle Times* in 1959. He is holding a Berkeley P-40 Warhawk. Every collector I have known has mementos like this; it is a nice way to add character to a collection. *Courtesy of Bob Parker.*

"Checkala Roma," exact replica of Davy Slagle's model used to win the 1946 National Championship and Walker Cup. Dave Slagle is now part of the colorful history of model aviation and now resides in Maine. *Courtesy of Bob Parker.* $700-1000.

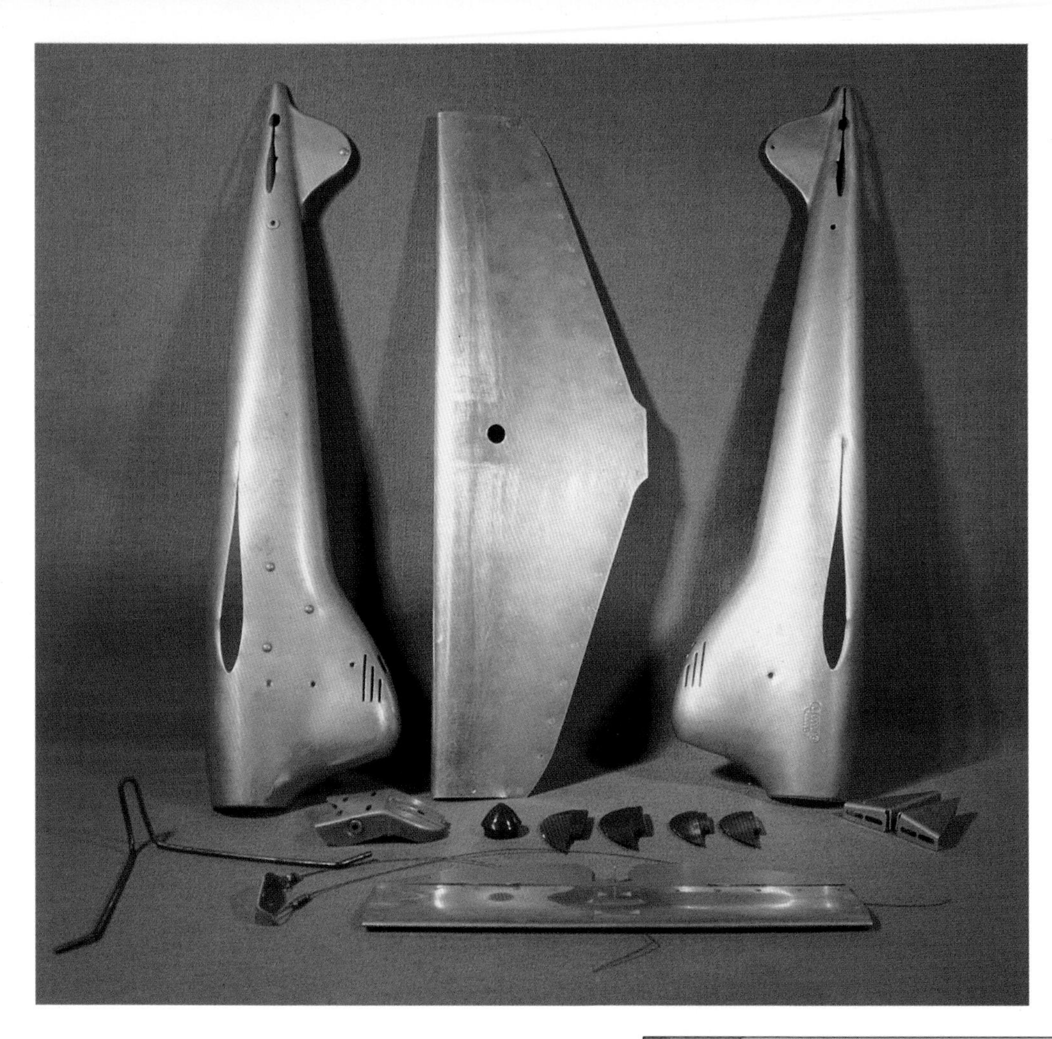

Topping Models, "Topping 100," prefabricated all-aluminum control line model for B and C engines, c. 1945, never assembled, with a box in average condition; examples with better boxes are at the higher end. Advertisments of the period said "suitable for any power from Bantam .19 to Hornet .60." The plane came with red plastic wing tips and a three bladed prop, spinner, and 2 1/2" Heliarc wheels. It sold for $10 in 1945 without an engine. Examples can be found complete with engine but no box. *Courtesy of Mike Hazel.* $300-700.

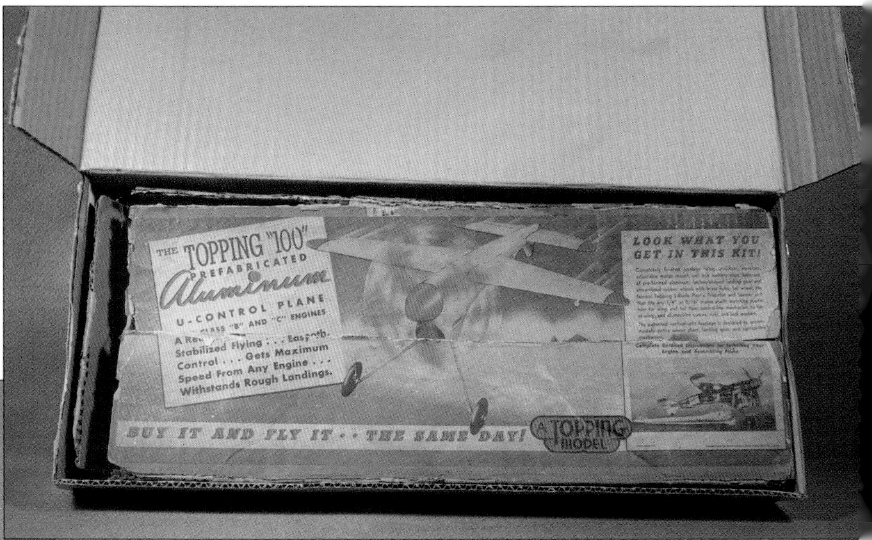

"Topping 100" box, a little worse for wear but still nice graphics.

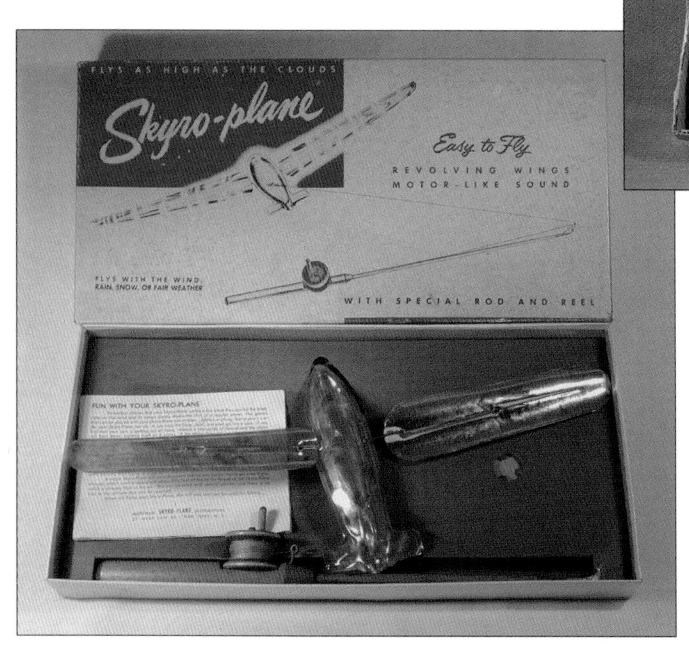

"Skyro-plane," plastic with the appearance of chrome, c. 1950s. According to the manufacture, the rod and reel can also be used for fishing. In good condition, $30-55.

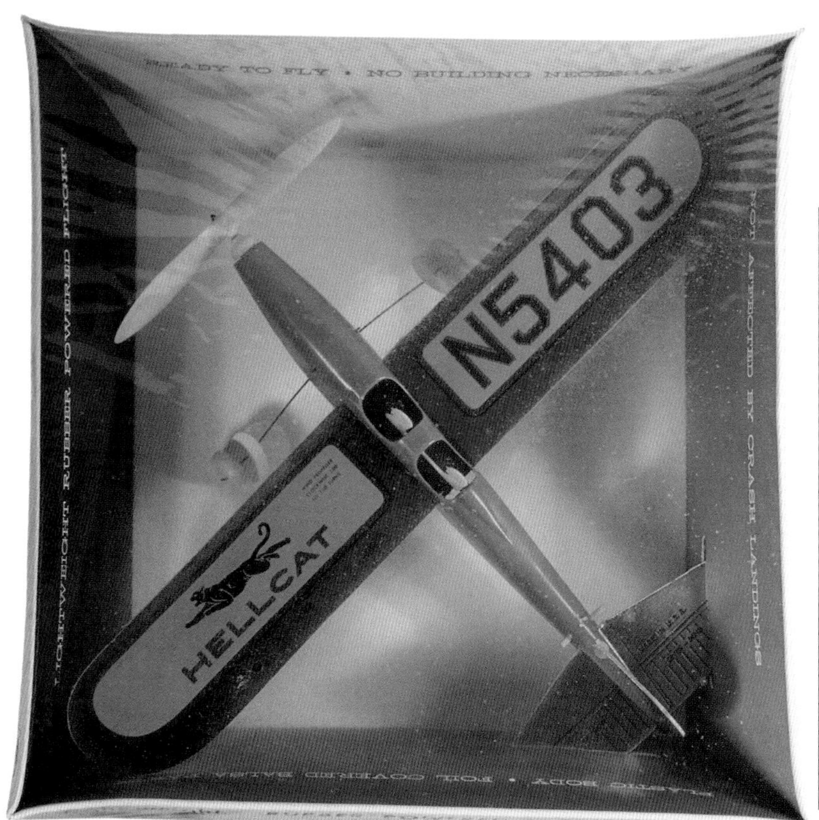

Comet, ready to fly rubber powered plane, "Hellcat," c. 1970s, new, $20-30.

Superior Products, "Sky Dicer," ready to fly rubber powered plane, c. 1970s, new, $20-30.

Comet and Superior Products box ends showing the other planes available.

Victor Stanzel & Company, "Super "V" Shark," c. 1940. This model was bought in 1945 being shipped in the kit box. Shown are the kit wheels, cement, and dope that came with every kit. Good condition, $40-65.

Victor Stanzel & Company, "Shark G-5," c. 1947. "When operated with the new "Thumb-it" and "Control-it," the racy Shark G-5 has no equal for ease of control and maneuverability." *Air Trails*, June 1947. The plane is Bob Parker's exact replica featuring the "Control-it" mechanism along with an original kit. Kit in mint condition, $80-130.

Victor Stanzel & Company, "Sharkadet," c. 1947, exact replica with Ohlsson .60 sideport, kit in mint condition, $80-130.

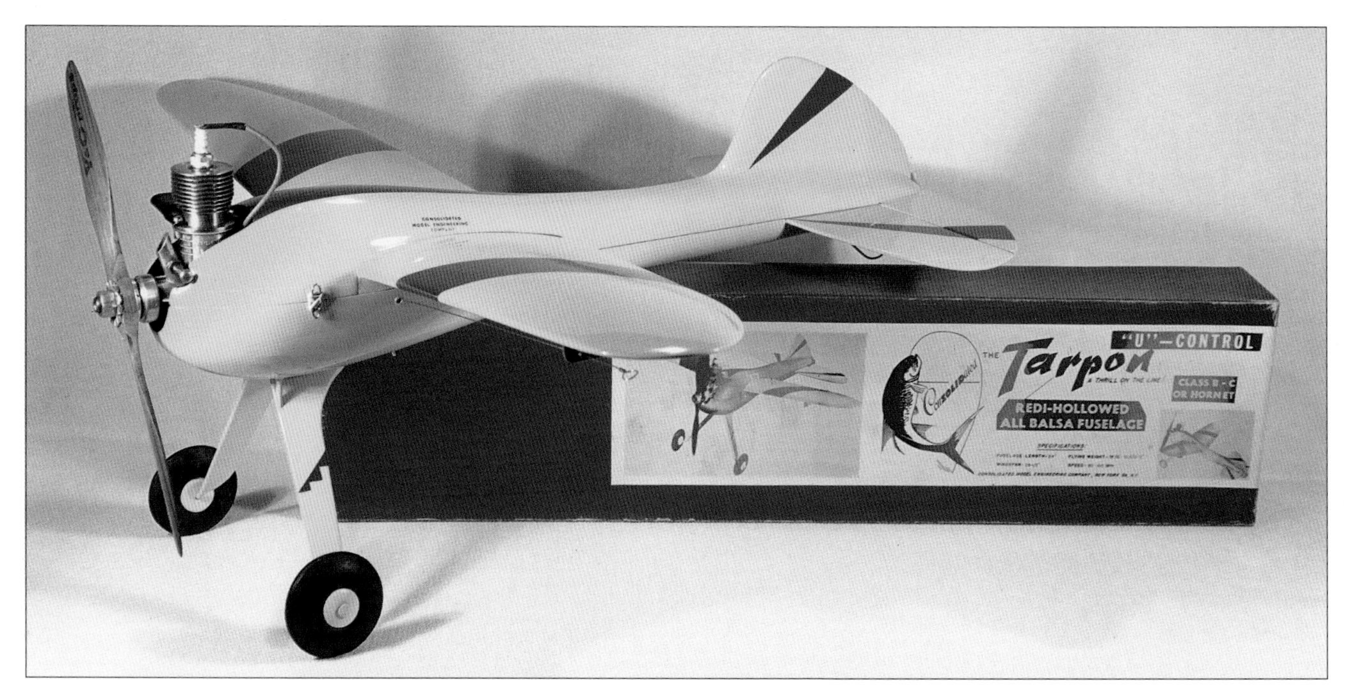

Consolidated, "The Tarpon," c. 1945, exact replica powered by an OK .60 sideport, along with the kit in mint condition. *Courtesy of Bob Parker.* The kit is valued at $90-125.

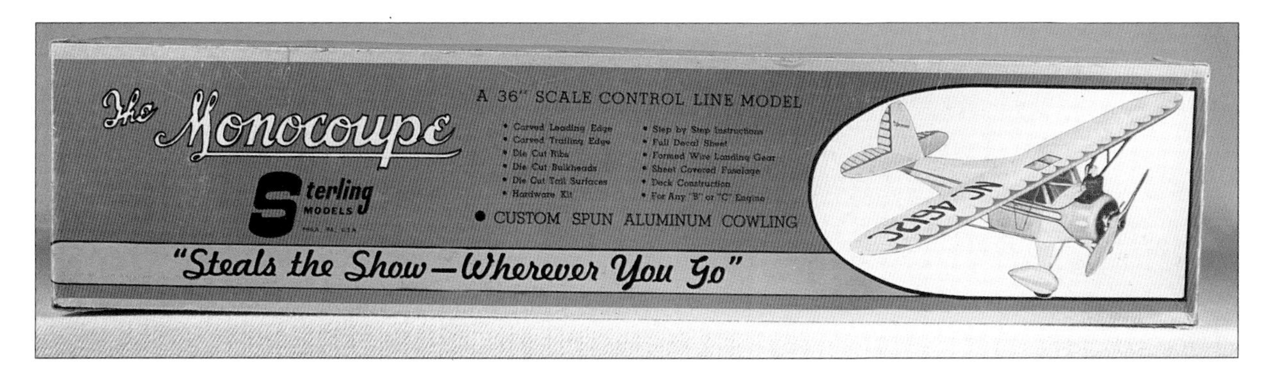

Sterling Models, "The Monocoupe," c. 1948, control line scale kit. This kit was one of first Sterling kits, the other was the "Pete." In mint condition, $ 85-130.

Bob Parker's replica of the Monocoupe with an Ohlsson .23 sideport, the original kit shows the Stanzel mono-line unit for control.

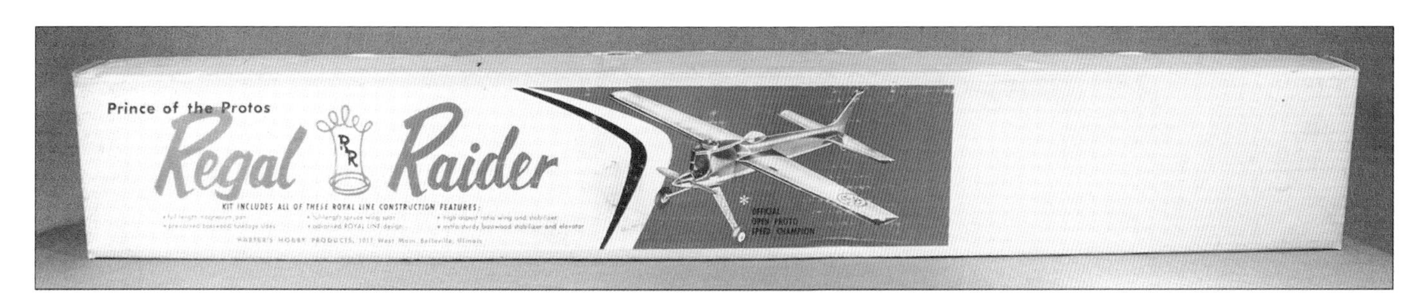

Harter's, "Regal Raider," c. 1957-1965, 2nd version depicting the model on the box, designed by William Mitchener, plans call for Dooling .29 or Fox .29R. *Courtesy of Mike Hazel.* Mint condition, $60-70.

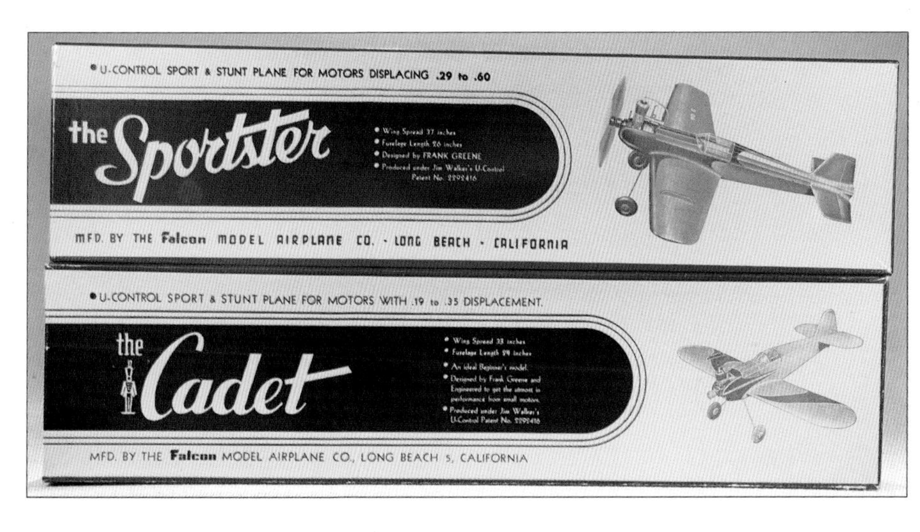

Falcon Model Airplane Company, "The Sportster and The Cadet," c. 1946, control line kits designed by Frank Greene. *Courtesy of Bob Parker.* Both are in mint condition, $65-85.

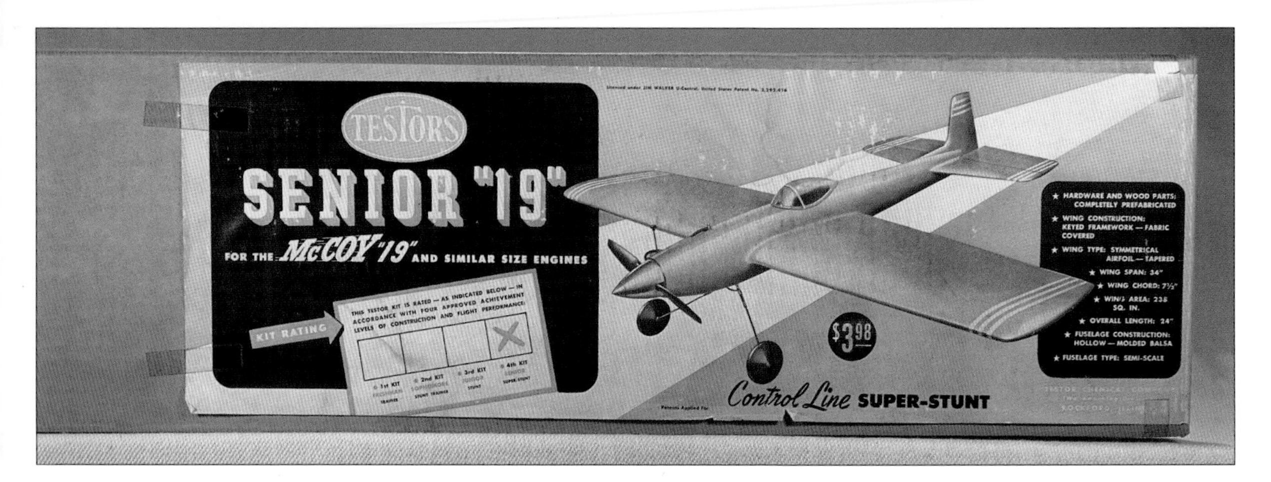

Testors, "Senior 19" c. 1950, control line trainer. The Testors Senior was designed by Nathan Bast. *Courtesy of Bob Parker.* Mint condition, $85-120.

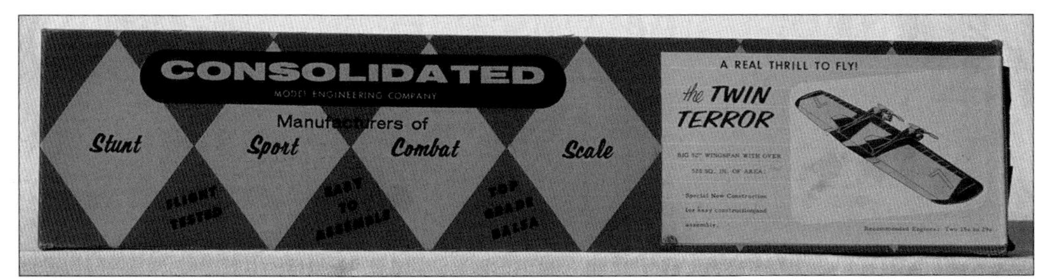

Consolidated, "Twin Terror," c. late 1950s, control line sport plane. *Courtesy of Bill Darkow.* Complete and in good condition, $45-75.

Guillow's "Barnstormer," c. 1950-51, control line stunt plane designed by Lou Andrews used to win the National Championship in 1950, kit came out a little later, mint condition, $100-135.

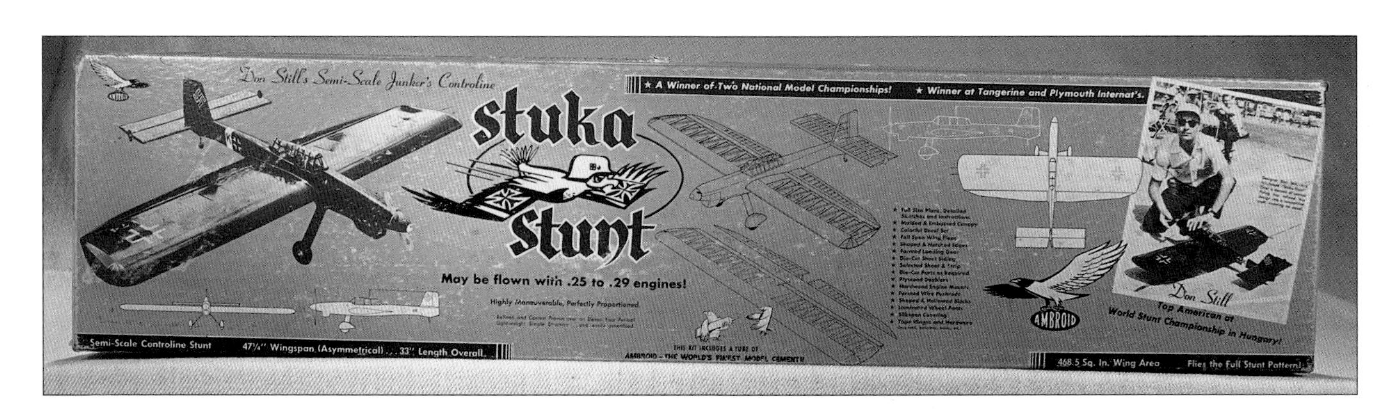

Ambroid, "Stuka Stunt" c. 1961, several planes were developed and designed by Don Still before it appeared in kit form. The first design was featured in *Air Trails,* April 1952. *Courtesy of Bob Parker.* Almost mint, $200-300.

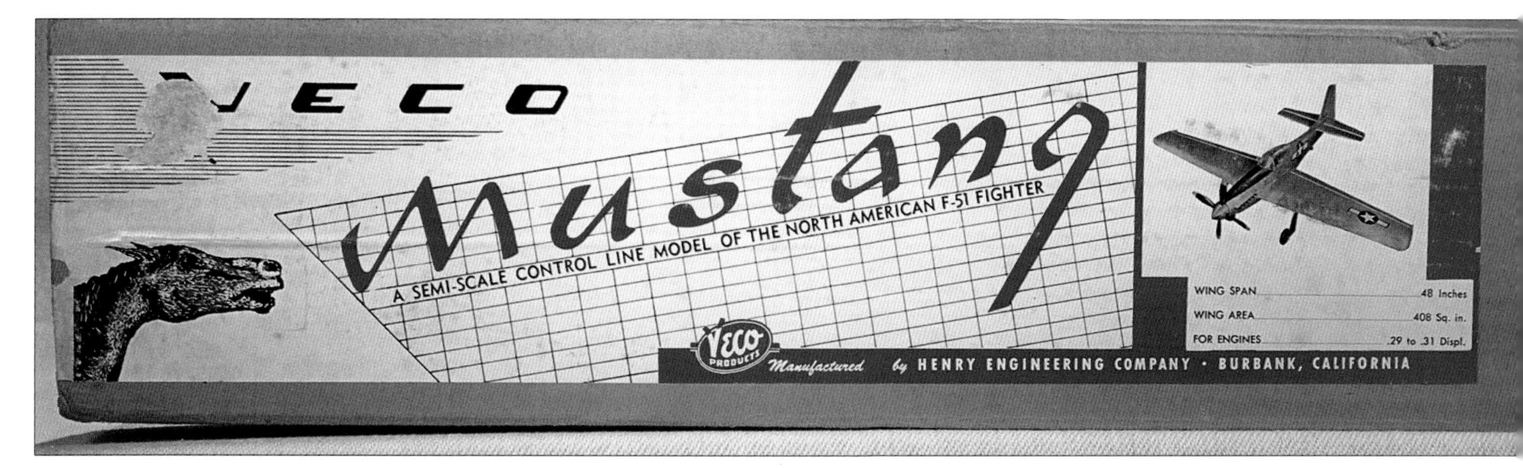

Veco, "Mustang," c. 1955. This is a rarely seen early Henry Engineering version. *Courtesy of Bob Parker.* The contents are mint with price sticker removed from the face of the box, $250-350.

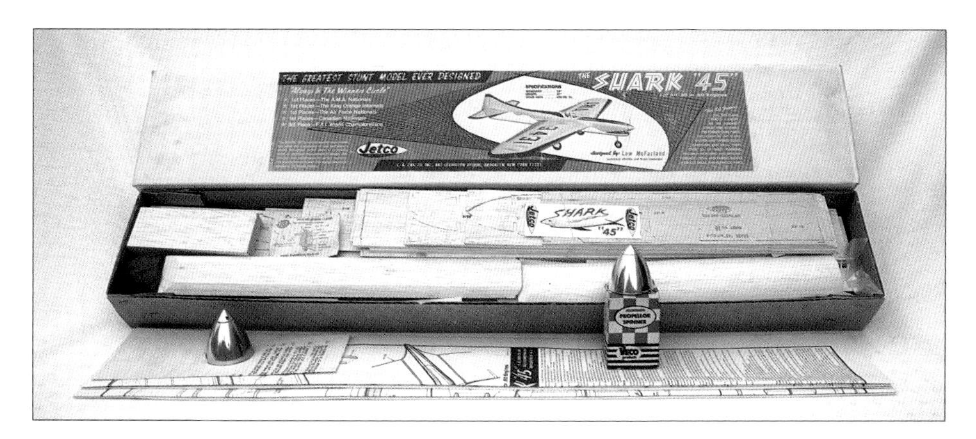

Jetco "Shark 45," c. 1965-1970s, designed by Lew McFarland and used to win the 1962 National Championship. This plane is credited with starting the trend toward larger stunt planes and is much modeled today, a timeless design. An article on this model appeared in *American Aircraft Modeler*, October 1961. Kits are still common but highly desirable. This one is opened so readers can see what a mint in box kit should look like. Most kits are compact and after removing the contents, you may wonder how the manufacturer was able to get all the stuff in the box. The contents of this kit have never been removed. Mint condition, $125-175.

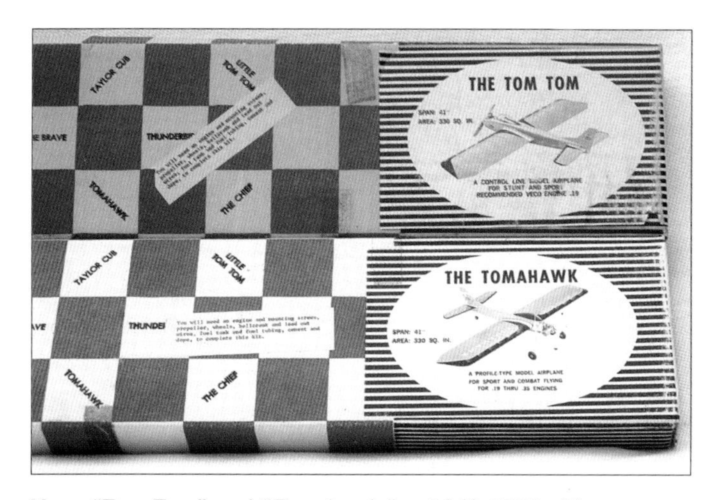

Veco, "Tom Tom" and "Tomahawk," c. 1960-1970s. These are the 2nd versions and the ones most remembered, the wing is the same on both designs. Kits are mint condition. Tom Tom, $65-90; Tomahawk, $40-70.

Sterling, Ed Southwick "Skylark" S-27, c 1963. This was a very popular kit. A magazine article appeared in *Model Airplane News*, December, 1963. Sterling's Ed Manulkin is quoted as saying "The best stunt control line model I've seen in nearly 35 years of experience." Ed Southwick built several different versions. This is another design with simple elegance and is timeless. Mint condition, $125-175.

Sterling, "Imperial Ringmaster" S-18, c 1959. *Courtesy of Bob Parker.* This is the early box and is in mint condition. $150-300.

Imperial Ringmaster decals, somehow Bob acquired these without a kit. *Courtesy of Bob Parker.* $10-15.

Sterling, "Customized Ringmaster" c. 1963, a short lived kit that is highly sought after. The kit was an out-growth of custom Ringmaster designs by Dave Holland starting in 1959. The story is featured in the *American Modeler Annual 1962*. Early 1964, Ed Manulkin of Sterling Models initiated a national contest, "Let yourself go" in custom designing the Ringmaster. The winners were announced in the July/August 1964 issue of *American Modeler* with Robert Mele of Philadelphia, Pennsylvania and Walter Schlesinger of St Petersburg, Florida sharing first place in the customizing contest. The Ringmaster series of model airplanes have been one of the all-time favorites for more than fifty years. Matt Kania designed the original Ringmaster around 1950. This kit can sell for $175-300.

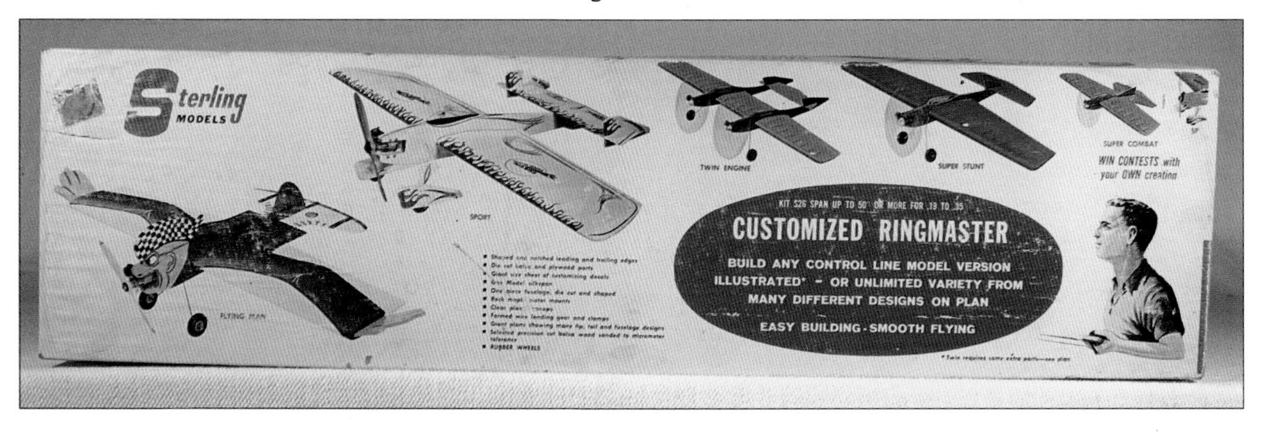

Midwest "P-63 King Cobra," c. 1970s, small version with a 33 inch wingspan. Midwest kitted the King Cobra in a 48" wingspan version along with a ME-109, Douglas Skyraider, and Mustang all using the same basic wing structure. Vince Micchia designed the P-63 and it was featured in the May 1969 issue of *Flying Models*. The Midwest kits were very popular and still easy to find. The small version in mint condition is worth, $35-50. The larger versions of these kits in mint condition. Courtesy of Bill Darkow. $50-100.

Chapter 3
Magazines

Since October 1928, when *Air Trails* and *Flying Aces* began to be published, and in June 1929 when *Universal Model Airplane News* appeared, magazines dedicated exclusively to model aviation have been a big part of a modeler's life. ("Two Decades of Progress" *Air Trails*, October 1948, 28, 102-104). They have provided stories, models, up-to-date details of new products, highlights of major contest results, upcoming meets, and advice to beginner and expert alike. Advertisements inspired the dreams of American youth. I found myself sometimes waiting in anticipation a whole month for the next issue to hit the stands. I purchased my first model airplane magazine, *Flying Models,* in February 1969, for fifty cents and still have the issue, in heavily read condition.

With today's huge interest in the history of model aviation, plus the desire to recreate models of the past, magazines have become enjoyable collectibles. Today's collectors want whole issues in good readable condition. Missing pages or covers change the magazine's value significantly. One of the trends in the antiques and collectible market that bothers me is cutting up magazines for their covers, articles, and advertisements. I believe this is done for two reasons: the first being money and the second, more space for dealer inventory. A message to dealers: **Modelers want the whole magazine**! You may sell cut up copies but not to knowledgeable collectors of model airplane memorabilia. Hard to find copies appear on eBay regularly. This has depressed the magazine market for sellers but is a boon to buyers.

There have been four excellent articles written in the past three years that detail the history of model airplane magazines. Jim Alaback wrote 108 columns for *Flying Models* beginning in September 1992; his last one was in the August 2001 issue. Most notably, Alaback started Kits And Models Antiquitous (KAPA) and is a member of the AMA Hall of Fame, inducted in 2001. His "Old Time Topics" articles have inspired many modelers to enjoy their "roots" once again and new modelers to find joy in the simple beginnings of aeromodeling. (Frank Fanelli, *Flying Models,* August 2001, 4). Jim recently published a three-part article on model airplane magazines. The first, an article on *Flying Aces* and *Flying Models* outlined their history and was published in the September 2000 issue of *Flying Models.* The second article detailed the history of *Model Airplane News* and *Air Trails* and appeared in the June 2001 issue of *Flying Models.* Jim finished his three part series in July 2001 highlighting *Popular Aviation* and other short-lived publications. Dick Sarpolus, writer for *Model Aviation* and *Flying Models* wrote a nice article titled "75 Years of Model Magazines" in the June 2002 issue of *Flying Models.* Dick has been a writer and builder for over forty years and has done much of his own photography for his articles. He was elected to the AMA Hall of Fame in 1985. Jim and Dick are both very experienced modelers; between them, they can cover just about every aspect of model aviation.

The impact of model airplane magazines is only now being appreciated. The cover art and advertisements have shaped at least three generations of modelers. As a teenager, I would use the American's Hobby Center ads as a wish list. Their ads ran two to four pages every month in my favorite magazine at the time, *Flying Models.* They were clearly geared to the kids that read them as they offered entry-level engine and kit combinations. From 1954 to the early 1970s LM Cox, OK, Comet, Enterprise, Berkeley, Guillows, Scientific Models, Testors McCoy, Top Flight, and Sterling regularly bought full- and two-page ads. Berkeley introduced their new line of products in April 1954 with two, six-page ads placed in the first issue of *Air Trails For Young Men.* These were highly detailed and are amazing to read still today. Duke Fox was a marketing genius often scattering small ads through out *Model Airplane News* announcing new engines, fuels, and planes from 1958 to 1964. In the early 1970s, he used four-page color ads to introduce another new line of engines, fuels, and accessories. Undoubtedly, advertising influenced a young boy's mind, we all wanted to be like the big boys.

Cover art of the past seventy-five years was also used to increase sales, and was aimed at the youthful market. The four most remembered early cover artists were August Schomburg, *Flying Aces*, Jean Oldham, and Josef "Jo" Kotula, *Model Airplane News*, and Frank Tinsley's creations on the *Air Trails* covers. Jo Kotula's artistic talents graced the covers of *Model Airplane News* beginning with the June 1933 issue and continued until the middle 1960s. (Jim Alaback, *Flying Models*, September 2000, 34-35; June 2001, 76-77; July 2001, 44-45). New artists and illustrators began to appear after the war and into the 1950s; most of them also built and flew model airplanes. This aspect changed cover art, as actual model airplanes became subjects often with an article about the plane featured on the cover included in the issue. The names of S. Calhoun Smith, Harold Stevenson, and Gil Evans along with British artists C. Rupert Moore and C.D. Carrick are among the best-remembered artists. C. Rupert Moore's model airplane renditions on the covers of *Aeromodeller* are classics. He also produced many illustrations within the pages of *Aeromodeller*. Carrick's art adorned the covers of the *Aeromodeller Annuals* starting 1949. Cover artists began depicting stories of modelers in their triumphs, trials, and tragedies. The stories portrayed activities every modeler had experienced during the great adventure of flight through model aviation.

Prolific illustrators H. A. Thomas and Cal Smith were geniuses with the pen and brush; their artistic talents took complex modeling ideas and formed them into something a young man could understand. Douglas Rolfe's fine illustrations of full-scale aircraft, model plans, and cut-away drawings graced the pages of *Air Trails* in the late 1940s. Another master illustrator was Lee Scott whose plans and engine cut-away drawings are phenomenal. He drafted the *Air Trails* plans and cut-away of

Davy Slagle's famous stunter Checkala Roma. The Fixit Wright illustrated stories featured in the early 1950s issues of *Flying Models*, by Bruce Wennerstrom are still beloved today. Wennerstrom, along with Gil Evans are the best-remembered illustrators drawing the Fixit Wright comic book style stories. Bob Buragas wrote the text while Gil Evans illustrated. Frank O'Connor also did some of the Fixit Wright strips in 1954. Other artists who did covers and illustrations from 1948 to mid-1960s were Jon Dahlstrom, Robert Lapshire, Robert Martin, Roger Metcalf, P.E. Norman, Alfred Owen, R.L, Patterson, Jim Triggs, Albert Vela, Gaylord Welker, and John Zeboyan. Scottish artist Laurie Bagley is best remembered for his wonderful renditions of the actual model airplanes featured in *Aero Modeller* from the late 1950s into the 1960s. Another great illustrator and draftsman was Hank Clark, drawing the anecdotal cartoon adventures of Chuck Wood featured in the early 1980s issues of *Model Aviation*. Artists and illustrators created the commercial successes enjoyed by model magazines and often the model airplane designers. Our lives are richer because of their creative gifts.

Robert Benjamin's marvelous paintings graced the covers for *Model Builder* and *Model Aviation* from 1982 to 1992. Bob lives in Olympia, Washington and is a master modeler who now competes at the National Scale Championships. Bud Gardinier from Richmond, Virginia created the cover art on *Model Builder's* 15th Anniversary issue and the Walt Good Commemorative Issue from August 1988. Les Hoy has done some nice covers for the Society of Antique Modelers yearbooks. All cover artists and illustrators have had one thing in common, their love of airplanes and desire to bring them into the lives of modelers. Historically, publishers paid the artists very little for their efforts and most of the covers' original paintings were thrown away. I have researched this for several years, searching for original cover art, and little exists today. Some cover art was given away as gifts during the 1950s, to those who supported and contributed to the world of aeromodeling. The Harold Stevenson painting used on the December 1953 issue of *Flying Models* was presented to Bill Effinger in recognition for organizing the Long Island Hydro Meet. (*Flying Models,* February 1954, 28). In retrospect, the hobby, sport, and industry of model aviation owes much to the artistic individuals who have touched the hearts and minds of modelers every month for the past seventy-five years.

From 1928 to 1975, magazine editors have guided and shaped the direction of model airplane magazines for the benefit of modelers. In 1975, *American Aircraft Modeler* went under and this led editors to begin making decisions that would insure their publication's survival in a tightening market for advertising dollars. Radio control manufacturers began to dominate the content and layout of magazines as more modelers started experiencing R.C. The role of today's editor is often a difficult balancing act trying to satisfy all disciplines associated with model aviation. Bill Winter is the most famous and prolific of all the great editors over the years. Other editors deserve mention as they, too, have had a huge impact on the industry: Al Lewis of *Air Trails*, Howard G. McEntee and Walter L. Schroder of *Model Airplane News*, Walter Holze and Don McGovern of *Flying Models* (Dick Sarpolus, *Flying Models*, June 2002, 74-77). Continuing the tradition of model magazine editing today is Robin W. Hunt who guided *Flying Models* from December 1980 to June 1996. He is now editor of the Academy of Model Aeronautic publication, *Model Aviation*. All of these men have been elected to the AMA Hall of Fame and their legacies are still being felt today. The reasons for collecting magazines today are as varied as the collector. The revival and preservation of model airplane history continues to be one of the most important reasons for amassing a library, one to enjoy for many years.

The American Boy, June 1930, cover by Harrison Cady, depicting model aviation adventures of the time. $10.

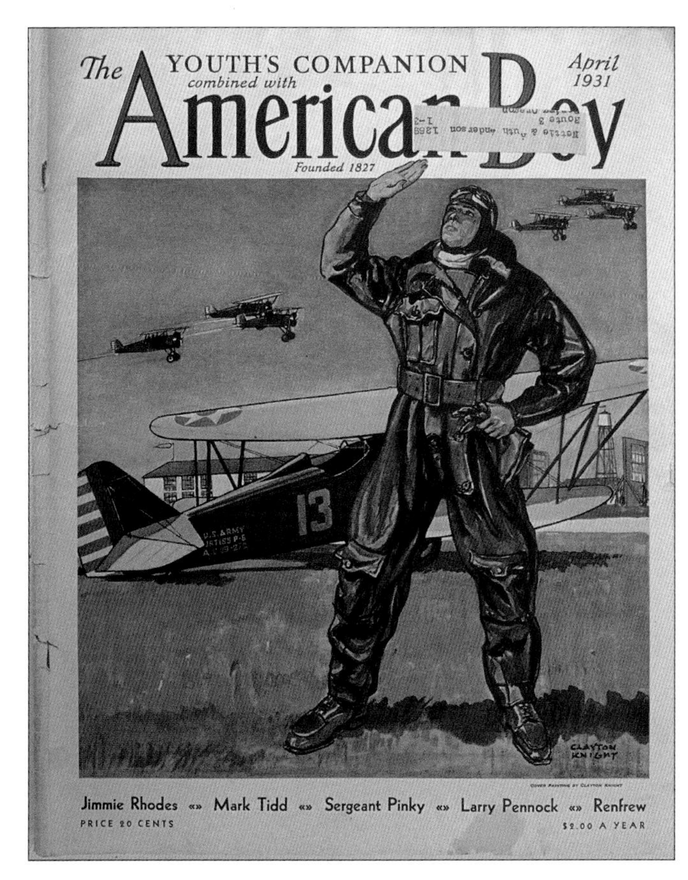

The American Boy, April 1931, cover by Clayton Knight. This issue contains the cancellation of the 1931 Nationals sponsored by the AMLA (Airplane Model League of America), $10.

Model Aircraft Builder, April 1936, cover by Marnac. This is volume 1, number 1 published by National Scientific Publications. Condition always varies on pre 1940 magazines as it is hard to find pristine copies of much read issues. This copy is in average condition. $10-30.

THE AMERICAN BOY—YOUTH'S COMPANION 71

25c a Week Club

ZANZIBAR PACKET FREE

SCARCE PAPUA! 5c

ILLUSTRATED STAMP ALBUM 25c

LARGEST STAMP IN THE WORLD

100 STAMPS FREE!

BOYS WANTED AGE 12 TO 20 YEARS

EARN $5 TO $15 SPARE TIME; MORE FULL TIME

A FAMOUS FOOD....FOR A FAMOUS DOG

KEN-L-RATION THE DOG FOOD SUPREME

February by stamps in values of ½, 1, 2, and 3 annas and 1 rupee presenting several Government buildings and a war memorial arch.

Italy: The trans-Atlantic flight by the squadron of planes from Rome to Rio Janeiro was commemorated postally.

Rumania: The recent national census brought commemoratives. *Recensamantul Populatiei*, signifying "the counting of the people," is inscribed. A map of Rumania is on the 1 leu, and a native woman carrying a baby is shown on the 2, 4, and 6.

Russia: The 25th anniversary of the ill-starred revolution of January, 1905, has been recalled with 3 kopecs, 5k, and 10k stamps with designs of military character.

Salvador: An earlier hero has been remembered—General Francisco Menendez, once a President of the republic, who was born a century ago. A picture of the monument which is over his grave is the design, the values being 2, 5, and 10 centavos. The dates 1830 and 1930 are inscribed.

South West Africa: A new definitive series shows a gom pauw (a species of bird) on the ½-penny; Cape Cross and the Portuguese coat-of-arms on the 1p; Bogenfels, a natural rock arch, on the 2p; Government structures at Windhoek on the 3p; and various scenes, animals, waterfalls, trees, and buildings on other values. Adjoining stamps in each sheet are inscribed alternately in English and Afrikaans.

Here's Your Yellowstone Park Contest! (Continued from page 26)

1. Your entry must be in by May 10!
2. You must be under 21 to be eligible.

The results of the contest will be published in the July issue. The two top placers will leave home about August 1. If you're to be one of them, write for that booklet now!

Honorary judges of the contest: Charles Donnelly, president of the Northern Pacific Railroad; Frederick E. Williamson, president of the Burlington Route; James Willard Schultz; Albin Henning; and Griffith Ogden Ellis, editor of *The American Boy*, who will be executive judge.

Do You Know That—

Meteorites each year add 100,000 tons to the weight of the earth? Thank goodness most of them disintegrate before they hit the surface!

* * *

A road runner—a bird built like a hen, and fast on his feet—seldom flies, but depends on his speed in running to get away from danger?

* * *

Not long ago, three men and a dog traveled 5,280 miles—all but a few miles by motor boat—from the mouth of the Columbia River on the Pacific Coast, all the way to New York City?

An Announcement to Airplane Model Fans

THERE will be no national A. M. L. A. contest in Detroit in 1931. The officers of the Airplane Model League of America have reached this decision only after much consideration, and it's with sincere regret that they make the announcement. And they wish you to know just why it has been necessary to take this step.

Previous contests have been supported in the following way: The Detroit Board of Commerce has generously contributed $7,500, or about half of the total cost. *The American Boy* has contributed its staff for the management of the contest; it has paid for the trips to Europe, and the final banquet; it has solicited from interested people added funds for the support of the tournament. In addition, *The American Boy* has supported and conducted the activities of the League throughout the year.

This year, however, the Board of Commerce, with money enough only to carry on its own activities, is unable to contribute its $7,500. The Board has approached other organizations, without success. And without this support, the officers of the League feel it best not to hold the contest in Detroit this year.

The following contests, however, will be conducted in Dayton, Ohio, this summer, under the direction of Merrill Hamburg, secretary of the A. M. L. A.: the Mulvihill Outdoor, The National Scale Model, the Stout Outdoor Fuselage, and the international contest for the Sir Charles Wakefield cup. The last two contests are for fuselage models—ships with built-up fuselages that entirely enclose the rubber motor. The Wakefield contest, which has never before been held in the United States, took place last year at Halton, England, and was won by Joseph Ehrhardt, American outdoor and fuselage champion. The date will be Monday, June 29. The place, Dayton, Ohio.

For further information on the above contests, and for general airplane model information, address Merrill Hamburg, Secretary, Airplane Model League of America, 300 Davis Ave., Dayton, Ohio. Until further notice, this address will hold good for all communications with the A. M. L. A.

Although *The American Boy* is not conducting the contests this year, the magazine will continue to publish airplane model articles. The magazine will still be your authority for the newest and most up-to-date ships. And during the coming year the magazine will publish the best planes developed in 1931.

On behalf of its membership of 400,000, the League wishes to thank the Detroit Board of Commerce, the hundreds of interested individuals, and *The American Boy*, for the impetus they have given model aviation during the past four years.

—THE OFFICERS.

They Wouldn't Believe Him

—And No Wonder!

GUESTS in Yellowstone National Park stand spellbound before erupting geysers, marvelling at their stupendous power; gaze in awe-inspired reverence at the beauty and immensity of the Grand Canyon; exclaim in amazement at the hundreds of other natural phenomena in this magic region.

Small wonder old Jim Bridger's stories failed to gain credence among the skeptics of his day. For even now one must SEE—to fully appreciate the glories of Yellowstone.

Jim Bridger, famed frontier scout and mountain man, explored the Yellowstone more than a hundred years ago. Finding people would not believe him, Bridger deliberately elaborated his stories. A few have been reprinted in a booklet. You may have one, also full information on Yellowstone tours and a Yellowstone album, by filling out and mailing the coupon.

NORTHERN PACIFIC

Article of the cancellation of the 1931 Nationals in Detroit, Michigan.

Model Aircraft Builder, May-June 1936, featured the much publicized "Crusader" as a model design, Irwin S. Polk editor of this issue. $10-25.

Model Aircraft Builder, August 1936, cover by John Zeboyan, contained a petition to bring the first airplane ever to fly, the Wright Brothers' original Kitty Hawk plane of 1903, back from the Science Museum in South Kensington, England. Dr. Orville Wright donated the plane in March 1928. This is the easiest to find and last issue of a great little publication. $10-25.

Model Aircraft Engineer, August 1934, $5-20.

Model Aircraft Engineer, November 1934. This issue is an advance copy of the October issue. Some months are missing and this magazine was sporadic beginning in April 1934. Only eight issues were published. $5-20.

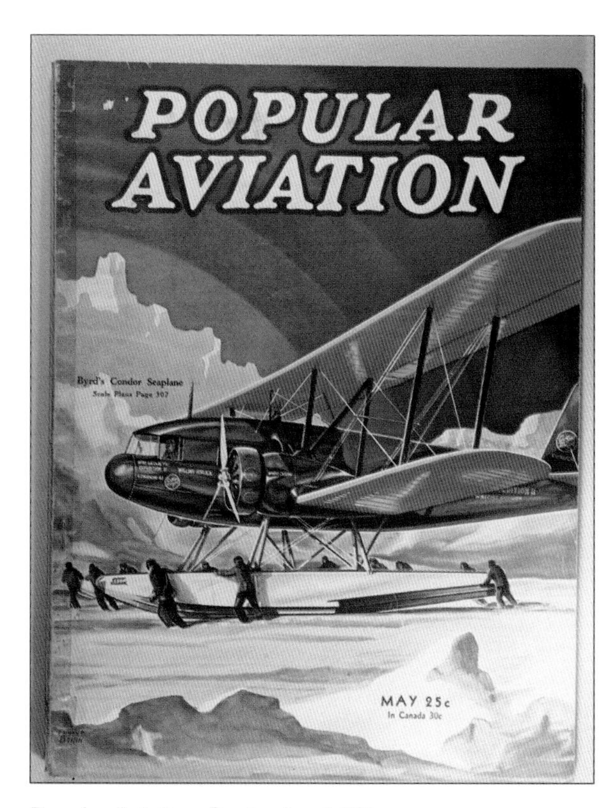

Popular Aviation, September 1934, cover by Herman R. Bollin, $8-15.

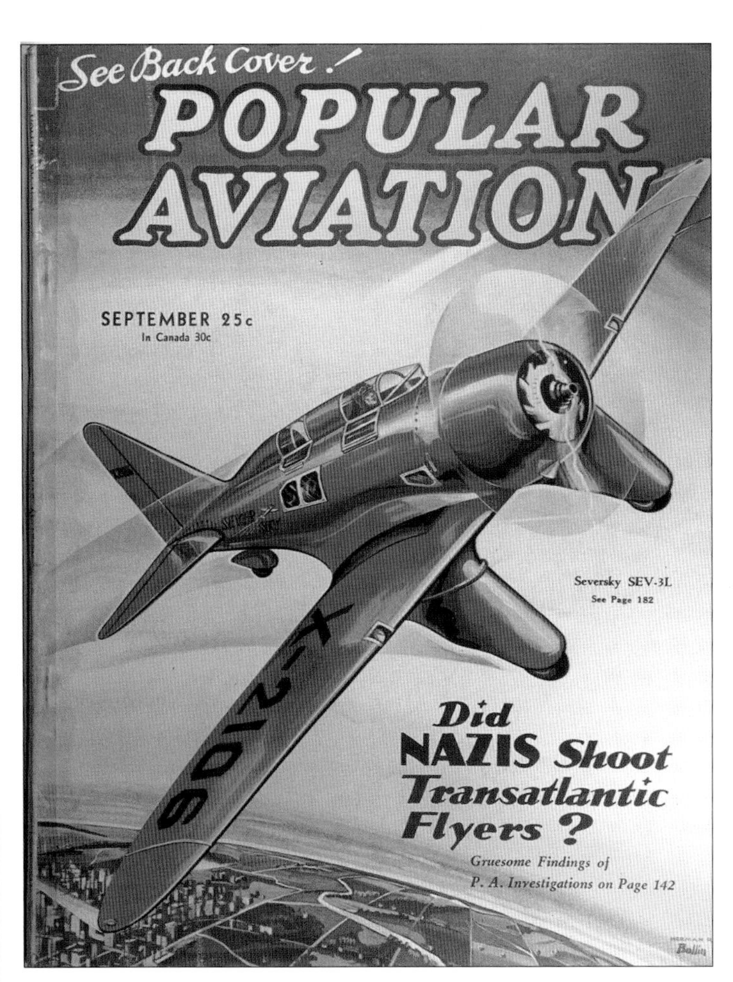

Popular Aviation, May 1934, cover by Herman R. Bollin, $8-15.

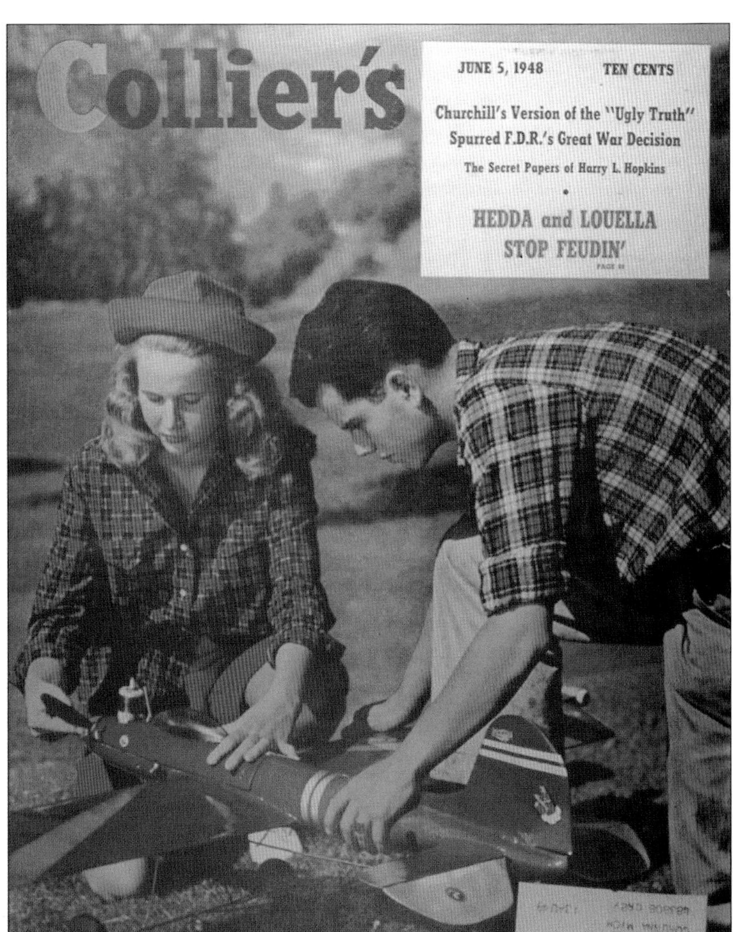

Collier's, June 5, 1948, $10.

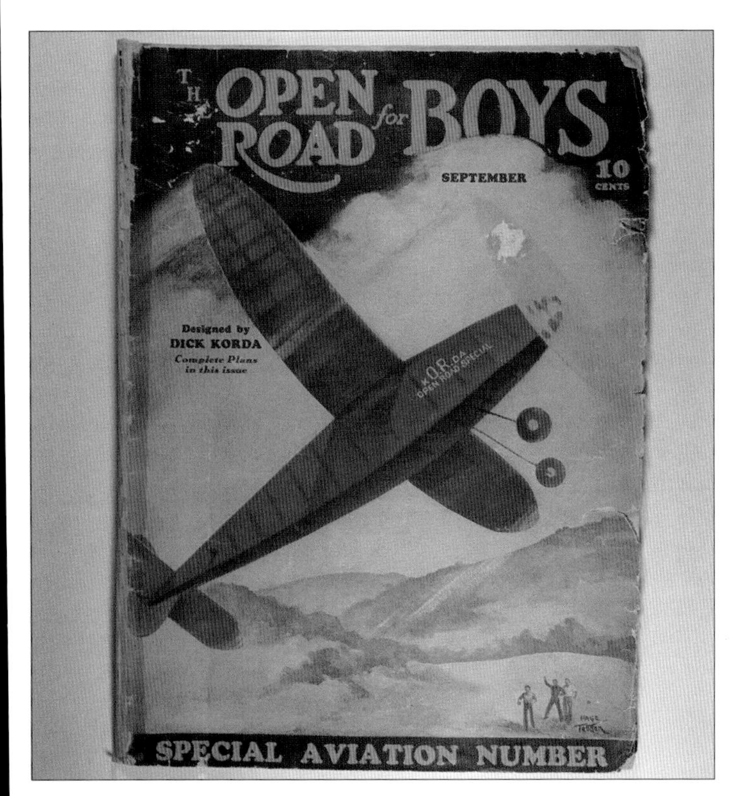

The Open Road for Boys, September 1941, cover by Page Trotter, special aviation issue featuring Dick Korda's winning Wakefield design. *Courtesy of Bill Darkow.* $15-25.

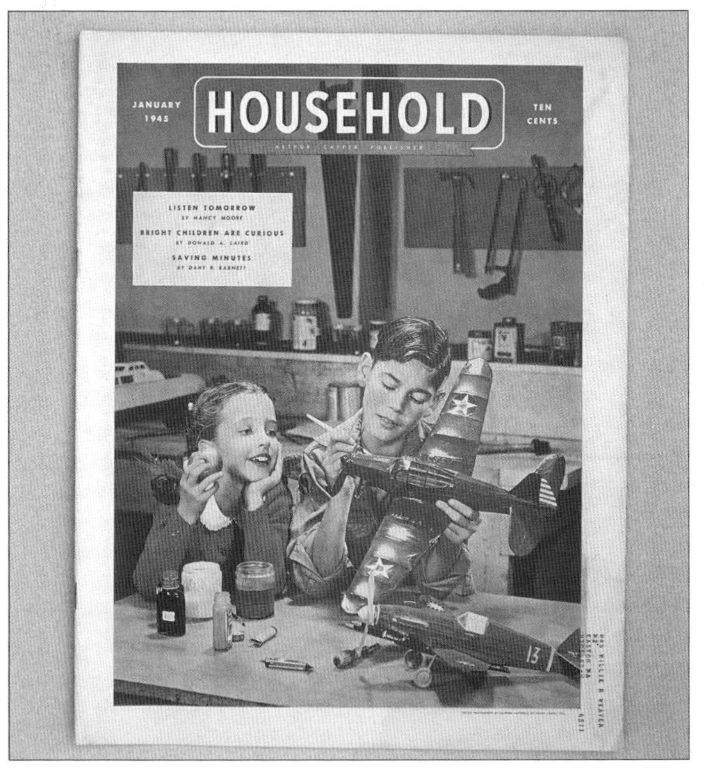

Household, a magazine printed newspaper style in January 1945, possibly on recycled paper due to shortages caused by the war. $10-15.

Modern Mechanix, April 1937, article and plans of plane featured on the cover, $10-20.

Mechanix Illustrated, May 1941, features the plane on the cover as a modeling project. $3-5.

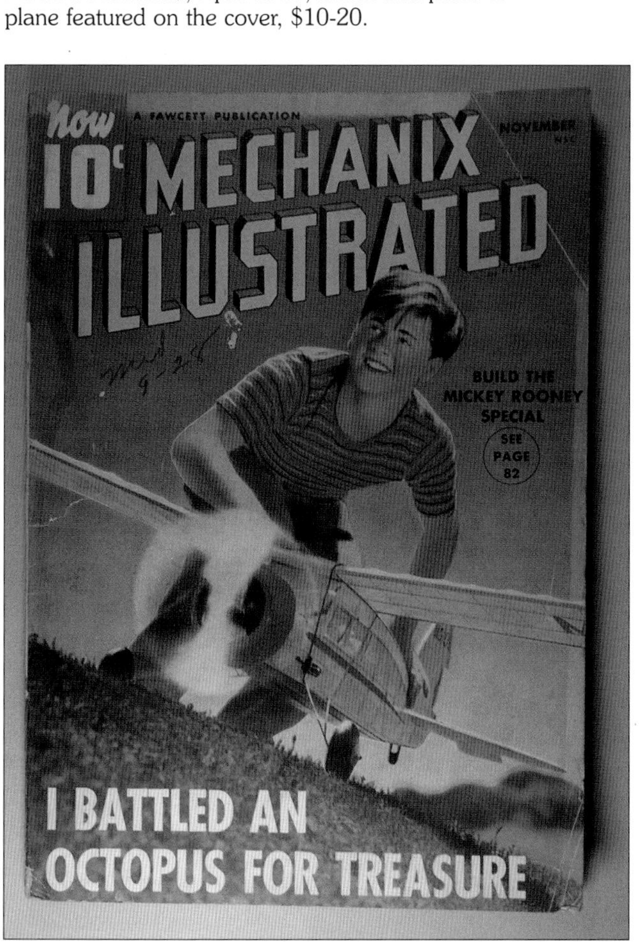

Mechanix Illustrated, November 1939, featuring the "Mickey Rooney Special," $5-10.

Popular Mechanics, December 1948, $2-4.

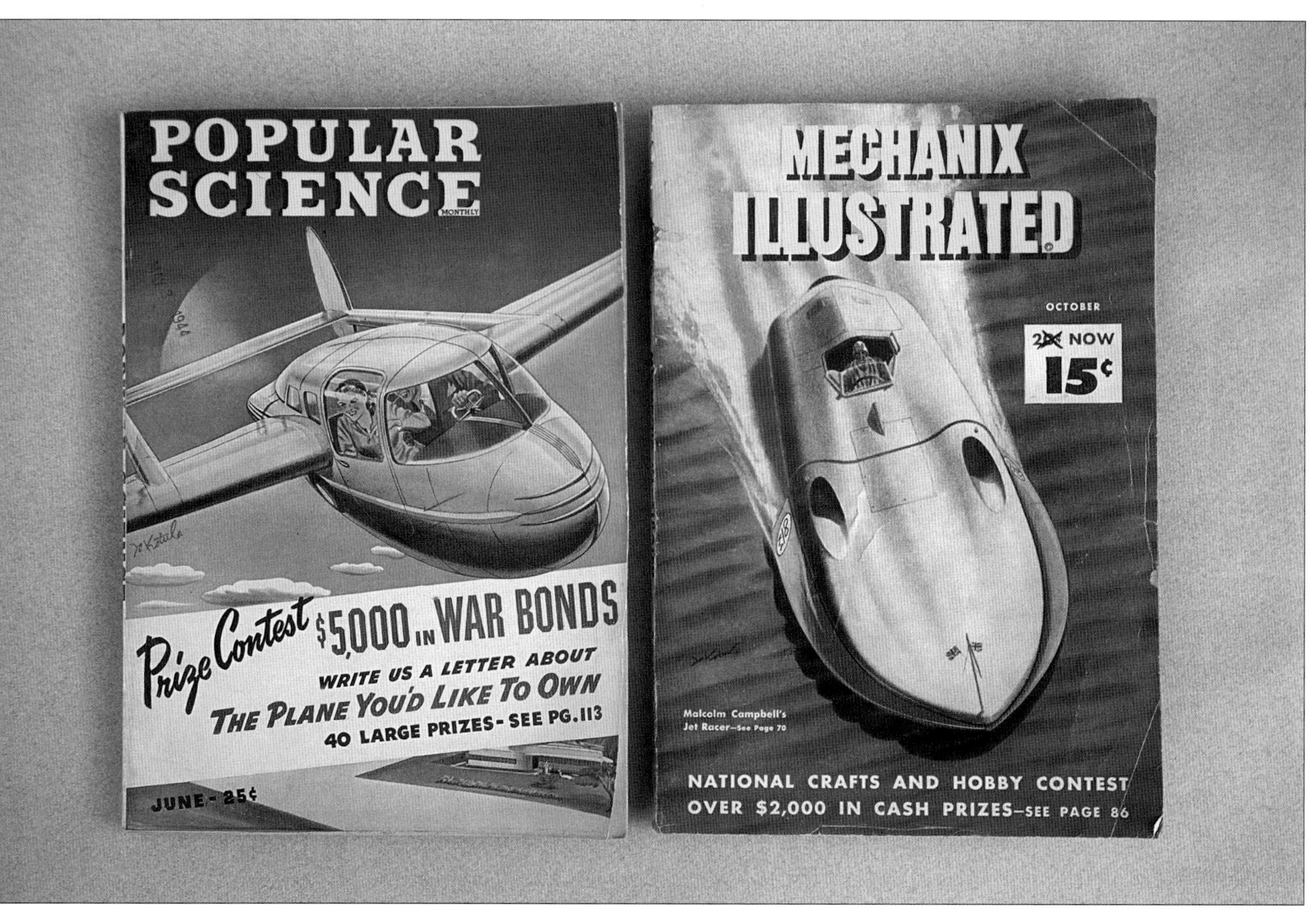

Popular Science, June 1944, and *Mechanix Illustrated*, October 1947, featuring covers by Jo Kotula. These were included to show some of the other cover art done by this famous aviation artist. *Mechanix Illustrated* featured regular articles on gas powered model aircraft. The October issue included the MI Acrobat, a 32" wingspan bi-plane designed by James Noonan for the Drone diesel, $2-4.

Popular Electronics, November 1954, May 1955. This magazine premiered in October 1954 with Bill Winter as editor of radio control electronics. Issues featured planes and electronics projects, $3-10.

Magazine Flag Covers – A Salute to Old Glory

Six months after the December 7, 1941 attack on Pearl Harbor, a plan was devised to rally the nation. Paul McNamera, a young reporter for the Hearst Corporation, came up with a contest idea using the American Flag and the slogan "United We Stand." The aim was to encompass all of America, making it almost impossible not to be touched by this young man's inspired idea. The publishers were seeking to stir the conscience of Americans, thus becoming a unique fusion of patriotism and consumerism. (*Newsweek*, July 1942, 68).

Nearly five hundred magazines responded with their July and August 1942 issues using this theme on the covers. Some magazines commissioned artists and others opted for photography. Street and Smith, publishers of *Air Trails* and a dozen other magazines used the same cover design on all their periodicals for this contest. The cover art, created by Rogers, appeared on at least ten magazines published by Street and Smith. This cover depicts a rising sun symbolizing hope of the new days ahead. August Schomberg, long time cover artist for *Flying Aces*, did an original cover for the 1942 issue just as he had been doing for many years. The contest winner was *Home and Garden* magazine.

In 1943, the United States was pushing through the fourth and fifth War Bond drive efforts that would continue until the end of the war. Magazine publishers mounted another campaign using this theme, but it didn't have nearly as much participation as the first one. For this second contest, *Model Craftsman* used the same cover design it had used in the 1942 contest; this was the first time it had ever used the same cover more than once. The Magazine Publishers of America were responsible for contributing more than forty million dollars worth of free advertising toward the war bond efforts. In all, $189.7 billion worth of securities were raised to fund the war effort toward victory.

Model Craftsman, July 1943. This was a repeat cover of the one used in July 1942. $10-25.

Flying Aces, August 1943, August Schomburg cover, $5-15.

Boy's Life, July 1942. Almost every issue of *Boy's Life* carried information on modeling activities of the times, $40-50.

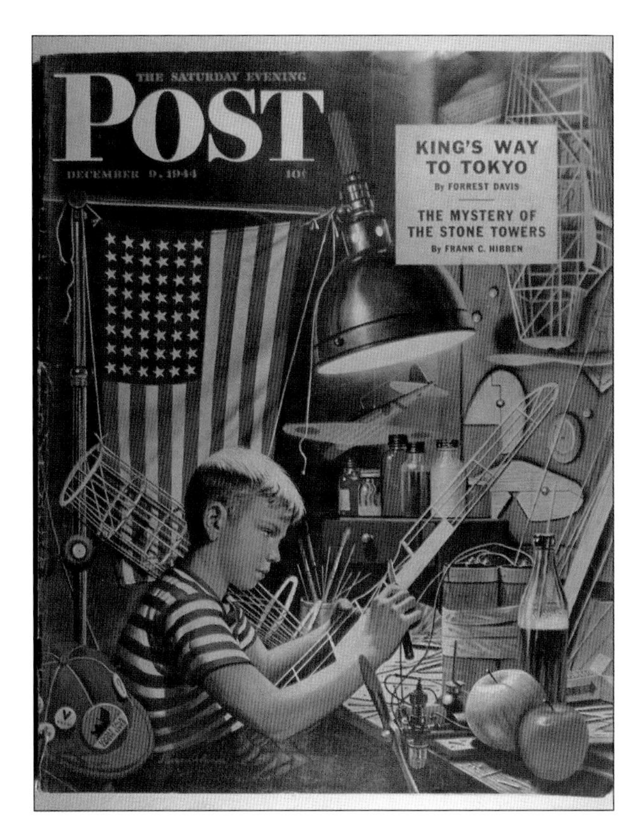

Saturday Evening Post, December 9, 1944, Stevan Dohanos (1907-1994) focused on the location and trappings of the American Dream, not those who populated it. In the 1960s, after the Post ceased to show art on its covers, Dohanos moved to a comparable position – chairman of the National Stamp Advisory Committee, to select art for postage stamps. Stevan Dohanos is pictured in the January 1946 issue of *Air Trails* on page 82 in an ad for X-acto knives and tools. $8-20.

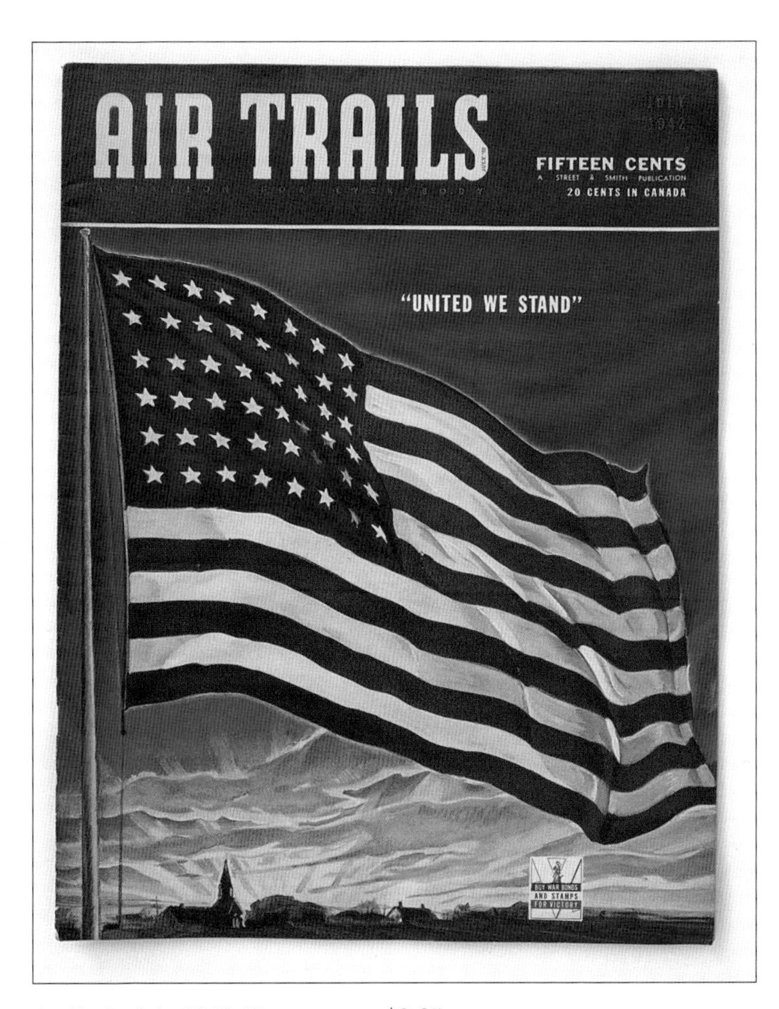

Air Trails, July 1942, Rogers cover, $8-25.

Model Airplane News, August 1944, Jo Kotula cover, $5-10.

Flying Aces, August 1942, August Schomburg cover, $5-20.

Boy Scouts of America and Modeling

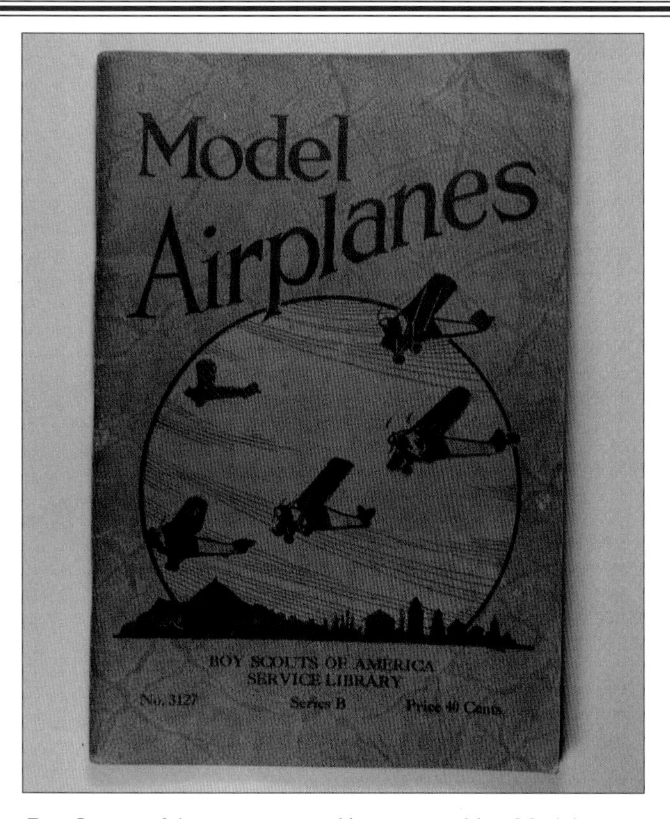

Boy Scouts of America service library pamphlet, *Model Airplanes*, c. 1929, featuring planes from the Ideal catalog and text by Elmer L. Allen, 52 pgs. $20-35.

Boys' Life, November 1940, $10-20.

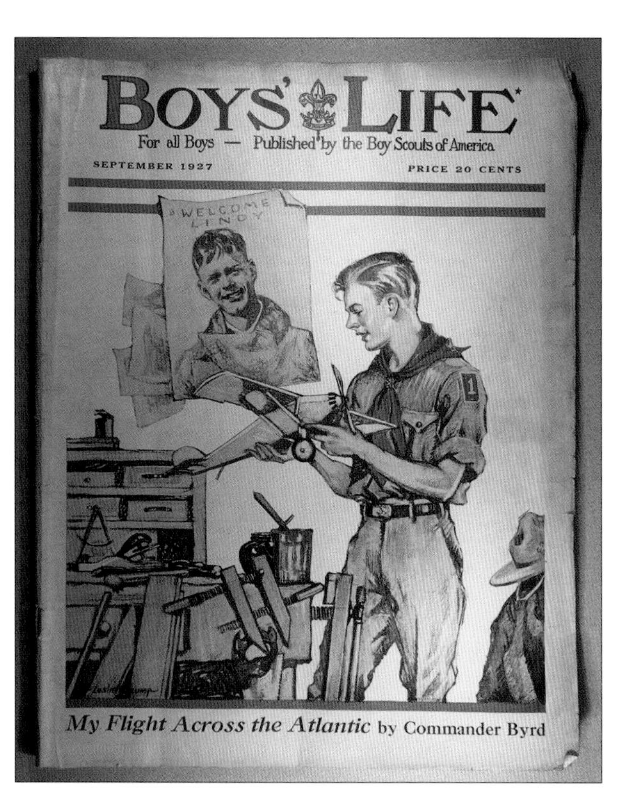

Boys' Life, September 1927, Leslie Crump cover, $15-25.

The Scout, September 4, 1952, weekly British Air Scout publication, was also read in Australia, New Zealand, and South Africa. $5-10.

Flying High, edited by Franklin K. Mathiews, Chief Scout Librarian, c. 1927-1930, with 192 pages of stories and modeling projects by various authors. $20-40.

Merit Badge books *Model Design and Building* c. 1964 and *Aviation,* c. 1958, with the merit badge for *Model Design and Building,* c. 1960s. I earned this merit badge by building my first scratch plane, Nick Ziroli's "Combat Zero." The whole group is worth $8-12.

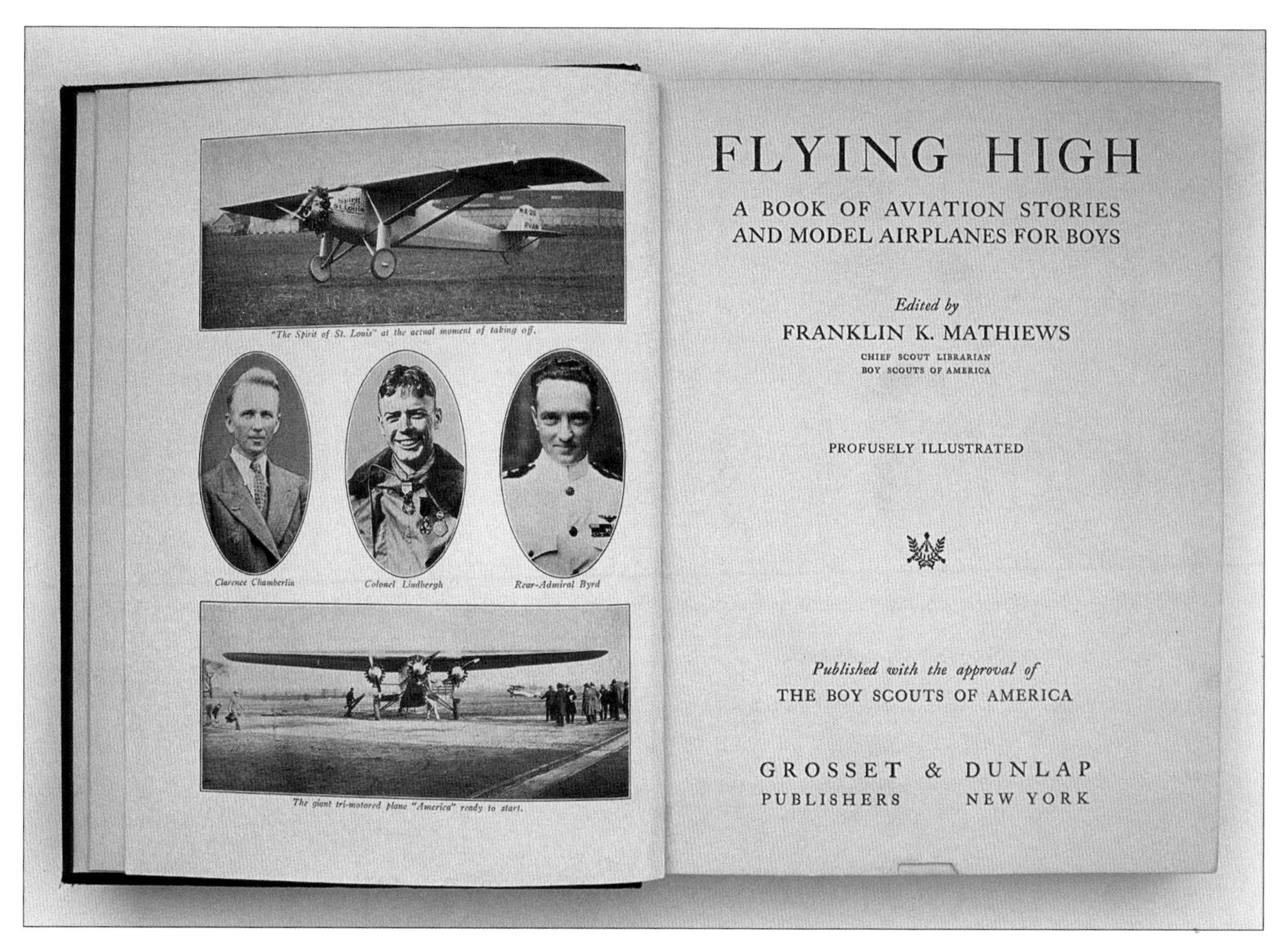

"The Spirit of St. Louis" at the actual moment of taking off.

Clarence Chamberlin — *Colonel Lindbergh* — *Rear-Admiral Byrd*

The giant tri-motored plane "America" ready to start.

FLYING HIGH

A BOOK OF AVIATION STORIES
AND MODEL AIRPLANES FOR BOYS

Edited by
FRANKLIN K. MATHIEWS
CHIEF SCOUT LIBRARIAN
BOY SCOUTS OF AMERICA

PROFUSELY ILLUSTRATED

Published with the approval of
THE BOY SCOUTS OF AMERICA

GROSSET & DUNLAP
PUBLISHERS NEW YORK

Introduction to *Flying High.*

Model Airplane News, August 1931, cover by Gerarld Muir, $10-20.

Model Airplane News, March 1932, cover by Gerarld Muir, this issue featured a model of a British WWI fighter the SE-5A by Howard McEntee. $10-20.

Model Airplane News, April 1932 cover by Gerarld Muir, this issue featured a Cessna Cabin monoplane by Howard McEntee. $10-20.

Model Airplane News, June 1931, cover by Gerarld Muir, $10-20.

Model Airplane News, September 1936, Jo Kotula cover. Kotula started drawing cowboys at the age of ten and soon discovered airplanes, the rest is history. He began his career as a commercial artist in 1926 and drifted around Oklahoma and Texas until moving to New York City in 1932. Soon after, he began doing cover art for M.A.N. He became a full-scale pilot and soloed after three and a half hours on a J-3 Cub. In 1986, Jo Kotula was one of five founding members of The American Society of Aviation Artists. He hasn't been inducted into the AMA Hall of Fame but most likely will be in the near future. His impact on model aviation is still being felt today because of over 35 years of cover art for *Model Airplane News.* $8-12.

Model Airplane News, June 1943, Jo Kotula cover, $5-10.

Model Airplane News, January 1944, Jo Kotula cover, $5-10.

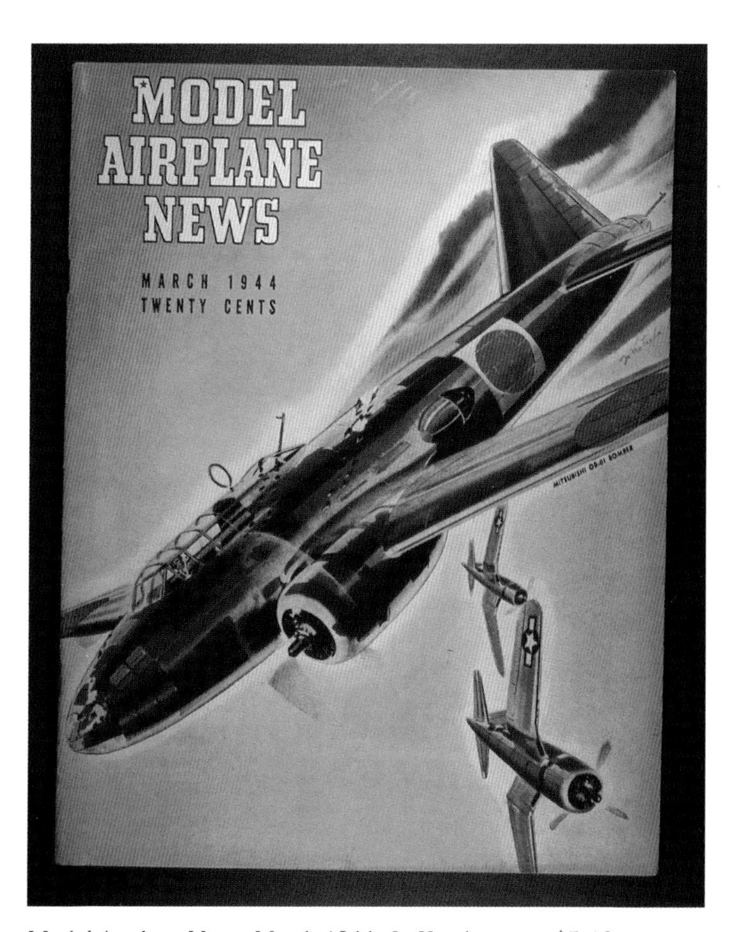

Model Airplane News, March 1944, Jo Kotula cover, $5-10.

Model Airplane News, July 1944, Jo Kotula cover, $5-10.

Model Airplane News, April 1949, Jo Kotula cover, $5-15.

Model Airplane News, September 1944, Jo Kotula cover, $5-10.

Model Airplane News, September 1949, Jo Kotula cover, depicting the Good Brothers flying at the Nationals, $5-10.

Model Airplane News, June 1949, Jo Kotula cover, $5-10.

Model Airplane News, April 1953, Kotula cover, $3-5.

Model Airplane News, July 1949, Kotula cover celebrating 20 years of *Model Airplane News,* $5-8.

Model Airplane News, November 1953, the Fokker DR-1 tri-plane has been a modeling favorite for many years and has graced the covers of several model airplane magazines over the years, $3-5.

Gee Bee R-1 Sportster Covers

Model Airplane News, January 1949, photo of an exact copy of the Lowell Bayles piloted Gee Bee racer, first powered with an Ohlsson .23 and switched to a Bullet engine. This was the black and yellow version of the famous racer. $5-15.

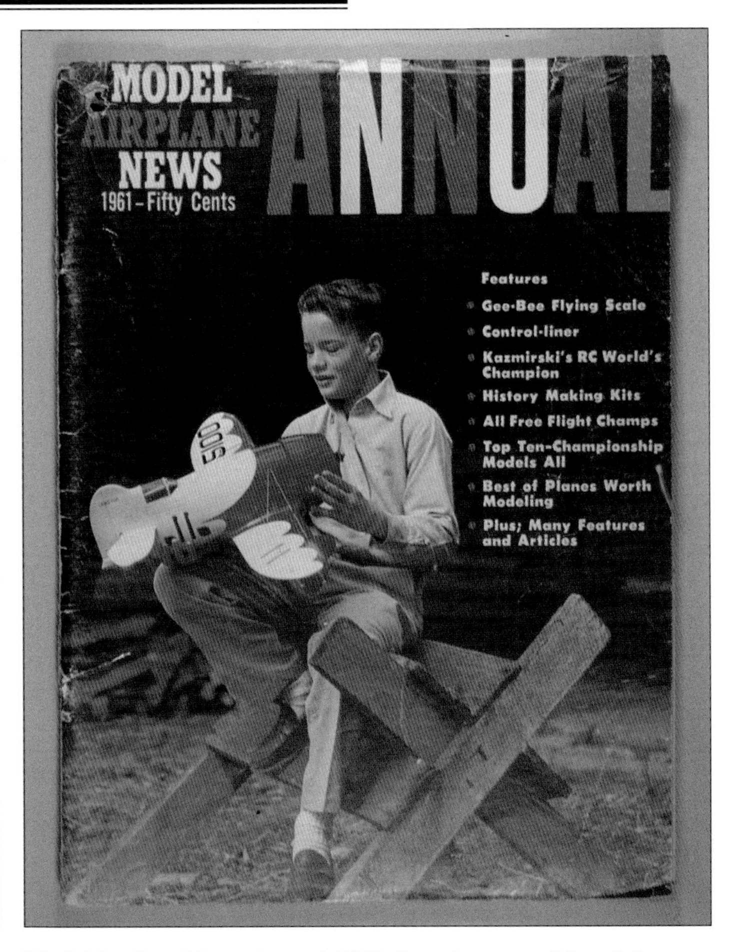

Model Airplane News, Annual 1961, featuring one of the all time great modeling projects the Gee Bee R-1 racing plane, $5.

Model Airplane News, September 1953, Kotula cover. The Gee Bee Super Sportster, dubbed the Flying Silo, once lapped all entrants to win the Thompson in 1932. Its achievements were many, but it could be a man killer. $5-10.

American Modeler, July 1958, Jim Triggs cover of the Gee Bee R-1 Sportster, $3.

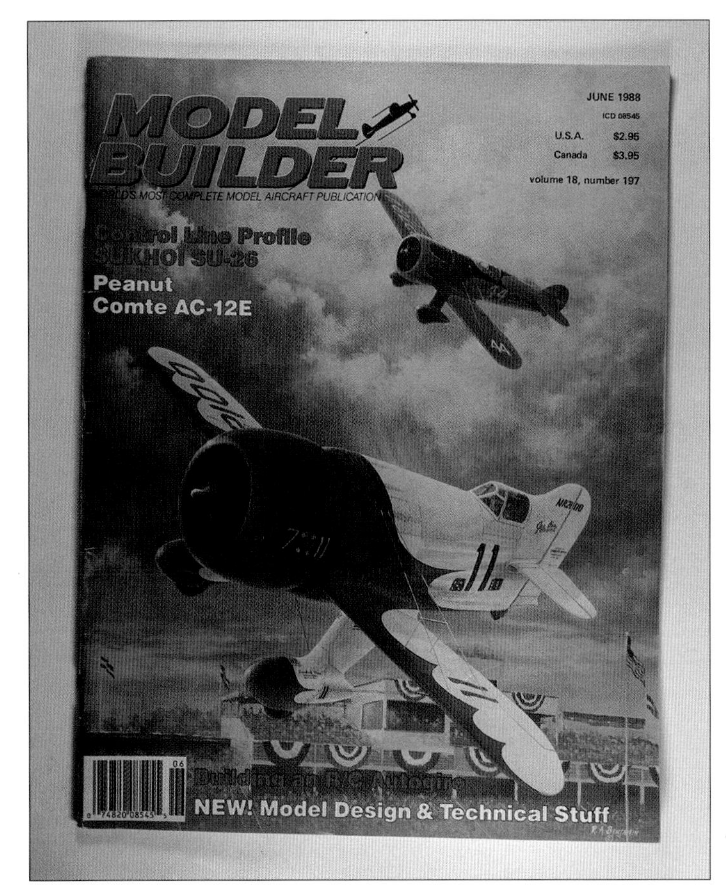

Model Builder, June 1988, featuring Bob Benjamin's rendition of the Gee Bee R-1. In the hands of Jimmy Doolittle, the R-1 won the 1932 Thompson Trophy race. Doolittle also set a new world landplane speed record of 296 mph in the Shell speed dash, a straight-line course. Lee Gehlbach, flying the R-2, (basically the same plane with the number 7 on it) finished fourth in the Bendix due to oil leak problems and fifth in the Thompson. Magazine $1-2.

Bill Barnes, Air Trails, June 1936, cover by Frank Tinsley. *Courtesy of Bill Darkow.* $5-15.

Air Trails, June 1937, Tinsley cover, $5-15.

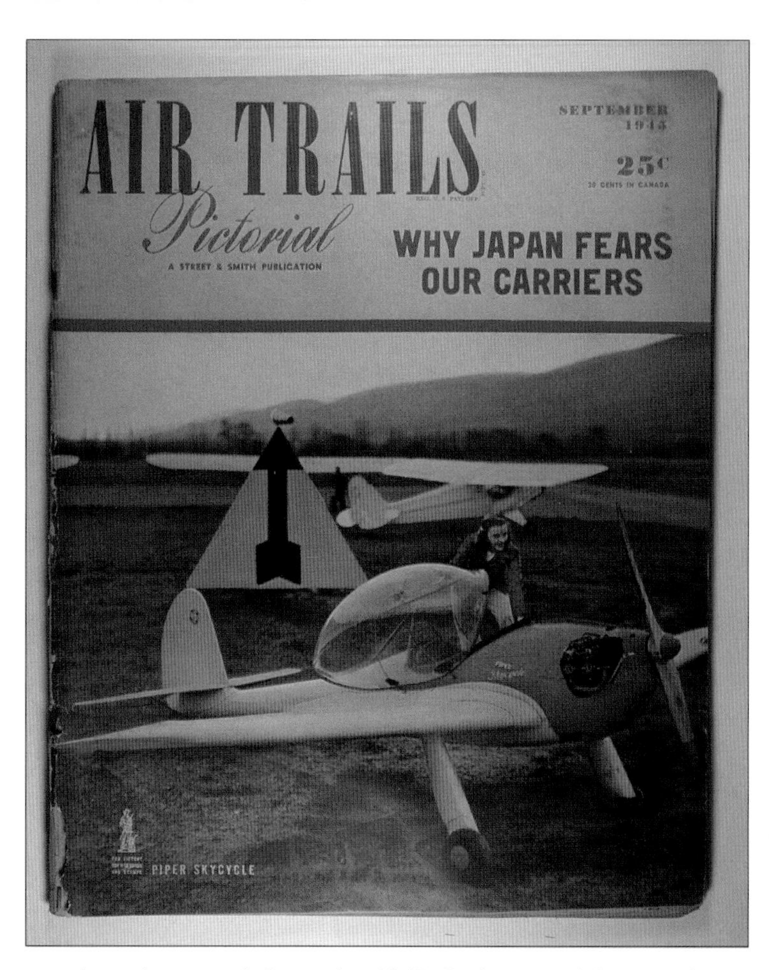

Air trails, pictorial, September 1945. Civilian aircraft began to be featured on covers as the war was coming to a close, $5-10.

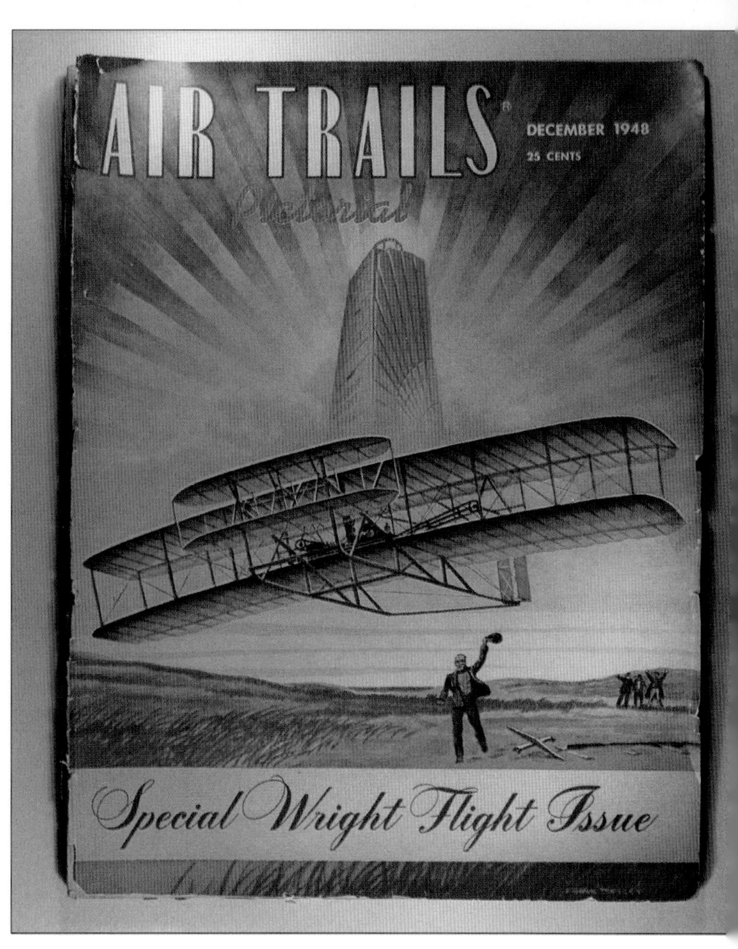

Air Trails, December 1948, Frank Tinsley cover, $4-8.

Air Trails and Science Frontiers, February 1947, $4-8.

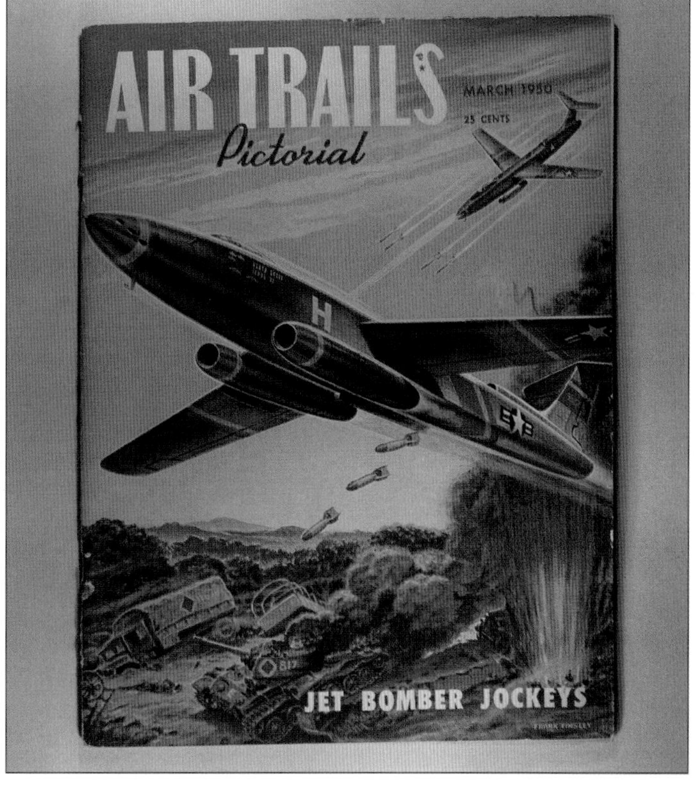

Air Trails, March 1950, Frank Tinsley cover. 1950 marked the beginning of jet aircraft appearing on covers. $4-8.

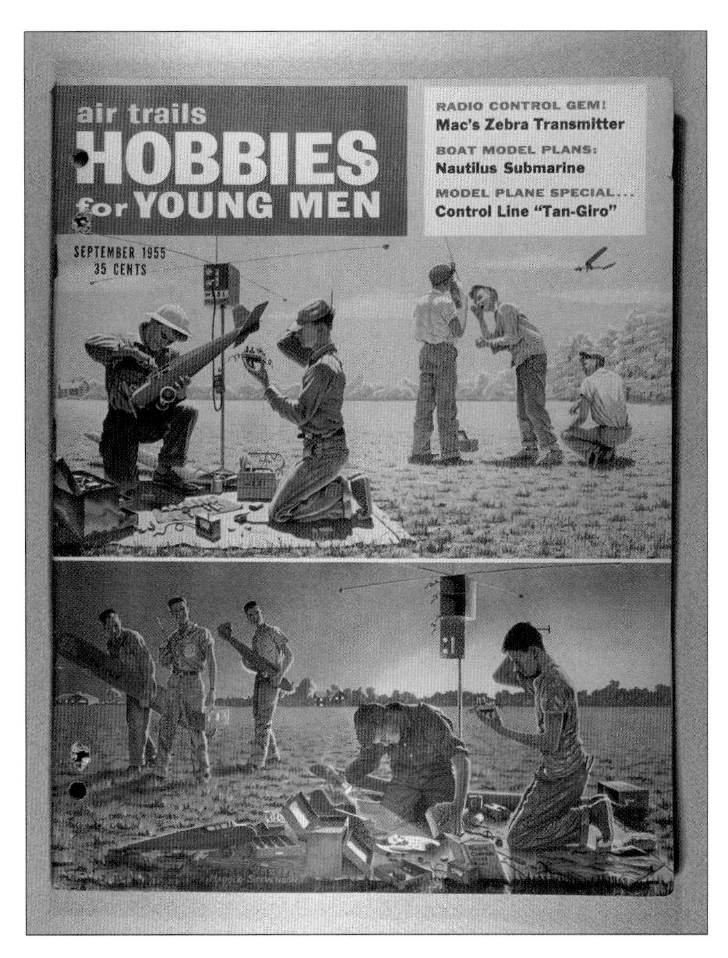

Air Trails, Hobbies for Young Men, September 1955, cover by Harold Stevenson. His covers are some of the best stories told through artistic talent. $2-5.

Young Men, December 1955, Stevenson cover, Merry Christmas! How many can remember that special Christmas when mom and dad bought you that special gift? $2-5.

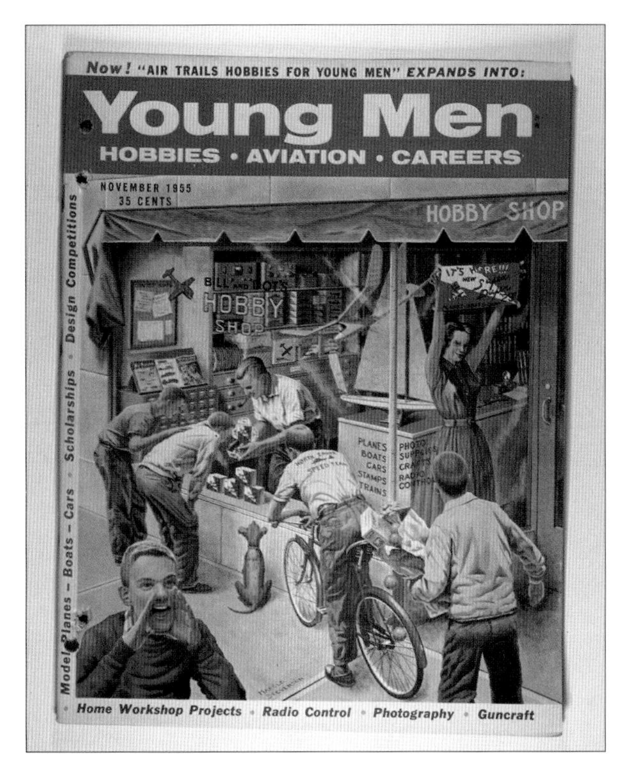

Young Men, November 1955, Stevenson cover. *Air trails* continued to change the face of their publication; the content expanded to cover hobbies including collecting, shooting, cars, and boats. $2-5.

Air Trails, Classic Flying Models, summer 1977 is its first issue, continued quarterly with reprints from old *Air Trails*, Challenge Publications, $3-6.

American Modeler, August 1959, Cal Smith cover, $2-4.

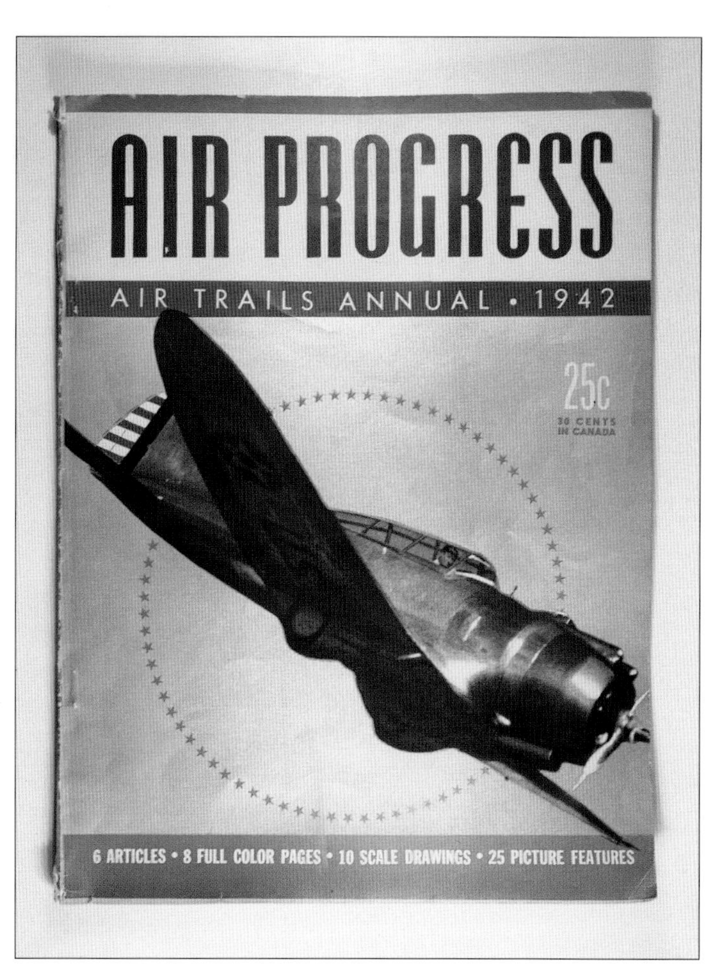

Air Progress, Air Trails Annual 1942, $5-10.

American Modeler, June 1962, Cal Smith cover featuring the then new Boeing 727, $2-4.

Air Trails Model Annual for 1943, $5-15.

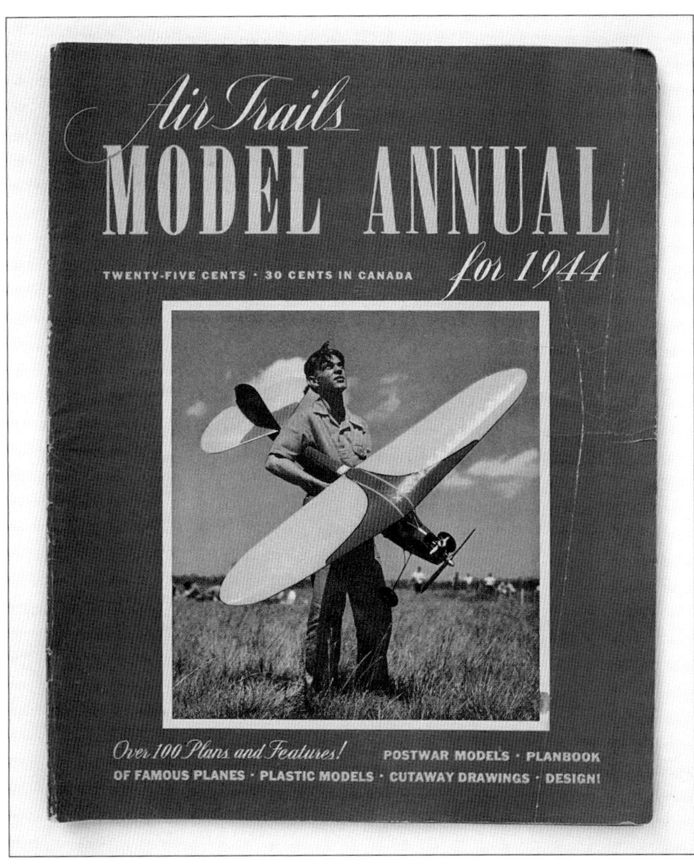

Air Trails Model Annual for 1944, $5-15.

Air Trails Model Annual for 1951, $5-12.

Air Trails Model Annual for 1946, $5-15.

Air Trails Model Annual for 1952, cover by Cal Smith, $5-12.

Air Trails Model Annual for 1954, cover by Cal Smith, $5-12.

Air Trails Model Annual for 1956, cover by Cal Smith, $5-12.

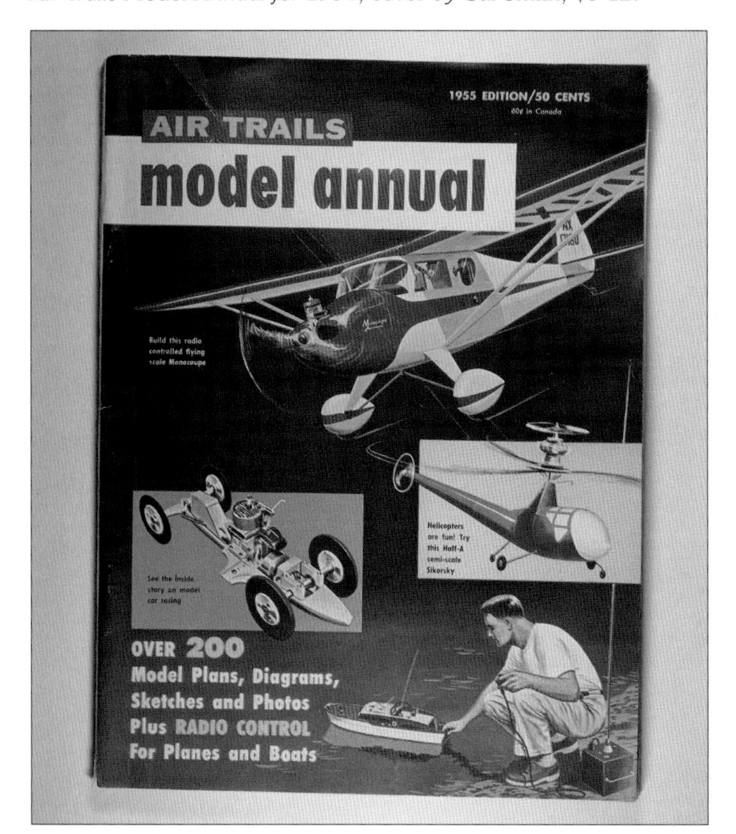

Air Trails Model Annual for 1955, cover by Cal Smith, $5-12.

Air Trails Model Annual for 1957, $5-10.

Air Trails Model Annual for 1958, cover by Jim Triggs, $5-10.

Air Trails Model Annual for 1960, cover by Cal Smith, $5-10.

Air Trails Model Annual for 1959, $5-10.

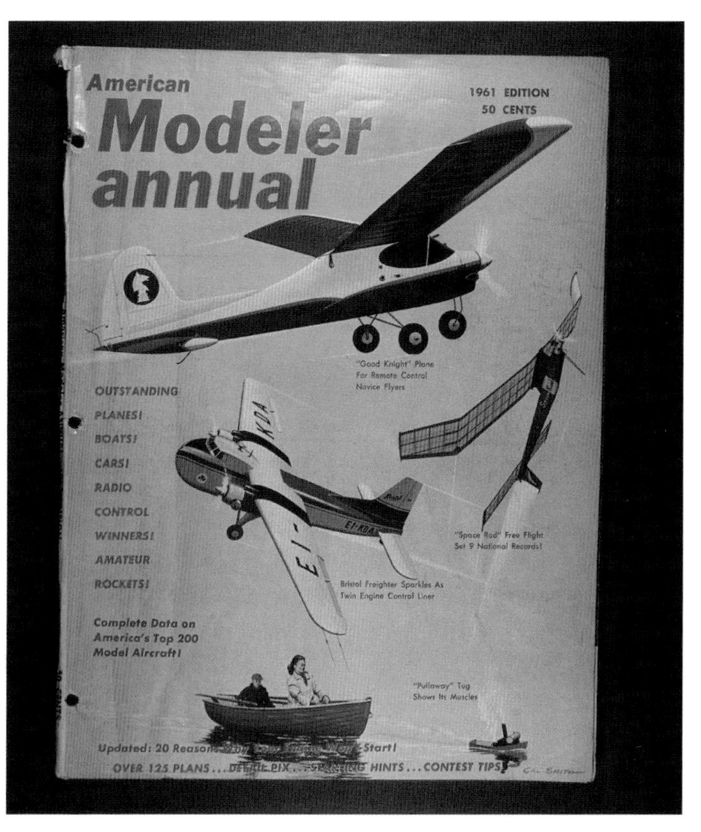

American Modeler Annual for 1961, cover by Cal Smith, $5-10.

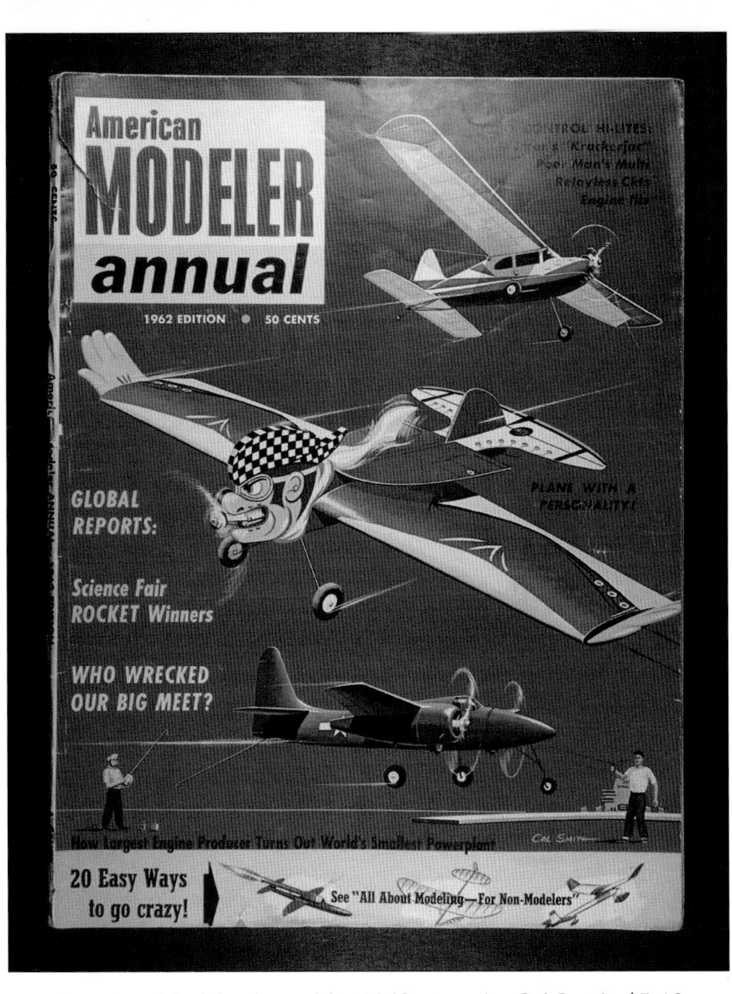

American Modeler Annual for 1962, cover by Cal Smith, $5-10.

American Modeler Annual for 1964, cover by Cal Smith $5-10.

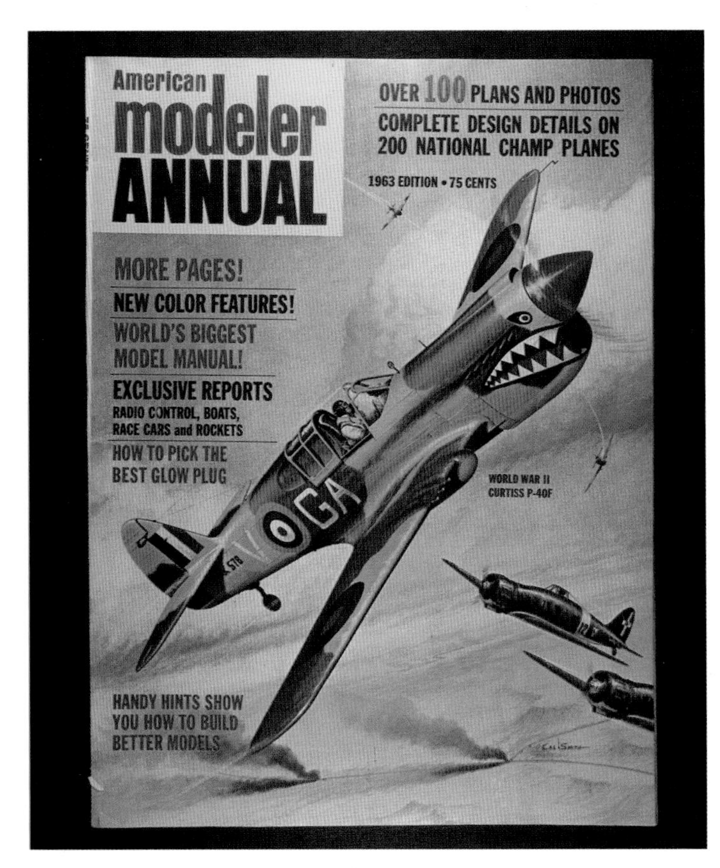

American Modeler Annual for 1963, cover by Cal Smith $5-10.

American Modeler Annual for 1965, cover by Cal Smith $5-10.

American Modeler Annual *for 1966*, $5-10.

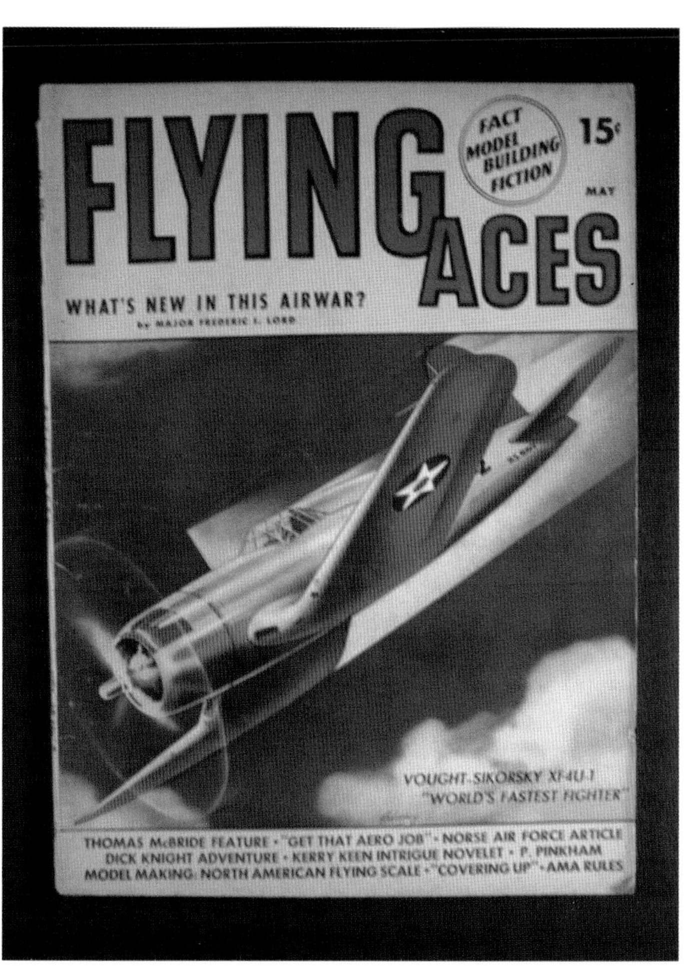

Flying Aces, May 1941, August Schomburg cover, $5-15.

American Aircraft Modeler Annual 1969, $4-5.

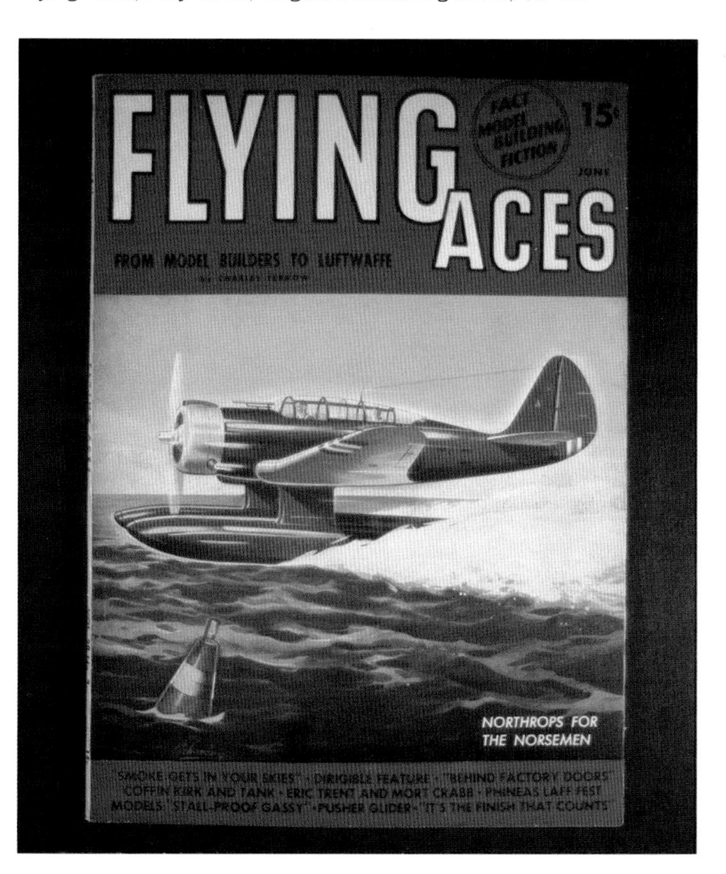

Flying Aces, June 1941, August Schomburg cover, $5-15.

Air-Age, April 1943, August Schomburg cover, No. 1, volume 3, $5-15.

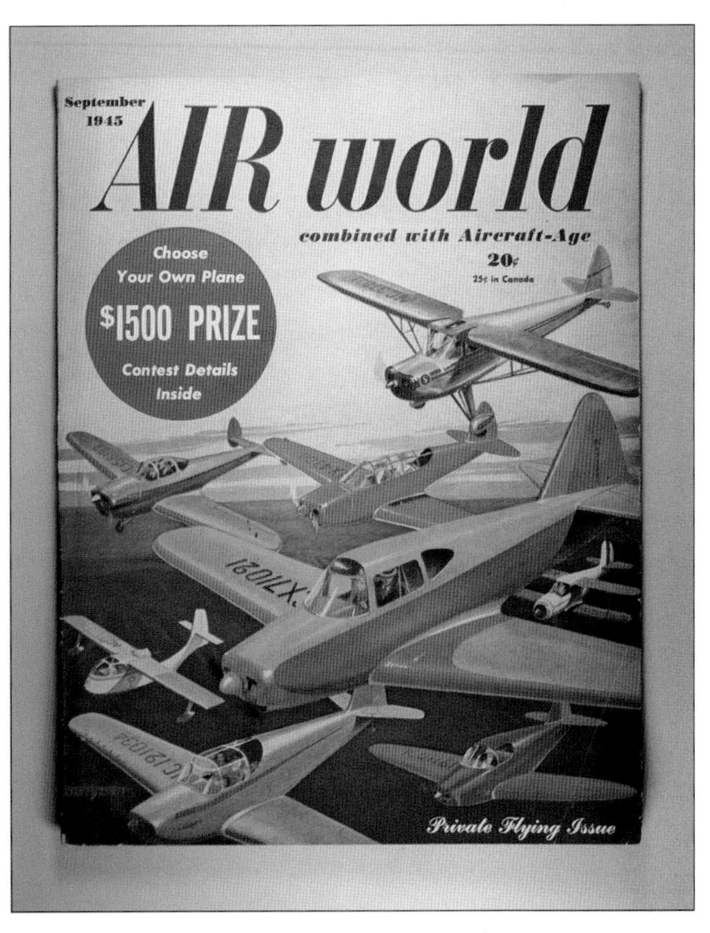

Air World, September 1945, Barry Bart cover, $4-8.

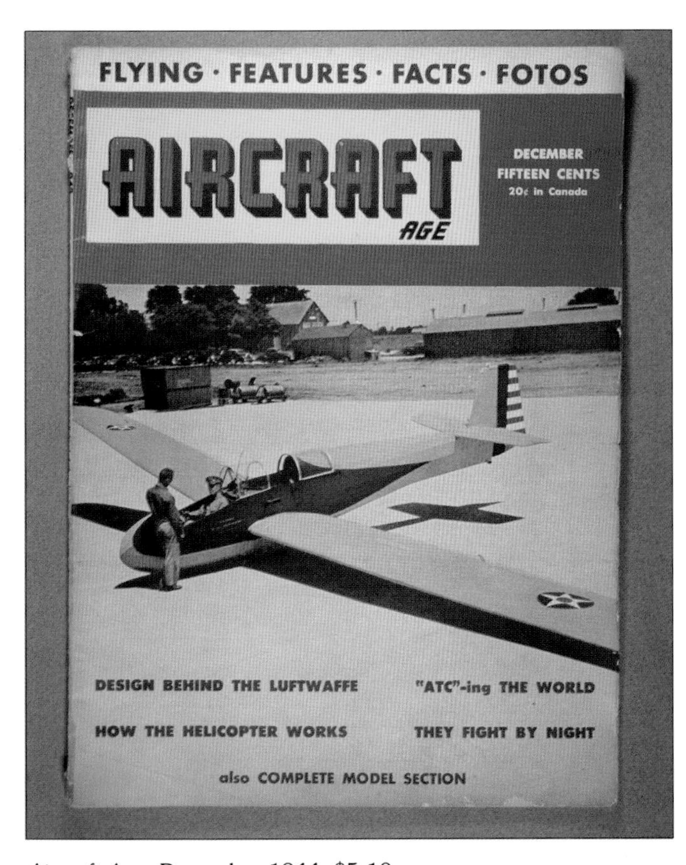

Aircraft Age, December 1944, $5-10.

Air World, July 1945, $4-8.

Flying Models, June 1947, the first issue of *Flying Models* and the August 1947 issue. This would end the changes *Flying Aces* went through. This publication continues today using the same name. $10-35.

Flying Models, June 1950, $5-10.

Flying Models, October 1948, $5-10.

Flying Models, May 1954, the comic book issue. This is the hardest copy to find. $15-40.

Flying Models, September 1957, Gil Evans cover, $3-6.

Flying Models, August 1957, Gil Evans cover, $3-6.

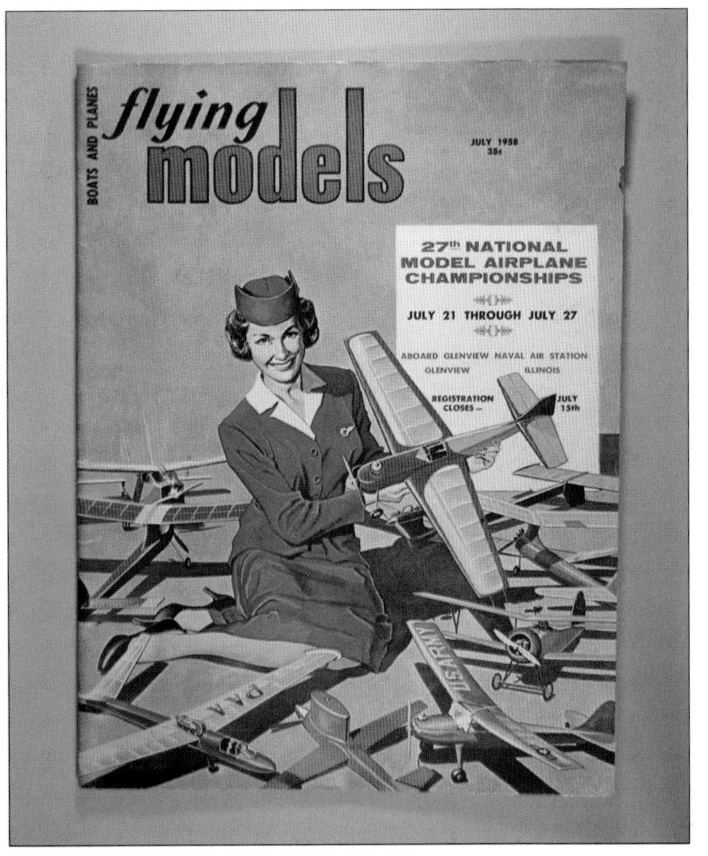

Flying Models, July 1958, Gil Evans cover, $3-6.

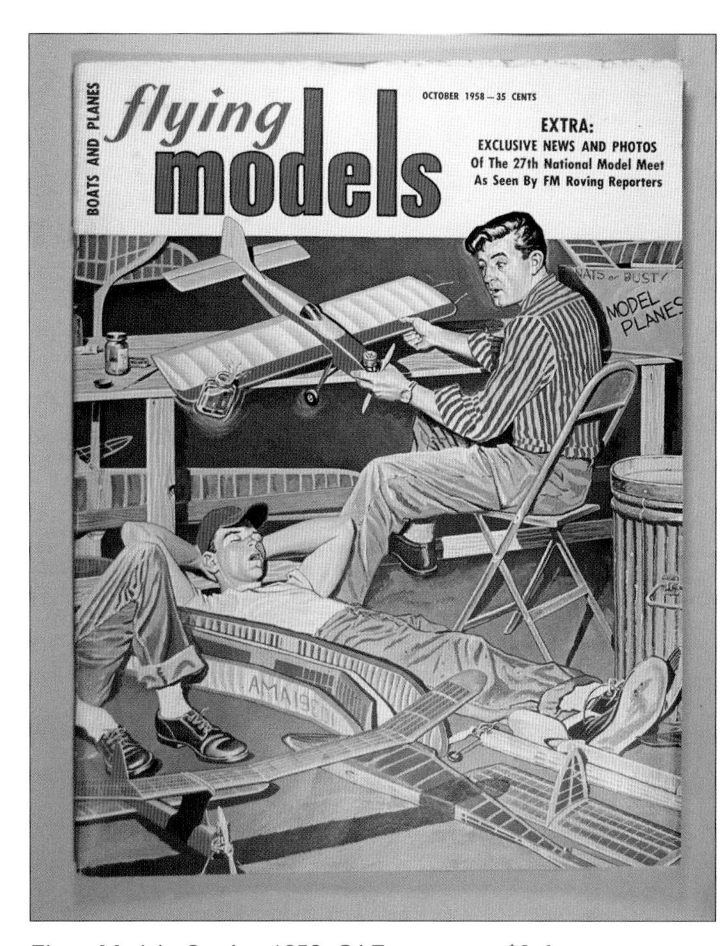

Flying Models, October 1958, Gil Evans cover, $3-6.

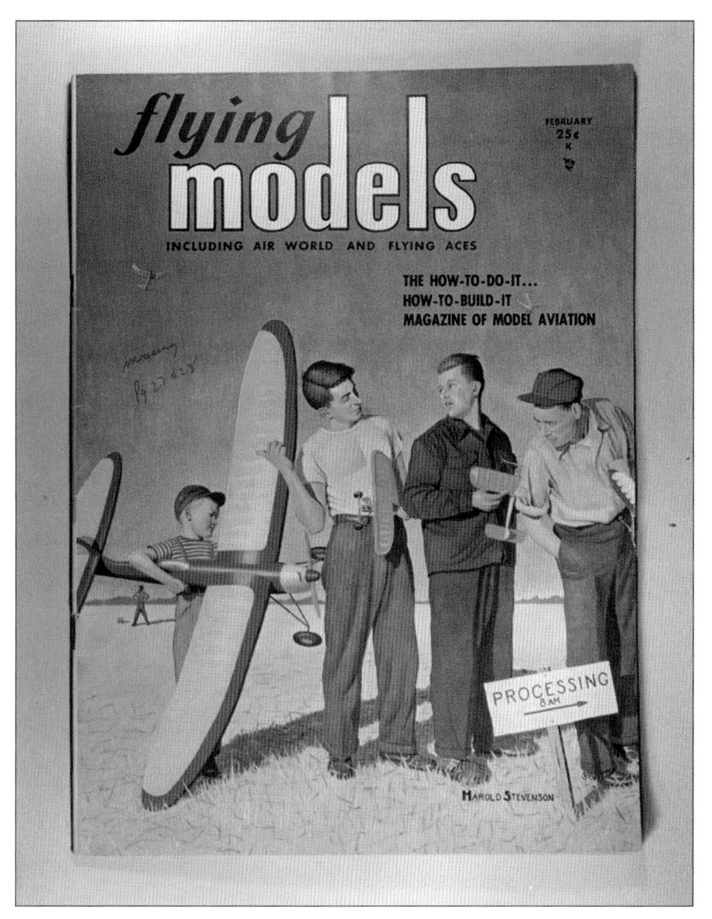

Flying Models, February 1952, Harold Stevenson cover. Everyone has a favorite cover – this one and the June issue are Bill Darkow's favorites. $4-7.

Flying Models, July 1959, cover by Alberto Vela. He was a well-known and well-respected modeler from Mexico; he competed in many meets during the 1950s, $2-5.

Flying Models, June 1952, Harold Stevenson cover, $4-7.

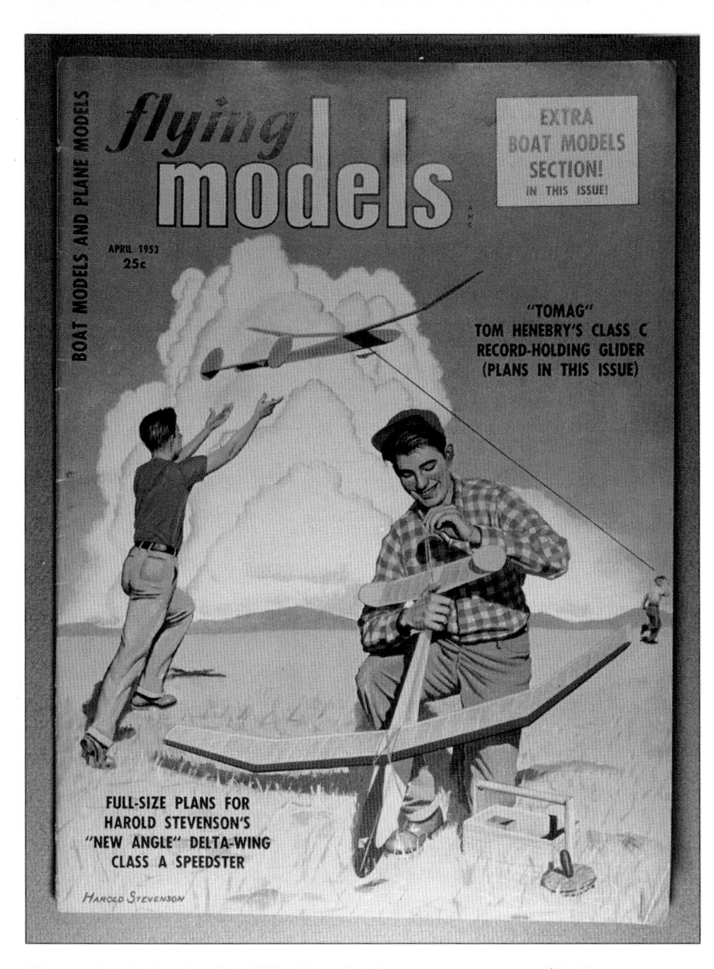

Flying Models, April 1953, Harold Stevenson cover, $4-7.

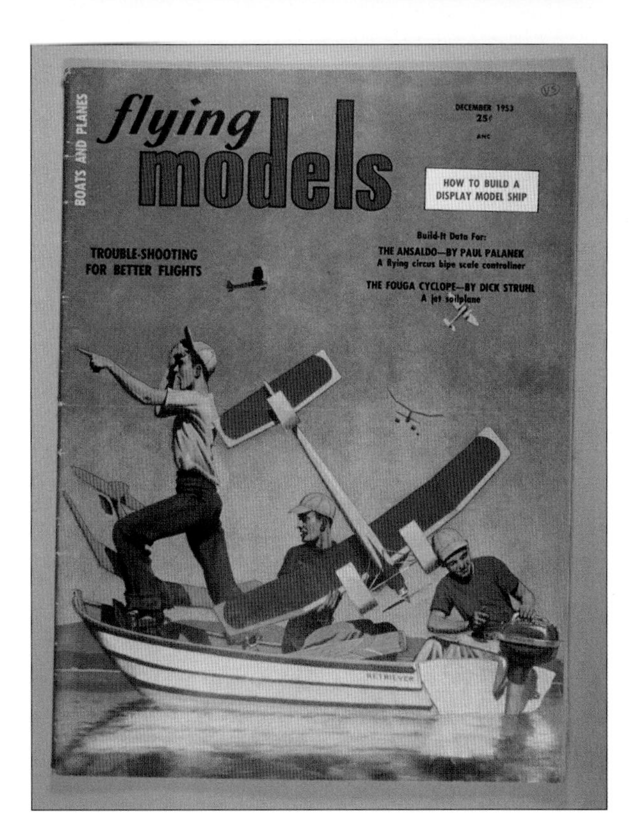

Flying Models, December 1953, Harold Stevenson cover. This cover was presented to Bill Effinger, president of Berkeley Models in recognition of his work in the field of model aviation. Joseph J. Hardie, publisher of *Flying Models* made the award. The painting was inspired by the 1st Annual Long Island Sound Hydro Championships at Bayville, New York and was sponsored by Berkeley Models. $4-7.

Flying Models, October 1953, Harold Stevenson cover, $4-7.

Flying Models, February 1954, Harold Stevenson cover. Walt Goods Royal Rudder-Bug flying in Central Park in New York City $4-7.

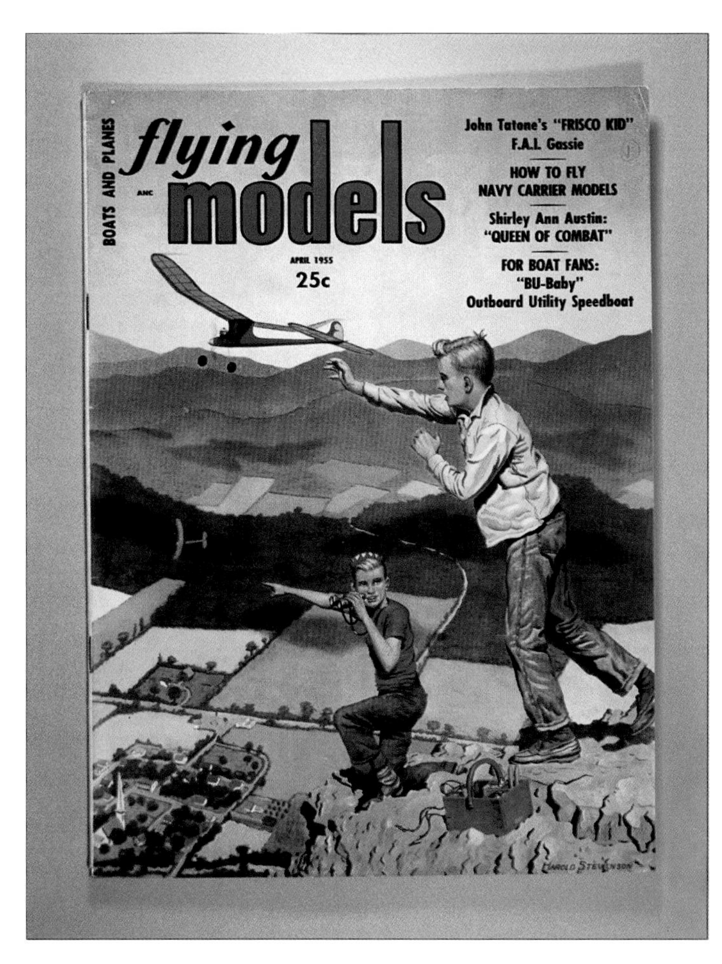

Flying Models, April 1955, Harold Stevenson cover, and my favorite cover, $4-7.

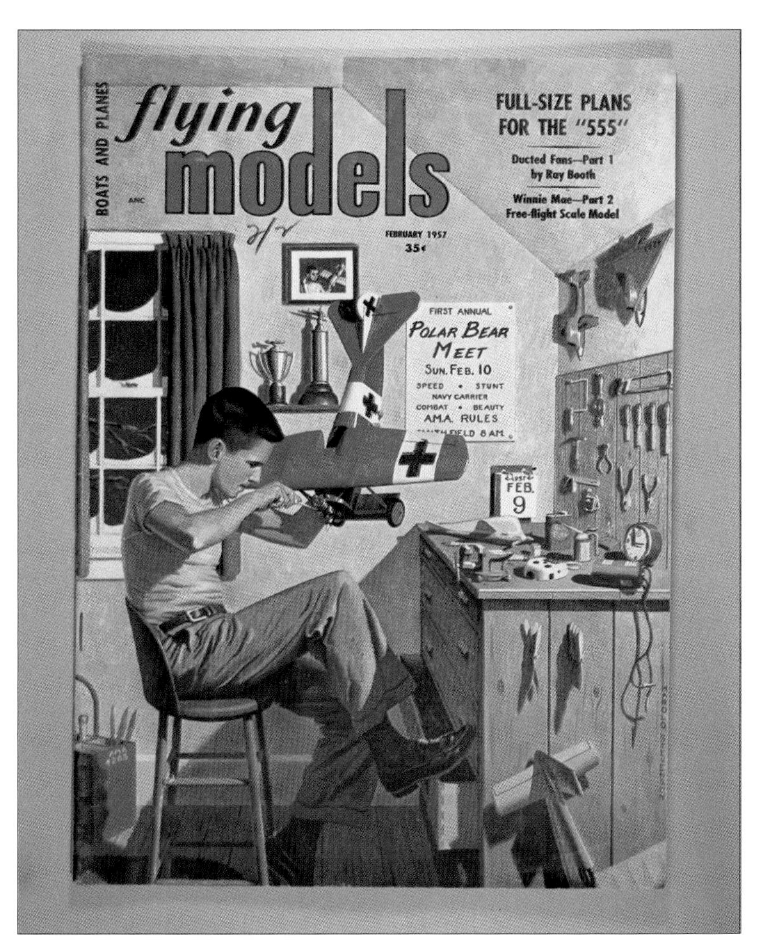

Flying Models, February 1957, Harold Stevenson cover, $4-7.

Flying Models, March 1957, Harold Stevenson cover, $4-7.

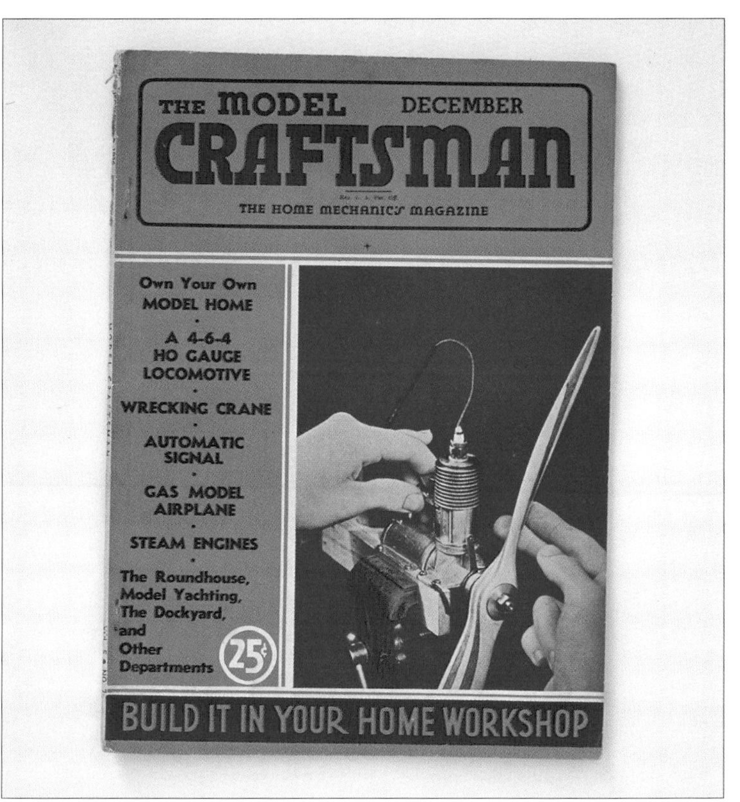

The Model Craftsman, December 1936, $5-10.

Model Craftsman, April 1941. Sex was used to sell model magazines more than sixty years ago, mainly to servicemen who had time and money for magazines, $5-10.

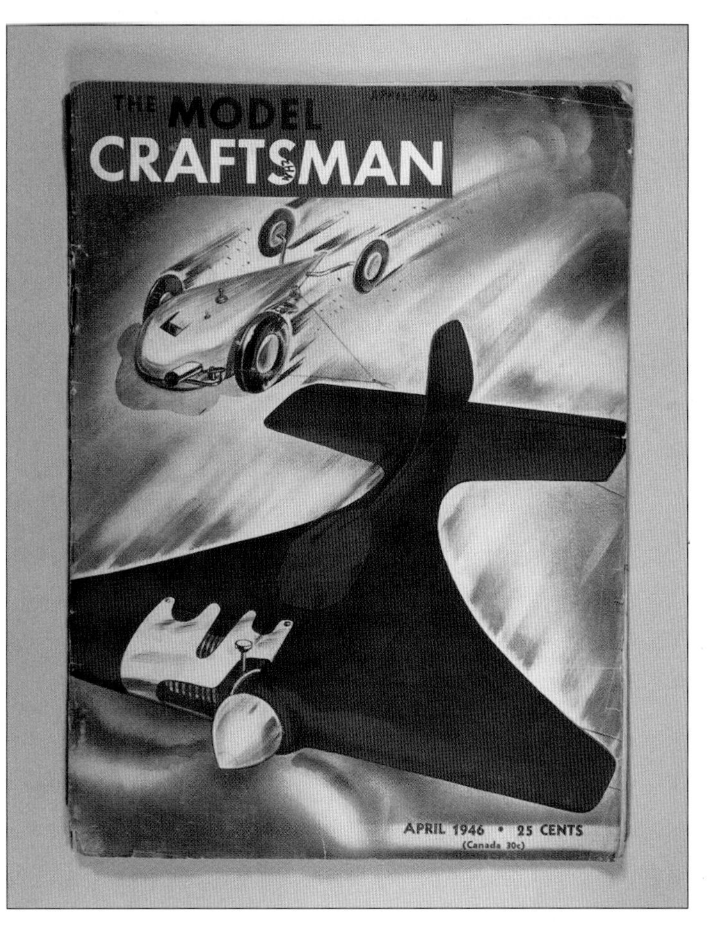

Model Craftsman, April 1946. Tether cars and control line speed were all the rage and contests swept the nation. Texans were particularly found of speed. Many new engines were developed for these new national pastimes. $5-8.

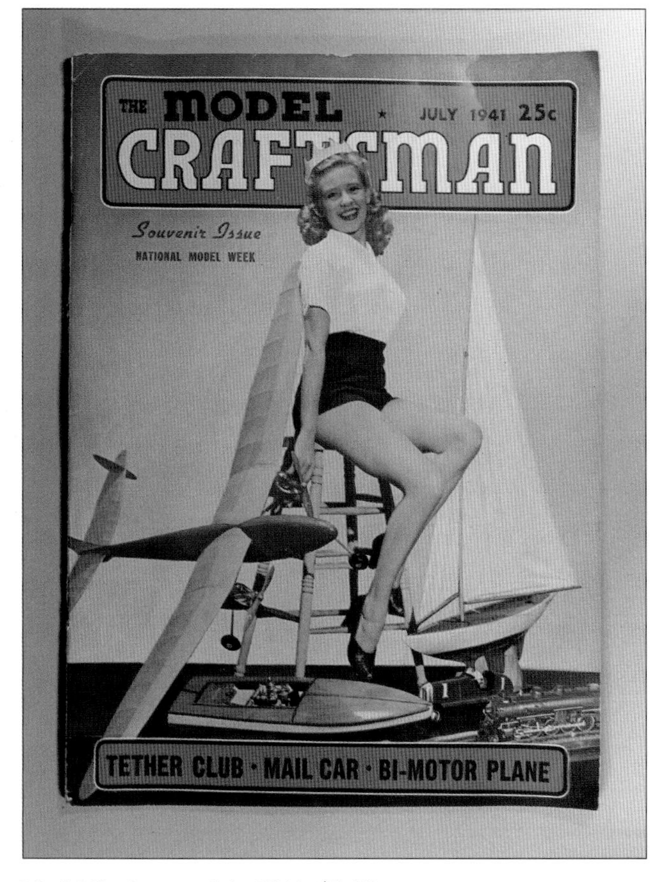

Model Craftsman, July 1941, $5-10.

Model Craftsman, June 1947, Walter Stalter cover, $5-8.

West Coast Model News, January 1953, official publication for the Western Associated Modelers. This magazine is hard to find as it was limited to the west coast. $4-8.

West Coast Model News, November 1963, $5-10.

West Coast Model News, October 1955, $5-10.

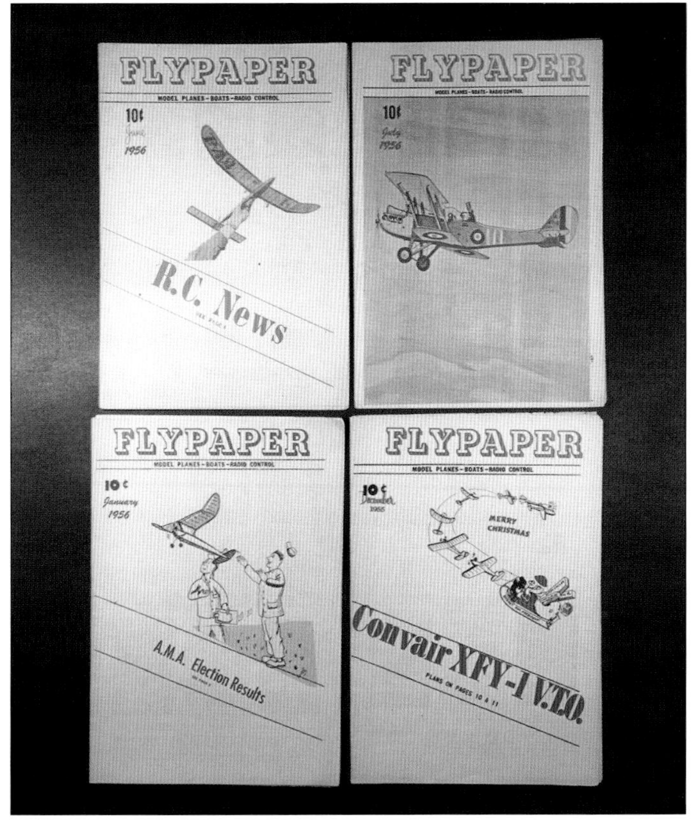

Flypaper, December 1955, January, June, July 1956. Early radio control publication from the east coast edited by Paul Runge. Rare, $3-5.

Grid Leaks, July-August 1964, one of the first publications solely dedicated to radio control modeling, $2-4.

Sig Air-Modeler, January-February 1967, Alberto Vela cover, $2-4.

Grid Leaks, January-February 1965, $2-4.

Model Builder, August 1988, Walt Good commemorative cover by Bud Gordinier of Richmond, Virginia. $1-2.

Model Builder, September 1986, 15th anniversary cover by Bud Gordinier, depiction of Sal Taibi's famous Pacer in flight. The Pacer was the first place winner in class C at the 1941 Nationals. $1-2.

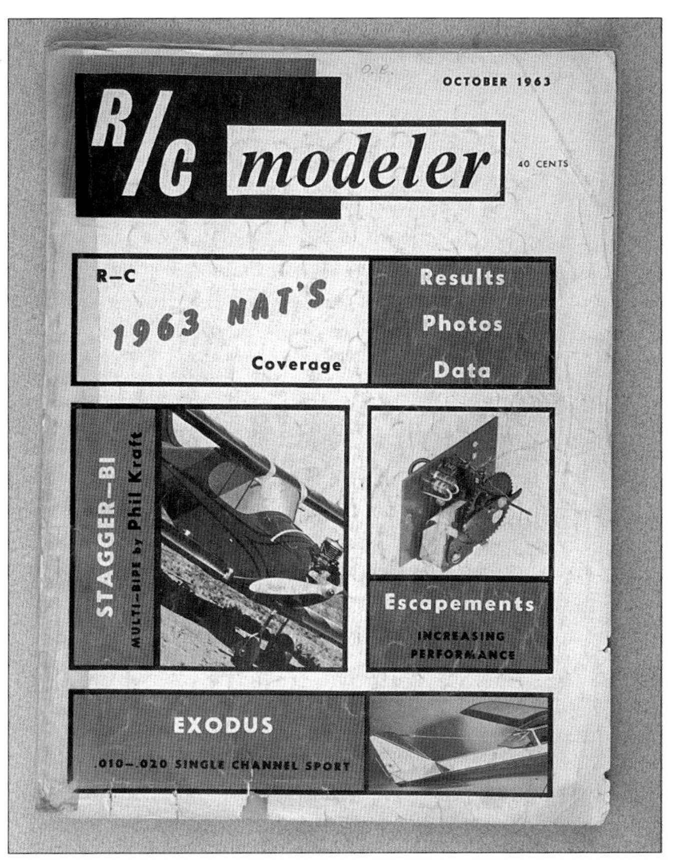

R/C Modeler, October 1963. This is the first issue of *Radio Control Modeler* (RCM), still being published today. This issue was edited by Don Dewey and featured an interview with Hal deBolt. The first couple of years of RCM are hard to find. $5-15.

Model Builder, July 1983, Robert Benjamin cover. Bob painted marvelous covers for Model Builder for about ten years and in time I believe he will join the ranks of famous and beloved model aviation cover artists, $2.

Radio Control Modeler, September 1964. The cover features a fantastic painting by Douglas Ettridge of the Dallas Nationals. $5-10.

Radio Control Modeler, May 1966, cover by Bill Polvogt, $2-5.

High Flight, official IMAA publication since 1980, issue number four on top, $2-3.

RC Sportsman, inaugural issue April 1975, $2-5.

Foreign Magazines

Aero Modeller, October 1937, $10-20.

Aeromodeller, May 1949, $4-7.

Aeromodeller, April 1949, C. Rupert Moore cover. In 1937, Moore designed a rubber powered model, the "Viper II" for Aeromodeller. He went on the do 125 consecutive cover paintings. His renditions are some of the most wonderful covers ever produced. *Courtesy of Bill Darkow.* $10-15.

Advertisement for Frog on the back cover from 1951.

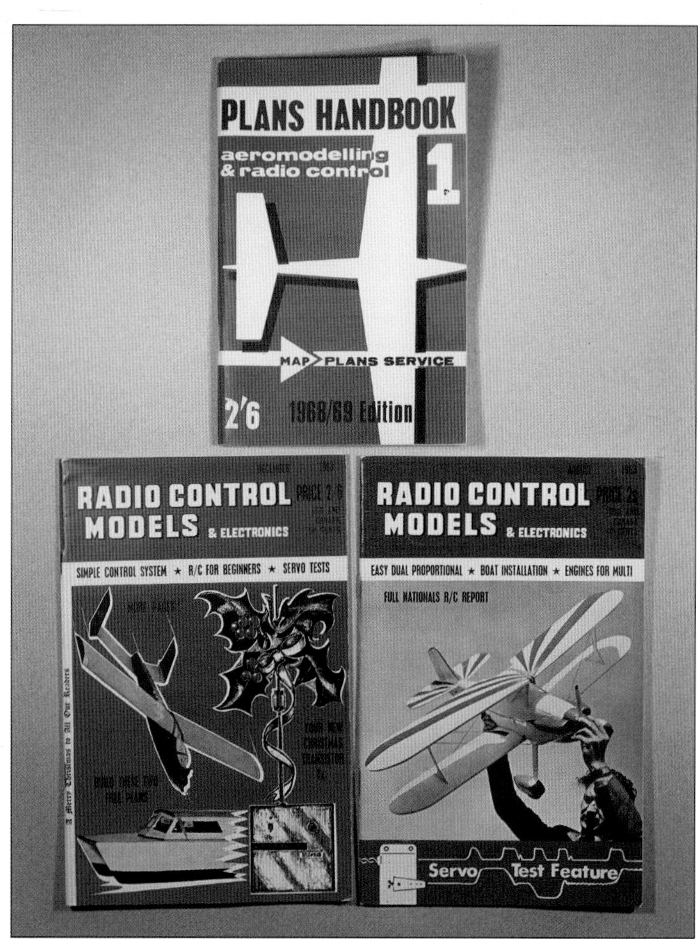

Plans Handbook, 1969, $5; *Radio Control Models and Electronics*, August and December 1963. $3-5.

Model Aircraft, November 1960, featuring Don Still from the World Championships and his famous Stuka Stunter in two color schemes. $3-5.

SAM Speaks, January-February 1989. This is the U.S. version with the cover art done by Bob Benjamin, $2-5.

SAM Speaks 35, February 1995 and August 1992. *Courtesy of Bill Darkow.* $3-5.

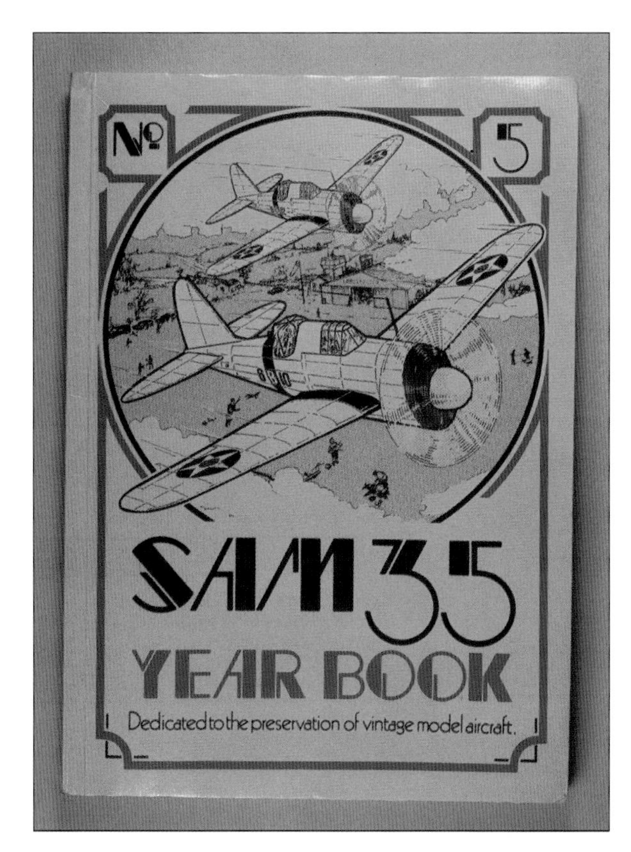

SAM 35 Yearbook, Number 5, December 1988, cover by Les Hoy. *Courtesy of Bill Darkow* $4-7.

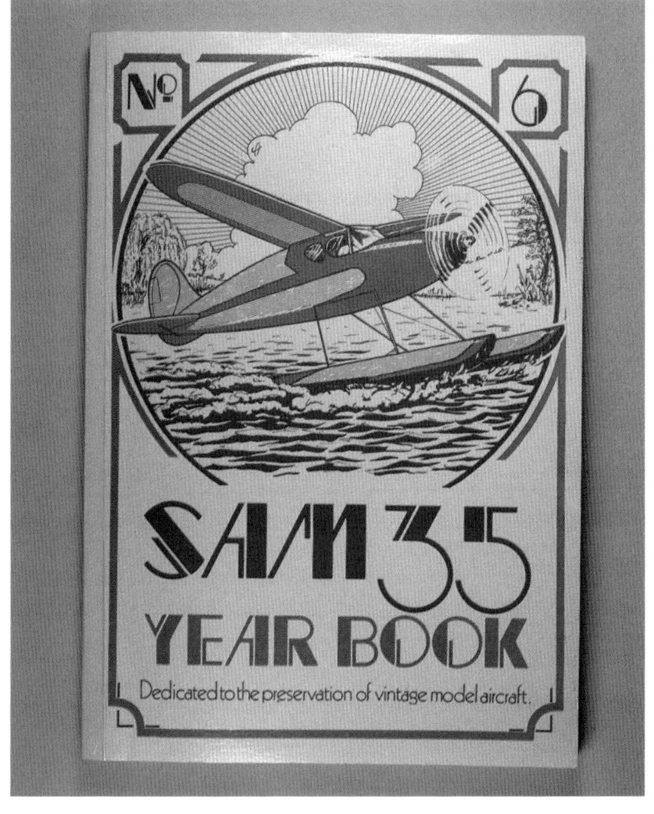

SAM 35 Yearbook, Number 6, November 1990, cover by Les Hoy. *Courtesy of Bill Darkow.* $4-7.

Model Avia, July 1959, from Belgium, $3-5.

Model Lismo, March-April 1993, Italian model magazine featuring cover art by Francesca DíOttavi. *Courtesy of Bill Darkow.* $2-4.

SAM 62 Annual, c. 1991, issue number one from Italy, edited and cover design by Cesare de Robertis. *Courtesy of Bill Darkow.* $10-15.

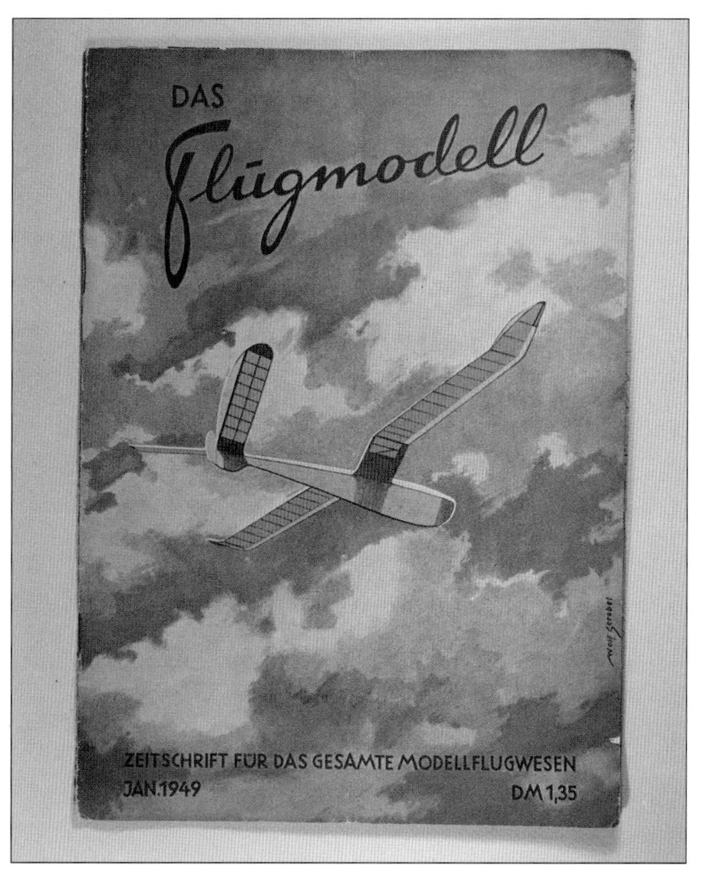

Das Flûgmodell, January 1949, cover by Wolf Strobel, $5-10.

Das Flûgmodell, February 1949, cover by Wolf Strobel, $5-10.

Hobby, December 1948, featuring the "Gran Premerio de Aeromodelismo 1948" and pictures of early modeling in South America, $10.

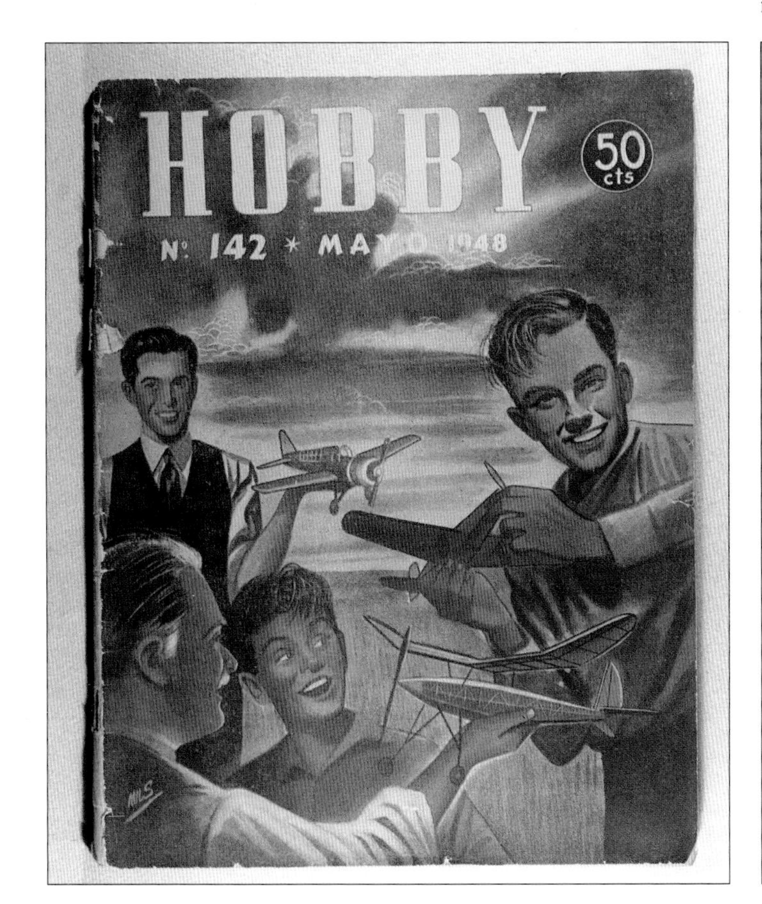

Hobby, May 1948, hobby magazine from Brazil. This issue featured control line aerobatics in Spanish, although Brazil's official language is Portuguese. $10.

Japanese model magazine from the 1950s. *Courtesy of Bill Darkow.* $10-25.

Japanese model airplane magazine from the 1940s. Bill and I dated these last two covers by the airplane designs shown. *Courtesy of Bill Darkow.* $10-25.

Chapter 4
Model Aviation Books

"Books are the ever-burning lamps
of accumulated wisdom."
—*G. W. Curtis*

The world of books about model airplanes is as diverse and colorful as the hobby. The history of model aviation has been documented repeatedly by an extensive list of authors that reads like the who's who of aero modeling. For almost one hundred years the writings and illustrations have inspired, encouraged, and transformed boys from every background. As full-scale aviation took to the air, the age of information was unleashed on just about every topic man could write about. Model airplanes were no exception. The first books to be published were aimed at the youthful market and this would not change until about 1940. As model competitions attracted more mature modelers and boys got older, the quest for information started an avalanche of excellent publications that are still enjoyable reading today.

modeling airplanes. Many early books contained a mixture of real aircraft and modeling; the information wasn't always the best as modeling was still growing slowly. (Bill Hannan, *Model Aviation*, April 1982, 33-36, 103-104).

Boy-Craft, a Whitman publication, c. 1928, 208 pp.; *Boy Builder*, c. 1930, Frank I. Solar, 208 pp, both books in excellent condition, $15-25.

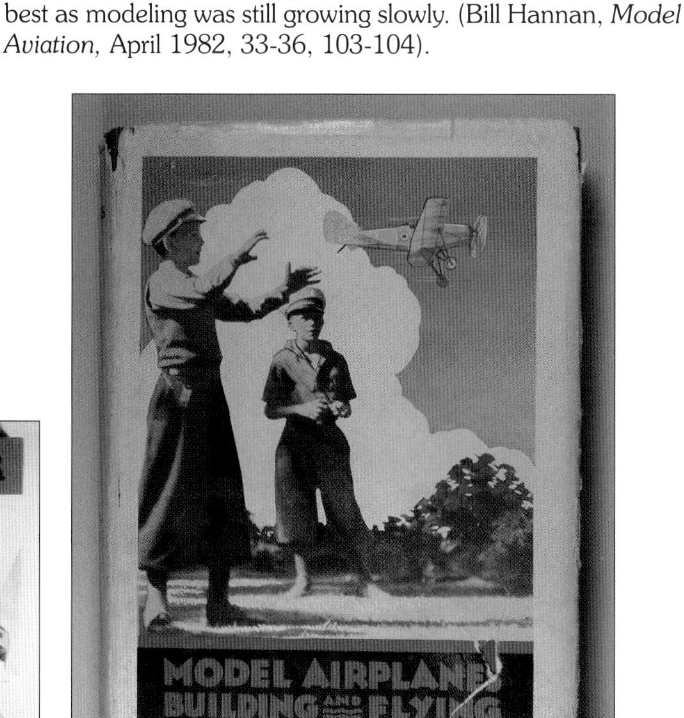

Model Airplane Building and Flying, c. 1931-32, Joseph S. Ott, 358 pp, $20-35.

The first book published in the United States was *The Boys Book of Aeroplanes*, authored by Francis A. Collins in 1910. This volume was successful enough to go to print in the original version six times and was revised in 1921 with five more printings. It was also published in England. Copies of this book are getting harder to find but it is not a rare book. The earliest exclusive book on model aviation is *The Theory and Practice of Model Aeroplaning* by Valentine E. Johnson; it was published in the London in 1910. Other notable books published before Lindberg's rise to fame include, *The Boys Second Book of Aeroplanes*, by F.A. Collins in 1911, *Harper's Aircraft Book*, by A. Hyatt Verrill in 1913, and *The Boy Mechanic*, by Popular Science Press in 1913 (this was part of a four volume set that remains a favorite among collectors today for the sheer content). The second volume of this set has a young modeler fabricating a twin pusher outdoors model on the cover. *The Boys Airplane Book*, Archie F. Collins, 1919 included a section on

With the explosion of interest in aviation after Lindberg's exploits, the floodgate was opened for writers to inspire a world of new modelers seeking knowledge as they became captivated with the mystery of flight. Several important works and authors appeared during this period. *Building and Flying Model Aircraft* copyrighted 1928 by Paul E. Garber, who worked closely with the Smithsonian Institution, listed and recorded early model aviation history. Elmer L. Allen wrote *Model Airplanes, How to Build and Fly Them* in 1928 and worked closely with the Boy Scouts of America in producing *Model Airplanes*, a fifty-two page booklet that included the Ideal Model Airplane Company plans. This little booklet seems to attract attention every time I see one as there are many Scout collectors wanting Boy Scouts of America aviation memorabilia. Edward T. Hamilton wrote his book, *Complete Model Aircraft Manual* in 1933 featuring over 500 pages of text, including Grants famous "Minute Man," a simple rise off ground (R.O.G.)

rubber powered model plane and several other small models for boys. This book went on to several printings and upgrades through 1938. Hamilton was a driving force in the modeling community with his writings, producing four classic books. Frank Zaic began his long running series of orange covered books that are still classics today, beginning with *1934 Junior Aeronautic Yearbook*. He went on to write sixteen similar books that have been reprinted and are still highly desired reading. (Bill Hannan, *Model Aviation,* May 1982, 37-40, 97-98).

Basic Principals of Airplane Control, Comet Model Airplane & Supply publication, c. 1942, 12 pp., written for the beginning full scale pilot. $7-15.

In 1941 two important works were published, Charles Hampson Grant's *Model Airplane Design and Theory of Flight* and William J. Winter's *The Model Aircraft Handbook.* Both of these books had several printings and were best sellers; they are still desired today as collectibles and for their content, much of which is timeless. Many volumes were printed and it is reasonably easy to find these two books. I have seen Grant's *Model Airplane Design and the Theory of Flight* listed as high as $90 on the ABE Books web site. If you are looking for books, this site had almost one hundred listings for books and magazines the last time I was in there. Other excellent books of the period are David C. Cooke's, *The Model Airplane Annual 1943, 1944, 1945* and *Guide to Model Aircraft* in 1945. This author has documented the history of pre-war, and war-time modeling with superb pictures and great detail.

British author Ron H. Warring started his prolific writing career in 1942 at the age of twenty-two. Warring wrote books, pamphlets, and articles until 1984 when he passed away at the age of 64. He wrote twenty-eight books and booklets; his three best sellers were *Control-Line Flying,* 1948, *Construction For Aeromodellers*, 1955 and *Design For Aeromodellers* in 1953. Listing and writing about all the books authored from 1910 to 1950 would be a whole volume alone. Many wonderful works were written and have found a wide readership among today's modelers.

From 1950 to modern times, other authors of note are Donald Foote, *Model Airplane Engines*, 1952, Walter A. Musciano, *Building and Flying Scale Model-Aircraft,* 1953, Edward L. Safford Jr. *Model Control By Radio*, 1951, and Howard G. McEntee, *Radio Control Handbook*, 1954. Another creative and prolific British writer is Ron G. Moulton. His books are sought after by modelers as they contain still useful information. His books *Model Aero Engine Encyclopedia* and *Control Line Manual* are highly sought after. Along with D.J. Laidlaw-Dickson, he helped keep the *Aeromodeller Annuals* going from 1963 to 1978. The annuals were produced starting in 1948 with the team of Laidlaw-Dickson and D.A. Russell continuing until 1950. Then the team of Laidlaw-Dickson and C.S. Rushbrooke continued until 1962. The annuals are favorites among free flight and control line modelers for the fantastic documentation of history and model designs spanning thirty years of aeromodeling around the world. They are collected for their cover art as well; the dust covers double the selling price. *Aeromodeller Annuals* with nice dust covers sell readily for twenty dollars and sometimes more.

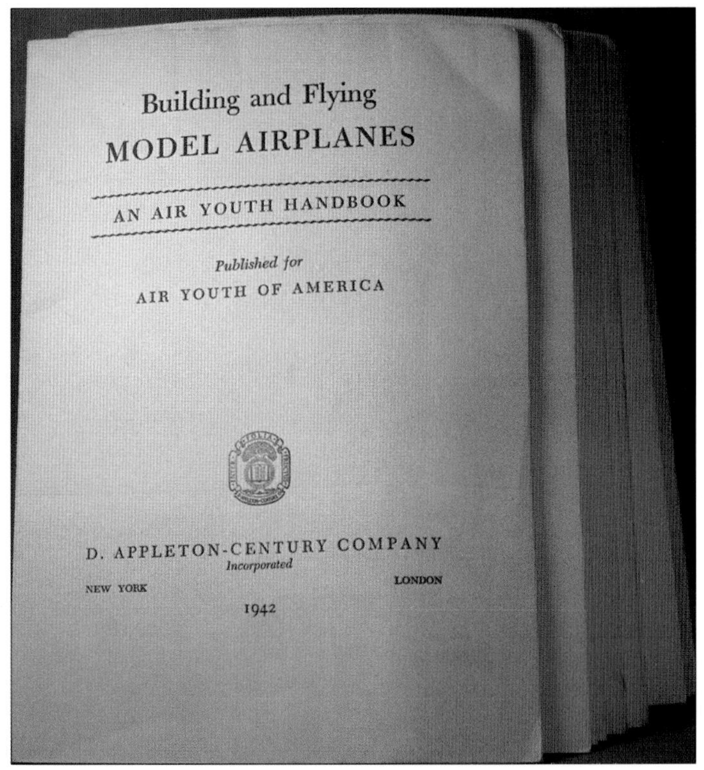

Building and Flying Model Airplanes, c. 1942, written for the Air Youth program during the war, $15-30.

Bill Hannan wrote an article in April and May of1982 featured in *Model Aviation* titled "Model Books." He took on this effort with the help of John Brown of Anaheim, California who has invested the past twenty-three years tracking down every book written in the English language on the topic of model aviation. I highly recommend reading this article for more information on the subject of writers and books referencing model airplanes. Authors continue to write on this ever-changing subject yet find room to include the rich history that has become part of our culture. Hannan is now among the list of notable authors who have observed the influences modeling has had on our culture the past one hundred years and are still finding something to give readers on this fascinating hobby. As this past time continues to evolve, modelers will keep wondering what else can be written. The amount of material already in print is an indication of why model airplanes can still capture the heart and imagination of those who take part in this great adventure.

Junior Aviation for Beginners, c. 1946, published by the University of New York, 100 pp. $10-30.

Junior Model Planes, c. 1945, James D. Powell and Ed Clark, 59 pp.; wonderful illustrations featuring five different model aircraft for beginning modelers, $10-25.

Collecting books and booklets on this subject is done for a couple of reasons. The first is for the pure enjoyment that comes from reading about days gone by. The second is needed information. Most modelers like to experiment and explore new ideas and designs. Modelers enjoy being different from each other by building unique designs of their own. Books give our collections a bit of flavor that reflects what we like about this subject. Almost every life-long modeler has some sort of "library" built up for reference and pleasure. Very few books about model aviation sell for huge sums of money but this seems to be changing slowly. If kept in good condition you can always get your money back when "cleaning" out your library. I hardly ever buy books as an investment collectible, only for the content and the pleasure they give.

Model Builders Manual, No. 4, c. 1950, Fawcett publication, 144 pp. Larry Eisenger editor, $10-20.

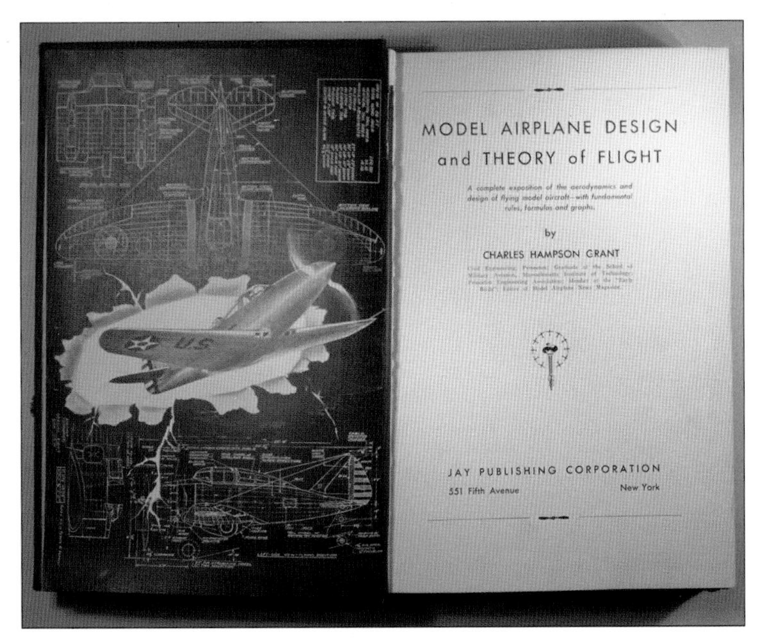

Model Airplane Design and Theory of Flight, c. 1941, Charles Hampson Grant, first edition, signed, Jay Publishing, 512 pp, $30-90.

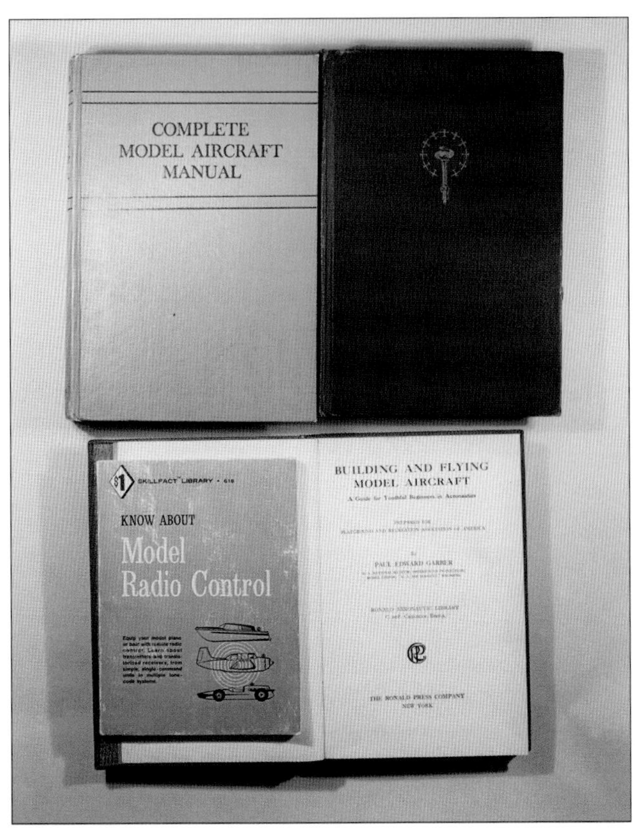

Complete Model Aircraft Manual, Edwin Timothy Hamilton, c. 1933, 578 pp. signed, $30-60; Cover of Grants book, *Know About Model Radio Control,* c. 1965 Allan Lytel, 96 pp. $5; *Building and Flying Model Aircraft,* c. 1928, Paul Edward Garber, 300 pp. $15-30.

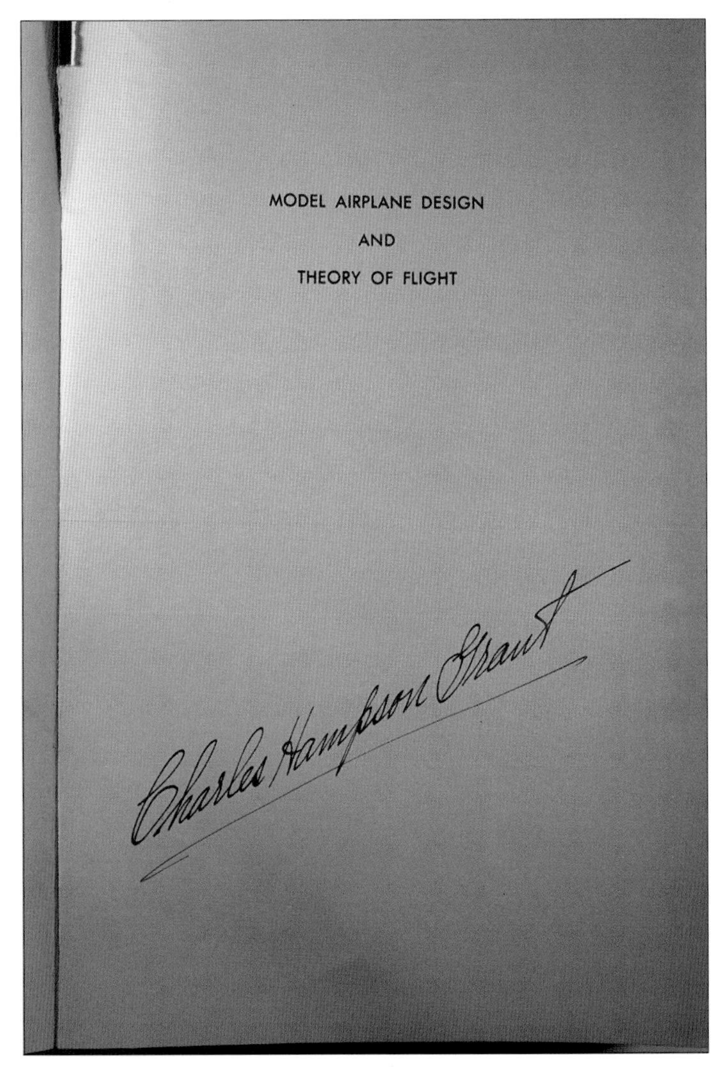

Charles Hampson Grant's signature. This book came out in a 2nd edition in 1942 by Air Age and was reprinted in 1943 and 1944. Unsigned books sell for about, $10-30.

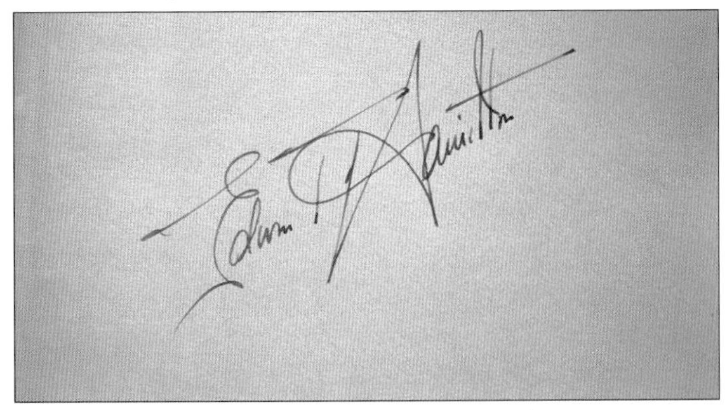

Edwin T. Hamilton's signature.

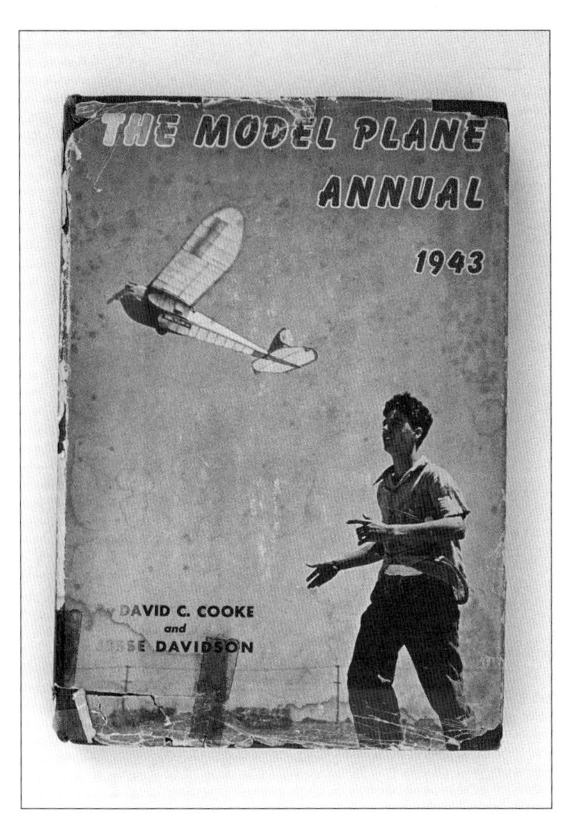

The Model Plane Annual 1943, David C. Cooke and Jesse Davidson, 224 pp, $15-30.

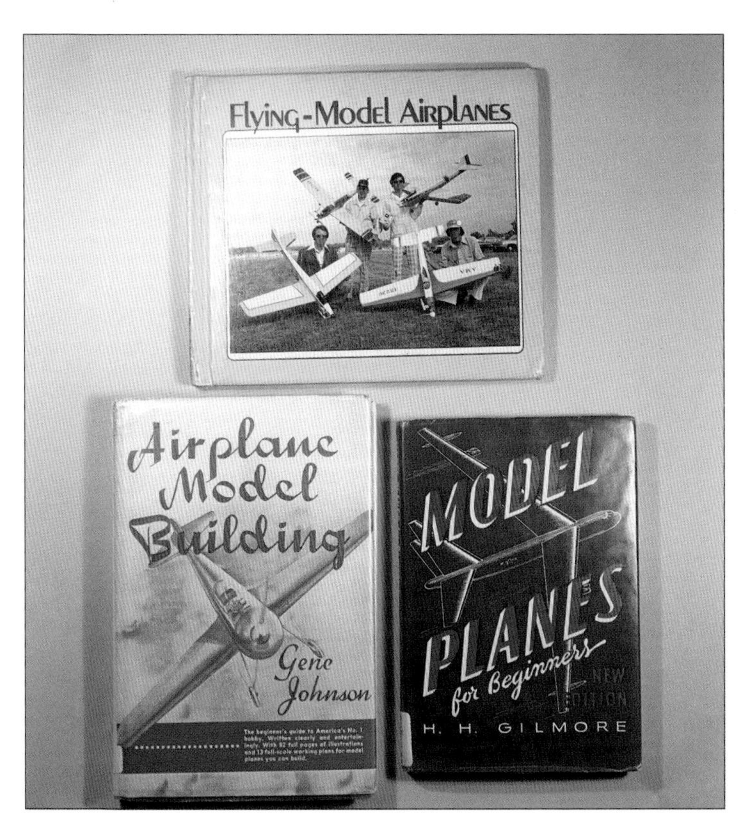

Flying-Model Airplanes, c. 1982, Don Berliner, current AMA President Dave Brown is in the checkered pants and hat. $5; *Airplane Model Building*, c. 1946, Gene Johnson, 141 pp. $10-15; *Model Airplanes for Beginners*, c. 1947, Horace Herman Gilmore, 95 pp. $10-15.

Model Glider Design, c. 1944, Frank Andrew Zaic, Model Aeronautic Publications, 192 pp. $10-20.

Musciano's Flying Scale Models Of Famous Aircraft, No. 1, c. 1954, Walter A. Musciano, 24 pp. $7-15.

Model Airplane Engines, c. 1952,
Donald K. Foote, 177 pp. $20-40.

Build Your First Flying Models, c. 1946,
Jesse Davidson, 33 pp. $7-15.

International Engine Review, c. 1957,
Peter Chinn, 24 pp. $5-15.

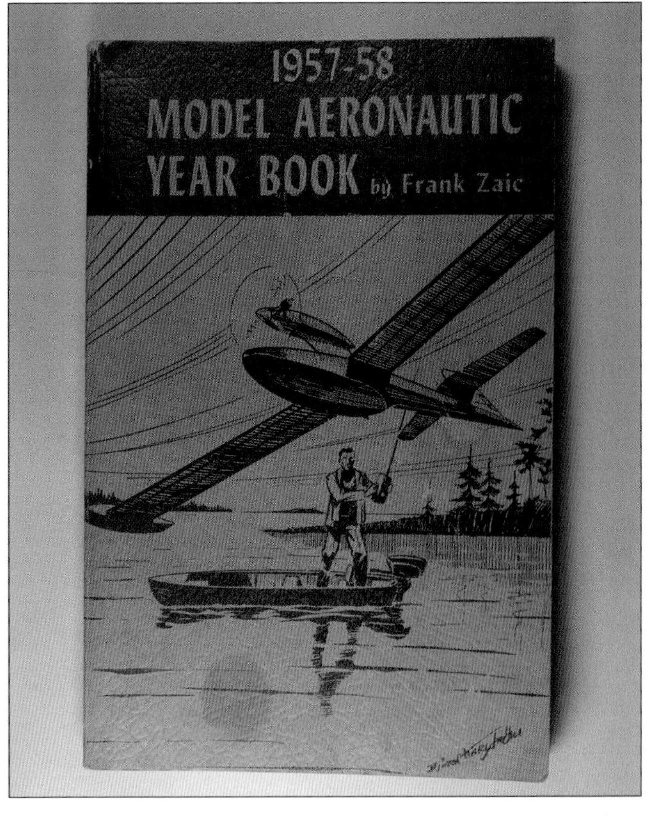

Model Aeronautic Yearbook, 1957-58, Frank Zaic, 223 pp. $10.

Model Aeronautic Yearbook, 1959-61, Frank Zaic, 288 pp. Frank Zaic's books are still widely read. He wrote about fifteen books with the signature orange covers, from 1934 to 1965. All have gone into reprints, 1970-1980s. Original copies of the early publications sell for more and some are signed. $10-20.

William John Winter, *The Model Aircraft Handbook*

"Let us endeavor so to live that when we come to die even the undertaker will be sorry."
—*Mark Twain*

It would be hard write about model aviation without mentioning Bill Winter. His book *The Model Aircraft Handbook* was first published in 1941 and went on to become a best seller. There were four editions and twelve printings, the last being revised in 1968 by Howard McEntee. Bill is remembered most of all for his service to the modeling community as an editor, writer, designer, and modeler. His style of writing is entertaining and informative with the keen understanding of the impact modeling has had on a nation of boys and men during his lifetime. He was one of first ten recipients to be inducted into the AMA Hall of Fame; the honor was bestowed in 1970.

Bill wrote twenty-one books and booklets covering every aspect of aeromodeling. He was a department editor with *Air Trails* from 1937-1946; at the same time was consulting editor for *Air World* and *Flying Models*. *Popular Electronics* hired him to write and edit the radio control column from October 1954 until the end of 1956. From 1951 through 1960 he was editor of *Model Airplane News*, and in 1960 he took over as editor of *American Aircraft Modeler*, a post he held until 1972. His last editing job lasted until 1980 for the Academy of Model Aeronautics publication *Model Aviation* but continued to write articles until 1986 when he fully retired. Bill Winter was most likely the most influential editor in the model airplane magazine business. (1998. R. Trumbull and J. Haught, *Model Aviation*, May 1999, 10-15). I once saw a picture of him wearing a t-shirt that said "May you live long enough to be a problem to your children." I liked it so much I gave one to my dad. Bill passed away December 11, 1998 at the age of 86.

Cal Smith on Model Building, c. 1952, Calhoun Smith, 144 pp. $10-30.

Handbook of Model Planes, Cars and Boats, c. 1965, William John Winter. On the cover is a picture of Cal Smith holding his famous radio controlled Sopwith Pup. 104 pp. $5-15.

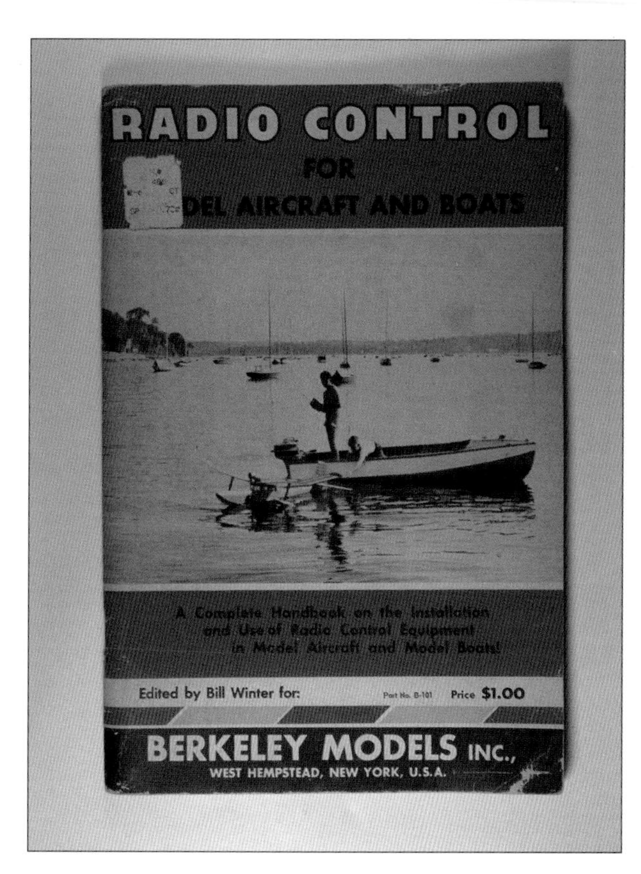

Radio Control for Model Aircraft and Boats, c. 1954, William John Winter, 72 pp. $5-10.

The Model Aircraft Handbook, c. 1957, William John Winter. There are many reprints of this famous and popular book. It is one of the best selling books on model aviation; the 1946 edition contained 345 pages making it the largest book with this title. 206 pp. $10-30.

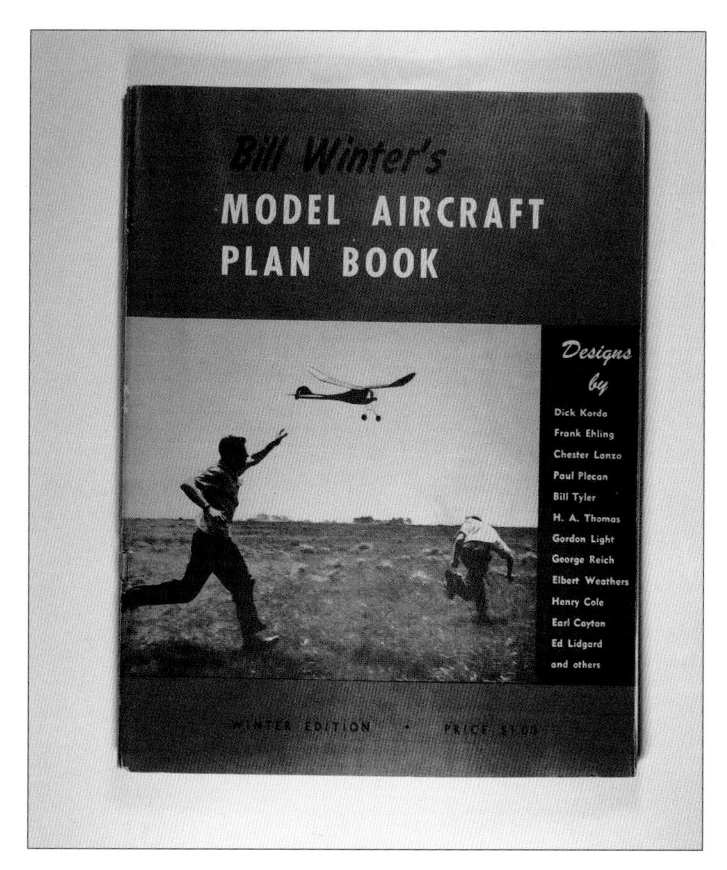

Model Aircraft Plan Book, c. 1947, William John Winter, 130 pp. $10-20.

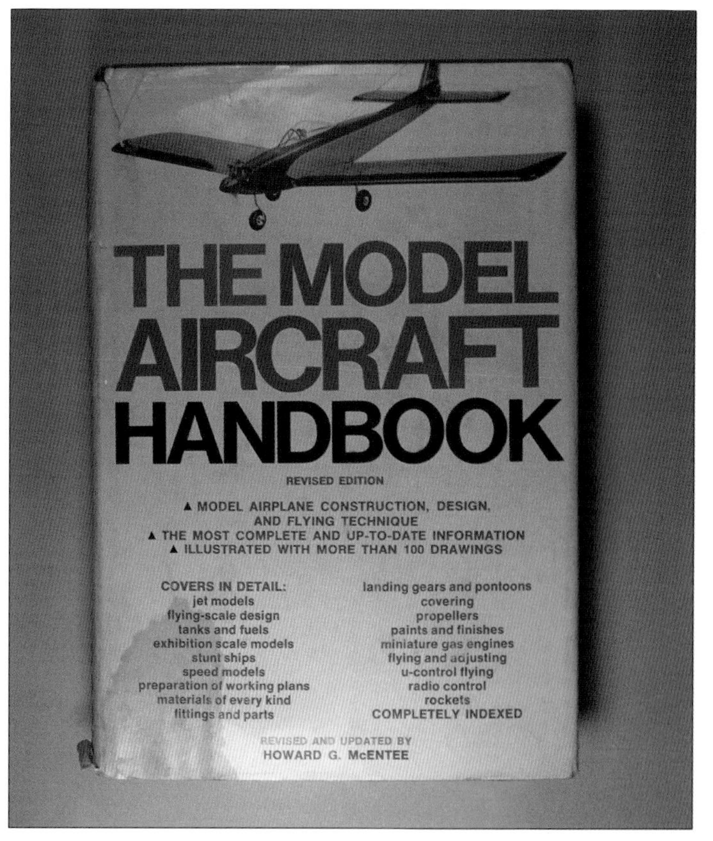

The Model Aircraft Handbook, c. 1968, Howard G. McEntee. This was the last version of Bill Winter's book. It was reprinted five more times, 1984 was the last year – almost forty-five years of continuous publication. 228 pp. $5-15.

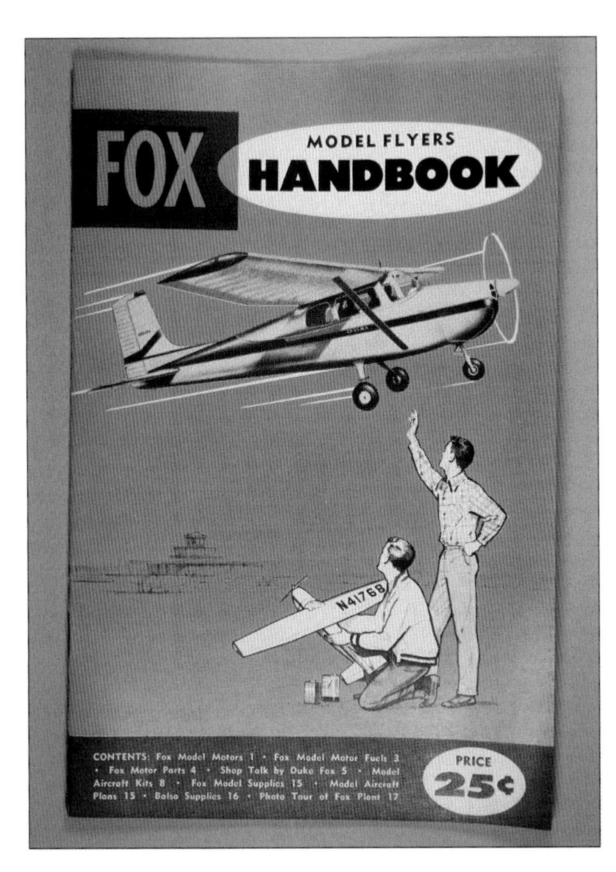

Model Flyer's Handbook, c. 1962, Duke Fox, 16 pp. $10-35.

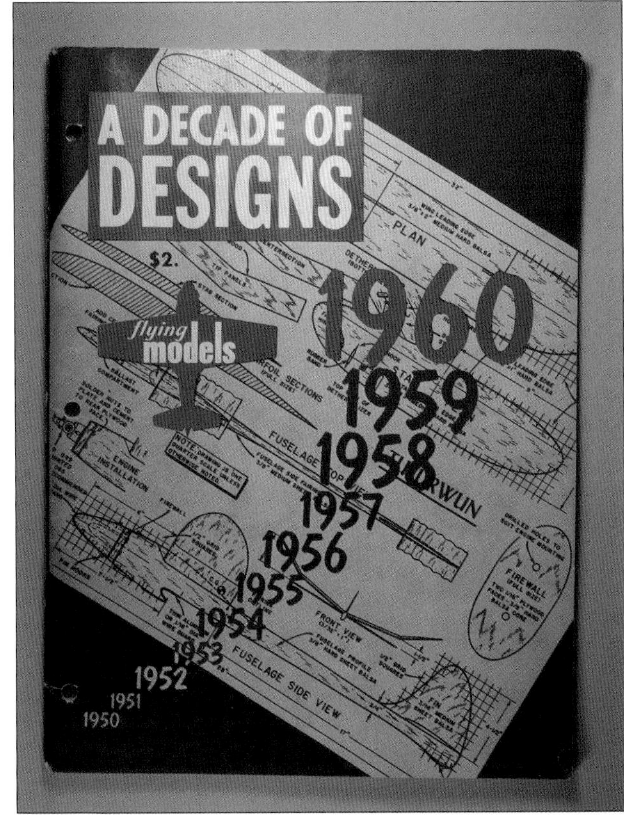

A Decade of Designs, 1950-1960, c. 1960, Don McGovern, 74 pp, $10-20.

Flying Models Reference Handbook, c. about 1960, may have been edited and written by Don McGovern, approx. 75 pp. $10-20.

Model Flying Handbook, c. 1976, Ottar Stensbol, 160 pp. $5-10; *Radio Control for Model Builders*, c. 1972, Fred Marks and Bill Winter, 151 pp. $5-7; *Radio Control for Model Builders*, 1st ed. c. 1960, William Winter, 220 pp. $5-10; *Radio Control Handbook*, c 1957, Howard G. McEntee, c. 1957, 4th printing, 192 pp. $5-10.

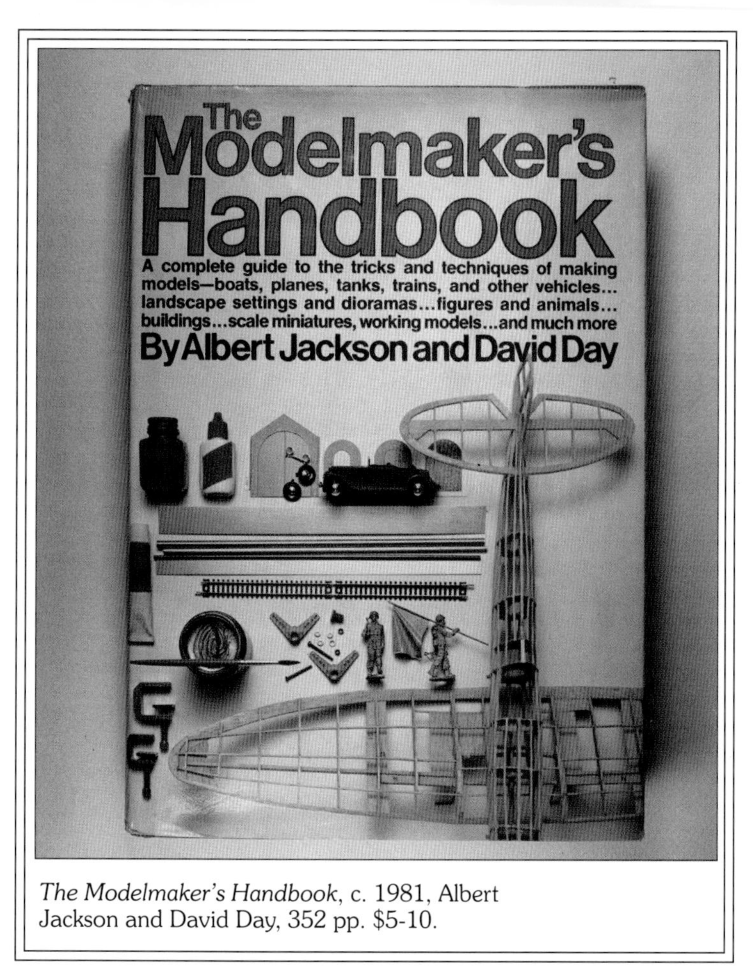

The Modelmaker's Handbook, c. 1981, Albert Jackson and David Day, 352 pp. $5-10.

Foreign Authors

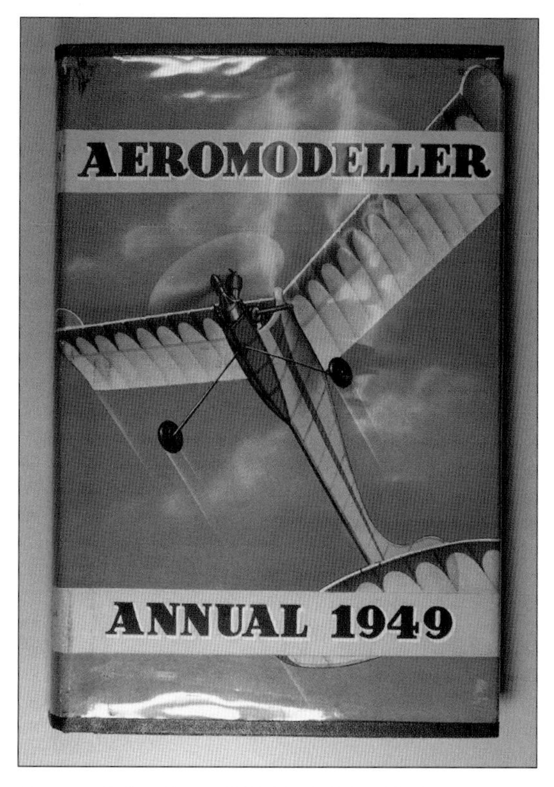

Aeromodeller Annual 1949, D.J. Laidlaw-Dickson and D.A. Russel, 192 pp. $20-30.

Aeromodeller Annual 1951, D.J. Laidlaw-Dickson and C. S. Rushbrooke, 160 pp. *Courtesy of Bill Darkow.* $15-20.

Aeromodeller Annual 1952, D.J. Laidlaw-Dickson and C. S. Rushbrooke, 192 pp. *Courtesy of Bill Darkow.* $15-20.

Aeromodeller Annual 1956-57, D.J. Laidlaw-Dickson and C. S. Rushbrooke, 160 pp. $15.

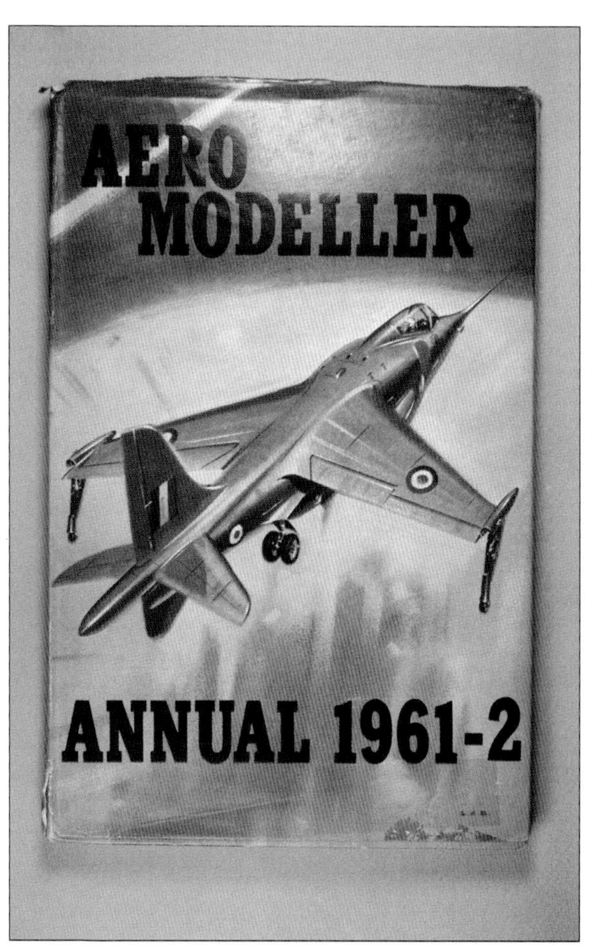

Aeromodeller Annual 1961-62, C. S. Rushbrooke and D.J. Laidlaw-Dickson, 160 pp. *Courtesy of Bill Darkow.* $15.

Aeromodeller Annual 1960-61, C. S. Rushbrooke and D.J. Laidlaw-Dickson, 160 pp. *Courtesy of Bill Darkow.* $15.

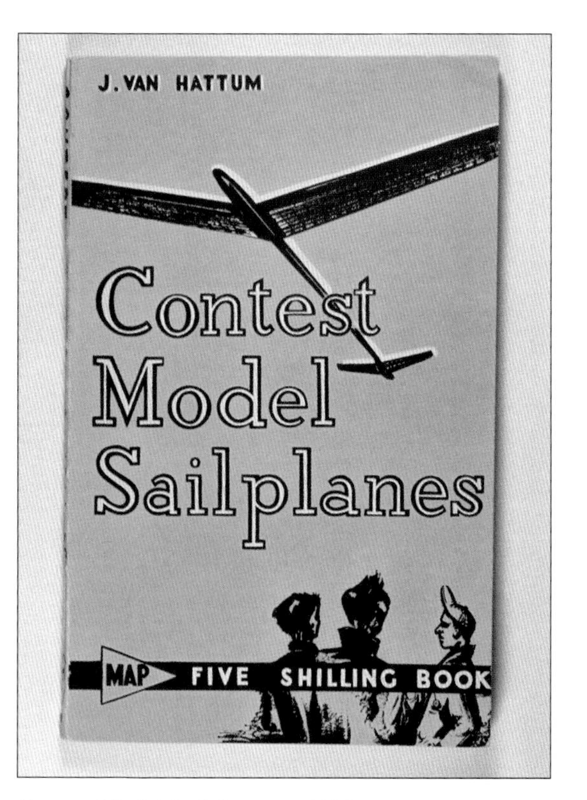

Contest Model Sailplanes, c. 1957, J. Van Hattum, $5-10.

Antique and Old Timer Model Aircraft, c. 1980, Danny Sheelds, signed, 84 pp. *Courtesy of Bill Darkow.* $10-30.

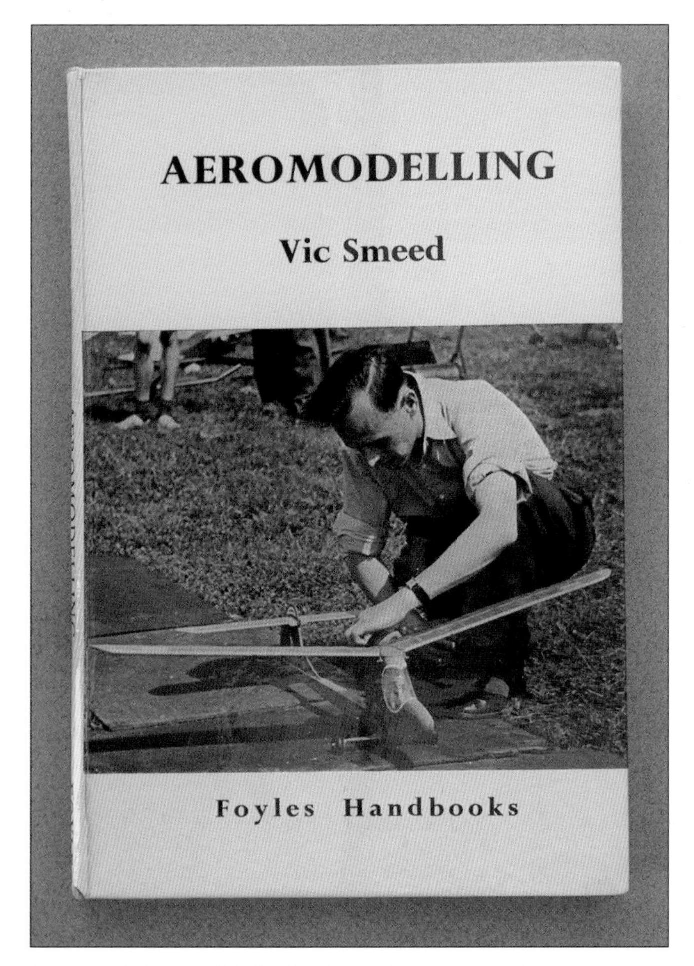

Aeromodelling, c. 1965, Vic Ernest Smeed, signed, 91 pp. *Courtesy of Bill Darkow.* $10-30.

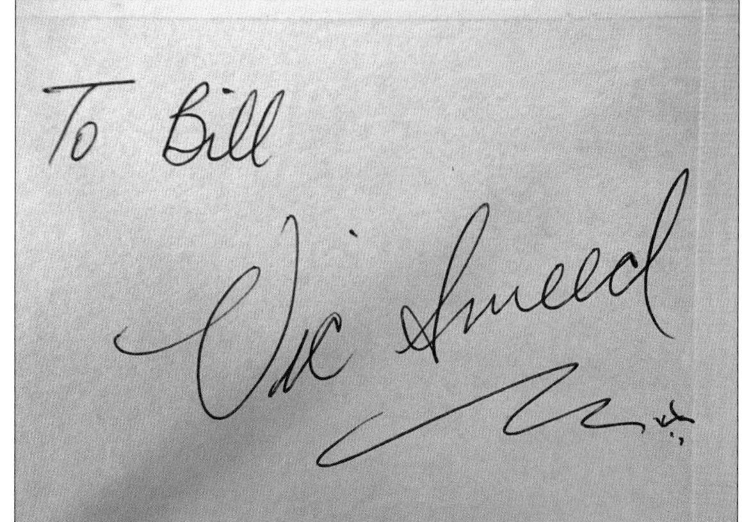

Vic Smeed's signature.

Model Flying, the First Fifty Years, c. 1987, Vic Smeed, 95 pp *Courtesy of Bill Darkow.* $10-20.

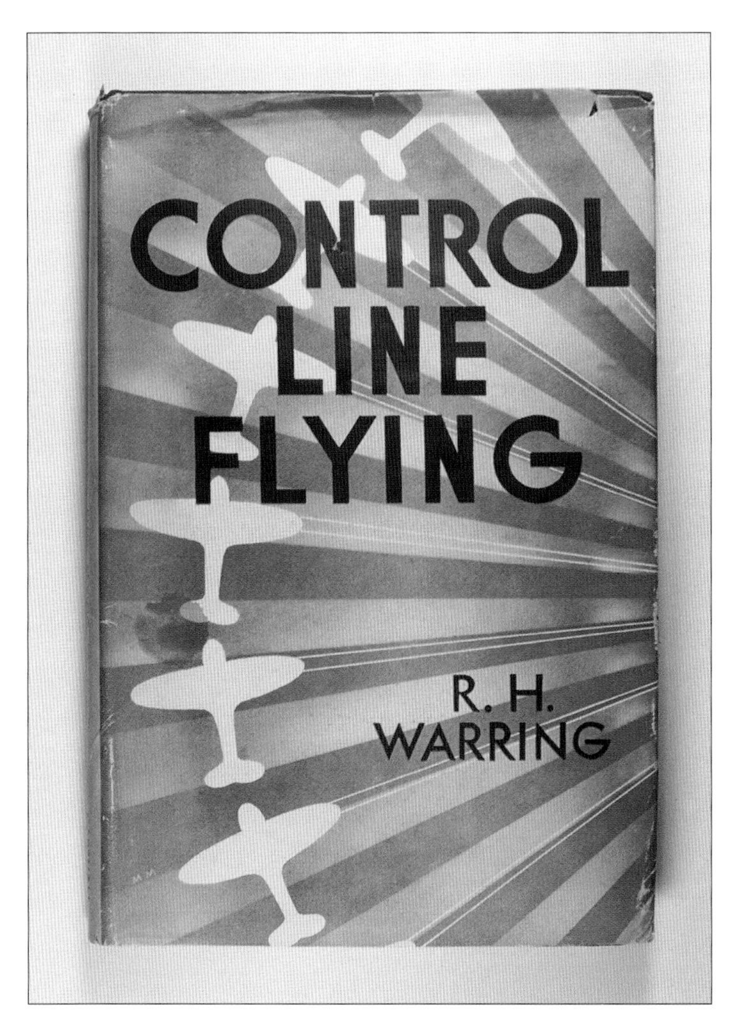

Control Line Flying, c. 1948-50, Ron H. Warring (1920-1984). British writer R.H. Warring is perhaps the most prolific author and noted authority on model aviation. His books have covered every imaginable subject from indoor models and engines, to radio control. Ron started with *Indoor Flying Models* in 1942 and produced more than fifty books and publications. *The Glassfibre Handbook* was his final book in 1983. The book sells for $15-30.

Radio Control For Models, c. 1981, R. H. Warring, 132 pp. $10.

Chapter 5
Radio Control and Accessories

Collecting early radio control gear has only recently come into its own as interest in the history of model airplanes has continued to gain ground. Along with vintage collector associations already established and the founding of the Vintage Radio Control Society in 1991, another subculture was created among model airplane collectors. Just about everything connected to vintage R.C. is being added to collections. This is a good example of the depth and directions collectors have taken in this ever-expanding category of collectibles.

Ten years ago, most old radio gear simply took up space or served as a conversation piece. Reminiscing about the "good old days" of escapements and reed radios is always a fun topic of discussion. I still have my first two radios: a C & S Falcon escapement set and an Ace Pulse Commander I drooled over for months. In 1971, I made a deal with my mother (who supported my modeling activities and used the Pulse Commander as the carrot at the end of my stick) that if I made Eagle Scout, she would buy the seventy-dollar radio for me. I made Eagle scout six months later and that radio went on to fly in an Ace High Glider – ah, success! These radios, in excellent condition, go for about $125 today; mine still occupies that special place in my hobby room.

Radio controlled model aircraft have dominated the model industry since 1970. Their impact has been felt throughout the hobby in the form of advertising dollars in all publications. With great strides in equipment, both in quality and price, over 90% of today's modelers have experienced the excitement of radio control flying. In the early 1980s, the industry trend was toward quarter scale model aircraft. Twenty years have passed and the industry has done a complete turn around with miniature radio controlled models dominating the market. Model aviation continues to find new ways to keep the dream of flight alive through innovation and technology.

Radio Control began in 1898 when Nikola Tesla invented and patented the radio receiver and transmitter. He demonstrated true radio control using a multi-channel radio system to control a submarine, which he also patented the same year. The circuits that Tesla used in his original remote controlled submarine are still being used in modern radio controlled transmitters and receivers today. History has recorded significant interest in flying by remote control before World War II. The first airplane flown by R.C. was a Navy N-9 seaplane. The N-9 was flown completely by radio control on September 15, 1924, a full 10 or more years before the first model airplane.

Debuting at the 1937 Model Airplane Championships, Chester Lanzo won the event with a simple single channel free flight stick model. By 1940, Bill and Walt Good were a national sensation. One of their more remarkable feats occurred at the 1940 Chicago Nationals. This did not involve flying. A day before the radio event their transmitter was stolen. They setup shop in a local radio laboratory and toiled through the night building another transmitter. They went on to capture first place convincingly over a dozen entrants. (Howard McEntee, *Air Trails Model Annual for 1952*, 68-70). Their historic R.C. model airplane, which they affectionately named the "Guff," was presented to the National Air and Space Museum in Washington, D.C., in May 1960, where it can be seen today. World War II called on most early pioneers to contribute their knowledge to support the war effort.

All early development was tied to ham radio bands and operators were required to be licensed and learn Morse code at a rate of thirteen words per minute. This changed in July 1951 to five words a minute for two new classes of radio control modelers. On June 26, 1950, approval of the 465 mc frequency band was granted. The first Citizen Band license was issued to Vernon C. Macnabb, producer of Citizen-Ship radio control equipment. The Federal Communication Commission eliminated the code and written examinations for users on the 465 megacycle and 27.255 megahertz bands in 1952. Chairman of the Contest Board for the AMA, Dr. Walt Good led this effort with countless letters, conferences, and demonstrations to the F.C.C. The postwar years (1945-1952) would be some of the most exciting in the history of model aviation. (Fred Marks, Bill Winter, *Radio Control for Model Builders*, 1-4; Dr. Walter Good, *Air Trails*, April 1954, 42-45; Howard McEntee, *Air Trails Annual for 1952*, 71-73).

The radio control event was still more of a novelty at the annual Nationals. Entrants included the Good Brothers, Jim Walker, L. Victor Brown, Clinton DeSoto, Ross Hull, Joseph Raspante, George Trammell, Leon Shulman, C. H. Siegfried, and Gene Foxworthy. The pioneers of early R.C. development along with their achievements became the foundations of what is enjoyed today. During this time, the first commercially produced radio sets became available.

Early manufacturers include Babcock, Bramco, Berkeley, Bonner, Citizen-Ship, and E.D. The Becon Electronics Company marketed the Good Brothers radio in 1947. Technological advancements would make all early radio gear obsolete a decade later as proportional radio control sets entered the market. Other significant manufacturers that left their mark on R.C. history were Ace, CG, C & S, Controlaire, Ecktronics, F & M, Kraft, Min-X, Orbit, and Sampey and Company. Some of these would go on to produce early proportional radios around 1960. This was the beginning of the modern era of model aviation. Escapement radio gear continued to be produced as an entry-level product. Getting a plane to fly using vintage radio gear was quite an achievement contrary to advertisements of the time.

Vintage radio gear now being acquired may be in working or non-working condition; most will never be used again. Frequency changes have made use of the old wide band radios illegal except on the 27 MHZ bands. The 27 MHZ band was added in September 1958 and experienced interference problems from Citizen's Band radios. The 72 MHZ band was added in 1966 to give radio control flyers relief from interference and overcrowding from the explosive growth R.C. experienced in the 1960s. Complete sets and accessories in their original packaging are the most desirable. Radio units manufactured overseas are also highly desirable among collectors. Some being currently collected are Aristocraft, ED, Futaba-MRC, Graupner, MacGregor, OS and R.C.S. Early proportional radios made by Kraft, Orbit, R.S., Expert, Proline, Citizen-Ship, and Bramco are gaining a small following. Equipment made before 1965 is the most expensive, along with single stick units and those that were unique. Obsolete radio control items can be a nice way to spice up just about any flying model collections. There seems to be appeal worldwide, so expect a bit of competition when using eBay to purchase vintage radios.

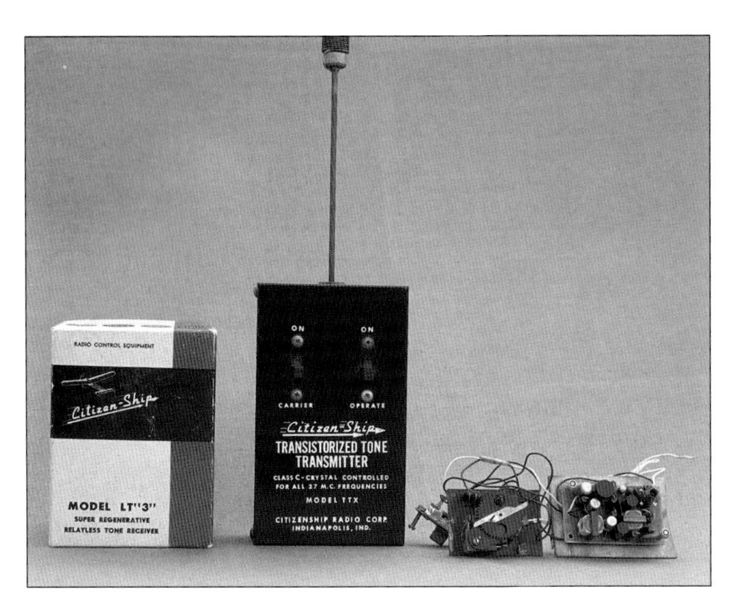

Citizenship TTX transmitter and LT-3 tone receiver with SE-2-M escapement, early 1960s, in new condition $75-100.

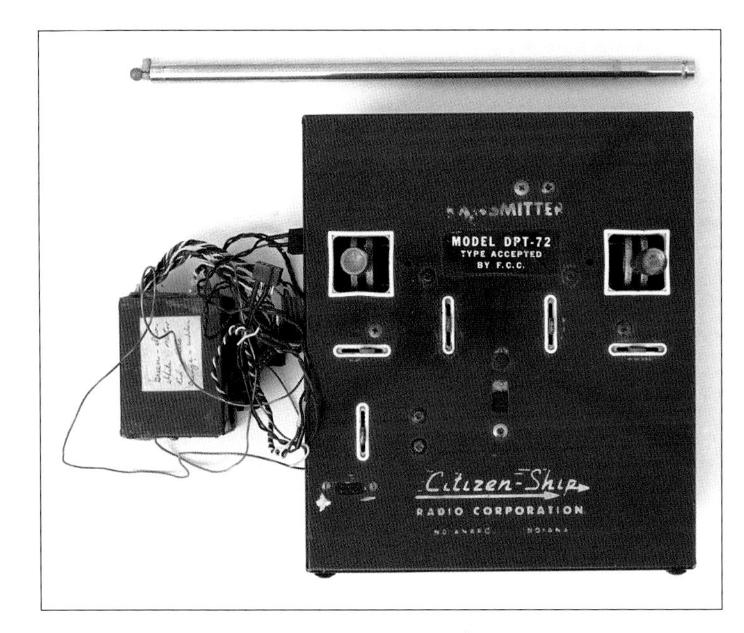

Citizenship DPT-72 five channel set used, $50-75.

Citizenship FLX transmitter in the box, on 27.225, near new condition c. 1954-1958, $35-45.

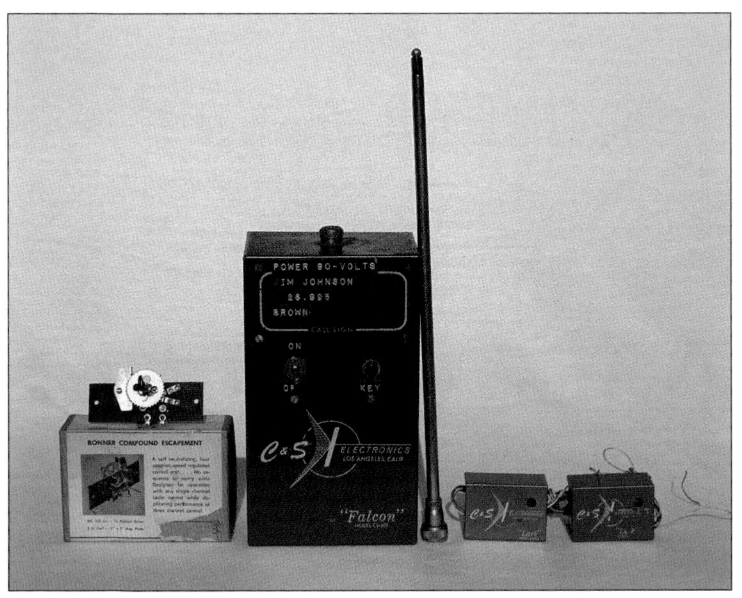

C&S Electronics Falcon CS-502 transmitter and Lark CS-503 receivers, c. 1963-65, used very little, this is my first radio, purchased at a garage sale in San Diego for $15 in 1968. It used two Burgess 45 volt batteries to power the transmitter and they cost almost as much as I paid for the set. C&S Electronics was founded by Bill Cannon and Bob Hunter joined as partner forming the company in 1961. The equipment was produced first in Phoenix, AZ, before moving to Los Angeles in 1963. $100-125.

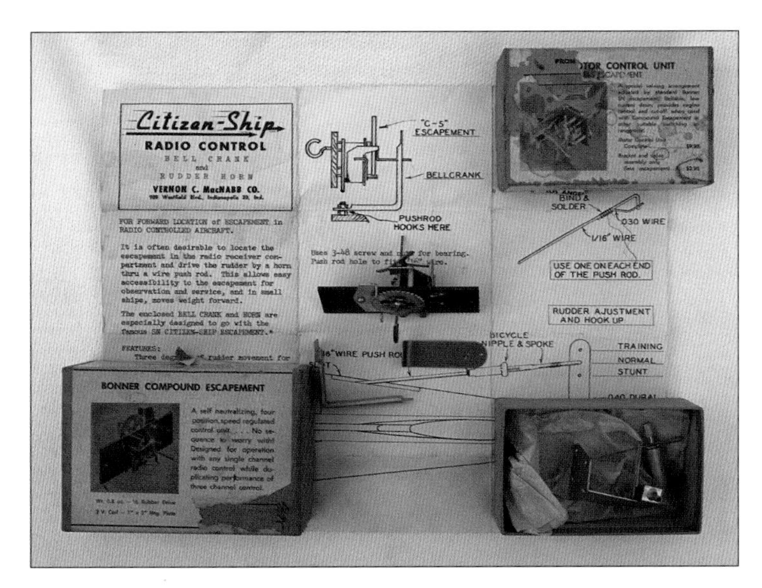

Bonner Compound escapement and Citizenship bellcrank and elevator horn, c. 1956 components are new, $15-25.

Japanese SN escapement for the single channel "Orient" c. 1965, $10.

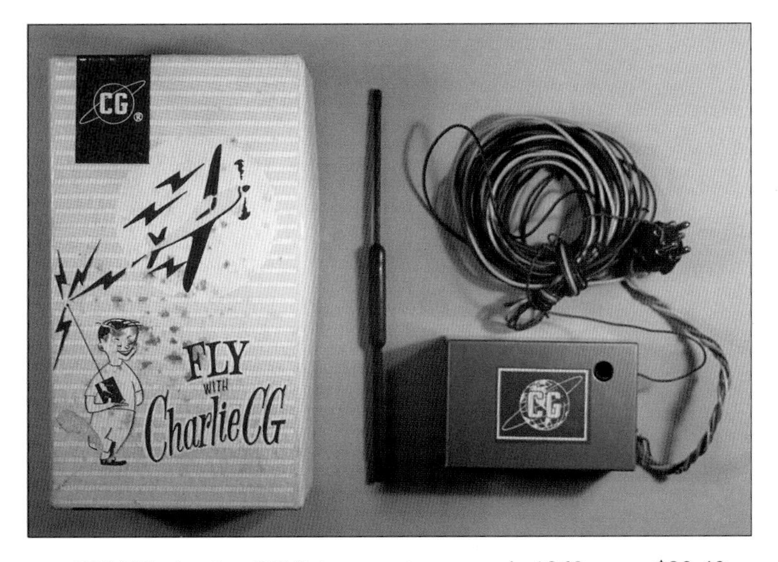

F&M Electronics, CG Saturn receiver, c. early 1960s, new $30-40.

Ideal Models, Tower Engineering Division, Selectronic fuel tank, c. late 1950s, used as an engine throttle, comes with built in escapement, new, $15-20.

Citizenship SE-2-M transistorized escapement, new $15-20.

Transmitters *left to right:* Pro-Line Competition Six, c. 1976-1980, the rest of this radio is still in a model built in 1984, $50-100; Venus CG transmitter, not much left here c. 1961, $15-20; Kraft Commander tone transmitter, marketed by Ace R.C. around 1960, $15-20.

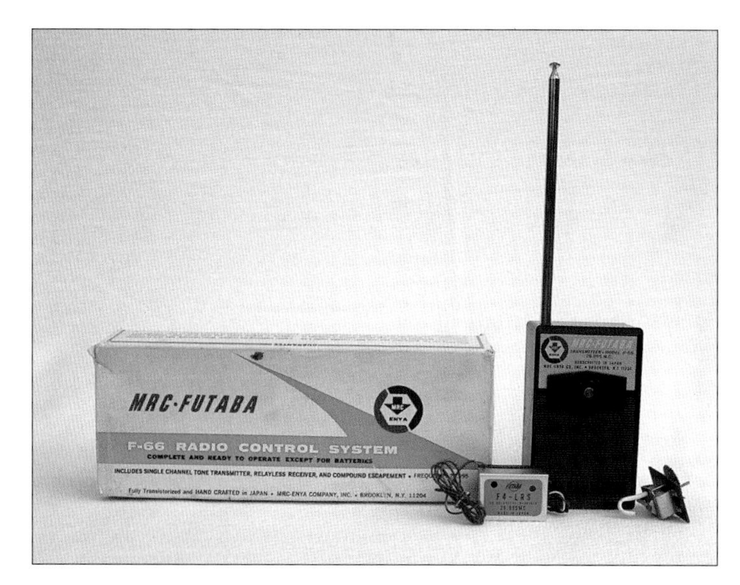

Model Rectifier Corporation, Futaba, F-66 single channel escapement set, c. 1965, new, $75-100.

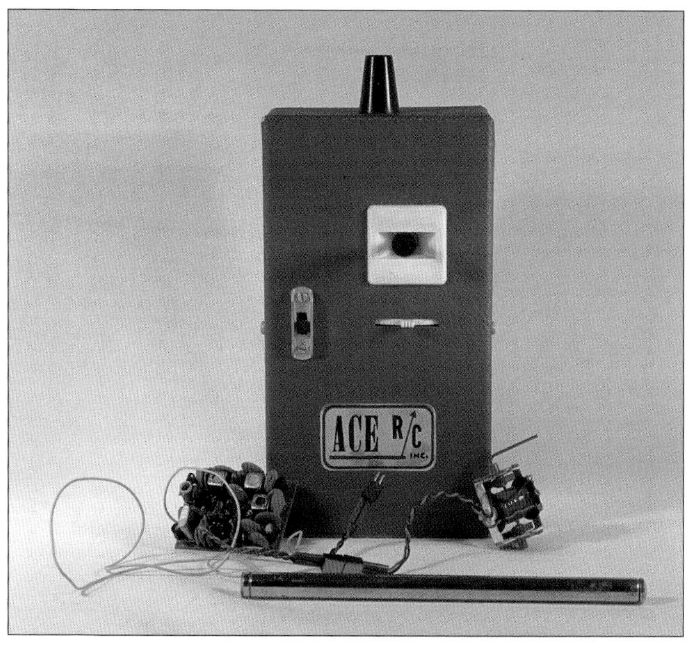

Ace R.C. Pulse Commander, c. 1972. In 1972, they sold for about seventy dollars. When proportional pulse radios were introduced, the single channel escapement sets went to a quick death, new sets sell for $100-135.

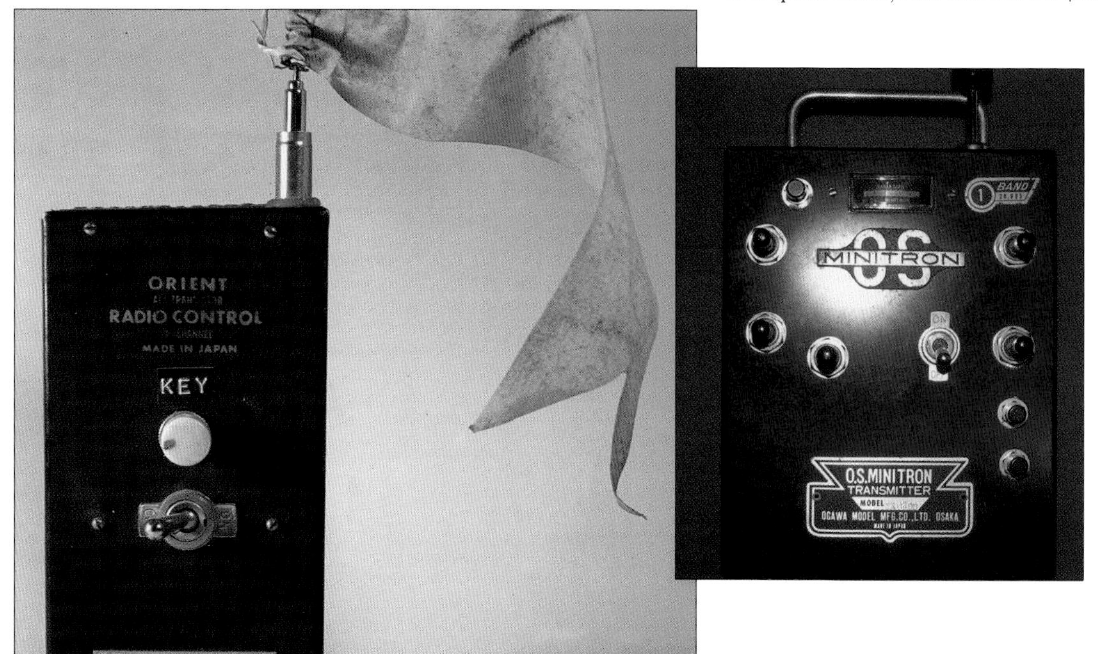

O.S. Minitron 12 channel transmitter, c. 1964, a leather case could be ordered as an optional accessory, like new condition. *Courtesy of Injae Chung Ph.D.* $75-125.

Orient single channel escapement transmitter, receiver is in a small black metal box (not shown) and was installed in my first radio controlled airplane, a Carl Goldberg 1/2 A Skylane. Dave Brown, a helicopter crewmember at NAS Imperial Beach, gave the set to me. He was my flying partner in 1969 and mentor while my dad was in the Gulf of Tonkin on the U.S.S. Kitty Hawk. I believe this set to be from 1965-68, $50-75.

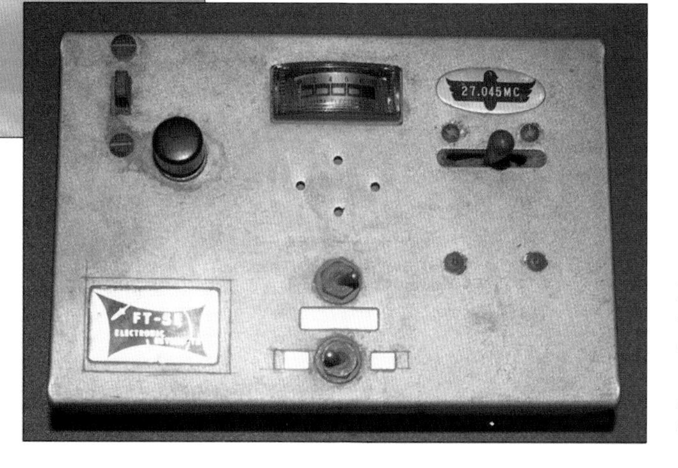

Futaba, FT-5E transmitter, 2 channel system, c. 1960s. *Courtesy of Injae Chung Ph.D.*, used, $ 20-30.

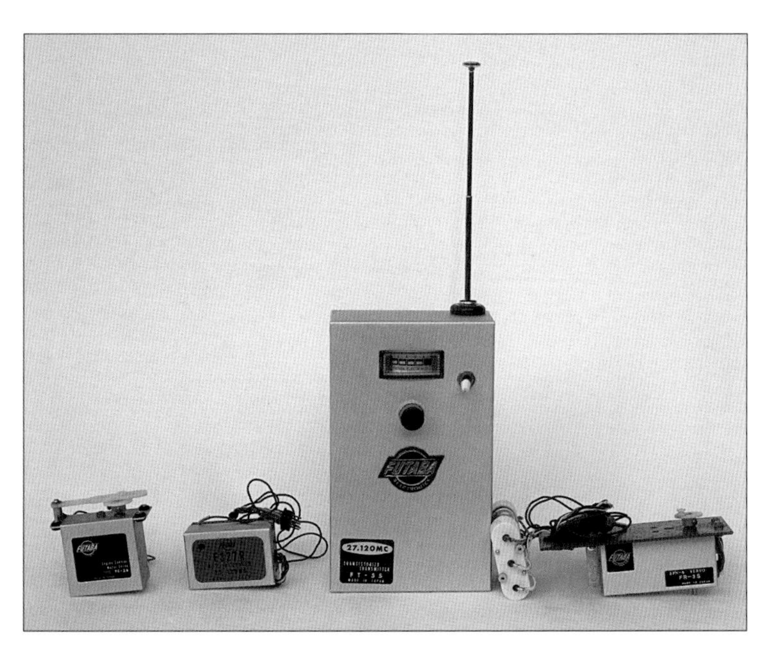

Futaba FT-5S transmitter and F327R receiver, c. 1960s, simple proportional two channel system, like new condition, $70-90.

Early proportional Futaba transmitter, c. 1968-70. *Courtesy of Injae Chung Ph.D.,* used $20-30.

World Engines, Digit Migit transmitter, c. 1968-70, used and in good condition. *Courtesy of Injae Chung Ph.D.,* $25-35.

EK Products, Logictrol 5, proportional transmitter, c. early 1970s, featuring open gimbles, used in like new condition. *Courtesy of Injae Chung Ph.D.,* $ 30-40.

Royal Tech RC, single stick proportional transmitter, c. 1980s, single stick radios are the most desirable of radios from the 1970s and 1980s. In 1990, the Federal Communication Commission added many new frequencies with a five megahertz separation. The result was felt throughout the modeling community as many fine radio control units produced in the 1980s and all the units produced in the 1970s became illegal to use. The higher end units are just starting to be collected. *Courtesy of Injae Chung Ph.D.*, $30-60.

Kraft seven channel transmitter with a Kraft Channel Master, series 1978. The Kraft name meant quality and reliability for thousands of radio control flyers in the 1970s. This radio may have been "upgraded" as this was a common practice on high end equipment. Kraft is now gone but their legend lives on. *Courtesy of Injae Chung Ph.D.*, $25-60.

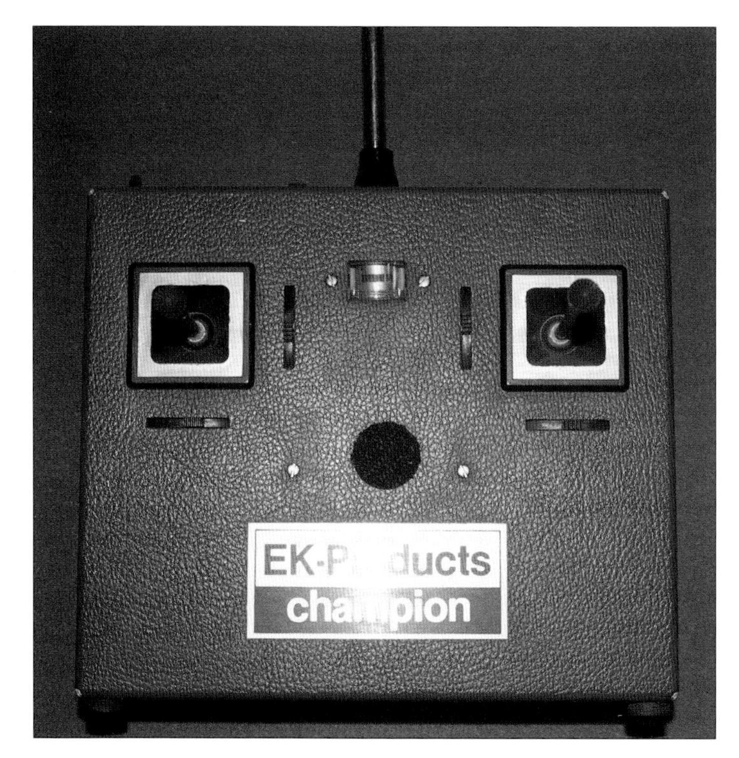

EK Products, Champion, five channel proportional transmitter, c. 1970s, used and in good condition. *Courtesy of Injae Chung Ph.D.*, $20-35.

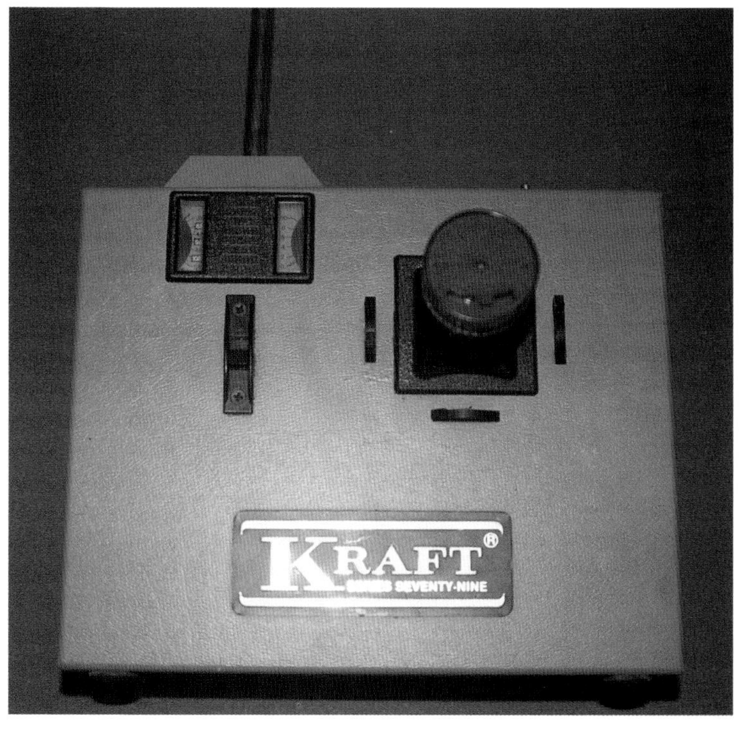

Kraft single stick, five channel transmitter, series 1979. *Courtesy of Injae Chung Ph.D.*, $25-35

Chapter 6
Catalogs, Organizations, and Other Memorabilia

Since the formation of the first aeromodeling club in New York City in 1909, competition has been the fuel of dreams for model flyers, young and old alike. The first recognized national contest sponsored by the American Model League of America in 1928 launched the beginning of a modeling tradition. Merrill C. Hamburg formed the AMLA in September 1927. Hamburg was the model airplane editor for *American Boy* magazine. He continued to write articles using his own designs until 1934. By then, more than 400,000 boys were members of the AMLA. Membership cost a mere two cent stamp.

The 1928 national championships awarded prizes to 259 participants, with national champion trophies, $3,000 in cash prizes, 198 medals and certificates, trips to Europe and the National races, which were held annually in Los Angeles. The second Nationals hosted more than 400 boys who showed up to compete for thirty-inch first place silver cups in six events, 198 gold, silver, and bronze medals, and other awards, plus trips to Europe and cash. By the fourth National contest, the effects of the great depression were felt by the *American Boy* magazine; they were unable to finance the 1931 Nationals. Future championships were held with much less extravagant prizes awarded. (Frank Anderson, *Golden Age of Model Airplanes*, 172-173).

The 1933 Nationals saw changes for future contests as Maxwell Bassett won the Mulvihill, Stout, Moffett, and Texaco awards. This sweep of the Nationals was done with a gas powered fuselage model. After this historical feat, rubber and gas became separate events. The pre-war contests were a proving ground for new leaders in aviation and the model airplane industry. The names of Carl Goldberg, Joseph Kovel, Gordon Light, Maxwell Bassett, Dick Korda, Bill and Walt Good, and Frank Zaic, William Atwood, are forever etched on the history of model aviation along with all the other participants of these pre World War II National contests. Their tireless devotion to the sport and hobby is still felt today.

By the 1950s, several things were common in cities and towns throughout the United States. Almost all of them had drive-in theatres, roller rinks, bowling alleys, motorcycle clubs, Boy Scout troops, and a model airplane club. Local contests were plentiful; it was common to be able to compete every weekend at a different contest throughout the entire summer. The club decal became proper attire for all model airplanes. Local contests between clubs were highlighted in all the major model magazines; clubs would often sport a team of participants.

All of modeling seemed to change around 1960 with the introduction of proportional radio control. Maybe it was not just this introduction, as many things began to change throughout the United States. We left the jet age and entered the space age. Astronaut John Glenn, a modeler in his youth, became an overnight hero by circling the earth three times in his Mercury capsule. The escalating conflict in Viet Nam may have been partially responsible. For whatever reason, participation in model airplane competitions began to drop off. Recent statistics have revealed that only 5% of all radio control modelers participate in competition. Participation among control line and free flight modelers is about 85%.

Over the years, model clubs, publications, contests, and manufacturers produced awards, programs, pins, patches, decals, new clippings, photos, and other memorabilia. These items are gaining interest among collectors today. Just about anything related to model aviation can be added to a collection. As to value, that remains to be seen. Most items are very affordable and will add immensely to the character of your collection. Historical items are starting to make it into museums, the largest being the National Model Aviation Museum in Muncie, Indiana. Another new museum recognizing Jim Walker and American Junior memorabilia is located in McMinnville, Oregon. The collection is maintained and continually being upgraded by Frank Macy. Frank is pictured on the AMA website holding his red American Junior Fireball on floats. The near-by Evergreen Aviation Museum is home to the famous Howard Hughes Spruce Goose, and together are well worth traveling to go to see. The Victor Stanzle Museum in Schulenburg, Texas, is dedicated to the Stanzel Brothers and their significant contributions to Model Aviation. Each museum has its own guidelines for contributions to their collections. If you have interest in contributing, please contact the museum directly.

Manufacturers produced quite a number of items that have a wide following. My good friend Herman Chairez collects just about everything connected with Brown Junior motors and Scientific Models. Newsletters were put out by Brown Junior motors around 1934 and are a hard to find publication. The Brown Junior engine appeared two years before model airplane kits came on the market! Cleveland Models published seven newsletters in 1933-1934 supporting the growing hobby. Manufacturer catalogs have become nice additions to collections. The cover art on Comet catalogs is especially attractive. Other collector items include promotional posters and flyers, hobby shop displays, and model pilot wings from Jimmie Allen, Flying Aces, Air Adventurers, and Cox. There seems to be an endless amount of printed material to view and enjoy. Modeling brochures, old plans, instruction, and advertising sheets can be found quite easily to the delight of those wanting to enhance the personality of their collections.

The value of these items can range dramatically when these particular collectibles show up at antique shows. While model engines, kits, and magazines stay mainly in the modeling community, all other model airplane collectibles can be cross collected. Collectors of aviation, advertising, automobilia, transportation, hobby and toys, and old tins and boxes are actively seeking the same items for their collections. Values listed in this book for these items will reflect all markets where these objects can be found.

Remember, just attending and browsing an antiques show, swap meet, or estate sale can be fun even without a purchase. Meeting new people, sharing stories, and getting reacquainted with dealers you haven't seen since the last show are as important as your acquisitions. Collecting is a journey through our memories of times gone by and should be treated with a certain reverence. I believe that items can be bought and sold for great profit, but a degree of respect is warranted. After all, a collection, large or small, is a reflection of someone's life. These things brought joy to that person, let them also bring joy to your life.

Model Airplane Catalogs and Brochures

Ideal catalog, c. 1922, with original order envelope, founded 1911, $20-30.

Ideal catalog, c. 1928, with order form, this is the easiest of the Ideal catalogs to find as the company's production had peaked. $20-30.

Selley Manufacturing Company catalog, c. 1932, in the back of the catalog shows a picture of the factory and states "Largest Exclusive Model Airplane Factory in the World". Founded by pioneering modeler, Armour Selley. $20-30.

U.S. Model Aircraft Corporation catalog, c. May 1929, included two and four cylinder compressed air motors selling for $15 and $20 respectively. Catalog, $15-25.

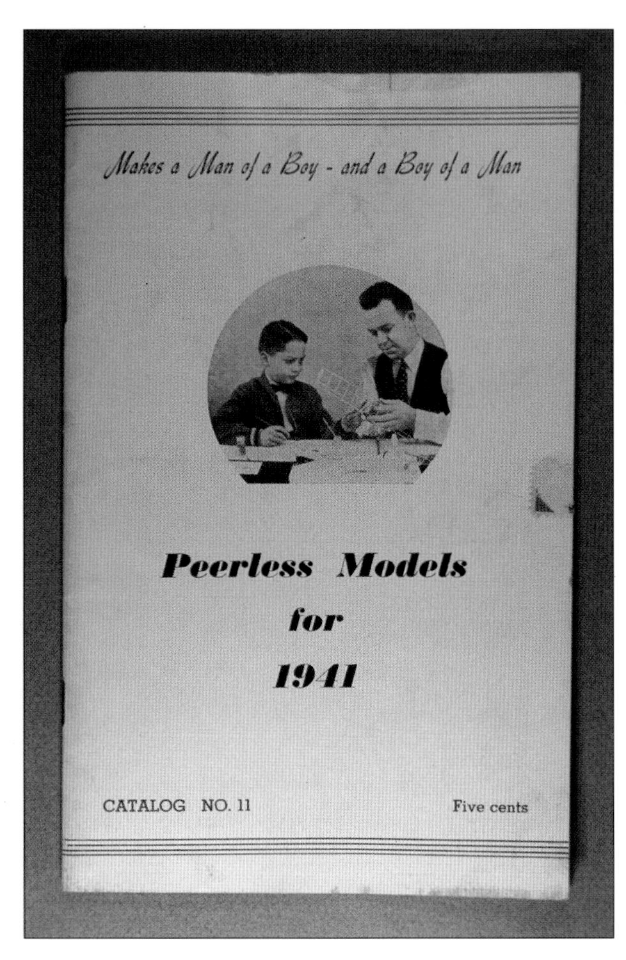

The Peerless Model Airplane Company catalog, c. 1941, founded 1930, $15-20.

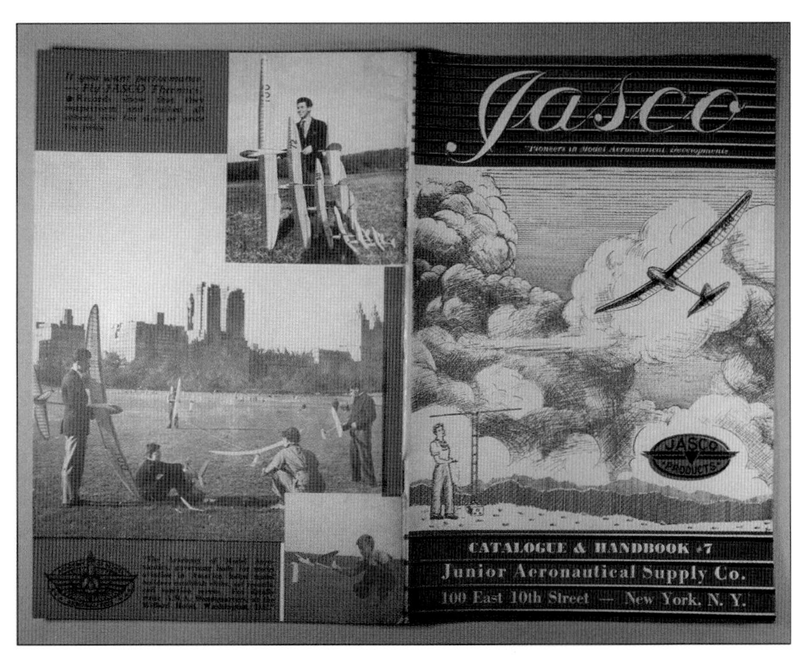

Junior Aeronautical Supply Company, c. 1940, founded 1934. $10-20.

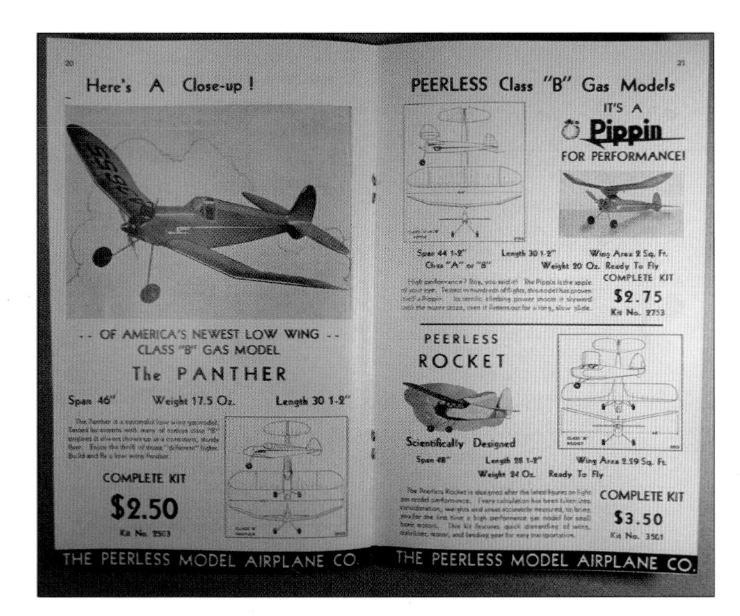

Peerless model airplanes; the Panther is one of their timeless designs, and is still being modeled today.

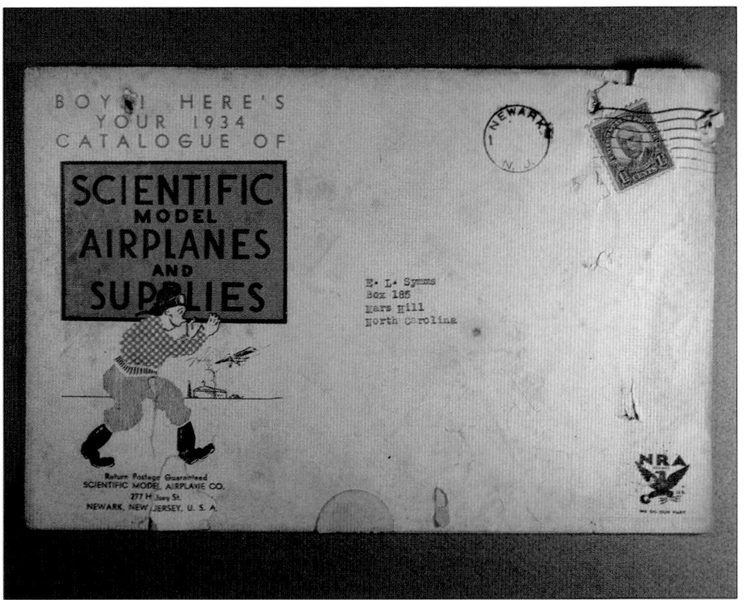

Scientific Model Airplanes and Supplies catalog, c. 1934. $15-25.

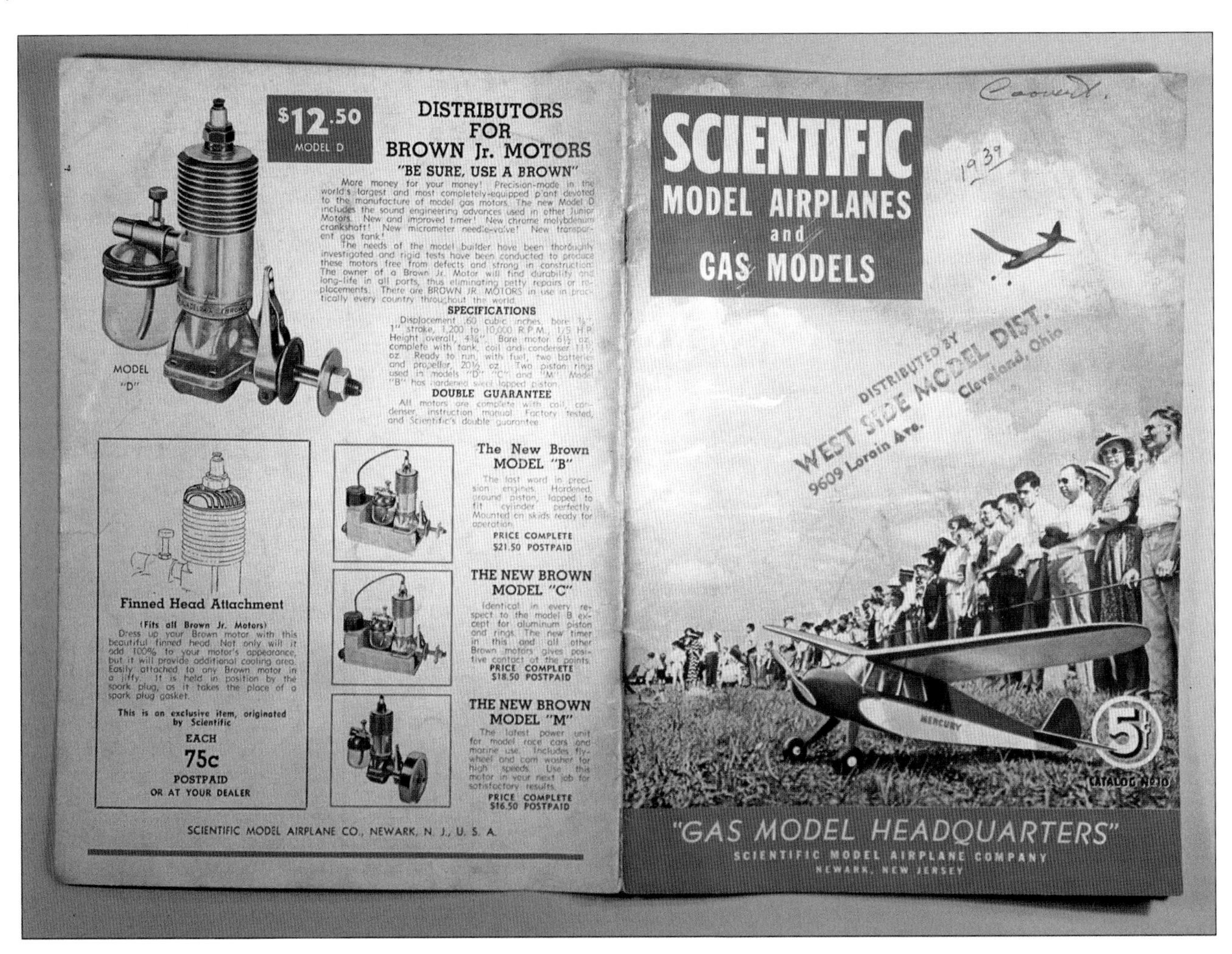

Scientific Model Airplanes and Gas Models, catalog, c. 1939. John D. Frisoli started The Scientific Model Airplane Company in 1929 at the age of sixteen. Notable designers Frank Zaic, Paul DeGatto, Bill Winter, and Walt Musciano did much to guarantee the company's success. Scientific is best remembered for the line of 1/2A control line kits designed by Musciano beginning in 1948. By 1957, the kit line had grown to no less than fifty-four airplane kits. John Frisoli was inducted into the AMA Hall of Fame in 1999. He was instrumental in initiating young and inexperienced modelers to a successful adventure into the marvelous world of model airplanes through the kits he marketed. *Courtesy of Herman Chairez.* $20-25.

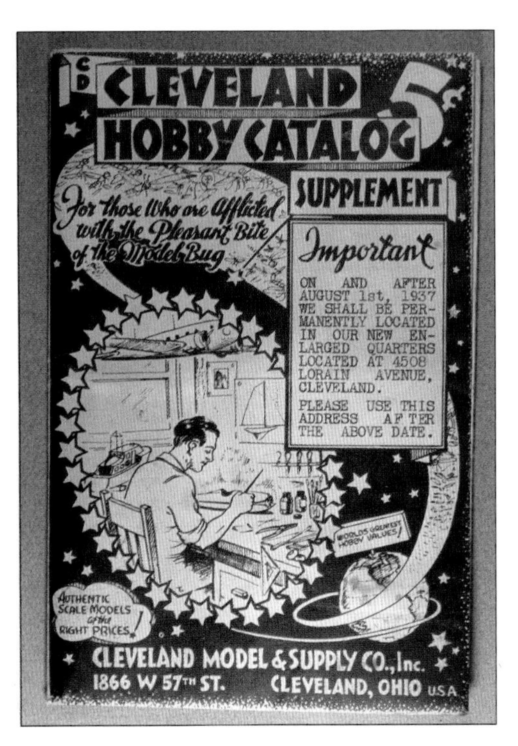

Cleveland Hobby catalog, c. May 1937. This supplement opens up to 17" x 21" and features trains and the Hand-ee Grinder and accessories. $10-15.

Cleveland Model and Supply Company catalog, c. 1942, $20-30.

Cleveland Model and Supply Company catalog, c. 1943, $20-30.

Motors for Gas Models from the Skyway catalog.

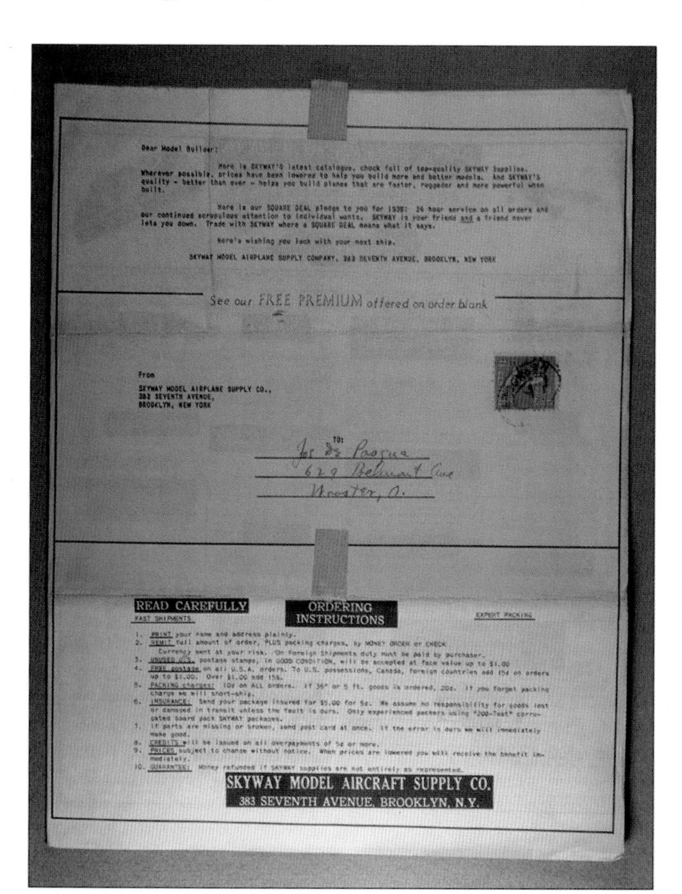

Skyway Model Aircraft Supply Company catalog, c. 1939, $10-15.

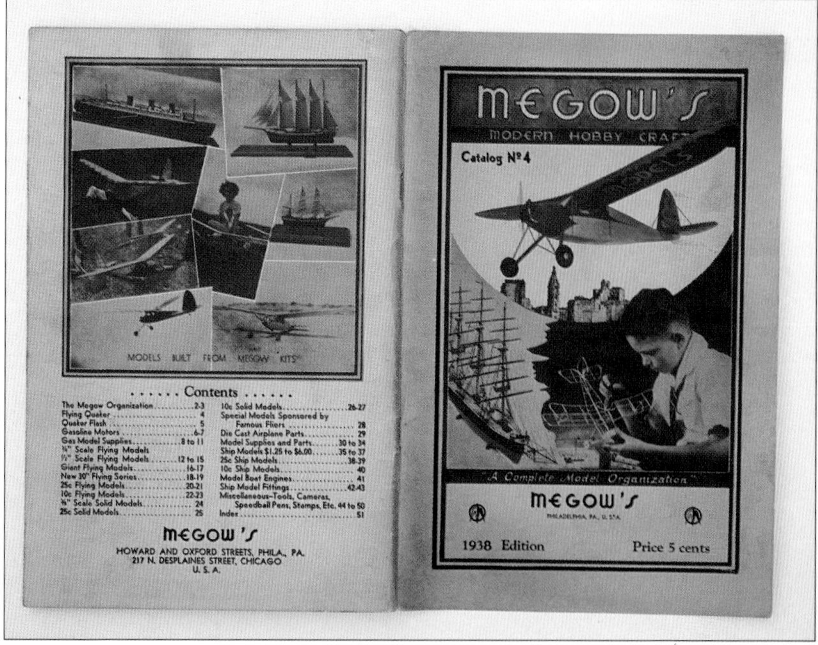

Megow's Modern Hobbycraft, c. 1938, *from the estate of Robert Baker.* $20-30.

Megow's Modern Hobbycraft, c. 1939. By the beginning of World War II, Fred Megow had built his company into the largest hobby and model airplane company in the world. $20-30.

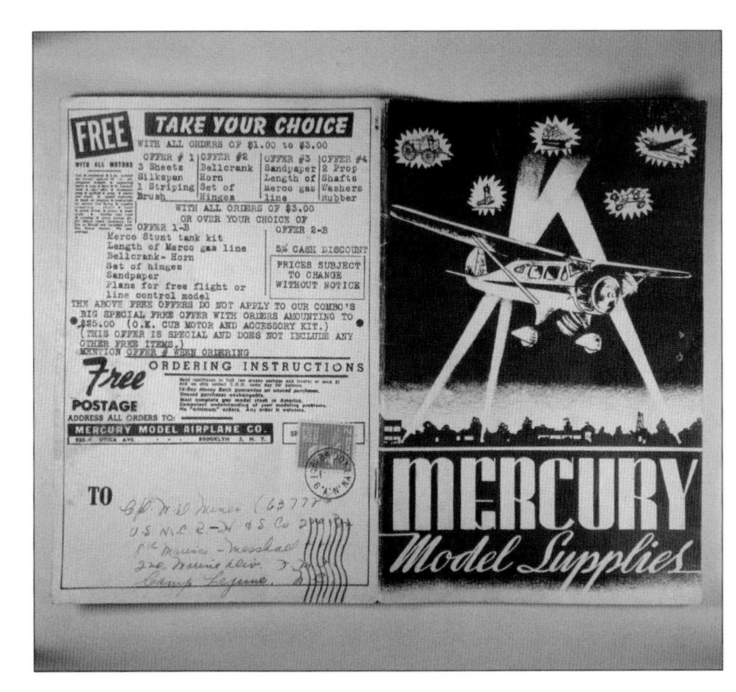

Mercury Model Supplies catalog, c. 1951. Pictures and layout are similar to the America's Hobby Center catalog and was most likely printed by the same company, 32 pages. $10-20.

Ace Model Plane Company, c. 1945. Pat Morrissey states, "If it's made we've got it." This is a nice wartime catalog with Ideal, Comet, Berkeley, Joe Ott, Cleveland, Stanzel, Hawk, and Eagle solids, and other wartime kits and vehicles. $15-25.

Central Camera Company wholesale catalog, c. 1945, $15-20. Everyone was getting on the hobby bandwagon. One of my favorite hobby shops was Kay Cee Drugs in Suitland, Maryland. They sold Sig products and you could sit at their giant 1950s soda fountain style counter and get real ice cream milkshakes. Many model planes hung from the ceiling.

Modelcraft Distributors Inc. catalog, c. 1950. A dealer's catalog that carried everything for hobby shops, planes, trains cars, engines, paint, props, and every imaginable accessory. $10-20.

Comet Model Airplane and Supply Company, c. 1941, $20-40.

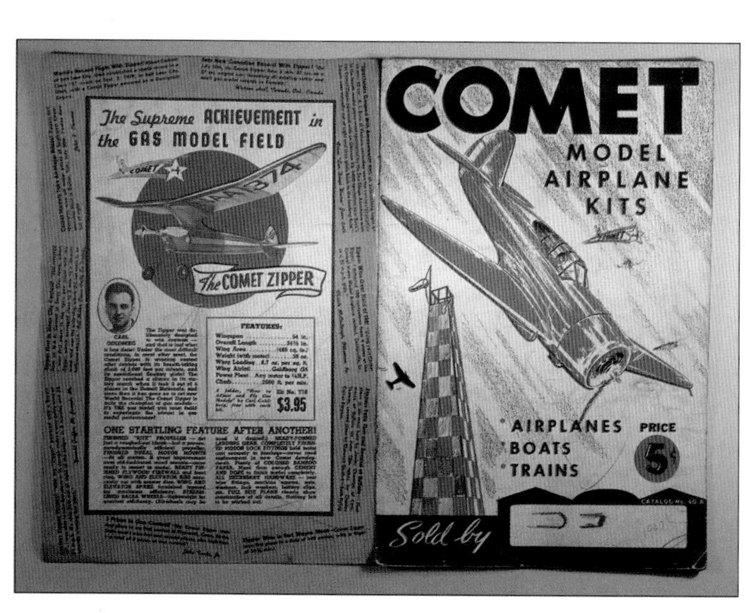

Comet Model Airplane and Supply Company, c. 1940, thirty-six pages of excitement, announcing the new Brownie .29, Speed King race car, Zipper "A," *from the estate of Robert Baker*, $20-40.

Comet Craft, Model and Hobby Industry dealer publication, c. May 1952, the latest news on the hobby industry with tips on increasing sales. $10-20.

Comet Craft, Model and Hobby Industry dealer publication, c. August 1952, $10-20.

Comet Model Airplane and Supply Company, c. 1960. Back cover states, "Model building builds model boys." Featuring the Sabre 44 ready to fly all plastic control line gas model and struct-o-speed flying and scale model kits. $20-40.

Comet Model Airplane and Supply Company, c. 1954. *Courtesy of Herman Chairez*. $20-45.

Sterling Models, Secrets of Model Airplane Building, c. 1960, pamphlet instructing new builders on the fine art of model aviation. $5-10.

K&B Torpedo engine brochure, c. 1952, *from the estate of Robert Baker*, $5-7.

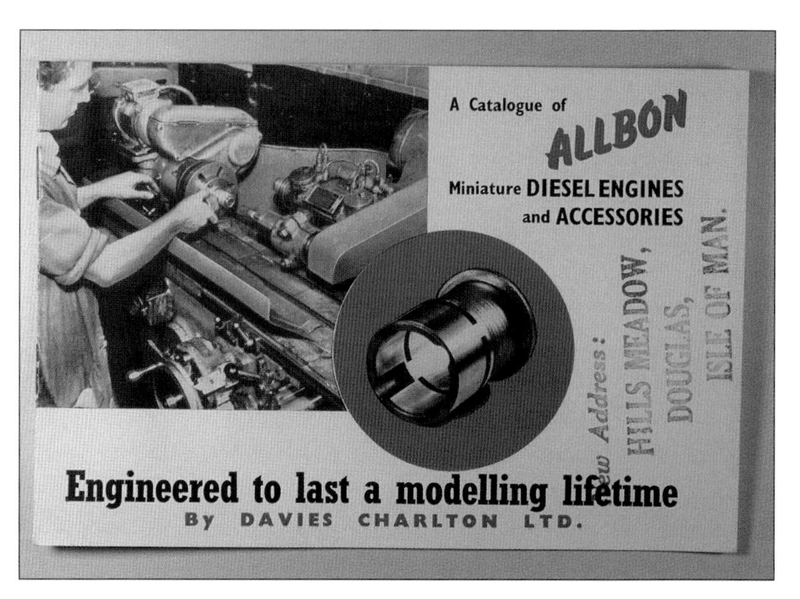

Allbon engine catalog, c. 1955, $5-10.

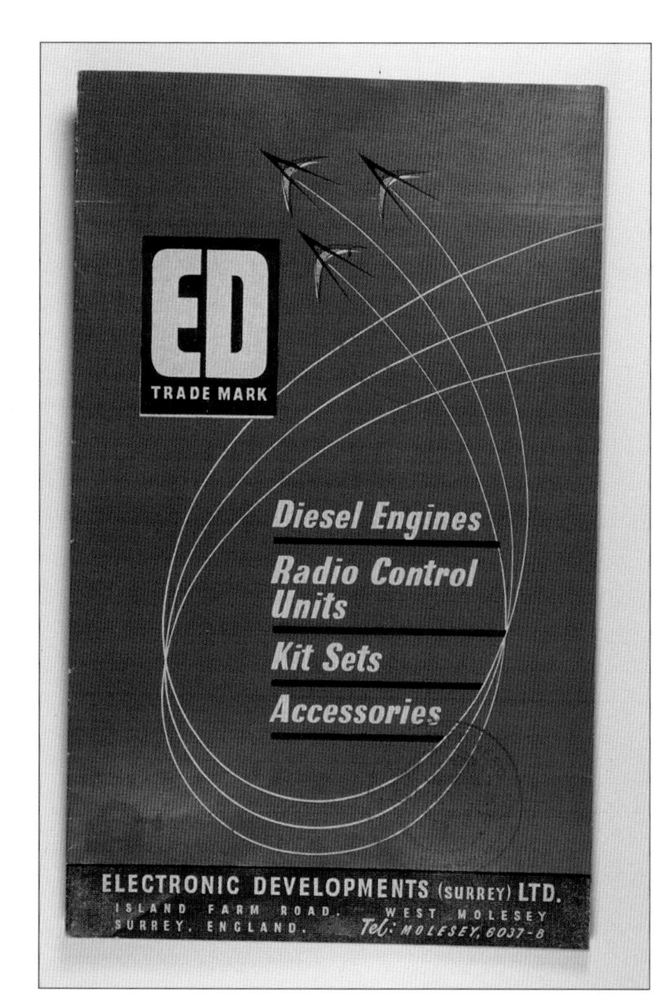

Electronic Developments catalog, c. 1955, opens to 15"x 19", *from the estate of Robert Baker*, $5-10.

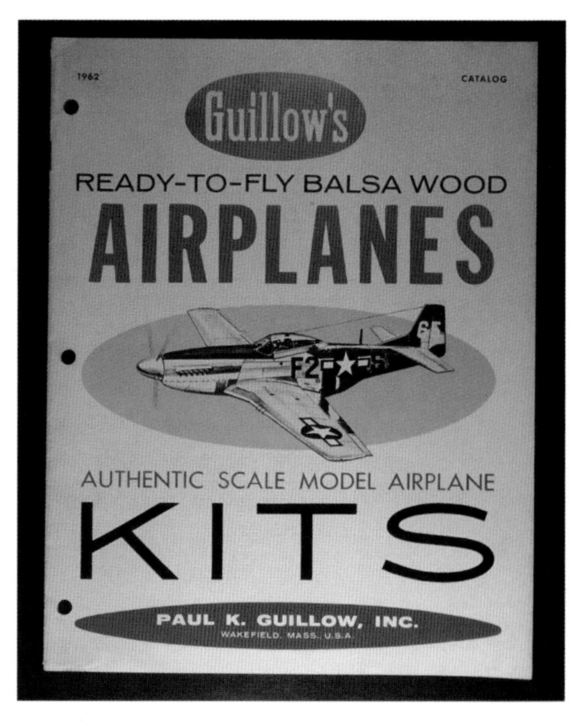

Paul K. Guillow, dealer catalog. c. 1962, $5-7.

Paul K. Guillow, dealer catalog. c. 1962. Dealers could show and order for modelers from the three-ring copies carried by many hobby shops. $5-7.

America's Hobby Center catalogs, c. 1950, 1958, and 1966 with supplement catalog. Founded in 1931, Bernard B. Winston was an advertising genius; each month his ads were the first to appear in most modeling magazines, most of the time with two to four pages of bargains. The ads were targeted to young modelers and entry-level radio control. He may have been the first to recognize if you sold an engine and kit at near cost all the other products and accessories would be where the money was made. $10-20.

America's Hobby Center catalog, c. 1969, $3-5.

Ace Radio Control catalog, c. 1962. The Nomad glider is pictured on the cover, $5-10.

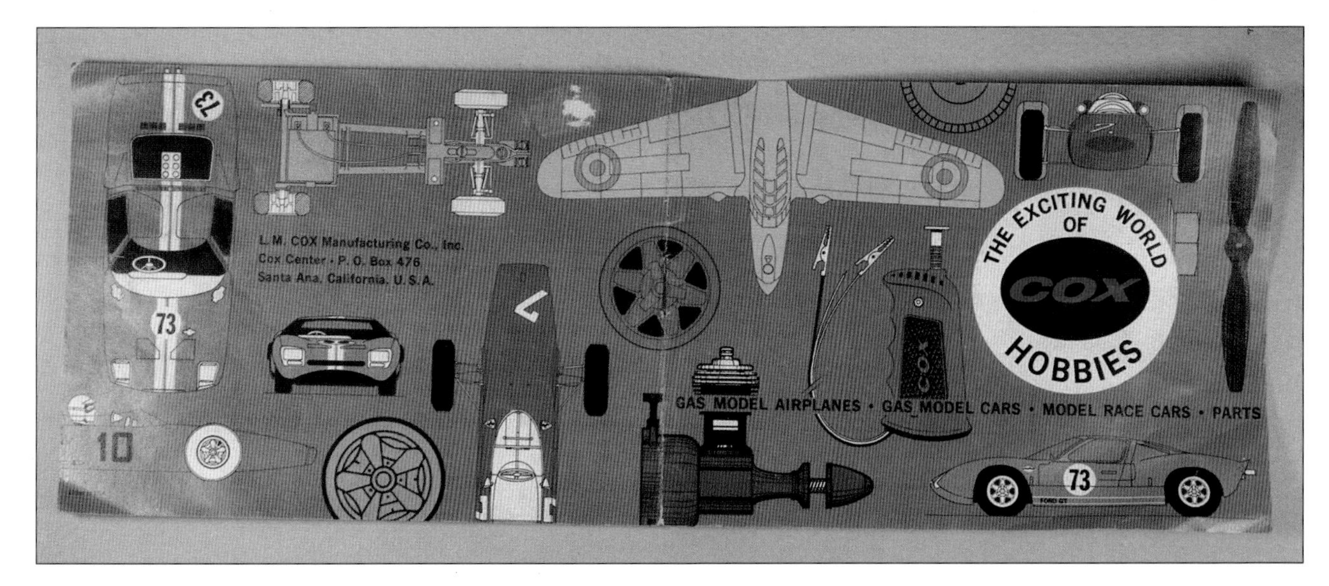

The Exciting World of Cox catalog, c. 1962, a small colorful brochure type catalog with 14 pages, $10-15.

Fuel Cans

Comet starter kit with OK Cub lighter fluid top, 4 oz, c. 1959, $10-15; OK Cub Diesel fuel can, c. 1956-1962, $10-20.

Phillips 66 Model Motor fuel can, 16 oz, c. 1942-1950, $40-75; Sportco Super Duper fuel can, 16 oz, c. 1945-1950. During the war, non hi-way use ration coupons were need to buy these fuels. $30-60.

Testors 39 fuel cans, the small 4 oz can came out in 1956 and sold for .39 cents, $5-10; the pint can, c. 1950-60s, $10-15; 1/2 pint can, c. 1950-60s. $5-10.

O&R fuel cans, c. 1950s, $15-25.

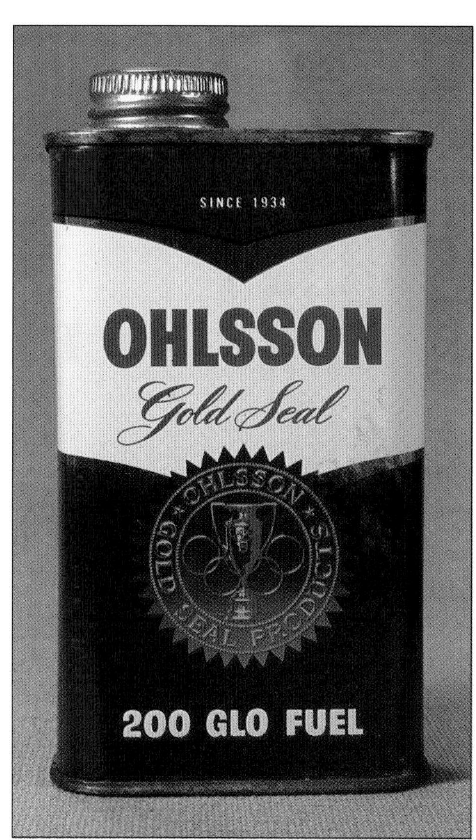

Ohlsson Gold Seal 200 fuel can, c. 1953. In August 1953, Ohlsson announced a slogan contest for two new 1/2 A fuels with the top prize being a 1953 two-door Mercury auto and twenty-five additional prizes. This fuel was one of the new fuels being introduced as small model airplane engines began to reach the market. $15-25.

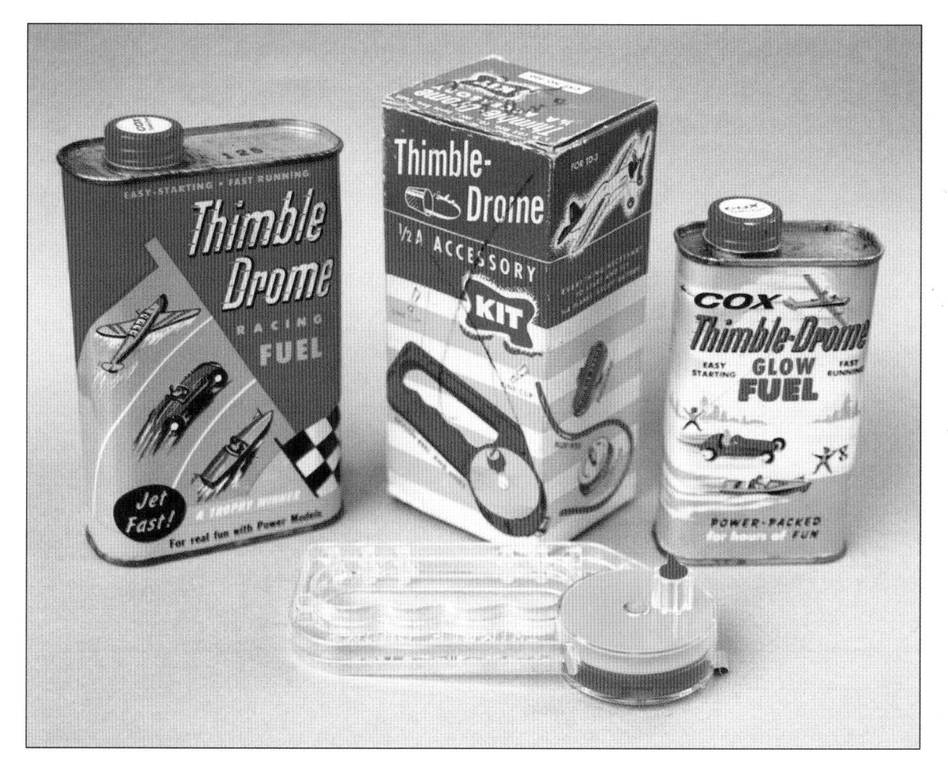

Cox Racing fuel can pictured with a Thimble Drone 1/2 A accessory kit, Skylon reel handle shown. Leroy Cox knew the value of colorful packaging and sold millions of engines, ready to fly planes, and accessories from 1952 through 1968 using these graphics. The accessory kit sells for $20-35.

L.M. Cox fuels cans, one pint Racing fuel, $15-30; 1/2 pint glow fuel can, $5-10; 1/2 pint custom blend fuel, $10-15. These were produced for almost twenty years. The Racing fuel can is what started the ball rolling for *Flying Model Collectibles*. While attending the Portland Antique Expo in 2001, I saw this can for sale for $65. It was priced too high and I knew no book existed for model airplane collectibles. My wife suggested I write one; until that time, I had no intention of writing a book.

Cox Thimble Drone starting kit, early 1960s, $20-30. The little blue Cox can came in ready to fly gas model planes in the early 1960s. *Courtesy of Bill Darkow.* $4-10.

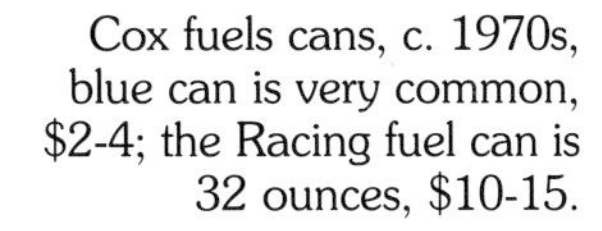

Cox fuels cans, c. 1970s, blue can is very common, $2-4; the Racing fuel can is 32 ounces, $10-15.

K&B Supersonic Flight Pack, c. 1960s, $10-20.

Wen-Mac Accessory Kit, c. early 1960s, $20-30.

Francisco Racing fuel can, c. 1950s to early 1960s, $15-30; Power Mist racing coolant additive, $10-15.

Pactra Power fuel can, c. 1956 – 1965. Famous stunt flier, Bob Palmer, promoted this fuel in advertisements during this period. $15-25.

K&B Supersonic 1000 1/2 pint fuel can, c. 1950s - early 1960s, $10-20.

Midwest Products, Nitro X fuel can, c. 1954-1965. Gallon cans were introduced in 1955. $15-25.

K&B quart sized fuel cans, the two end cans are from the 1970-80s and are common; $3-5, the center can is from the early 1950 to 1960s, $15-25.

Fox Manufacturing Company, Missile Mist quart fuel can c. 1970s, $10; the gallon can in mint condition, $ 20-25.

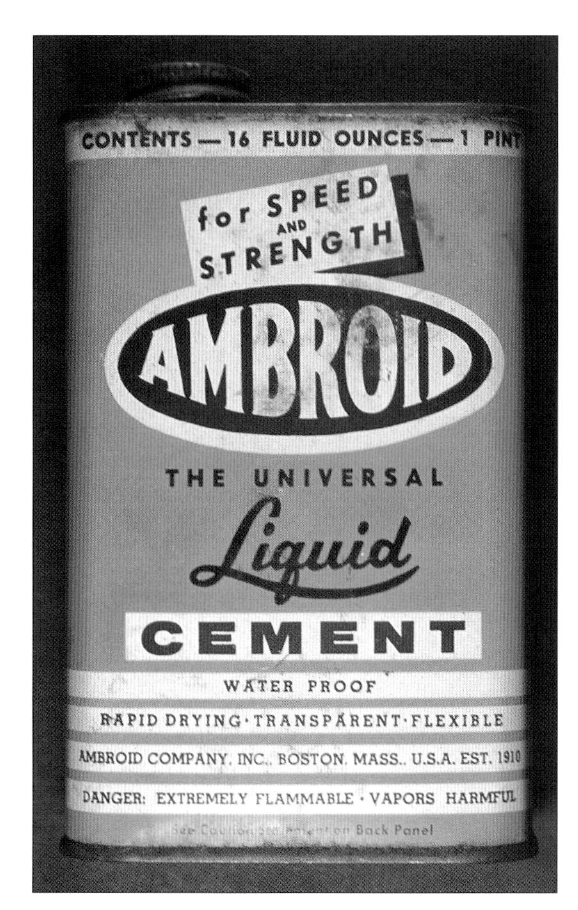

Ambroid liquid cement pint can, c. 1960s, $5-10. In 1962, glue sniffing had become a problem and federal law required the manufacturers to add isothiocyanate or "oil of mustard" to all glues. I had a hard enough time buying Ambroid in the tubes. In 1970, one hobby shop wouldn't sell to me without a note from my mom. I couldn't imagine anyone wasting glue. The smell of this glue is memorable and still sold today. This company was started around 1930.

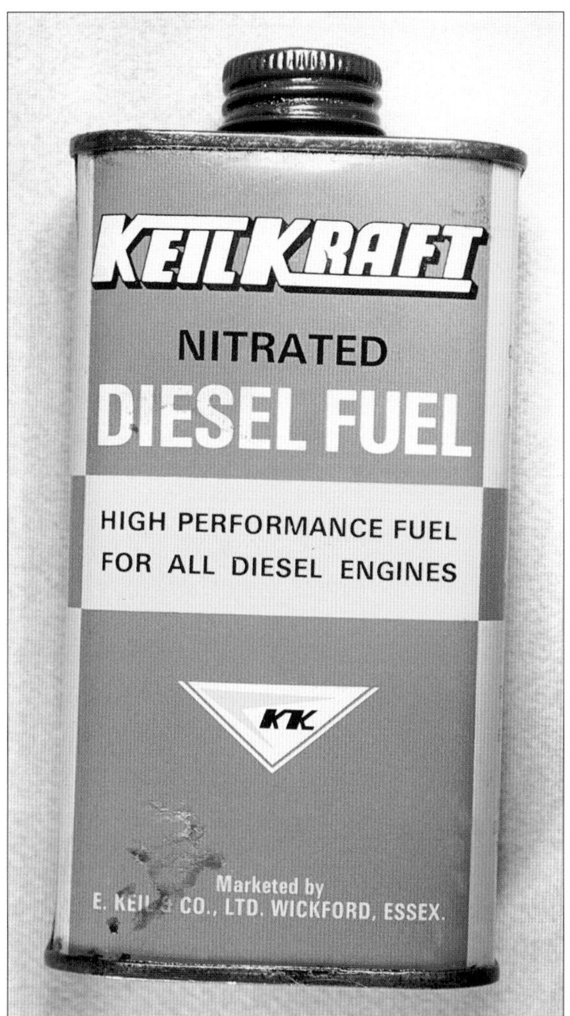

Kiel Kraft Diesel fuel can, c. 1960s, $20-30.

Accessories and Supplies

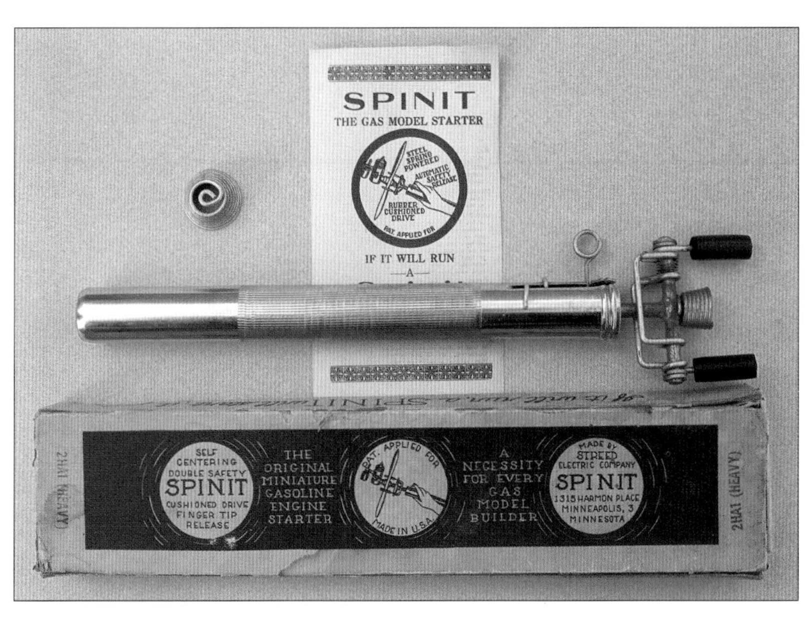

Spinit Gas Model starter, c. 1945-1950, $10-20.

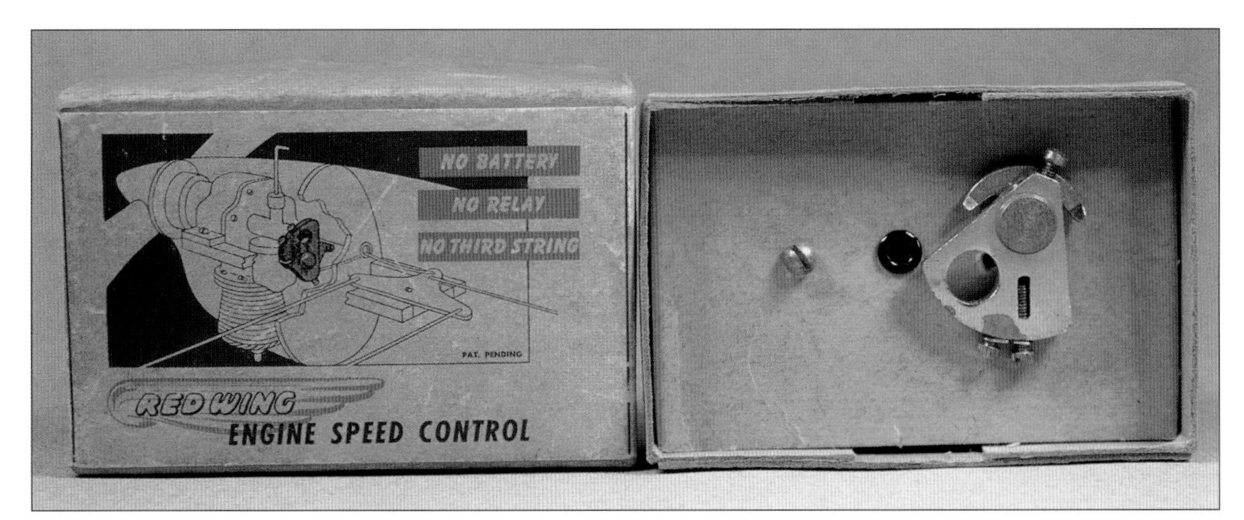

Redwing Engine speed control, c. 1945-50. *Courtesy of Bob Parker.* $7-15.

Towline glider reel, c. 1958, $10-25.

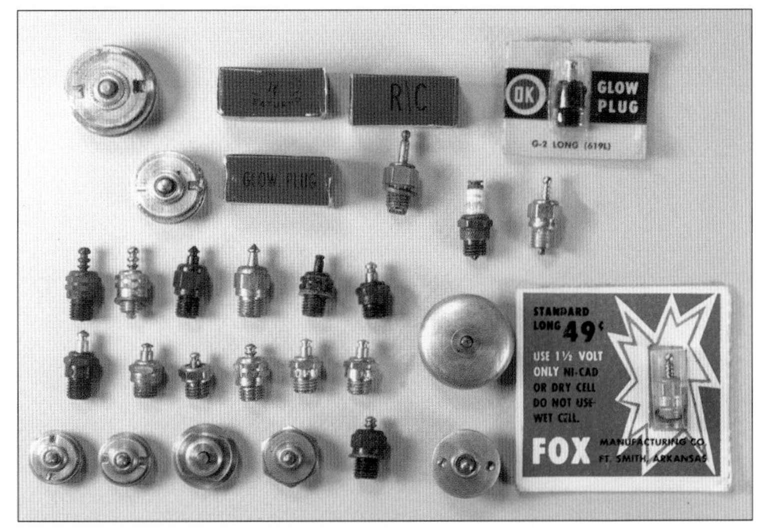

Glow plugs, c. 1949- 1970s. Manufactures names were many but almost all glow plugs were produced by a few makers. "Veco glow plugs had been made by Fred Schortt (who also made them for other engine manufacturers), and in 1958 joined the Henry organization and expanded his plug business. His death a few months later was a sad blow to his many model business friends." (William Netzeband, *American Modeler,* September 1960). The result of Fred's passing left a huge gap and the quality of "farmed out" work produced an inferior product. Veco went on to develop equipment to make their own glow plugs. Veco became a large producer of electrical connectors as an outgrowth of developing glow plug seals. The plugs pictured are Cox, Champion VG-3, c. late 1940s, Super Tigre, Fox, Anderson Spitfire, Ok ceramic and regular, and Wen-Mac, $1-5.

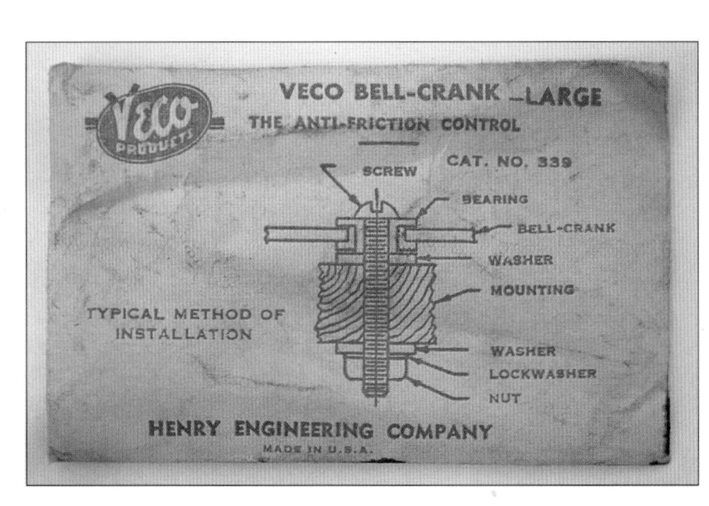

Veco Bell-crank, Henry Engineering Company, c. 1950s, new $3-7.

Enya glow plugs, c. 1957, 10 (ten) new in the box, $40-60; Champion V spark plug, c. 1950 $5-10; Veco #109 glow plug, c. 1960s, $3-6; other plugs are $1-3.

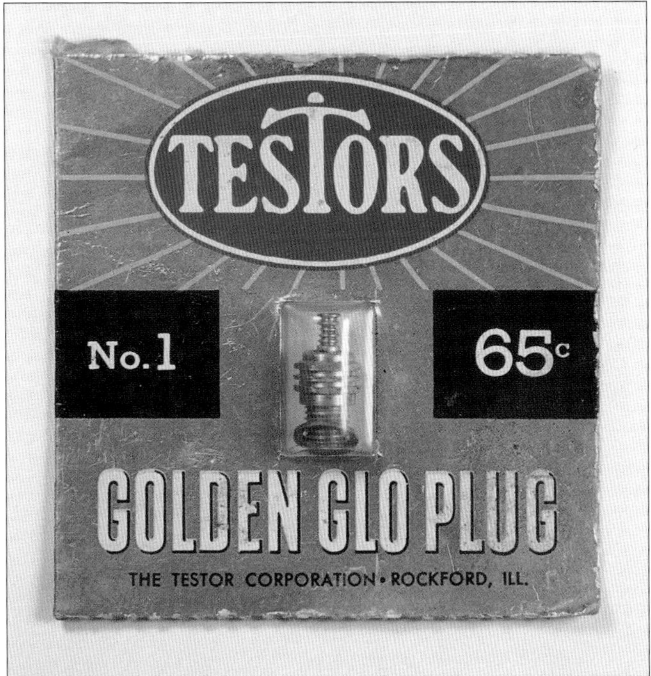

Testors Golden Glo Plug, c. 1960s. In the September 1960 issue of *American Modeler,* William Netzeband conducted tests on glow plugs produced at the time; this list was revised in the 1964 *American Modeler Annual.* Almost all of the early plugs had been replaced by new designs. Bill has tirelessly pursued scientific data on many aspects of model aviation. New, $3-5.

Anderson Spitfire glow plugs, 10 (ten) new, c. 1950, $ 45-75.

Various Nose Spinners, Froom, Veco, MG, Super Tigre, and Scamper plastic spinners, c. 1940-50s. Randall E. Froom patented the prop spinner in the 1940s. Veco eventually absorbed Froom around 1956. New spinners are preferable as many are used for classic era modeling projects. No one puts a beat up spinner on a new model. *From the estate of Robert Baker*. $5-30.

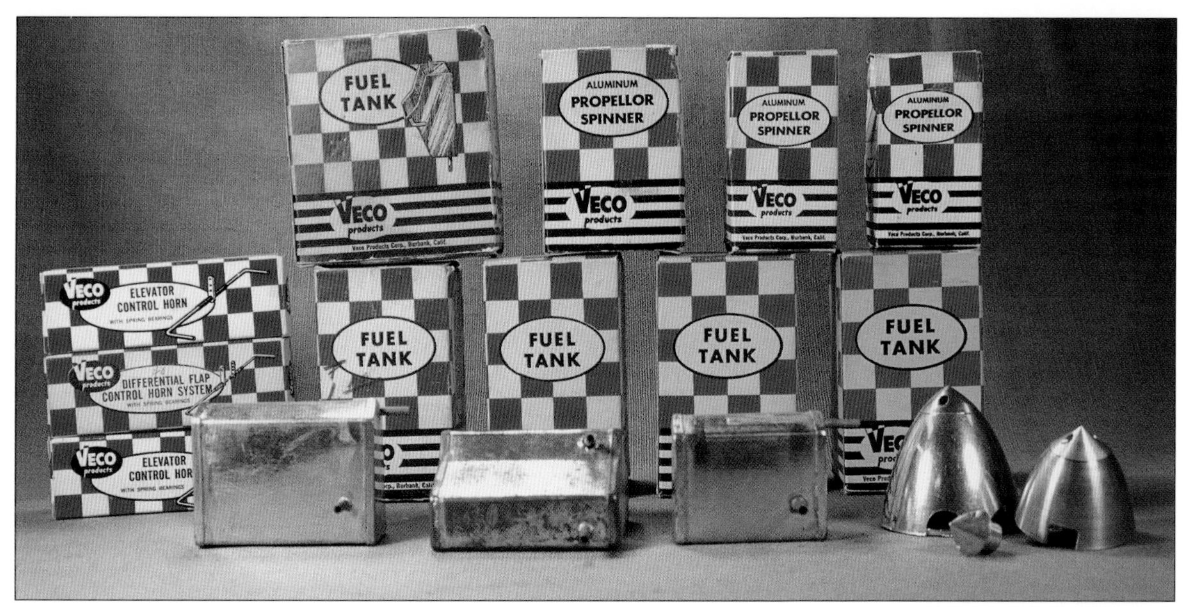

Veco control horns, c. 1960, $3-5; new control line tanks, c. 1960s, the larger 2.5 to 4 oz tanks are the most desirable, $4-10; nose spinners, c. 1960s, the most used are the 1.75" to 2.25" and go for $10-25 in new condition.

Various control line gas tanks, c. 1950-1960s. Kap-Pak, Froom, Acme, K&B, Fox, and Veco. New condition is very important as used tanks are usually junk, $5-10.

Model dope, Testors, Aerogloss, Peerless, mostly used for display though can still be used if in liquid form. The Peerless dope c. 1940, most likely came from a kit due to their size, $1-3; the whole lot might sell for $10-15.

Mechanical Free Flight Timers, Austin Craft Timerette, c. 1940-50s, $10; KSB shut-off timer, c. 1980s, $10-20; Tatone DT Timer, c. 1960-70s, $15-25; Timet fuel shut-off, c. 1940s, Lud Kading Specialty Company, $10; K&B fuel shut-off, c. 1950s, $10; Austin Craft fuel shut-off, $5.

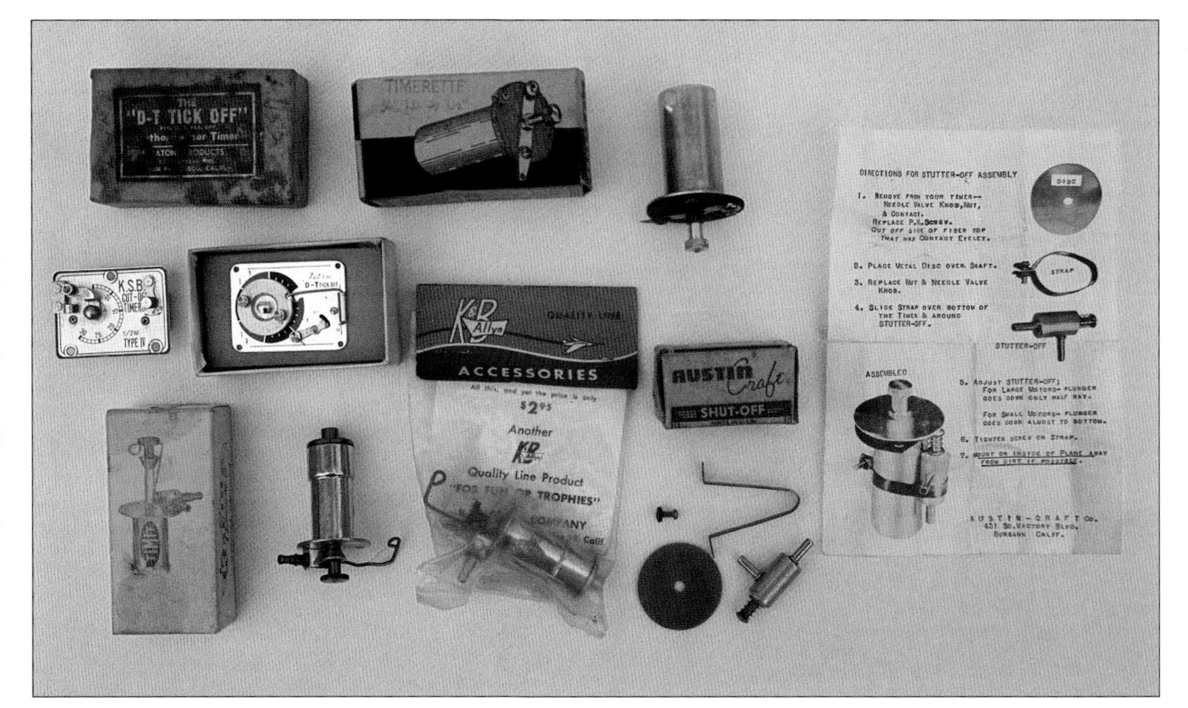

Russian fuel filters, c. 1980s. These were a gift from Dan who is one of the great characters and supporters of model aviation here in the Northwest. *Courtesy of Dan Rutherford*, $1-2.

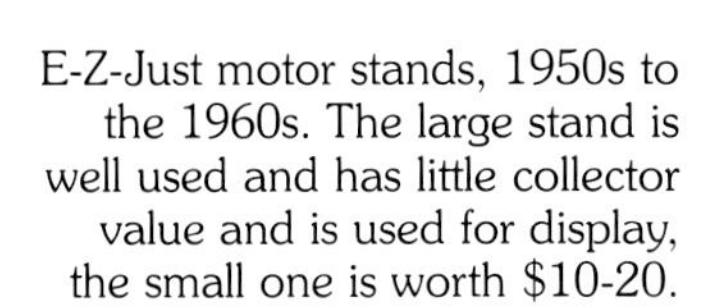

E-Z-Just motor stands, 1950s to the 1960s. The large stand is well used and has little collector value and is used for display, the small one is worth $10-20.

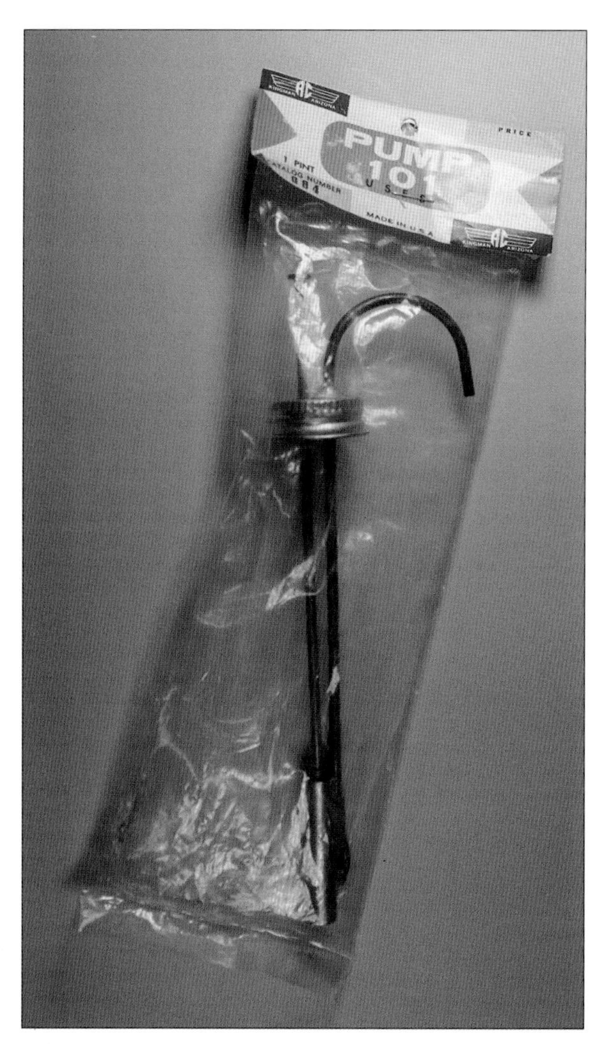

Austin Craft fuel pump, c. 1960, new, $5-10.

Banner 1 3/4" wheels, c. 1950-60s. These date from around 1958 and were some of the best wheels produced for model airplanes. New, $10-15.

Cox Junior Pilot wings, c. 1960, $20-25.

Advertisement from 1960 instructing boys on how to become a Junior Pilot.

Cox Thimble Drone Flight Engineer Case, c. 1959. The case was sold through many retail giants and is pictured in the 1959 Sears Christmas catalog. This case came with a rare paper label fuel can; the battery is from a 1970s ready-to-fly gas model and not original to the case. An earlier battery with the Cox logo was included. A black version appeared in the 1970s. This case appears to be in almost new condition, $50-100.

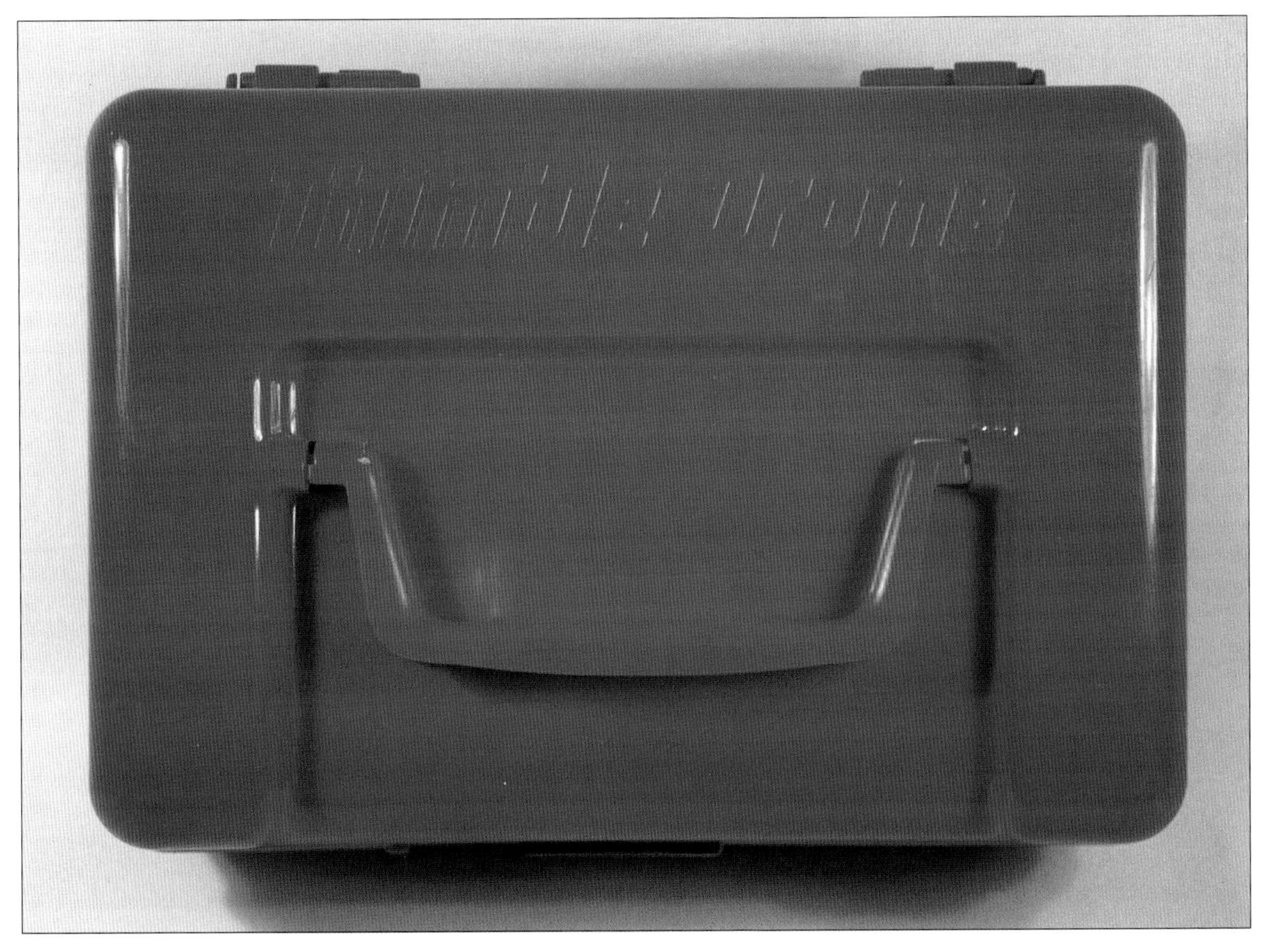

Cox Flight Engineer Case, top view. The hard plastic breaks easily, so inspect carefully if you want a nice one for your collection.

Propellers

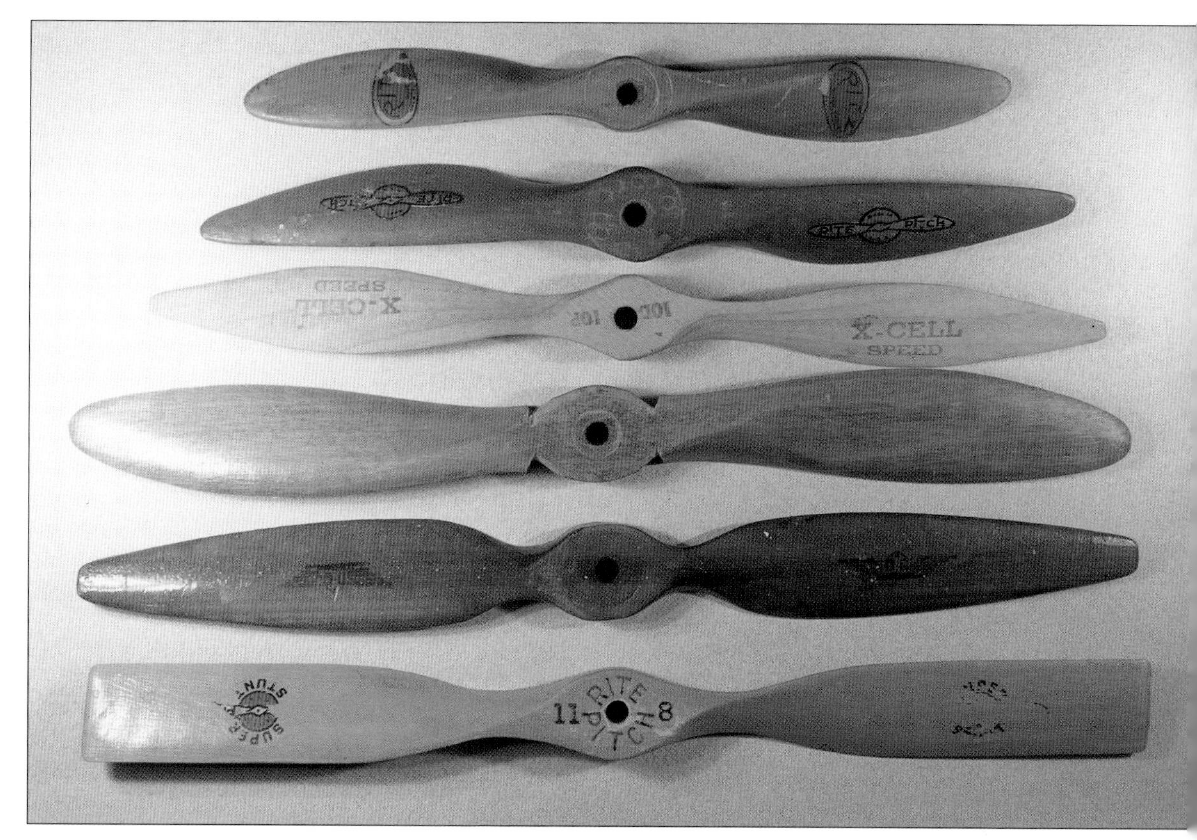

Model airplane propellers c. late 1940s. Bob Roberts Rite pitch, X-Cell speed, modified Flo Torque Hi-Ball, DG, and square tip Rite Pitch Super Stunt, all are used except the X-Cell. *From the estate of Robert Baker.* $1-5.

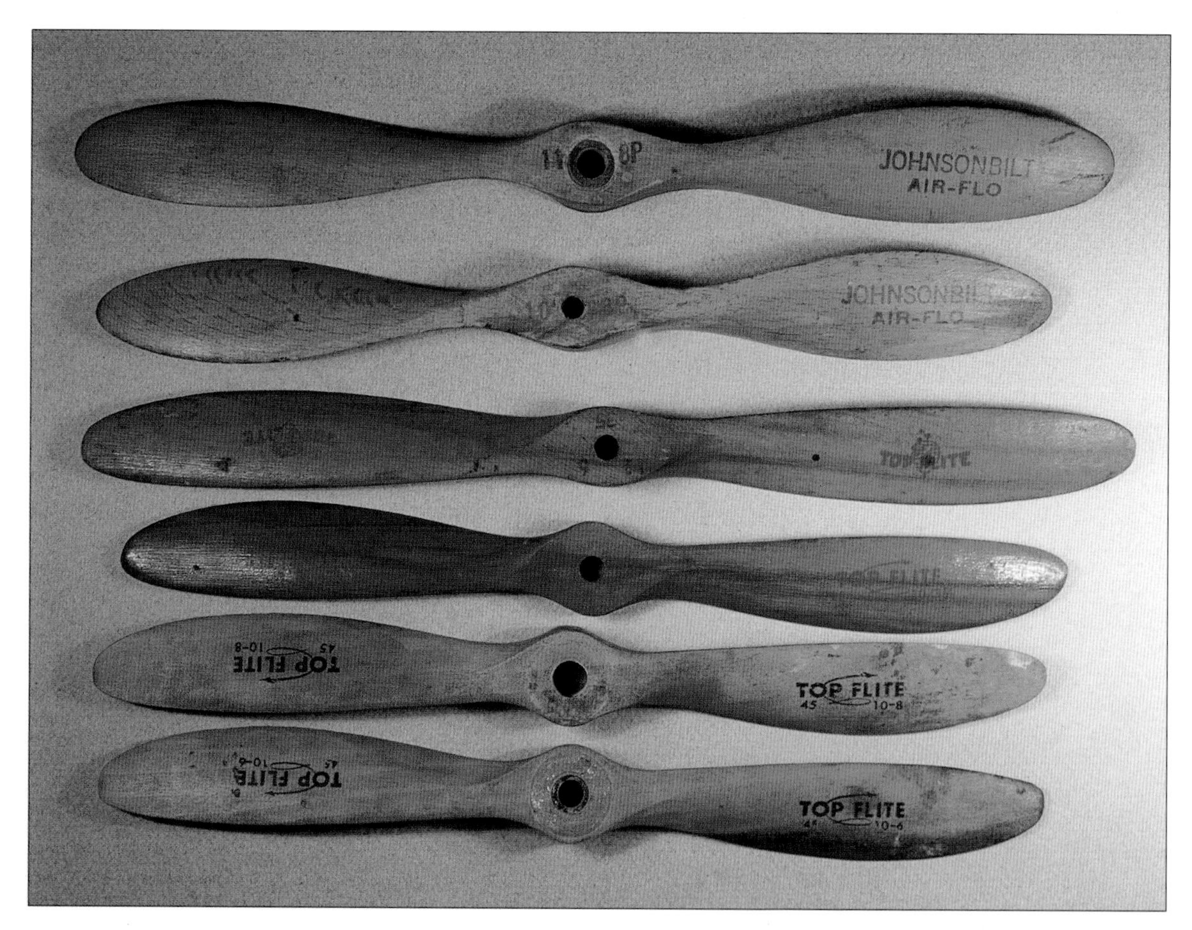

Model airplane propellers, Johnson Bilt Air-Flo, late 1940s, also produced the Yates "Madman" and Palmer "Go-Devil" stunt kits and were sold by Crescent Model Shop in Los Angeles, $3-6; Top Flite Red Top, c. early 1950s and Top Flite 45 props designed for the 1959-62, Green Head 45 engine. *From the estate of Robert Baker.* Props in new condition are the most preferred and sell for $1-5.

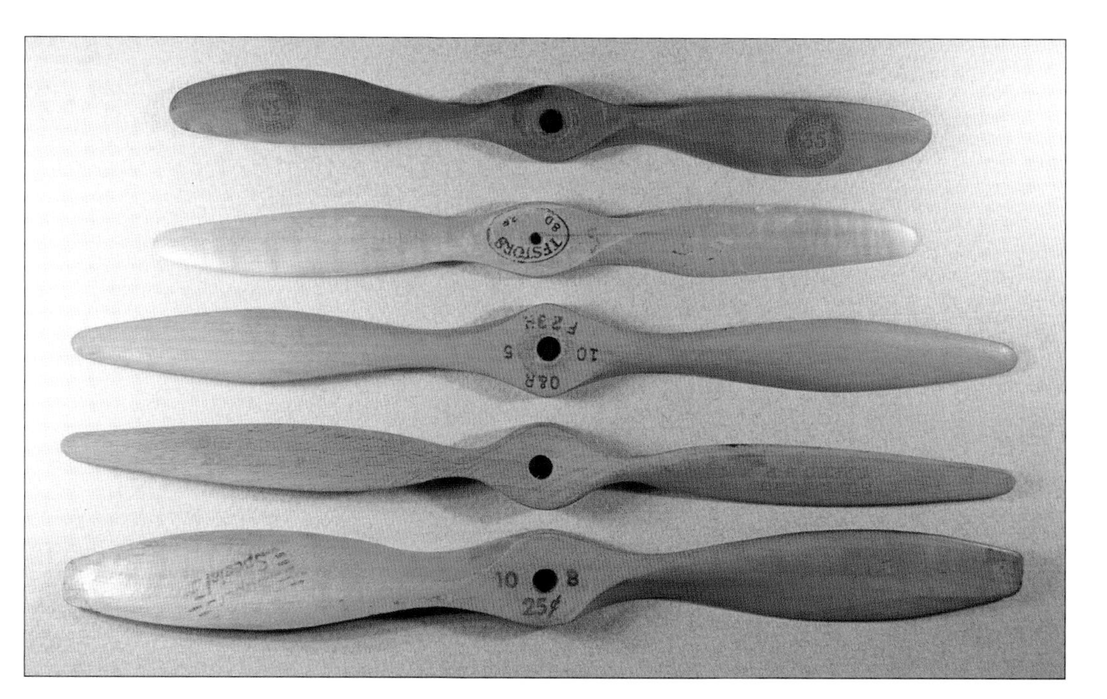

Model airplane propellers, c. late 1940s to 1950s, Super Dynamic, Testors, O&R for the front rotor .23, Super Scru speed, and Super Special. *From the estate of Robert Baker*. $1-5.

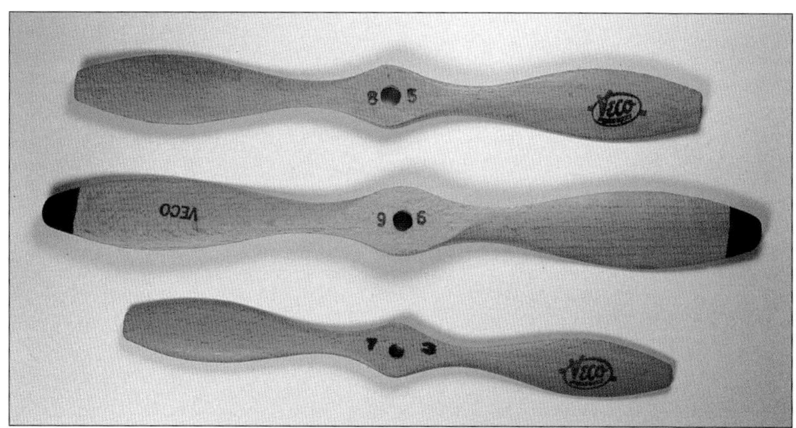

Veco model airplane propellers, c. 1950s, $2-5.

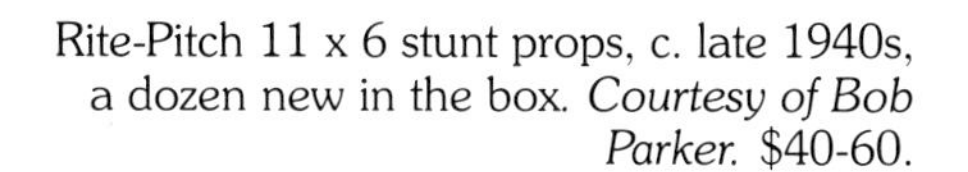

Rite-Pitch 11 x 6 stunt props, c. late 1940s, a dozen new in the box. *Courtesy of Bob Parker.* $40-60.

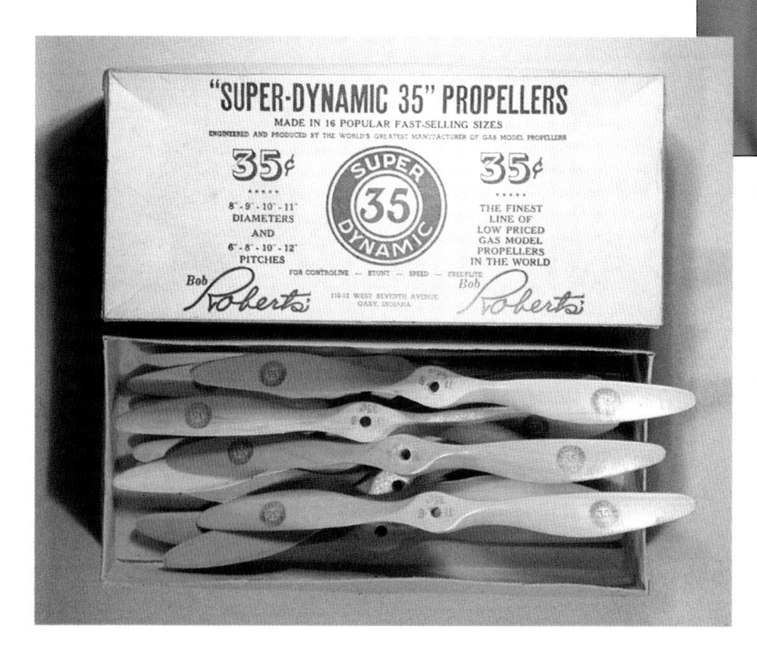

Bob Roberts Super Dynamic 35 propellers, c. late 1940s, 13 props new in the box, $40-50.

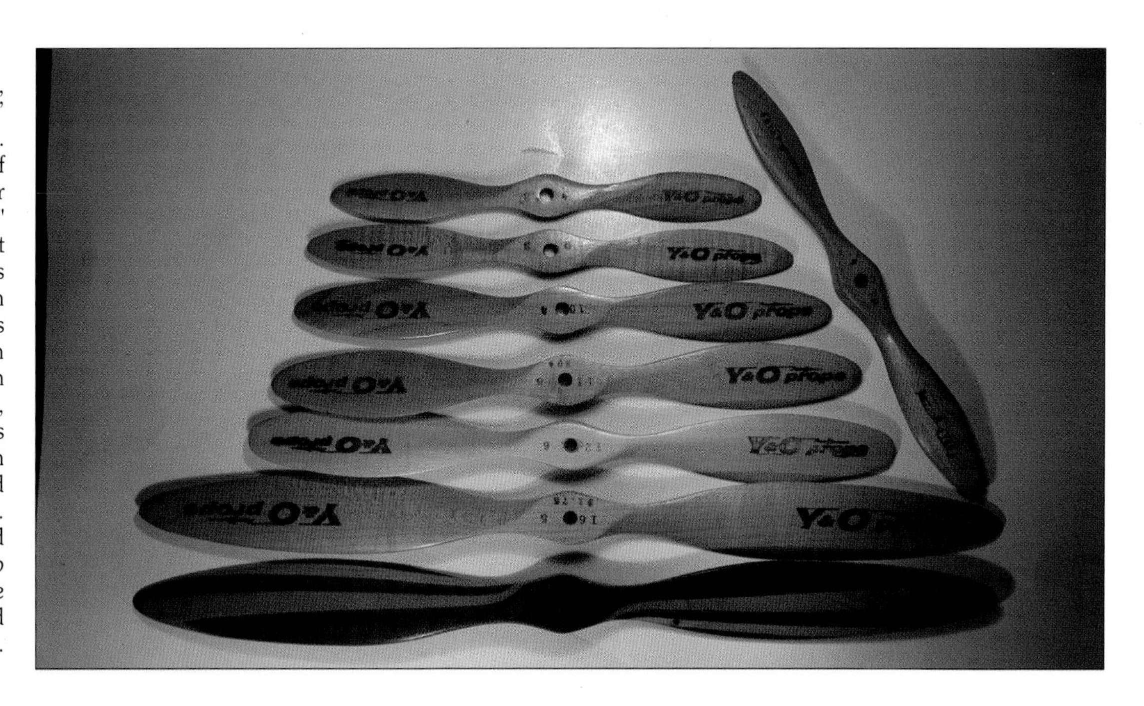

Y&O propellers, c. 1950, designed by J.C. "Madman" Yates and Henry Orwick. The Y&O props are some of the most sought after propellers, with the 9" to 12" props being the most desirable by today's modelers. Production stopped in the middle 1950s and temporarily resumed in 1965, distributed by Stanton R.C. for a while. In 1979, the Y&O propeller was offered by Bill Schagerman in 8" to 18" sizes. He offered the laminated propeller also. The design is timeless and beautiful. *Courtesy of Bob Parker.* $5-15. The large laminated prop is 16" and may sell for $20-30.

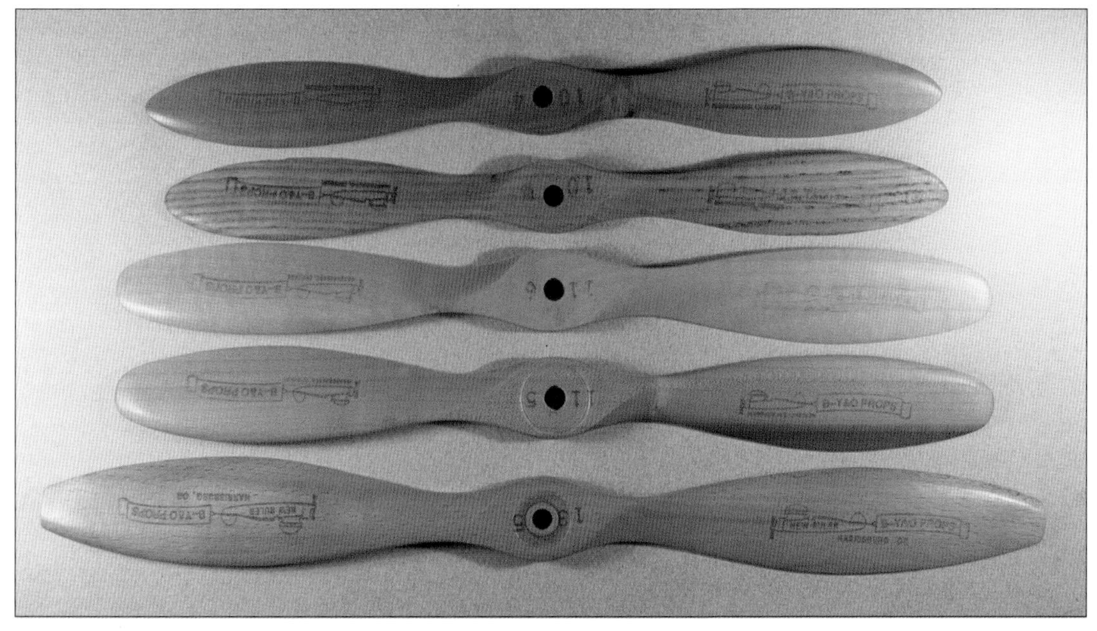

B-Y&O model Airplane propellers, 1990s, produced from the original Y&O equipment by the late Clarence Bull. These outstanding stunt props are now being produced by John Brodak. *Courtesy of Bob Parker.* $3-7.

Control Line Handles and Accessories

Jim Walker's U-Reely, c. 1943. This was the first production U-Reely, made of mahogany plywood and has never been unreeled, a rare example. *Courtesy of Bob Parker.* New condition, $100-200.

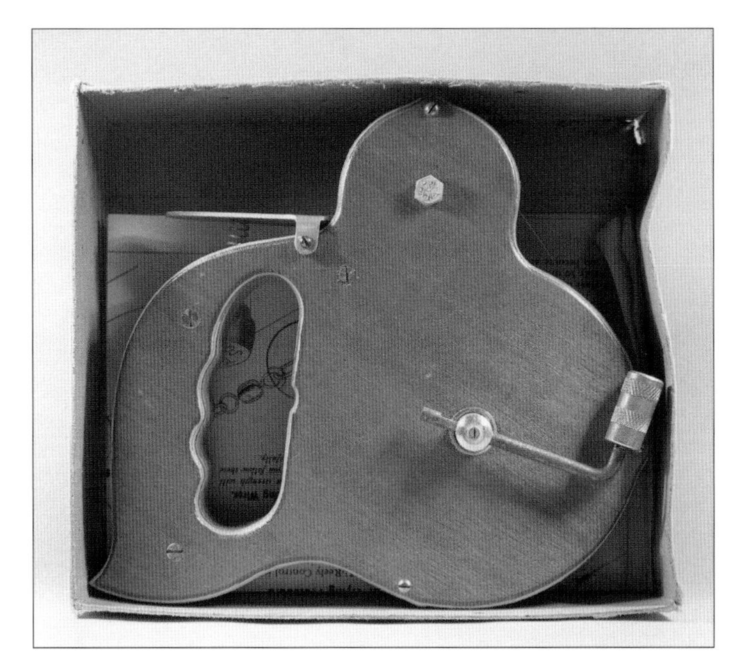

U-Reely control line handle.

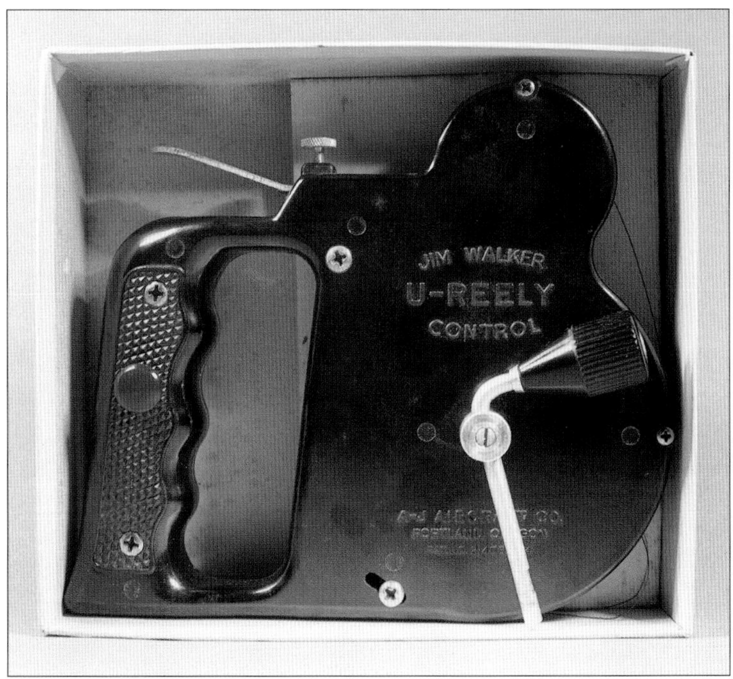

U-Reely control handle, notice the red plastic piece on the handle.

U-Reely control line handle, c. 1950s, manufactured by A. J. Aircraft Company, Portland, Oregon. *Courtesy of Bob Parker.* The box is a bit shop worn, handle is new, $40-75.

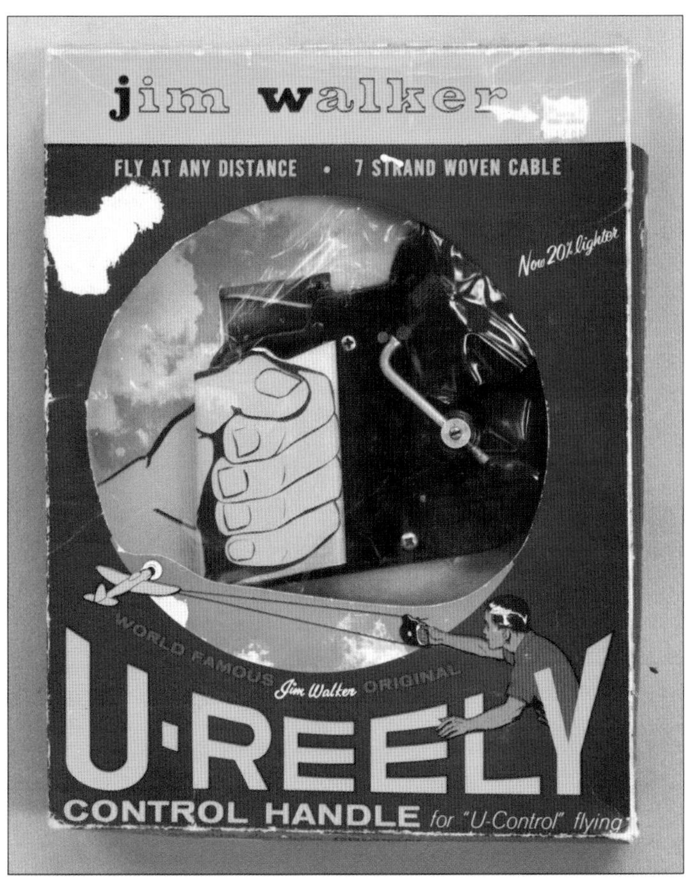

U-Reely control handle, c. 1970s. The U-Reely is one of the devices created by Jim Walker to promote control line modeling. They are quite common as many flyers received them as gifts and didn't use them that much. I still have the one my mother bought me in 1969. Without the box, $10-15, in the box, $30-40.

Various control line handles. The first one is unknown, $15; middle handle with reel, $10-20; U-Reely with Fireball pin, $10-15; E-Z-Just and lines, $10; the rest have minimal value and are made by Merco, c. 1957, Carl Goldberg, Guillow's, and Sullivan. $1-3.

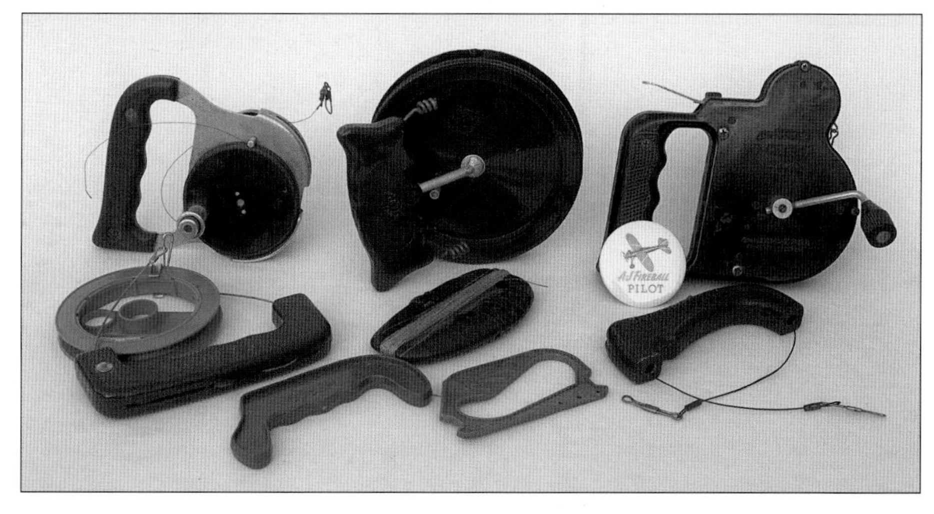

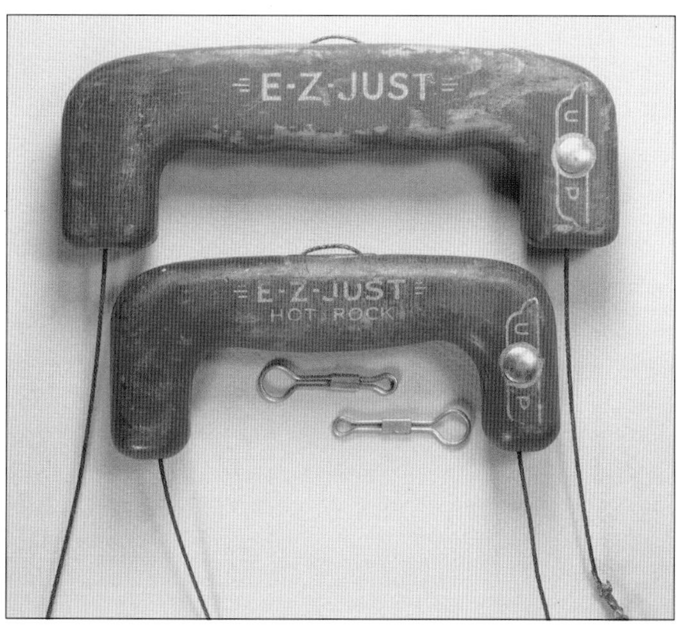

Original E-Z-Just control line handles, c. 1945, the first handles produced by Phil-Leys and were made of wood. Around 1946-1947, the handles began to be made of plastic, millions were sold, and every control line flyer in the United States would eventually use one. Sadly, a flyer flying his model near power lines was electrocuted and litigation caused the company to go out of business. I won't say the wooden handles are rare but they aren't seen that often. *Courtesy of Bill Darkow.* $15-25.

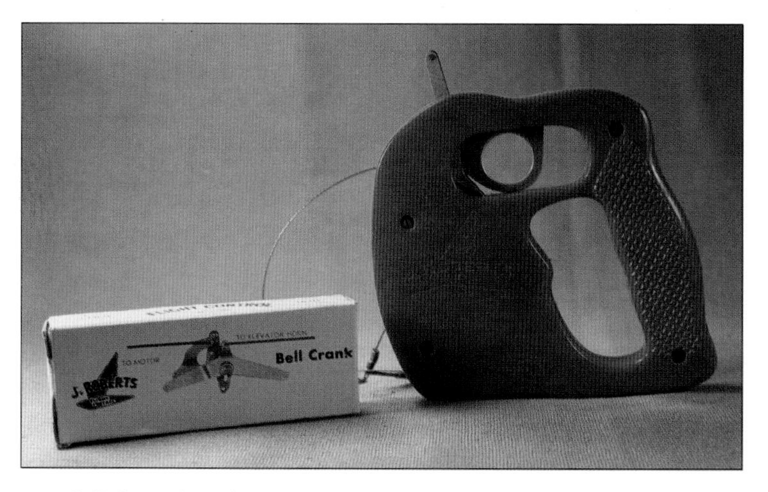

J. Roberts three line control handle, c. 1958, like new condition, $25-40, and bell-crank, $10-20.

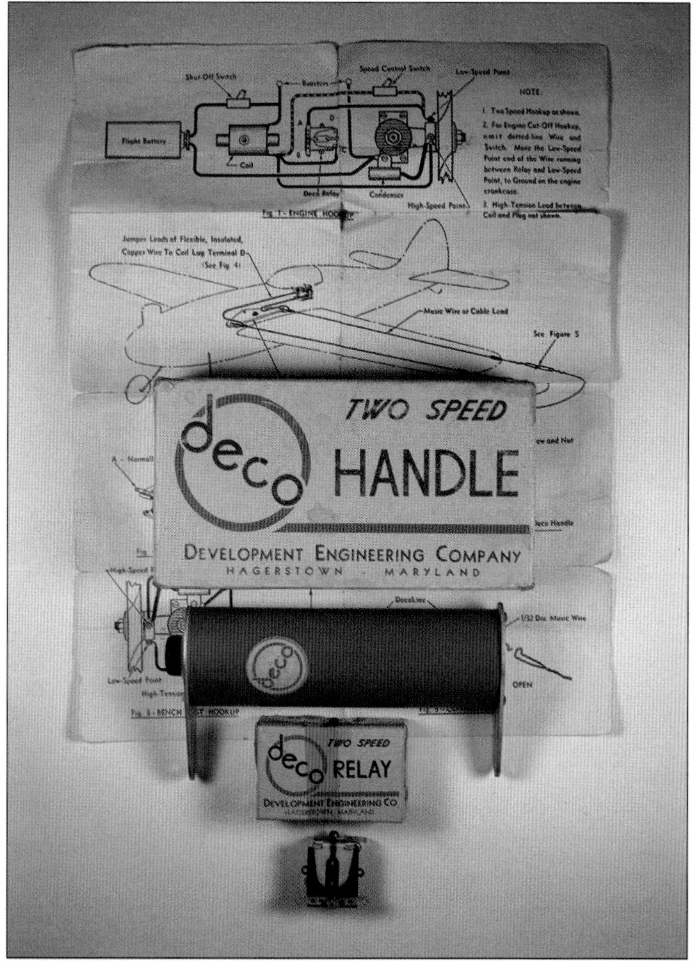

Development Engineering Company, two speed control handle, c. late 1940s. Insulated control lines were sold separately. They transferred electrical current to the model to control the engine speed. $10-15.

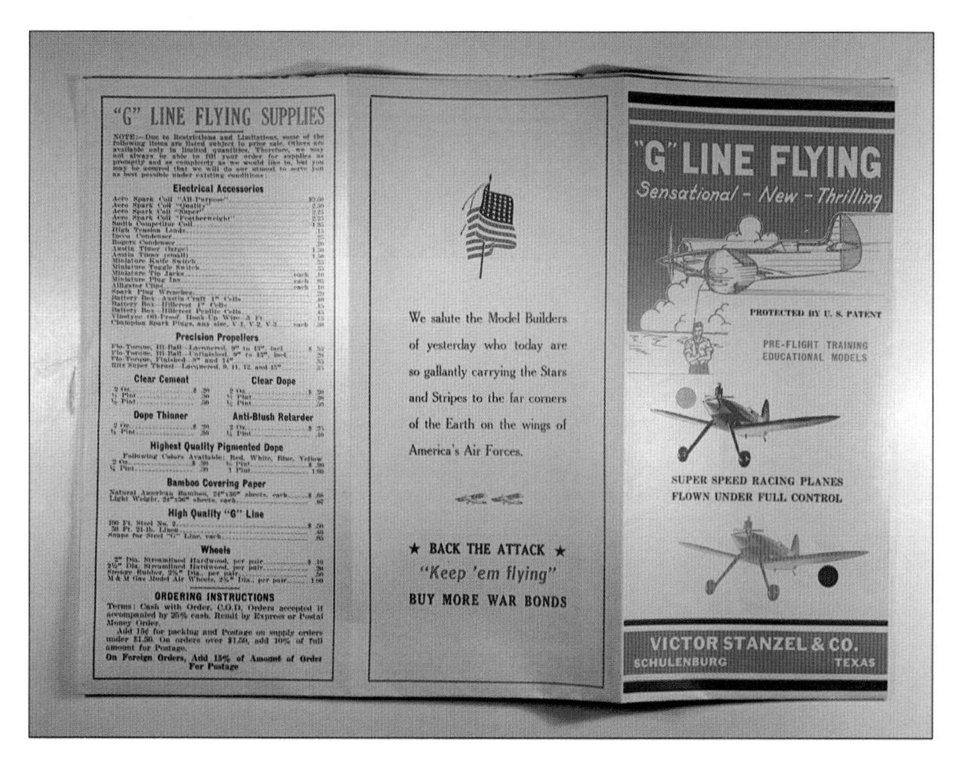

Victor Stanzel & Company brochure, c. 1941-1945. *Courtesy of Bob Parker.* $ 10-15.

Victor Stanzel's G-line Thum-it control line handle for mono-line, c. 1947. An excerpt from an ad in *Air Trails* stated, "The Thum-it offers finger tip control of any model. Eliminates tense wrist movements, fouled controls, reversing. It's foolproof!" *Courtesy of Bob Parker.* $15-20.

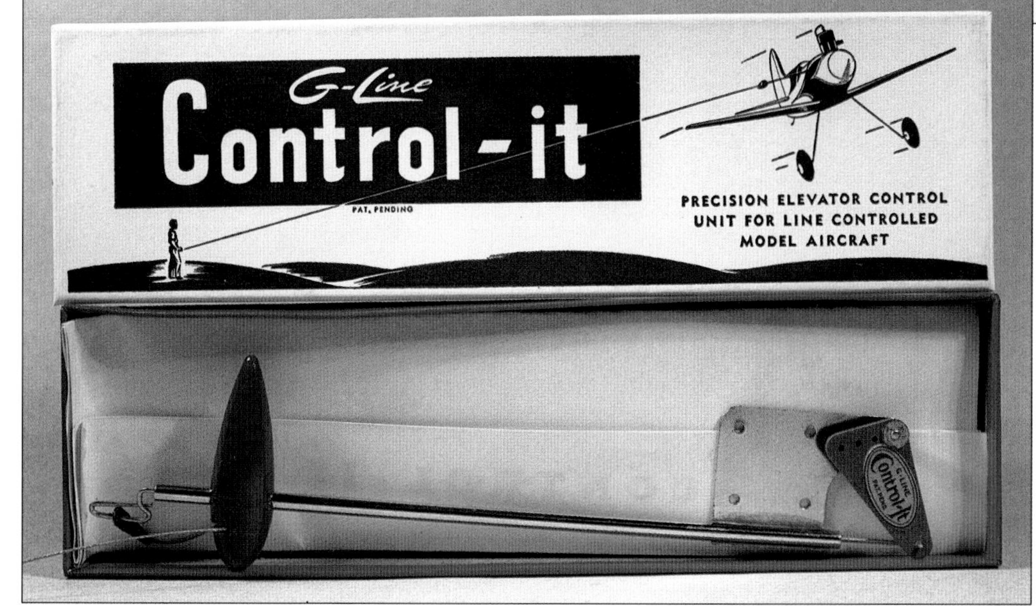

Victor Stanzel's G-line Control-it c. 1947, used in place of a bell-crank for mono line systems. *Courtesy of Bob Parker.* $10-20.

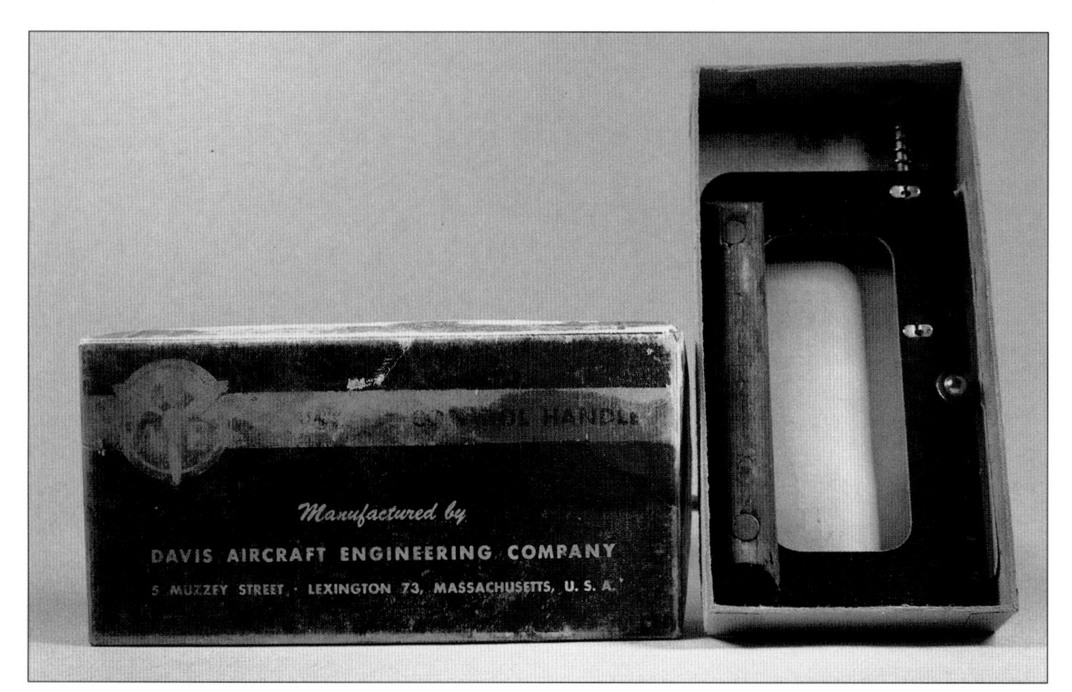

Davis Aircraft Engineering Company control line handle, c. 1950. *Courtesy of Bob Parker.* $10-20.

Cox Thimble Drone Handy Reel. c. 1952. The Handy Reel was developed by Roy Cox and became the center of the lawsuit filed by Jim Walker in 1953, for patent infringement against his U-Reely. He won that part of the suit but lost on being the creator of the bell-crank with testimony by Oba St. Clair. Oba had created a bell-crank system a few years before Jim Walker's patent in 1940. New condition, $25-40.

Berkeley Flight Reel, c. 1950s, storage reel for control line flying lines, $10-20.

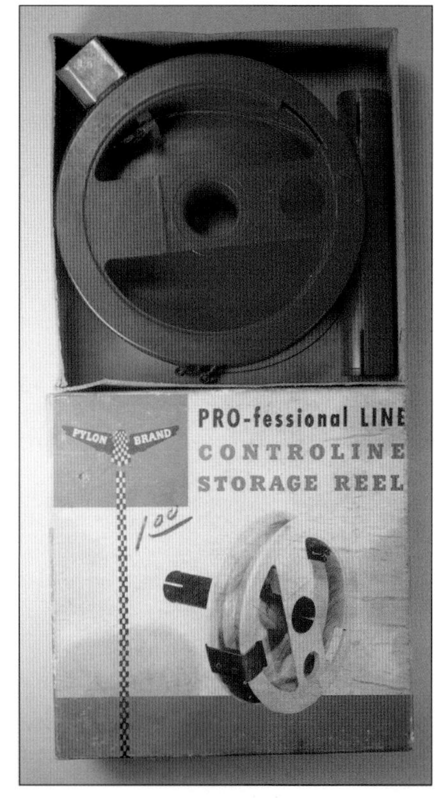

Sullivan storage reel for control line flying lines, c. 1958, $10-15.

Contests, Awards, and Other Memorabilia

Model airplane trophy, c. 1954. First place towline glider sponsored by the American Legion. National Trophies made this style of trophy. First place awards are more valuable than second and third. Awards from national, $15-40.

National Plane Exhibit trophy, c. 1954, $15-35.

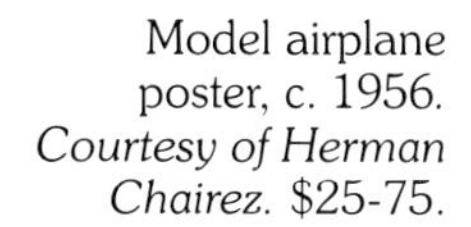

Model airplane poster, c. 1956. *Courtesy of Herman Chairez.* $25-75.

Mirror Model Flying Fair Official's pith helmet, c. 1950. The Mirror meets began in 1946 and attracted the largest crowd of spectators, never again equaled. The meet was held at the Grumman flying field on Long Island, New York. The first contest drew more than 200,000 spectators driving 50,000 cars. More than five and a half miles of snow fence was used to control the crowd. *Courtesy of Bob Parker.* Mint condition, $20-50.

Plymouth state meet trophy, c. 1951. Most of the Plymouth trophies were made by M. T. Lawrence Trophy Center in Detroit, Michigan, $25-45.

Plymouth state meet trophy from Baltimore meet, c. 1952, $20-40.

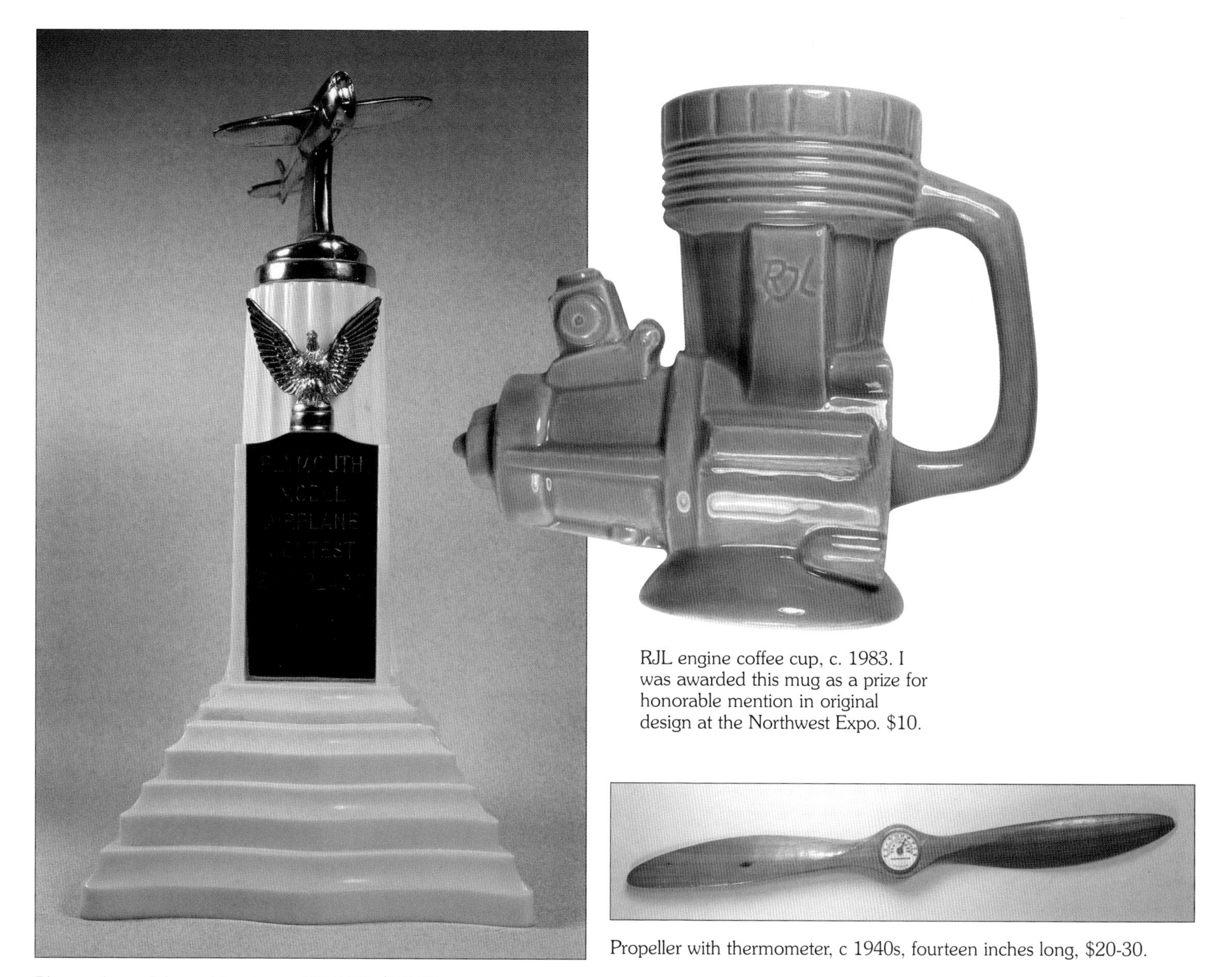

RJL engine coffee cup, c. 1983. I was awarded this mug as a prize for honorable mention in original design at the Northwest Expo. $10.

Propeller with thermometer, c 1940s, fourteen inches long, $20-30.

Plymouth model meet trophy, c. 1950-53, $15-30.

Letter and pictures from George Aldrich, showing old time free flight models on his work bench. As famous modelers pass on, cherished letters and correspondence take on a special meaning, finding a place in many collections. Most have only sentimental value but in time, they are sure to gain some monetary value. Aldrich did much to advance model aviation and is remembered for creating the modern stunt pattern around 1957, which is still used by flyers through out the world today. *Courtesy of Bill Darkow.*

Testor's award plaque, c. 1952, $10-15.

American Ace Spotter, c. 1944. This was one of five different sets manufactured by Reed and Associates, $5-15.

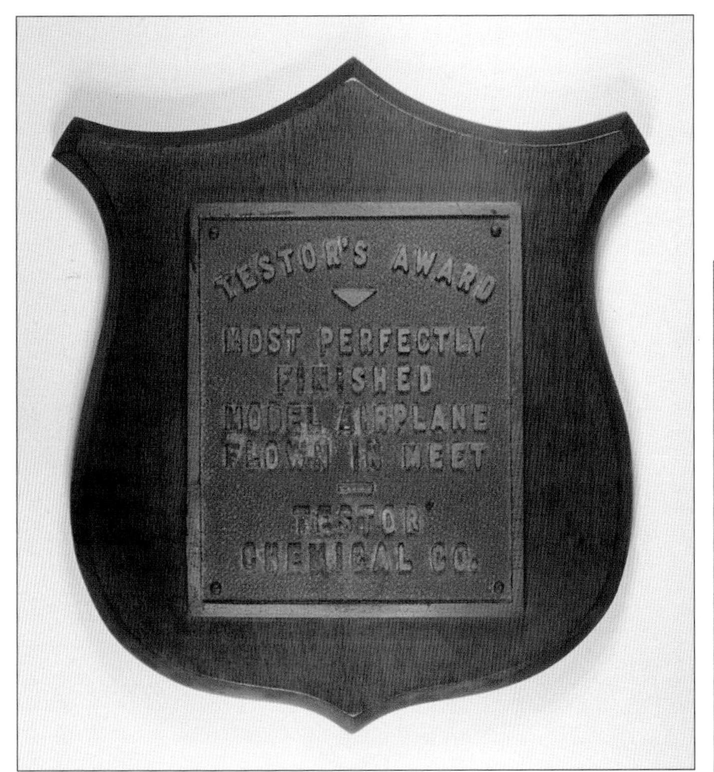

Testor's award plaque, c. 1950. This was presented to a modeler in San Diego, $10-15.

1953 International Competition Handbook, free flight rules for F.A.I. competitors. The Federation Aeronautique Internationale was founded in 1905 and still governs all aviation records worldwide. Bill Tyler was the cover artist, $10-15.

PAA Free Flight Payload Event

Dallas Sherman, as Educational Director of Pan American World Airlines and an avid modeler, was able to persuade the airline to sponsor the first PAA event in 1948. George Gardner took over in 1949 when Sherman was transferred to the Far East. Gardner tirelessly promoted the event. While Sherman was overseas the event gained popularity in Japan, Hong Kong, Indonesia, and India. Modelers constructed airplanes designed to carry a weighted "passenger." Berkeley produced the first PAA kit in 1948. The winner was determined by amount of weight carried for the longest amount of "air" time. Models had to take off from the ground and stay aloft for at least 40 seconds. Herbert Kothe was the first national contest winner with a best time of 361 seconds. The 1954 Glenview Nationals saw over half of the fourteen hundred entrants signifying their intention to compete in one of the PAA categories. About 300 actually flew in one or more of the PAA events. The payload event was popular for over fifteen years; Pan Am quit sponsoring the free flight event in the early 1960s. Many designs and kits were produced to accommodate the event, which grew from one category to several as it gained popularity. (George Garner, *Air Trails Hobbies for Young Men,* August 1955, 20-23, 81, 85).

PAA Load Event Official patch, c. 1950, 3.5"x 7.5", from the Red Costlow scrapbook. *Courtesy of Bob Maschi,* $20-40.

Vintage Valentine postcard, c. 1920s. Dating this item was hard but I believe this was manufactured after the first World War and before Lindberg made his famous flight because of the bi-plane, $5-10.

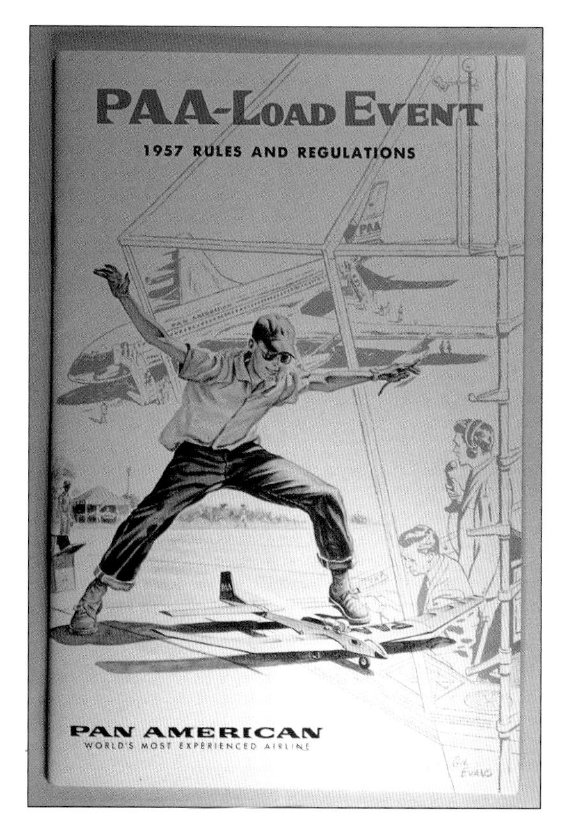

PAA Load Event rule book, c. 1957, cover by Gil Evans depicting the launching technique that caught on around 1956 and that many flyers used at the 1956-57 Nationals. Phil Grau was the National winner in the Junior/Senior division at the 1957 Nationals. He is pictured in the 1957 *Air Trails Model Annual* launching his model this way. $10.

Airplane Model League of America pin back, c. 1928-34. The AMLA was founded September 1927, William B. Stout became the president. Hundreds of thousands of these were made and are the easiest vintage modeling pin backs to find, $5-10.

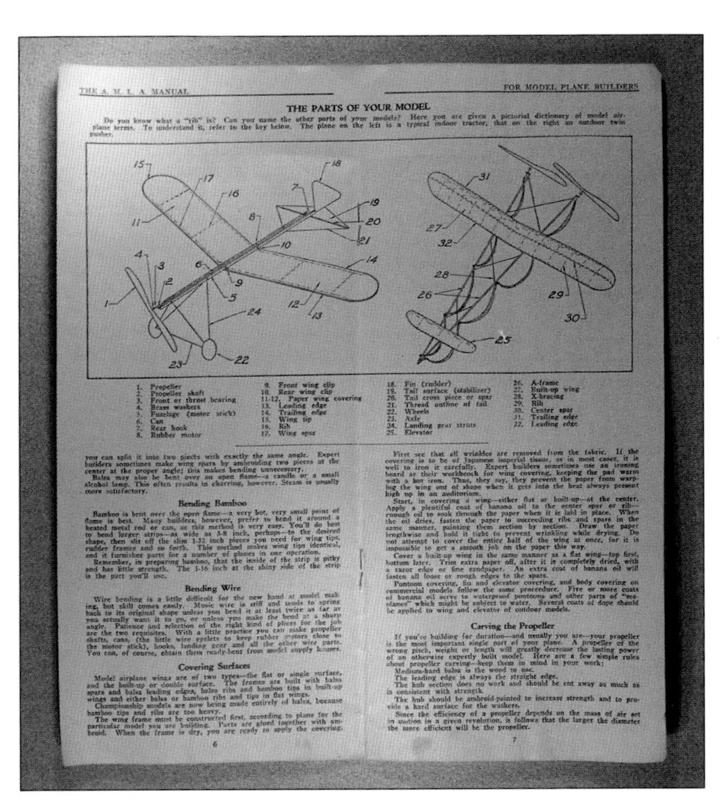
THE A. M. L. A. MANUAL — FOR MODEL PLANE BUILDERS

THE PARTS OF YOUR MODEL

Bending Bamboo

Bending Wire

Covering Surfaces

Carving the Propeller

Inside the AMLA Manual.

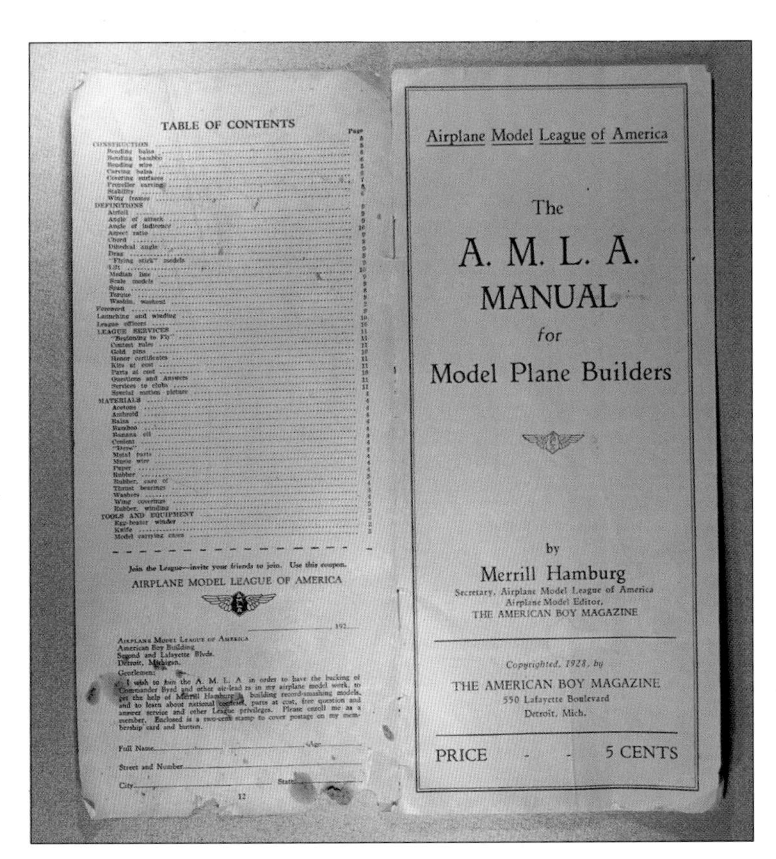
TABLE OF CONTENTS

AIRPLANE MODEL LEAGUE OF AMERICA

Airplane Model League of America

The

A. M. L. A.

MANUAL

for

Model Plane Builders

by

Merrill Hamburg

Secretary, Airplane Model League of America
Airplane Model Editor,
THE AMERICAN BOY MAGAZINE

Copyrighted, 1928, by
THE AMERICAN BOY MAGAZINE
550 Lafayette Boulevard
Detroit, Mich.

PRICE - - 5 CENTS

The A.M.L.A. Manual, c. 1928, written and compiled by Merrill Hamburg, $15-20.

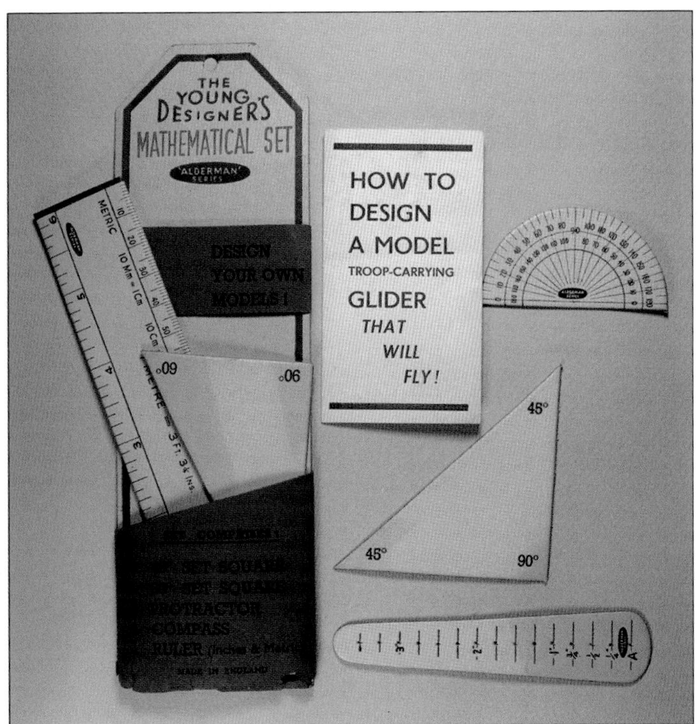

The Young Designer's Mathematical Set, c. 1940s, manufactured in England during the war, made of cardboard, new condition, $10-15.

Megow pin back, c. 1940, $15.

Berkeley printers block, c. 1950s. This was the printer's stamp that appeared on Berkeley model kit plans, rare. *Courtesy of Mike Hazel.* $75-150.

First Day Covers

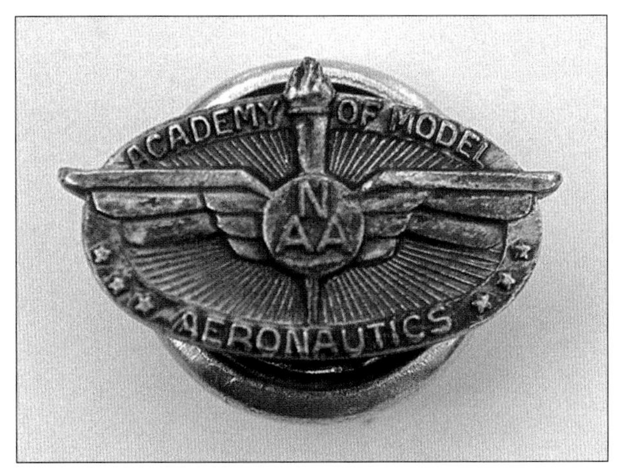

Sterling silver AMA pin, c. 1947, $20-30.

First Day Cover, Pacific Coast Miniature Aircraft League, Selma, California, May 30, 1926. $10.

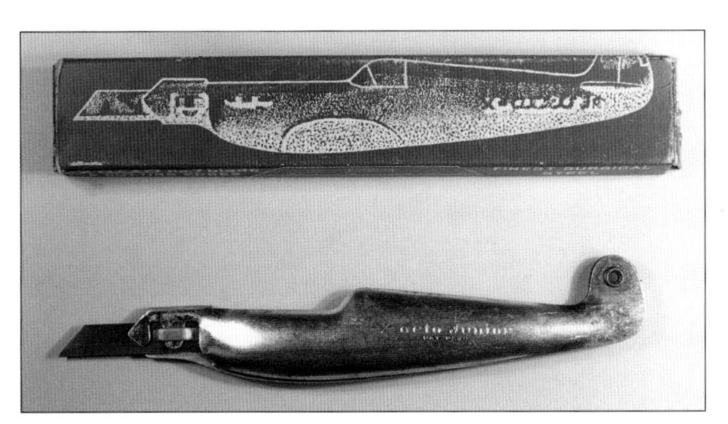

No. 7 all metal X-acto Junior modeling knife, c. 1940s. This was in the shape of a Spitfire fuselage, available from AHC 1942, and Central Camera Co. 1945 catalogs. $10-20.

First Day Cover, The Kansas City Miniature Aircraft Contest, Kansas City, Missouri, June 8, 1929. FDCs were popularly used to commemorate special events nationally and locally. $10.

First Day Cover, A.M.L.A.'s second contest in Detroit, Michigan, June 20, 1929, $5-10.

First Day Cover, Commemorating Gordon S. Light's 1932 win of the Lord Wakefield Trophy, this depicts the back of the envelope.

First Day Cover, Gordon Light drawing by D. E. Schucker, notice the hand stamped airplane on the stamps. Light would win again in 1935. Other notable U.S. Wakefield flyers of the time were Ehrhardt in 1930-31, Cahill in 1938, and Dick Korda in 1939. $8-12.

First Day Cover, Aero Club of Struthers, Ohio, July 1-4, 1931, $8-10.

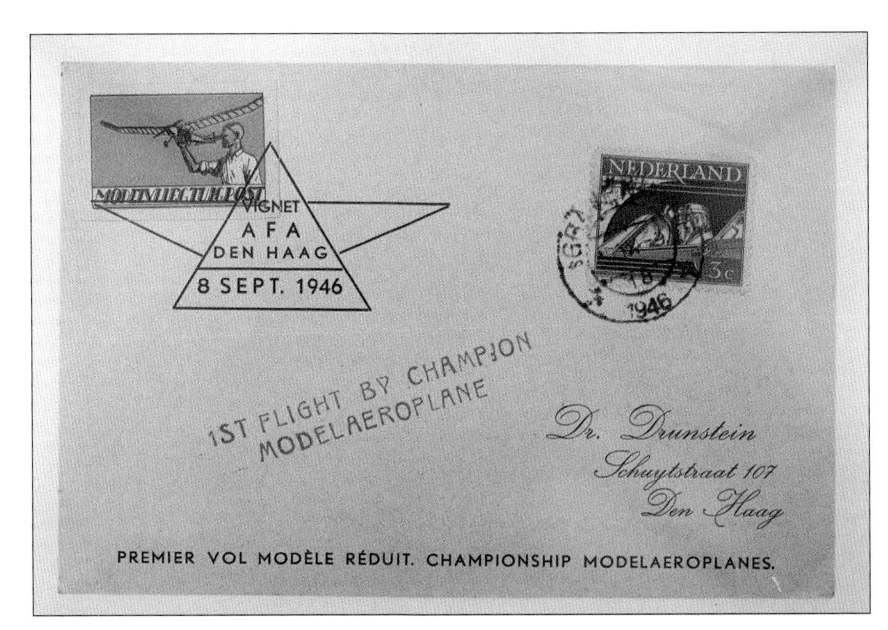

First Day Cover, Netherlands, September 8, 1946, celebration of model airplane contests after the war. 1946 was a grand year for modeling worldwide as everyone made efforts to return to normal after the devastation caused by the war. $10-15.

Modeling Stamp from the Netherlands.

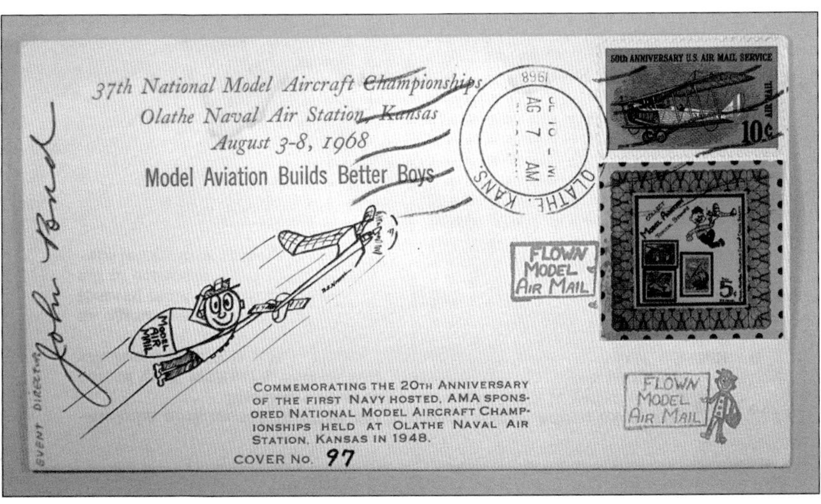

First Day Cover, commemorating the 20th Naval National Championships on August 7, 1968 sponsored by the AMA. The Navy Nationals are still talked about today; military personnel were used as timers and judges. The FDCs were actually flown in one of the competing free flight model aircraft in the old-timer event before being mailed. The first FDCs to be flown by model aircraft occurred at the 1949 Nationals using models in the first PAA event. This one is signed by event director John Pond, the founder of today's old time movement, the Society of Antique Modelers. He was elected into the AMA Hall of Fame in 1987. $10-15.

The stamp celebrating the 1968 Olathe Kansas Nationals. Inside the envelope contains the history of the first National Championships held in 1926. They were called the Philadelphia Air Races. In 1927, the New York Playground Association sponsored the National Championships. In 1928-29, they were held in Detroit sponsored by the AMLA and conducted by *American Boy Magazine.* In 1930, the national contest was called The First Chicago National Outdoor Model Airplane Meet. 1931 marked the beginning of the national championships being conducted by the NAA, a governing body now known as the Academy of Model Aeronautic which was formed in 1936 by Lieutenant W. H. Alden. Willis C. Brown became the first president. Alden served as secretary/treasurer, and Frank Zaic designed the first logo. "The Navy's interest in model aviation was to foster and encourage an increasing awareness of aviation among the youth of America. Most present day Naval Aviators and Astronauts gained their first exposure to the adventure of aviation by constructing and experimenting with model airplanes." Doc Nichol's *Model Aircraft Stamps and Covers.* 1968.

Academy of Model Aeronautics

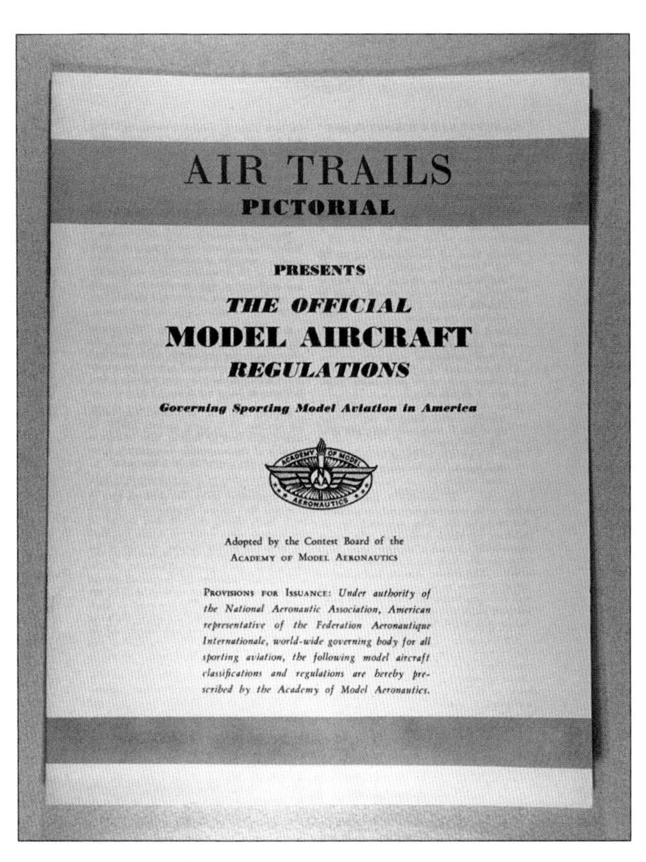

Air Trails Pictorial, Model Aircraft Regulations, 16 pp, c. 1947, $7-12.

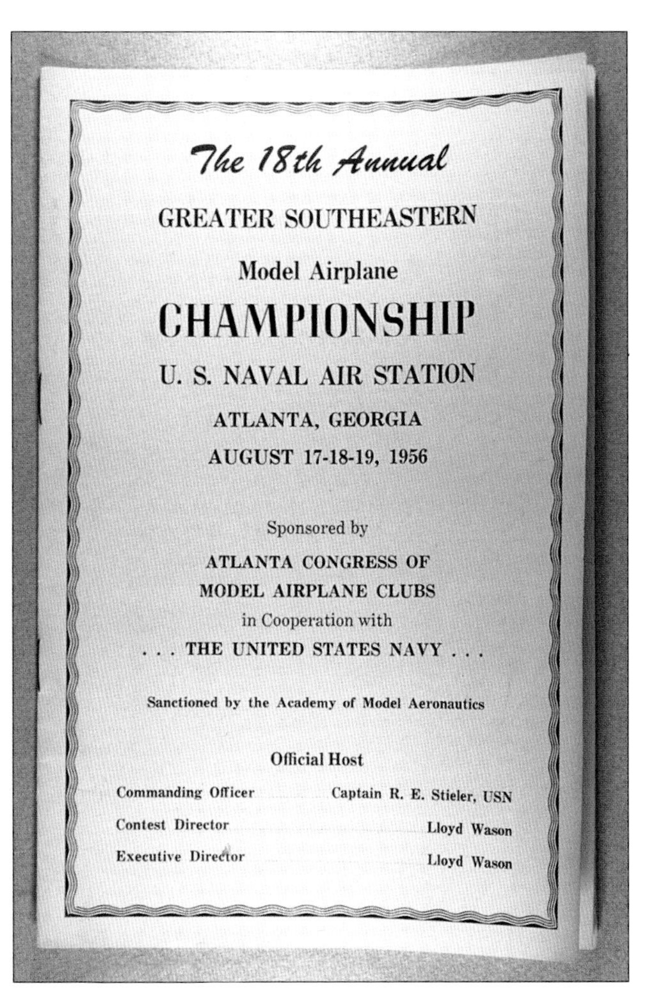

The 18th Annual Southeastern Model Airplane Championship program, c. August 1956, $10.

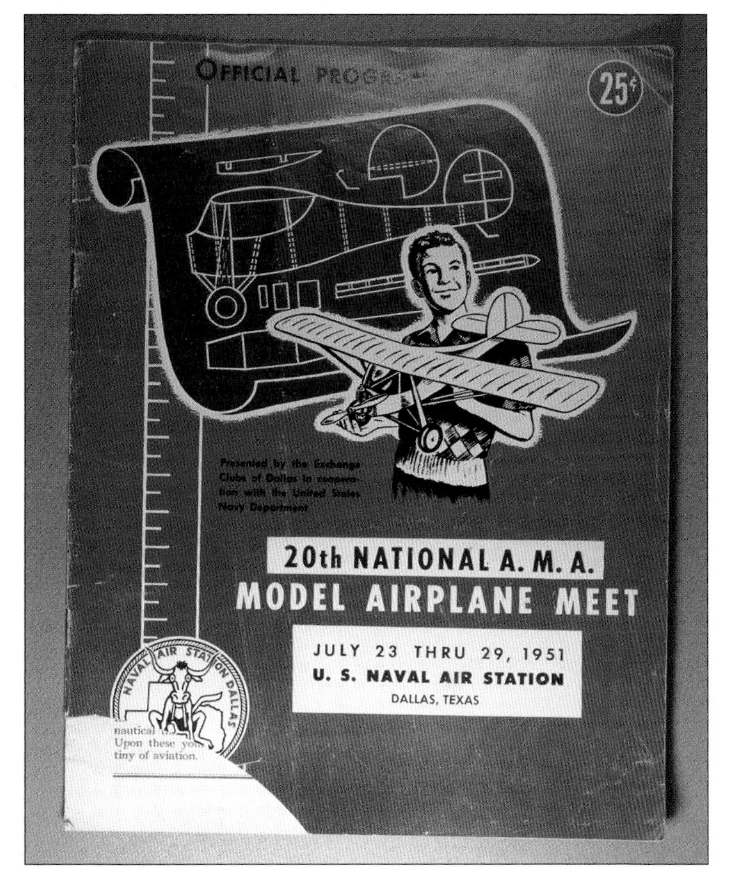

Program for the 20th National Model Airplane meet, c. 1951, $10.

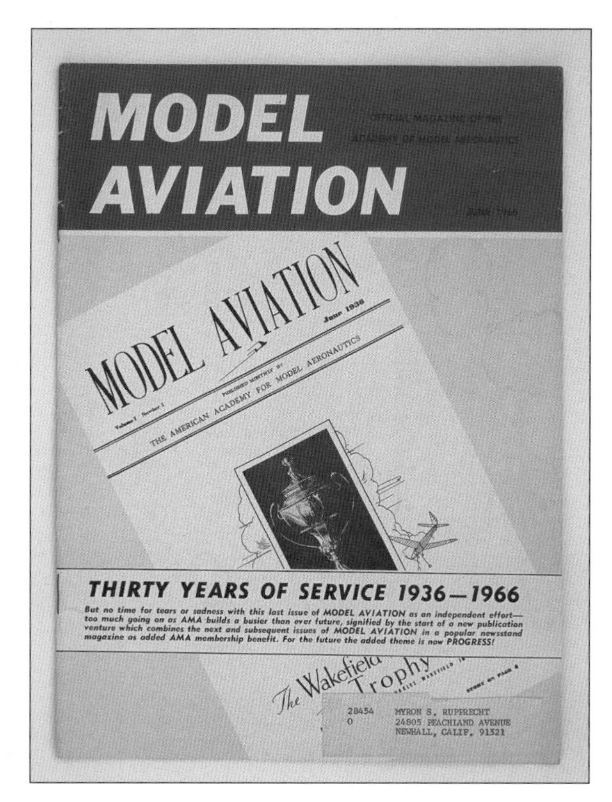

Model Aviation, June 1966, the last issue of MA, after thirty years of printing their own publication, *American Aircraft Modeler* would begin to carry AMA news to the membership. $2-5.

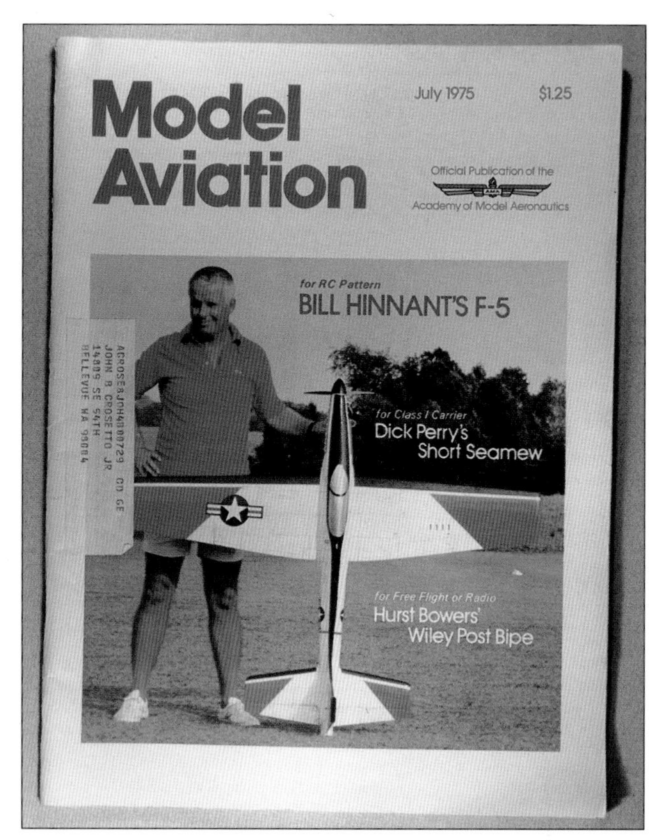

Model Aviation, July 1975. The AMA announced with this issue that it would resume publication of its own magazine again when AMERICAN AIRCRAFT MODELER went bankrupt. All AMA members can view every issue of MODEL AVIATION from this issue to 2001 online through the AMA website archives. $1-2.

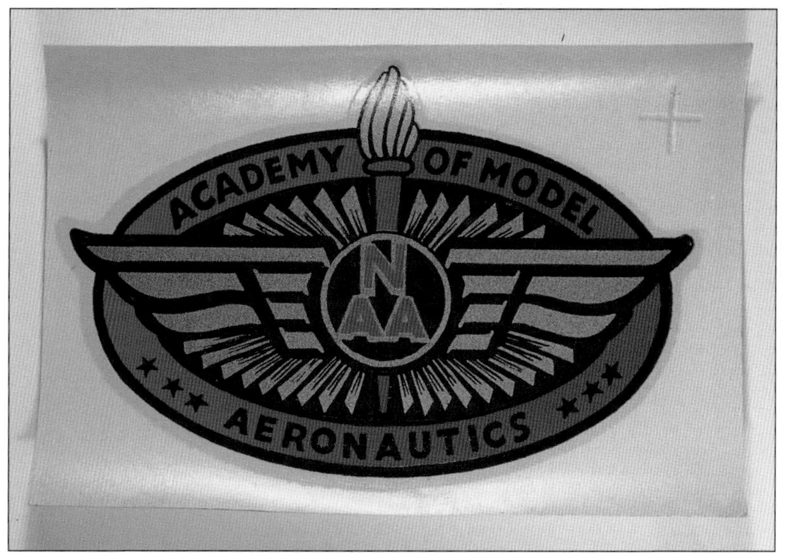

Original AMA decal, c. 1947. *Courtesy of Bob Parker.* $5-10.

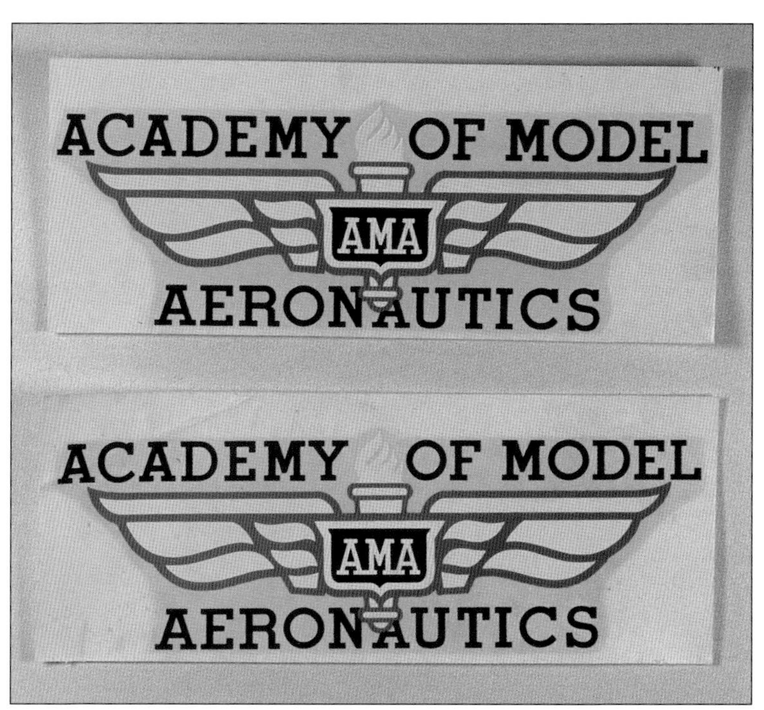

Original AMA decals, c. 1957, $5-7.

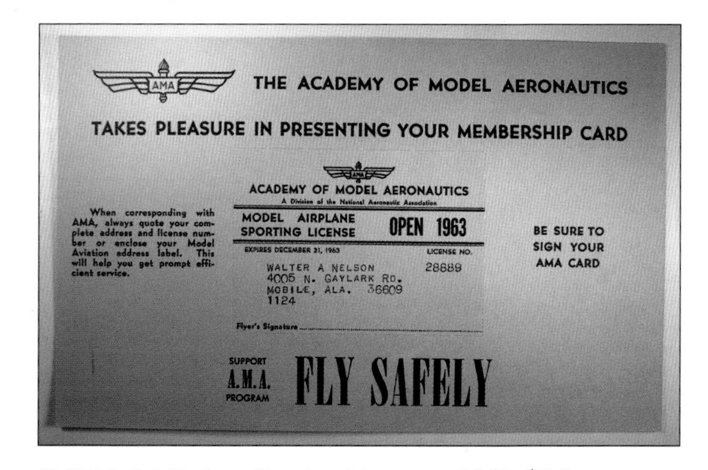
THE ACADEMY OF MODEL AERONAUTICS
TAKES PLEASURE IN PRESENTING YOUR MEMBERSHIP CARD

When corresponding with AMA, always quote your complete address and license number or enclose your Model Aviation address label. This will help you get prompt efficient service.

ACADEMY OF MODEL AERONAUTICS
A Division of the National Aeronautic Association
MODEL AIRPLANE SPORTING LICENSE OPEN 1963
EXPIRES DECEMBER 31, 1963 LICENSE NO.
WALTER A NELSON 28889
4005 N. GAYLARK RD.
MOBILE, ALA. 36609
1124
Flyer's Signature

BE SURE TO SIGN YOUR AMA CARD

SUPPORT A.M.A. PROGRAM FLY SAFELY

AMA Model Airplane Sporting License, c. 1963, $1-4.

My first AMA license, c. 1971. I was seventeen that year and became a member of the Prince George R.C. club that flew near Washington D.C.

AMA decal and patch, c. 1957, these were included in the membership package. $5-10.

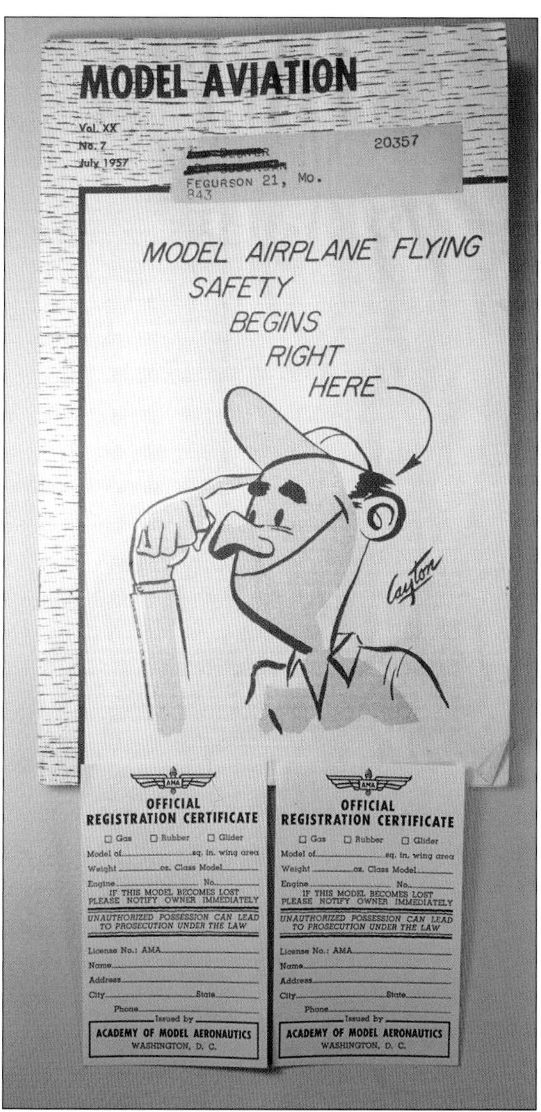

Model Aviation, July 1957, with registration cards, cover by Earl Cayton, $5.

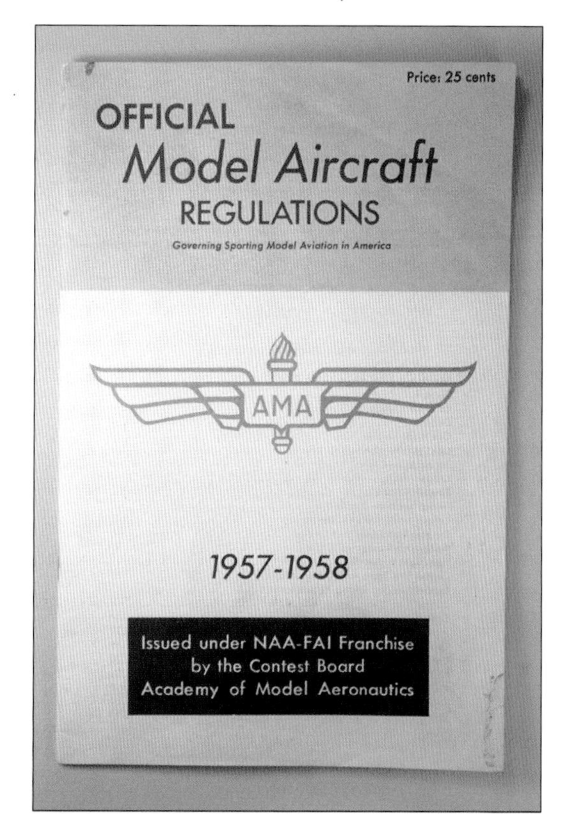

Official Model Aircraft Regulations, 1957-58, $5-10.

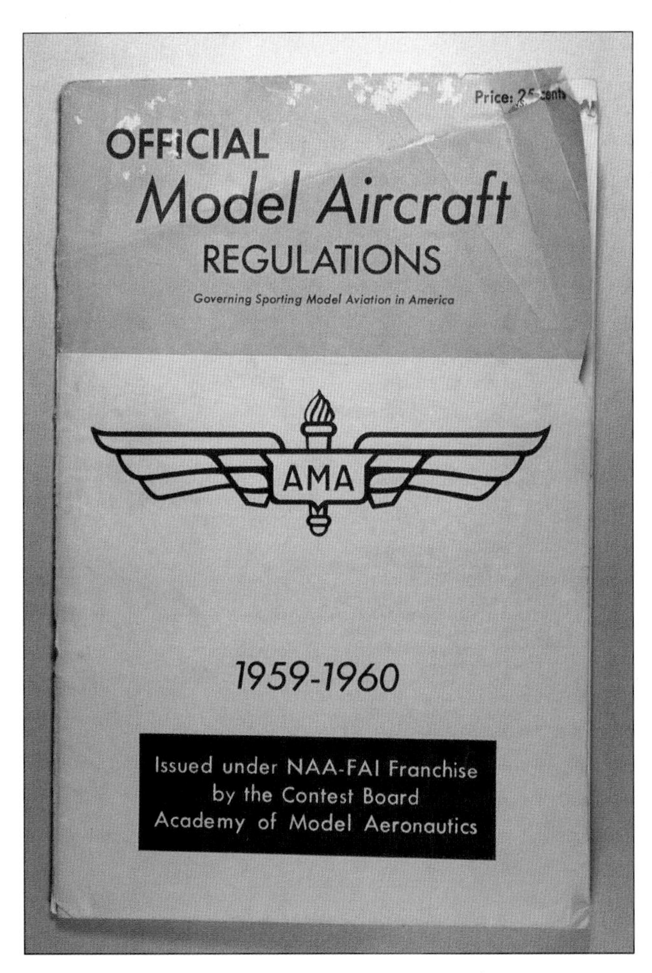

Official Model Aircraft Regulations, 1959-60, $5-10.

Official Model Aircraft Regulations, 1972, 1973, and 1984-85, $2-5.

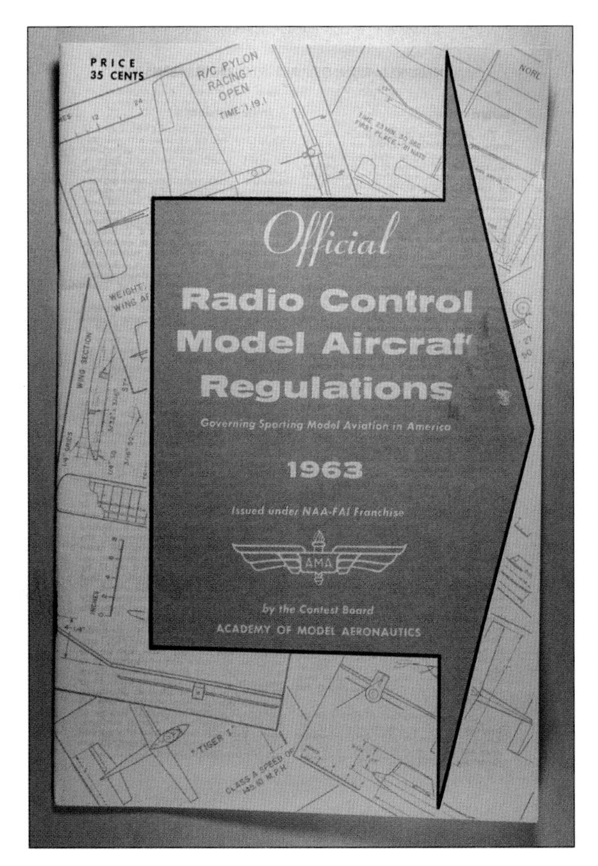

Official Radio Control Model Aircraft Regulations, 1963, $5.

Program, from the first Aerobatic Radio Control World Championship held in the United States in Doylestown, Pennsylvania. Governor Milton J. Shapp proclaimed the week of September 13-19, 1971 as International Radio Control Week. In 1971, it was estimated that 300,000 people throughout the world enjoyed radio control airplanes as a creative use of their free time. Sixty-two competitors took part in the weeklong event. Maynard Hill was the contest director. $5-10.

Decals and Patches

Model club decals, c. 1958. The Pittsburg ARCS decal is featured in *American Modeler*, November 1958. $5-10.

American Airlines club decal, c. 1958, $5-10.

Decals from Great Britain, c. 1980s. *Courtesy of Bill Darkow.* $3-6.

Italian SAM patch and decal, c. 1990 *Courtesy of Bill Darkow;* Kanto Modelaires club patch, c. 1980s $2-3.

Seattle Skyraiders Club decals. *Courtesy of Bill Darkow.* $2-3.

Seattle Skyraiders Club decals. The control line club was founded in 1963 and is now called the Northwest Skyraiders. *Courtesy of Bill Darkow.* $2-3.

Northwest Model Exposition patch, 1983, $5-10.

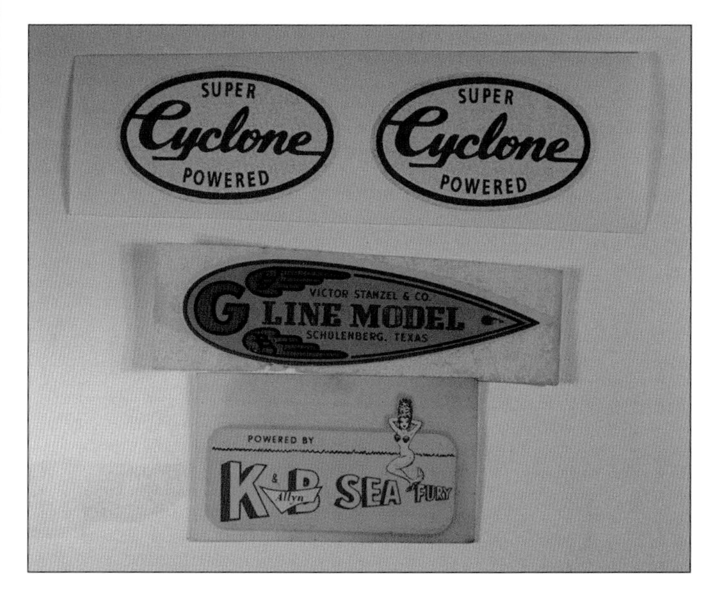

Super Cyclone, Stanzel G-Line, c. 1940s and K&B Sea Fury engine decals. *Courtesy of Bob Parker.* c. 1956, $5-10.

Drone Diesel decal, c. 1947; Bunch engine decals, c. 1940s. *Courtesy of Bob Parker.* $7-10.

K&B decals, c. 1960-70s, $1-4.

McCoy, Veco and O&R decals, c. 1950-60s. The dark red McCoy decal is a reproduction. *Courtesy of Bob Parker.* $5-10.

Model Aeronautics Association of Canada decal, c. 1990s; Scientific Cadet model decals, c. 1960s. *Courtesy of Bob Parker.* $5.

Sterling Jr. Ringmaster and Top Flite Combat Cat decals. Even the kit decals were designed to attract youthful modelers. If you saw one of these decals you had to build the plane. $3-5.

American Junior Super Firecat c. 1950s and Comet Zipper model airplane decals c. 1940s. Bob related that Walt Disney designed the Firecat decal. Model airplane flying was featured in 1957 when Disneyland opened in Los Angles. A special enclosed flying circle was built for control line flying in Tomorrow Land. *Courtesy of Bob Parker.* $5-10.

American Junior commemorative decals, c. 1990. *Courtesy of Bob Parker.* $5.

Plymouth Dealer Book

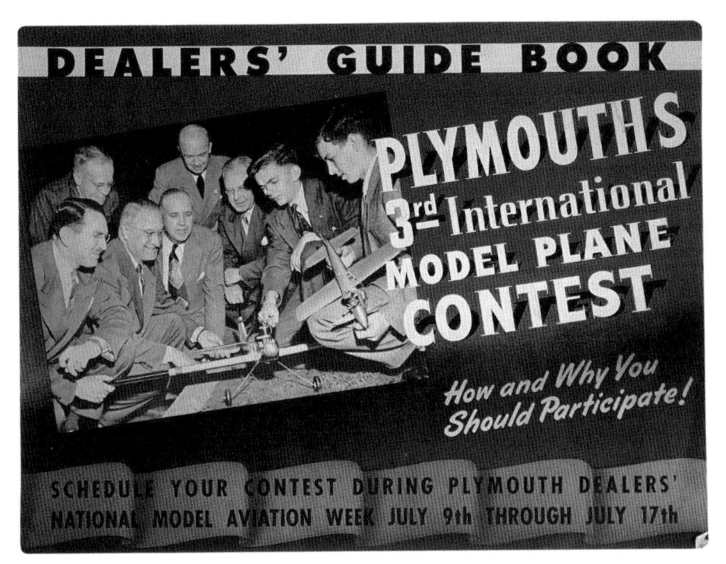

Plymouth Dealers Guide Book, c. 1950. The guide book measures 11.5" x 15" and contains everything needed for local Plymouth-Chrysler dealers to conduct and hold model airplane meets. The guide shows how to display models in the dealer showroom, arrange for a practice field, connecting with local hobby shops, and making displays in department stores. A dealer could also order sound movies of the 1949 International Model Plane Contest in color ($255) or black and white ($85) for promoting local contests. It gave information on how to approach local newspapers, radio, and television. Tom Lay of Los Angeles identified the young man pointing to the engine on the cover photo as "a young George Aldrich and the plane a Yates 'Dragon.'" $75-150.

16 MINNEAPOLIS SUNDAY TRIBUNE L June 27, 1948

R. E. COSTLOW SIGNS FOR MODEL AIR MEET
Ray Lagermeier waits center; Robert Thor holds jet

MODEL PLANE PRIZES POSTED

July 11 Contest Features 23 Events

about 30 inches from wingtip to to wingtip, are propelled entirely by the exhaust gases of internal combustion engines.

Contest headquarters are at 2395 University avenue, St. Paul. Entry blanks may be secured from Plymouth dealers or from hobby shops.

Original news article used in the *Plymouth Dealer Guide Book* of Ralph "Red" Costlow, Ray Lagermeir, and Bob Thor, signing up for the local state Plymouth contest on June 27, 1948, from the *Minneapolis Sunday Tribune*. The news clipping by itself is not worth much but would have value when added to the *Plymouth Dealer Guide Book*. From the Red Costlow scrapbook. *Courtesy of Bob Maschi,* $1-3.

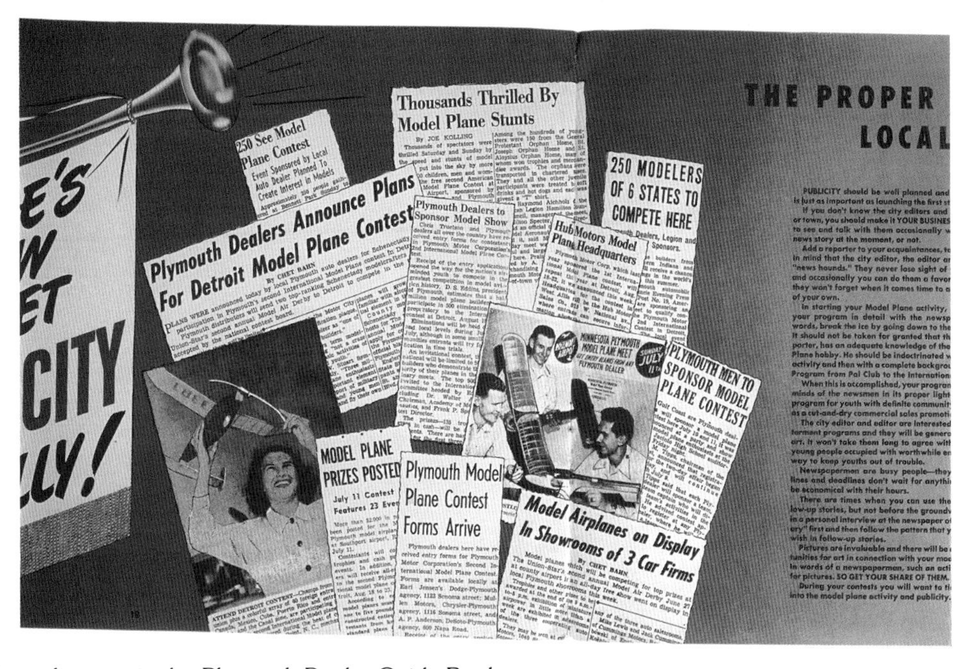

News clippings in the *Plymouth Dealer Guide Book*.

Items for the Plymouths contests. All contestants received these things; the dealerships spent a lot to promote local contests.

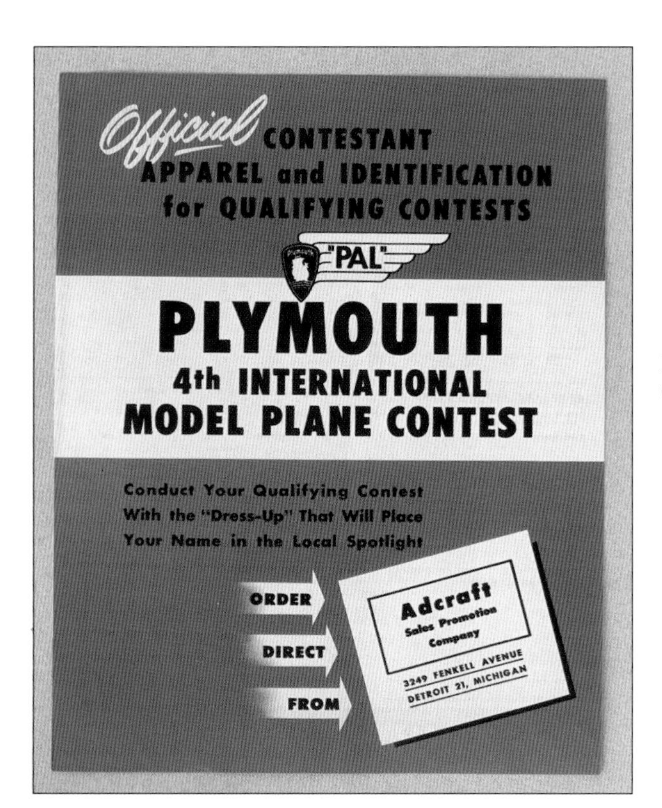

Official Plymouth Contest apparel catalog, c. 1950. In this catalog dealers could purchase t-shirts, flight caps, membership cards, lapel emblems, and celluloid buttons with the Plymouth Aero League logo. $5-10.

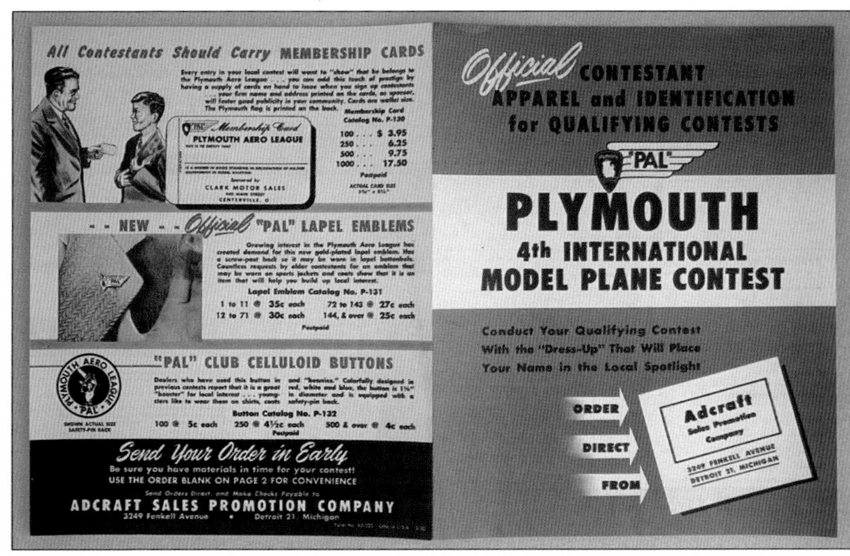

Fold out of the Plymouth Contest apparel catalog, c. 1950.

Plymouth International Model Plane Contest entry form and souvenir program, c. 1950, $15.

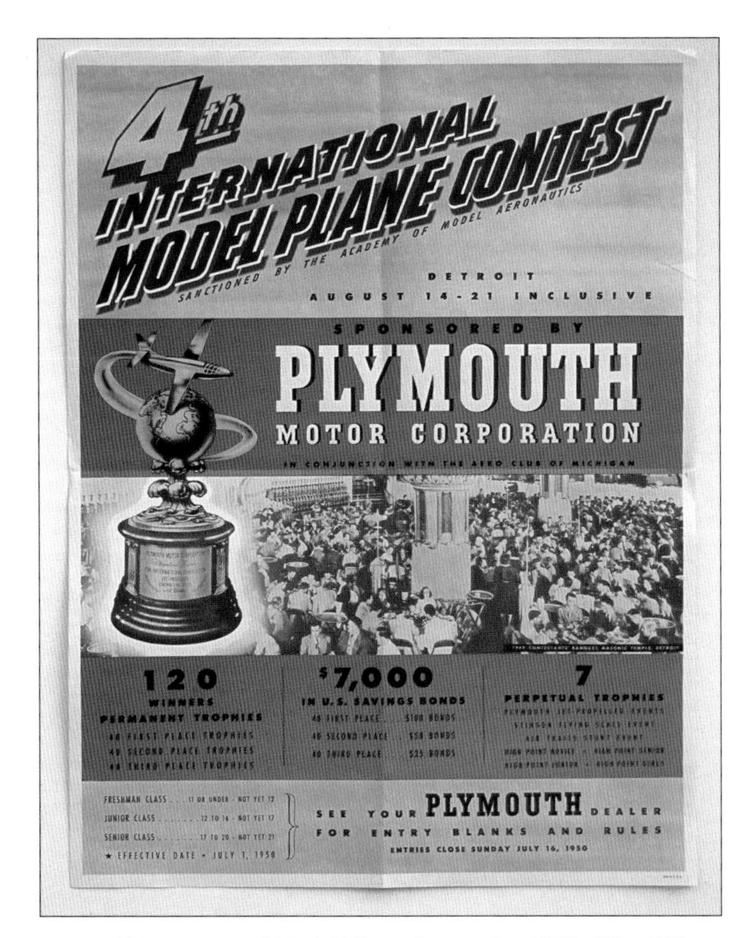

Poster. 4th International Model Plane Contest for 1950, 19" x 25", dealers displayed this poster in their windows. $30-75.

Plymouth catalog and brochure for ordering trophies for local contests. $5-10.

The Search for Jack Ritner

After flying radio control for ten years and another eight years not flying because of a resentment when all my radio gear became obsolete in 1990, the itch to fly again hit me. I returned to my modeling roots by becoming involved in control line flying and began research on the next model to build. In 1999, at the Palmer/Wirfs and Associates Portland Expo antique show, I found a collection of 280 old model airplane magazines and struck a deal with the seller. My new concern turned to how to get them home. I knew our car was already full of treasures my wife and her parents had purchased during this marvelous yearly show. When I got home, two weeks of steady reading only rekindled my love for model airplanes.

In this lot were two issues of *Model Airplane News*, November 1954 and December 1957, featuring articles and designs by modeler Jack Ritner. These designs were of interest because I believed they would qualify for the Old Time Stunt event, which had become popular during my absence from control line modeling. The cut-off date for design eligibility is December 30, 1952. The 1957 article gave hints that the design was built and flown before the cut-off date; this would make the 1954 plane even older. I estimated Jack's age and began wondering if he was still alive and what he was doing now. This began my search for the man who wrote the articles fifty years earlier.

Jack's modeling career began in San Francisco and an Internet search revealed a Jack Ritner living there. I called the number and the man answering the phone was way too young to be the guy I was looking for, but he raised my hopes by telling me he met a guy at a Lake Tahoe ski resort with the same name. Sacramento seemed the next logical place to search as it was between Lake Tahoe and San Francisco. The next Internet search yielded another Jack Ritner; with excitement, I dialed the new number. An older woman answered and immediately wanted to know what I wanted and who I was. After mentioning something about model airplanes, she yelled for her husband to come to the phone. Bingo! My heart was pounding, I had just located the author who had written those two articles fifty years earlier; we talked for almost an hour.

Mike Keville, old time columnist for *Stunt News*, had encouraged me to find Jack. I now had good news for him. I also contacted Gary McClellan, chairman of PAMPA's Competition and Judging Committee to get the designs officially approved for use in old time competition. Gary revealed that he flew with Ritner in the early 1950s when he was fourteen years old. The two designs, "Twelve" and "Thirteen" were subsequently approved. The discovered facts confirmed that these two designs were indeed built and flown in 1951-52.

Jack was a member of the San Francisco Vultures model airplane club during the late 1940s and early 1950s. He credited Norm Wilson for designing "Twelve" and "Thirteen." Jack won the Western Open Stunt Championship in 1952 using "Thirteen" and was urged to submit an article to *Model Airplane News*. This was just before the 1952 National Model Airplane Championships held for the first time on the west coast at N.A.S. Los Altimos. Jack's submission and accomplishments led to him getting credit for the designs.

Jack competed at contests supported by the Western Associated Modelers and Plymouth Motor Corporation. He made a name for himself at many meets all over California, from 1948-1950. Competing in the Junior division, Jack was the winner of the 22nd Annual Recreation Model Airplane Tournament in 1948. Another contest hosted by the Pterodactyls recorded that Jack won the Class A hand-launched stick contest. In the February 1948 issue of *Model Airplane News,* page 47, it states, "His superlight little stick model turned in an out of sight flight of 2 minutes and 45.2 seconds on the third attempt."

Today, John "Jack" Ritner is a retired state architect, loves sailing, has built a full scale Jodel homebuilt in his living room, and flies regularly. He is also a wonderful watercolor artist. On the way to Tucson, Arizona to attend the Vintage Stunt Championships in 2001, we finally met. I found his wife and him to be wonderful people. Jack continues to be active in modeling, now designing radio controlled sailplanes and gliders. Finally meeting Jack and his wife is a highlight in my modeling career. I was teary-eyed as I left the driveway and reflected on all that had happened during this adventure into a bygone era of model aviation history. I will always cherish this occasion.

I have included this adventure into the past as an example of what can happen to devoted collectors. Sometimes an item of interest comes to us and just owning it isn't enough. The stories and history about an item adds to the desirability and sometimes the value. A trip into the past will most likely uncover new treasures. Museums are enjoyable because of the history that is part of their collections. Discovering the history behind some of the unique items in your collection can be one of the most gratifying moments in your life. Anybody with money can accumulate things. Adding history to your accumulation is the difference between a group of objects and a real collection.

Jack Ritner holding "Twelve" a little more than fifty years after he first flew the design. Plane is powered by an early Fox .29 and tank built from the original plans. Published plans show a 44" wingspan; this should be corrected to 40" using a 36" spar for the wing. Jack said "I noticed the mistake when the November 1954 issue of *Model Airplane News* came out but there was nothing I could do to correct it." This picture was taken in March 2001.

THIRTEEN

by JOHN RITNER

ong-span stunter for .29-.35' engines has mpressive rack-up of wins on the coast. Outstandingly easy to fly through stunts.

► The Thirteen is the end product of a long series of stunt models. All of these models were of the same general design; long tail-moment arm, medium length nose-moment arm and slightly above average size. The Thirteen in the photos is five years old and has consistently been a winner in W.A.M. Contests. It weighs 24 ounces and flies 75 mph on 60-foot .012 lines with a Fox .35 running a 10 x 6 prop.' This basic design flies level with almost no corrections from the pilot, yet it is capable of very tight maneuvers, due to the light wing loading. Square eights, triangular eights, you name it, they are a snap with this model.

Construction is simple, even with a tapered wing, so don't let this part scare you away. These instructions are set up so that you can build straight through; that is, one

Model Airplane News, December 1957, signed article and picture of Jack Ritner, $10-15.

My version of Jack Ritner's "Twelve" signed by him in 2001 on the way to my first trip to the Vintage Stunt Championships in Tucson, Arizona.

The Fourth Plymouth International Model Plane Contest

The Fourth International Model Airplane contest was sponsored by the Plymouth Motor Corporation and was held in Detroit, Michigan on August 15, 1950. This contest has been heralded as one of the all time great contests of model airplane history. Over 180,000 people attended the eight-day affair, proving that the sport and hobby of model airplanes was firmly planted in American culture. The Fort Shelby Hotel was used as headquarters for 446 contestants; all were given red helmets and t-shirts. From the information gathered during research, I actually felt the air of excitement and the anticipation of the events planned for the boys attending. My imagination drifted back and wondered what it would be like to be part of this grand event. I realized the only way to go back in time was through the words of someone who had been there. *Plymouth Model Plane News* from 1950 listed the names and results of the top ten places in an effort to give all who participated recognition. *(Plymouth Model Plane News*, November 15, 1950, 1- 24). This became my starting point for another adventure into the past.

Having located and talked to three men who attended this competition, I am able to convey a little of how they remember this magnificent occasion. They all remembered the weather as being hot and humid. This was more than a contest, as old friendships were rekindled, with new ones being made. Three modelers who have shared their experiences are Jack Ritner of Sacramento, California, Fred Roberts of Dana Point, California, and recently, Jack Hudspeth of Auburn, Washington. Jack Ritner and Jack Hudspeth competed against each other in the junior towline glider event. All were afflicted with the fascination that comes from model airplane competition.

The 1950 contest was near the beginning of Jack Ritner's modeling career. The trips to the Plymouths contents were a big deal for boys flying back then. It was an all-expense paid trip and everyone wanted to go. Jack was flying hand-launched and towline gliders and decided to take up control line combat and stunt after attending the 1950 contest. He did this to improve his chances by being able to accumulate the points needed to win the state meets. At the 1950 Plymouth meet, he placed third in the towline glider event as a junior. He continued flying through 1954 and was part of the San Francisco modeling scene until he joined the Army in 1955.

Fred Roberts was sponsored by his hometown dealership in North Dakota and remembered in detail the event he flew in. I have found discrepancies in some of the records as to his placement but he told me he placed 10th in control line flying scale as a senior contestant. When it was his turn, he started his plane, a Fleet Bi-Plane, ran out on the field and began his flight. All was going well until he went into his wingover and the engine quit just as he attempted the maneuver. "The contest was in a walled ball park. I managed to get the plane down by whipping and running in all kinds of directions while maintaining flying speed. All the judges came out after I got the model down to compliment me on getting it down undamaged and without hitting anything or anybody." He pulled it out and made a smooth landing. The judges were very impressed with his flying ability and remarked they were sure he was going to crash. Fred's Fleet Bi-Plane is pictured on page 41 of the December 1951 issue of *Air Trails*. It was a real show stopper and a testament to his skills as a pilot. Fred went on to a career in scuba diving and became one of that fields pioneers, authoring several books on the subject.

On June 1, 2003, I was able contact one more contestant from the list of winners from the 1950 Plymouth meet. Jack Hudspeth was fifteen years old when he attended the 1950 International Model Plane meet and I spoke with him to get a few more details. He recalled the meet was more laid back than compared to contests of today. Fellow modelers always helped each other and were often willing to share secret winning techniques. Competitors were there to make new friends and hang out with their old ones. Jack also attended the 1947 Nationals in Minnesota, placing 2nd in the junior stunt contest behind David Slagle. Hopefully now Jack is remembered for his contribution to control line stunt history. (*Model Airplane News*, Nov. 1947 pgs. 9-11 and 70-72 '47 Nationals).

By all accounts, Jack was a fine modeler as his record indicates: he won 1st in Class C free flight, 1st in flying scale, 5th in control line stunt, 8th in Class A free flight, and 9th in towline glider. Jack was also the high point junior at the State Championships at Oregon's first state meet held in Portland in 1947. (*Model Airplane News*, Oct 1947, pg. 65). He used kits manufactured during this period for competition and was humble about his modeling past. He was a member of the Olympia Model Airplane Club, the "O-Macs." He no longer builds or flies but says he loved model airplanes; his participation lead to a career in aviation. Jack went on to fly F-106 fighter jets and later became a pilot for Northwest Airlines.

At last count, Jack said he had over eighty trophies stored at his parent's home in Olympia, Washington where his father was the local Plymouth Dealer. After they passed away, he had to make a decision as to the ones he wanted to keep. He kept about forty trophies and gave the rest away. His 1st place trophy from this contest still occupies a special spot in his display case at his Auburn, Washington home.

Many young modelers who went on to be well-known in the modeling community attended the 1950 Plymouth Model Plane contest. Noteworthy are Johnny Brodbeck Jr., Arthur E. Scholl, Dale Kirn, Leslie K. Bartlett, Donald E. Ferguson Jr., Carl R. Wheeley, Donald R. Zipoy, Harold Price, and Harold C. Reinhardt. *(Plymouth Model Plane News*, November 15, 1950, 1- 24). The knowledge and skills developed through the building and flying of model airplanes is immeasurable. No other sport or hobby builds the character of the devotee more than model aviation. The only other organization that comes close or equals this involvement is the Boy Scouts of America. The virtues of modeling are numerous: an ability to work alone and see a project through to completion, the humility that comes from contest participation and the inevitable plane crash. It creates resourcefulness, confidence, and the willingness to take chances by testing new ideas. The ability to use your head, heart, and hands is the foundation of craftsmanship. The pride of success can be felt even when your favorite plane thermals away never to be seen again. The Plymouth Motor Corporation not only sponsored some of the best-remembered model airplane meets, it helped create and mold the character of every participant of this grand event. The legacy is still being felt today.

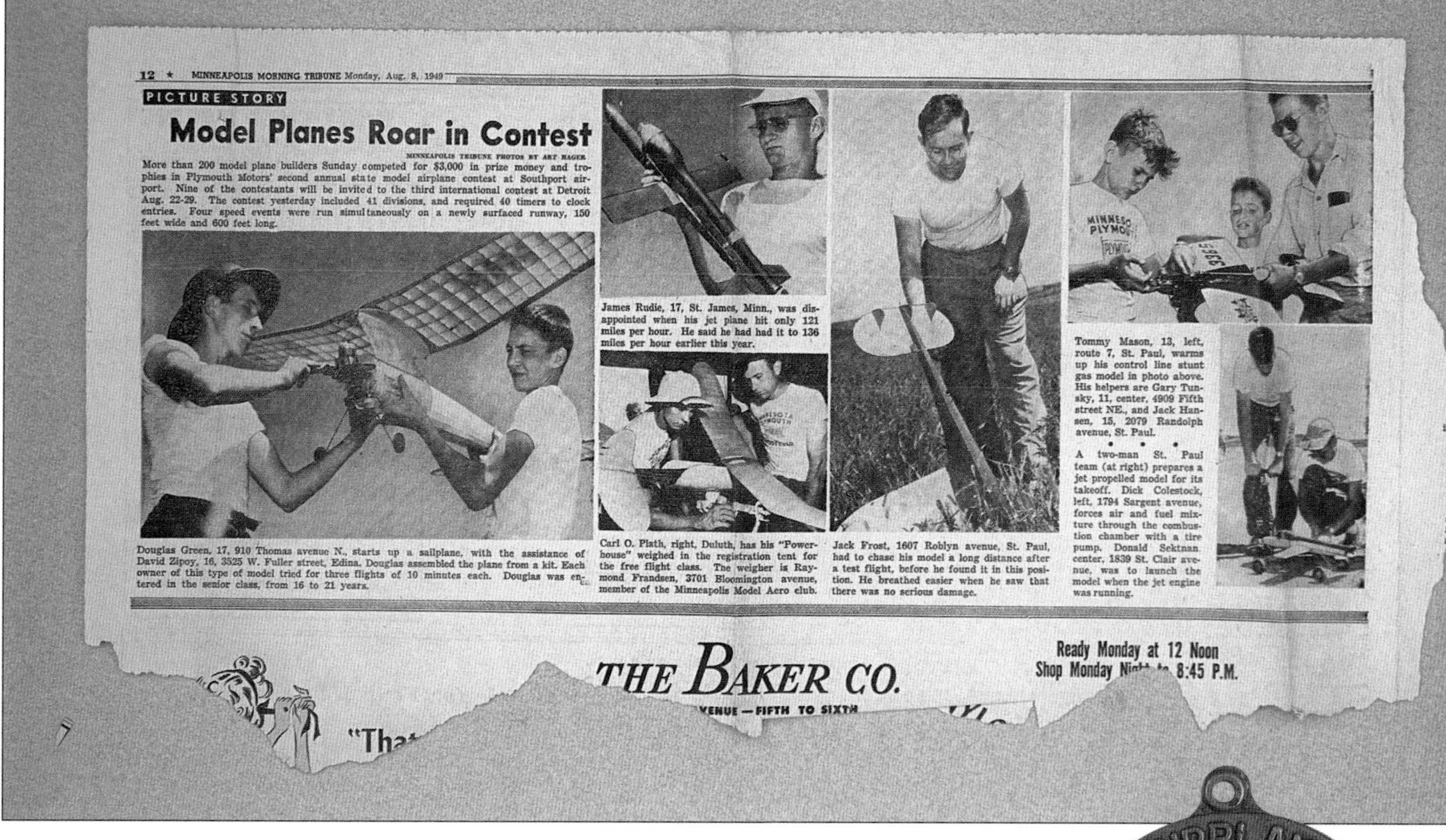

12 ★ MINNEAPOLIS MORNING TRIBUNE Monday, Aug. 8, 1949

PICTURE STORY

Model Planes Roar in Contest

MINNEAPOLIS TRIBUNE PHOTOS BY ART HAGER

More than 200 model plane builders Sunday competed for $3,000 in prize money and trophies in Plymouth Motors' second annual state model airplane contest at Southport airport. Nine of the contestants will be invited to the third international contest at Detroit Aug. 22-29. The contest yesterday included 41 divisions, and required 40 timers to clock entries. Four speed events were run simultaneously on a newly surfaced runway, 150 feet wide and 600 feet long.

Douglas Green, 17, 910 Thomas avenue N., starts up a sailplane, with the assistance of David Zipoy, 16, 3525 W. Fuller street, Edina. Douglas assembled the plane from a kit. Each owner of this type of model tried for three flights of 10 minutes each. Douglas was entered in the senior class, from 16 to 21 years.

James Rudie, 17, St. James, Minn., was disappointed when his jet plane hit only 121 miles per hour. He said he had had it to 136 miles per hour earlier this year.

Carl O. Plath, right, Duluth, has his "Powerhouse" weighed in the registration tent for the free flight class. The weigher is Raymond Frandsen, 3701 Bloomington avenue, member of the Minneapolis Model Aero club.

Jack Frost, 1607 Roblyn avenue, St. Paul, had to chase his model a long distance after a test flight, before he found it in this position. He breathed easier when he saw that there was no serious damage.

Tommy Mason, 13, left, route 7, St. Paul, warms up his control line stunt gas model in photo above. His helpers are Gary Tunsky, 11, center, 4909 Fifth street NE., and Jack Hansen, 15, 2079 Randolph avenue, St. Paul.

A two-man St. Paul team (at right) prepares a jet propelled model for its takeoff. Dick Colestock, left, 1794 Sargent avenue, forces air and fuel mixture through the combustion chamber with a tire pump. Donald Sektnan, center, 1839 St. Clair avenue, was to launch the model when the jet engine was running.

News clipping of the 2nd Plymouth state meet held in Minneapolis, August 8, 1948 from the *Minneapolis Morning Tribune*, from the Red Costlow scrapbook. *Courtesy of Bob Maschi,* $4-10.

Plymouth contest medal from Hill Air Force Base, Utah, c. 1950, $7-15.

PLYMOUTH MODEL PLANE NEWS

PUBLISHED AT INTERNATIONAL MODEL PLANE CONTEST HEADQUARTERS BY PLYMOUTH MOTOR CORPORATION

DETROIT, MICHIGAN, NOV. 15, 1950

FOURTH INTERNATIONAL MODEL PLANE CONTEST TOPS ALL FORMER MODEL AVIATION ACTIVITIES

6-YEAR-OLD STEALS SHOW

The axiom try, try again, paid off in a big way for blonde Freddie Sage of Independence, Missouri. Inspired by a second place in Stunt last year at the age of five, young Freddie resolved to win for himself additional glory in the Fourth International.

And Freddie carried out this resolve in a big way. For with a string of victories that far exceeded his fondest expectations, this six-year old veteran amassed a total of 58 points to win the highest award in his class . . . Freddie was the new Freshman High Point Champion!

To the delight of the more than 1,000 present at the award dinner, this diminutive champion accepted with youthful modesty not one, but six trophies and a total of $400.00 in U. S. Savings Bonds. Young Freddie, who hardly topped in height the trophies he had won, counted among his victories three first place and two second place awards; winning in Towline, Glider, Control Line Stunt, and Control Line Speed Class B; and placing second in Outdoor Stick and in Control Line Speed Class A.

Like a true champion, Freddie promises to be back next year to defend this outstanding Freshman record in the Fifth International and perhaps steal the show once again.

ANNOUNCING THE FIFTH INTERNATIONAL MODEL PLANE CONTEST

W. E. Bartlett, Plymouth Contest Manager, states that the Plymouth Motor Corporation, its Dealers, and the Academy of Model Aviation have settled upon the week of August 20 through 27, 1951, as the date for the Fifth International Model Plane Contest. As previously, these contests will be held at Detroit, and again, the locales will be Selfridge Field, U.S. Air Force Base near Mt. Clemens for free flight; beautiful Belle Isle for control line.

Due to the excellent facilities and the opportunity afforded for a grand day of fun—it is planned to once again hold the Victory Dinner at Bob-Lo Island Park. And because this island is situated in Canadian waters near the mouth of the Detroit River, the glorious 1½ hour boat ride aboard the steamer Columbia to and from the Island will again be a feature.

According to Mr. Bartlett, some con-

(Continued on Page 10)

PLYMOUTH SPONSORED CONTEST ATTRACTS MORE THAN 180,000 FOR NEW ATTENDANCE RECORD

On August 15, 1950, Detroiters awoke to an invasion by an air force of 446 youths smartly attired in red helmets and shirts. This air force had the day before, silently slipped into town, captured the Fort Shelby Hotel and established a headquarters base therein. And to the amazement of many, an airborne Armada was buzzing the downtown air.

From 44 states, the District of Columbia, and Canada the pilots and planes had assembled . . . by invitation of the Plymouth Motor Corporation. They were the 275 Seniors, 142 Juniors, 29 Freshmen and 4 girl champions from 162 local and 14 state contests sponsored by 2,734 Plymouth Dealers; 33 contestants were from Canada. Here were the "tops"—the best modelers of the year, competing for 129 trophies and $7,000.00 in U.S. Savings Bonds in the *Fourth International Model Plane Contest.*

And what a show they put on! More than 180,000 spectators thrilled to the 40 AMA santioned events. This great turn-out of model plane fans set a new all-time attendance record . . . in excess of 17,000 more than witnessed the Third International in 1949. With a full meas-

(Continued on Page 8)

Pictured above is a crowded portion of more than two-thirds of a mile of snow fence. Throngs of cheering spectators filled bleachers and lined the fence for four days at Belle Isle Athletic Field.

Plymouth Model Plane News, November 15, 1950. An amazing historical journey as one reads through this publication. It contains all the winner's through ten places and highlights in every event from the 4th International Model Pane Contest. $15-30.

Fred Roberts original pith helmet from the 1950 4th International Model Plane Contest, $20-40.

President, MoPar Division, Chrysler Corporation.

	Total Points	Name	Town	Total Points	Na
. J.	364	1. LEFEBVRE, David C. *(Sponsored by State of Washington Plymouth Dealers)*	Seattle, Washington	261.0	1. ZIPOY, *(Sponsor*
rnia	356	2. SMITH, Richard R. *(Sponsored by Penobscot County Plymouth Dealers)*	Bangor, Maine	247.5	2. DAVIS, *(Sponsor*
rsey	335	3. KIRN, Dale J. *(Sponsored by Salina Plymouth Dealers)*	Salina, Kansas	173.0	3. KIRN, *(Sponsor*
nois	333	4. RADA, Robert O. *(Sponsored by Chicagoland Plymouth Dealers)*	Berwyn, Illinois	149.7	4. KATKE *(Sponsor*
nois	312	5. SCHOLL, Arthur E. *(Sponsored by Milwaukee County Plymouth Dealers)*	Milwaukee, Wisconsin	147.0	5. GOUVE *(No spon*
ing	310	6. ROBERTS, Fred M. *(Sponsored by North Dakota Plymouth Dealers)*	Bismarck, N. D.	114.5	6. SCHUL *(Sponsor*
nois	304	7. JONES, Edwin O'Neil *(Sponsored by Plymouth Dealers of Owensburg)*	Owensburg, Kentucky	89.0	7. SEKTN *(Sponsor*
ass.	303	8. QUEL, Charles W. *(Sponsored by Greater Pittsburgh Plymouth Dealers)*	Pittsburgh, Pa.	84.5	8. STEBBI *(Sponsor*
nsas	301	9. GROVE, William C. *(Sponsored by Cheyenne Plymouth Dealers)*	Cheyenne, Wyoming	80.5	9. RUDIE, *(Sponsor*
. J.	300	10. SCHRELLO, Don M. *(Sponsored by Greater Pittsburgh Plymouth Dealers)*	Pittsburgh 16, Pa.	71.2	10. KEYS, *(Sponsor*

Fred's name appears in *Plymouth Model Plane News* lists of winners. c. 1950.

his Ike-
Fleet trainer from AT took 10th in sr. scale for F. Roberts, Bismarck, N. D. Scalers surprised judges with neatness, flyability.

Picture of Fred Roberts' "Fleet Bi-Plane Trainer" appearing in the December 1950 issue of *Air Trails*.

Fred Roberts original t-shirt from the 1950 4th International Model Plane Contest, each contestant had his name on the back of the shirt. $10-20.

● Frank L. Cummings, Los Angeles, Calif., sweepstake winner in open class (over 21) with Cl. A.
● Jack Hudspeth, 14, Portland, Ore., junior class point champ congratulated by C. D. Frank Sposite.

Picture of Jack Hudspeth from *Plymouth Model Plane News*. There were several pictures of Jack, as he won in a few events that year. His parents were some of the most supportive parents a kid could have. Jack and his father competed all over the Northwest and traveled to several National Championships. He lives in Auburn, Washington and still has the trophy in the picture.

RULES
Sixth International
Model Plane Contest
SPONSORED BY
PLYMOUTH MOTOR CORPORATION
and the nation-wide CHRYSLER-PLYMOUTH, DESOTO-PLYMOUTH
and DODGE-PLYMOUTH DEALER ORGANIZATIONS
IN CONJUNCTION WITH THE AERO CLUB OF MICHIGAN
DETROIT • AUGUST 1952
20 - 25
SANCTIONED BY THE
ACADEMY OF MODEL AERONAUTICS

Sixth International Model Plane Contest rulebook, sponsored by the Plymouth Motor Corporation in 1952. In 1953, Plymouth ended its sponsorship of the most remembered and written about model airplane contests in the history of model aviation. The rulebook lists past winners of perpetual trophies, builder of the model rules, and awards given to winners, $10-20.

Chapter 7
The Ralph "Red" Costlow Scrapbook

The Ralph E. Costlow scrapbook is an exciting piece of modeling history. It is presented in this book as a collectible and for its historic content. By courtesy of Bob Maschi, I am able to include memories and mementos of the exciting events that took place more than fifty years ago involving model aviation in the Midwest from 1946-1954. Included are modeling activities from the Minneapolis, Minnesota area and surrounding states. In 1947, the Model Airplane National Championships were held in Minneapolis. The event was a sensation for the community, local press, and modelers alike. Along with locally organized events, information about the second Plymouth state contest is also offered for your enjoyment.

After high school, Red studied the development and maintenance of helicopters at the Sikorsky training facility in 1944. He worked for Woodcraft Hobbies, Ace R.C. and as a salesman for Philco and Motorola Corporations. He was an amateur photographer, leather worker, played flute and jazz guitar, in addition to being an avid boat modeler and ham radio operator. In the late 1970s, he built and flew a 1/3 scale Christen Eagle bi-plane. Red passed away March 17, 2003; he was seventy-six years old.

Scrapbooks always reflect the personality of the owner. This collection of original news clippings, papers, photos, and memorabilia is no exception. It provides names, places, and dates that were part of Red Costlow's life as a modeler in 1947. At the time, free flight, team racing, and control line speed model airplanes generated the greatest interest among modelers. The pictures show Red and his friends deeply involved with these popular activities. He belonged to a community of modelers, mentors, competitors, and friends that are all part of this thrilling period of aeromodeling history.

All modelers have mentors and the Minneapolis group was no exception. Walt Billet owned and operated a hobby shop in the Twin Cities, supporting model aviation since Lindberg's trans-Atlantic flight. During World War II, he was responsible for a community project making wooden identification aircraft. He was the creator of a five-foot kitchenware loving cup known as the Walt Billet Trophy and jokingly, as the National Modelplane Washtub Trophy. Bill Effinger of Berkeley Models was the first recipient in 1952. Effinger passed this award on to Ted Clodius of Mirror Model Flying Fair fame and Clodius continued the tradition passing it on to George Gardner for his contributions supporting the PAA event. He was a dedicated promoter and fundraiser for the programs initiated by the Academy of Model Aeronautics. At age 73, he was most proud of getting an airfield established for local kids to fly. His home was the meeting place for the Minneapolis Model Aero Club. He organized the Flying Eight-Ball club, the fund-raising arm for the AMA and was responsible for the financial health of the AMA after World War II. Walt Billet was elected to the Academy of Model Aeronautics Hall of Fame in 1969, becoming one of the first seven recipients of this prestigious award.

Another supporter of model aviation and the Minneapolis Model Aero Club was Mayor Hubert Humphrey. From Red's notes, the mayor was the club sponsor and club meetings were held in his chambers. The club had about 125 to 150 members. It is noted by Red "when we needed help, we got it." At the yearly club banquet, the primary speaker was the mayor. Knowing the city mayor had its advantages, especially when complaining neighbors threatened to shut down a "super flying field" because of noise. "Rumor has it that the Mayor spread the word that an industrial complex was going in there. All of a sudden, the people that complained were protesting that the city was taking the flying field from these poor modelers. We never were able to prove it, but we had no more problems from the neighbors." (Red Costlow, in a letter dated 1980.)

The scrapbook contains twenty news clippings from 1947-1954, seventy-nine photos of modelers, airplane models, and contests, including seventeen photos of the activities at the 1947 Nationals. Also included are significant news articles of 1947 Grand National Champion, Frank Cummings and his wife, control line speed champions and Red's best friends, Bob Thor and Glen Temte, as well as a news clipping of Ralph, Bob Thor, and Ray Lagermeir signing up for the second Plymouth State meet. (This photo was featured in the *Plymouth Dealers Contest Guide Book)*. News articles on the local state Plymouth meet with pictures were also saved.

Photos of notable modelers include Leon Shulman and his diesel powered stunter. He produced the Drone diesel engines and was a pioneer of early radio control modeling. One nice group photo of early radio control planes and pilots is part of this collection. A photo of the famous J.C. "Madman" Yates fabulous "Dragon" stunter, that placed 2nd behind Bob Tucker at the 1947 Nationals is included. There are several pictures of Robert M. Thor who flew in the senior speed events, placing 1st in Class VI, 2nd in Class III, and 3rd in Class I and II speed events at the 1947 Nationals. Bob Thor and Glen Temte's jet powered plane, "BJ-6," held the world record briefly with a top speed of 179.03 mph. It is featured in the December 1948 issue of *Air Trails* and in the *Air Trails Annual for 1952*. Glen Temte is pictured in a news article holding the remains of the jet aircraft that broke loose from the lines and caught fire. (Glen Temte and Bob Thor, *Air Trails*, December. 1948, 45-47, 99-101). Ralph flew control line speed using a McCoy .49 and Class III open free flight with an original design powered with an Arden .19 at the 1947 Nationals.

There are several pictures from the 1958 National Championships featuring R.C. planes, the most famous being Fred Dunn's amazing Astro Hog design. Several were entered in the national contest. This design swept the first four places in aerobatics according to a Sig Manufacturing ad for the updated version of this plane. Another photo is of Dale Root of Oakland, California and his famous radio control design the "Low Ender." The original photo appears in the March 1958 issue of

American Modeler magazine as part of the article featuring the "Low Ender." Dale also designed the early 1/2 A radio control plane, "Little Freak 27" featured in the *Air Trails Model Annual for 1954*. (*Air Trails Model Annual for 1954*, 34-35). Dale was elected to the AMA Hall of Fame in 1988.

Red Costlow gained an early interest in radio control. There are photos of him on television from around 1957 along with Woodcraft Hobby Store owner Claude Newman. Newman sponsored an early Minneapolis television show featuring hobbies. Red is shown demonstrating early radio gear controlling boats and engines on the show. His wife Birdie took the pictures. He teamed up with Don Kamm in 1957 to produce an "Ace exclusive designer approved kit," the all transistor TR 4.5 Receiver Kit, selling through 1961. His name appears with Don Kamm on the front of the receiver; an ad for this kit is on page 51 in the February 1959 issue of *American Modeler*. In October 1980, his article "Building Radio Transmitters: The Case for Kits" appeared in *Craft, Model and Hobby Industry* magazine. From the pictures in the scrapbook and the letters he wrote, his relationship with Ace R.C. continued through 1985. In the June 1981 issue of *Scale RC Modeler*, Red is pictured with his 1/3 scale Christen Eagle in an Ace R.C. ad for Atlas servos. He worked for Ace R.C. for eight years, about the time when the Ace 4-20, 4-40, and 4-60 Doc Mathews designed model kits first came on the market.

Scrapbooks in general are overlooked collectibles; most are bought and broken up for profit. The Red Costlow scrapbook is included in this book for the reader's enjoyment and to give historical perspective to the collectibles of the model airplane craze that swept the nation during this time. Much of what is available to collectors today comes from this era, 1945-1965. Pricing items from a person's life was hard. It was a privilege to have even viewed this scrapbook and include it in this book. As my hands touched the items, and examined the photos of this storybook in time, I was able to look into the mind and life of the man who held these things dear to his heart. I truly believe the scrapbook came to me through providence as this book took on a life of its own as it neared completion. I dedicate this chapter to Red Costlow and all the modelers who aspired to be champions; no one remembers who came in second, but there would be no winners without them.

All images in this section are from the Red Costlow scrap book and are shown courtesy of Bob Maschi.

Original photo of Red Costlow with two trophies, Class B speed and the Browns' Hobbycraft Class C speed trophy. The name of the plane "Hell-n-Gore" was named by his wife Birdie, c. 1947-48. *Courtesy of Bob Maschi,* $2-5.

Red holding his control line speed creation using a McCoy .49. It went 101.3 mph on the first flight to win a second place finish, February 1, 1947. *Courtesy of Bob Maschi,* $2-5.

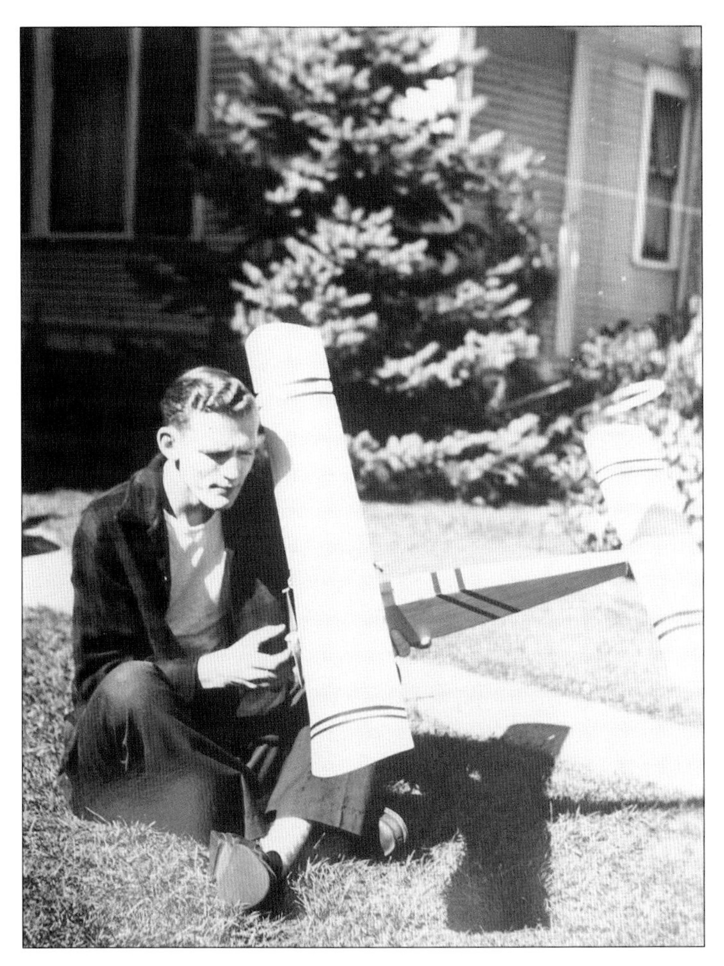

Photo of Red and his Arden .19 powered original free flight model airplane, c. 1947. He used this plane to compete at the 1947 Nationals. *Courtesy of Bob Maschi,* $2-5.

Photo of Red holding a team racer, c. 1949-50. The Team Racing event was developed around 1948-49. Keith Storey's "The Key" appeared in *Air Trails*, March 1949 making it the first published team race design. Berkeley Models eventually kitted "The Key." Red was one of the pioneers of this event in the Minneapolis area and gave talks on building, flying, and conducting the event. *Courtesy of Bob Maschi,* $2-5.

Photo of Red with another free flight plane, c. 1950. *Courtesy of Bob Maschi,* $2-5.

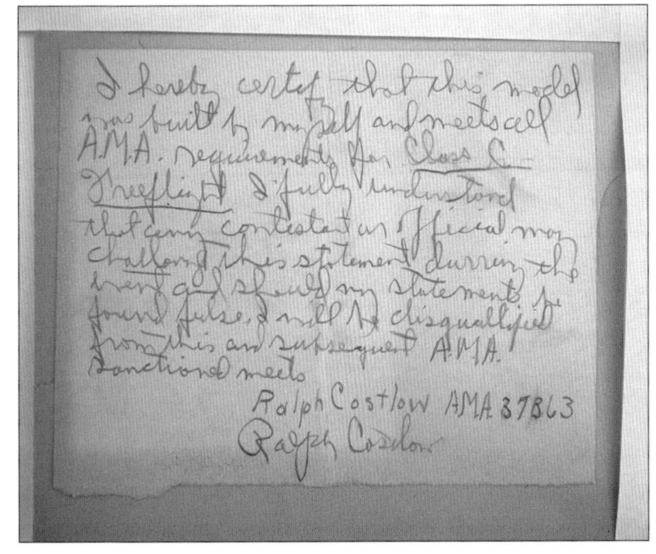

I hereby certify that this model
was built by myself and meets all
A.M.A. requirements for Class C
Freeflight. I fully understand
that any contestant or official may
challenge this statement during the
event and should my statements be
found false, I will be disqualified
from this and subsequent A.M.A.
sanctioned meets

Ralph Costlow AMA 37863
Ralph Costlow

Red Costlow's original declaration that he was the builder of his Class III free flight model at the 1947 Nationals. *Courtesy of Bob Maschi,* $5-10.

Photo of Red holding his "Satan's Special" speed plane, c. 1948. *Courtesy of Bob Maschi,* $2-5.

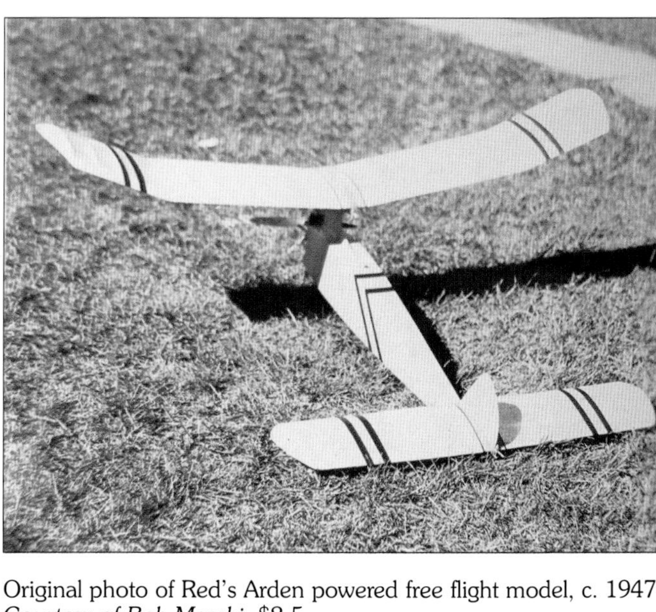

Original photo of Red's Arden powered free flight model, c. 1947. *Courtesy of Bob Maschi,* $2-5.

Photo of a Dyna-jet powered speed plane by Bob Thor. *Courtesy of Bob Maschi.* $2-5.

Original photo of famous speed flyer Bob Thor with the predecessor to the "BJ-6" jet powered speed plane. *Courtesy of Bob Maschi*. $2-5.

Photo of speed flyer Bob Thor getting pull tested at the 1947 Nationals. *Courtesy of Bob Maschi.* $2-5.

Photo of Bob Thor getting ready to fly his jet speed plane. *Courtesy of Bob Maschi.* $2-5.

Bob Thor receiving his trophy at the 2nd International Model Plane Contest in 1948.

Windshield admission sticker from the 1947 Nationals. When was the last time you saw one of these? *Courtesy of Bob Maschi.* $10-20.

AIR TRAILS PARADE OF WINNERS—Another National Record Holder

World's Fastest Model

BY GLENN TEMTE AND BOB THOR

HERE'S THE JET THAT DID 179.03 MPH IN RECORD TRIALS THEN MADE HIGHEST SPEED AT PLYMOUTH MEET

MINNESOTA winters are cold. That alone probably contributed more to the development of this record-breaking jet model than anything else.

During the winter months any extensive U-control flying in Minneapolis was limited to local club contests on alternate Sundays in the University of Minnesota field house. Reciprocating engines, even with good electric starters, just didn't run when confronted with ten-below-zero weather. From previous experience with a jet-powered race car, we knew of the simple operation

which was no doubt adequate for the purpose intended but which just didn't seem to fit into the speed picture.

Our first design thoughts were toward complete housing of the engine, but these were quickly given up when we discovered how great a frontal area would be required to streamline the necessary insulation. The present compromise design was evolved, with the engine half buried in the fuselage, and B. J. I was constructed as a rugged transition trainer.

Number I was built in two and a half days with the

Article on the worlds fastest jet by Bob Thor and Glen Temte from *Air Trails*, December 1948.

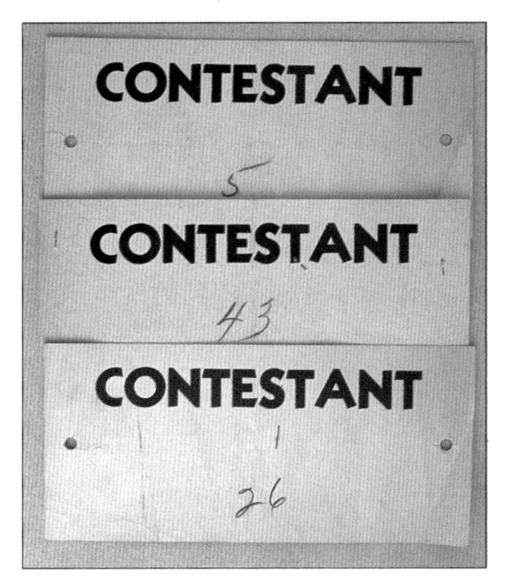

Red's contestant numbers from the 1947 Nationals. The contestant numbers have little value after being separated from the scrapbook. Many items is the scrapbook only have value collectively, as each one complements the other items. Many modelers have mementos that are sentimental and acknowledge their modeling careers. *Courtesy of Bob Maschi.*

Photo of Bob Thor with a McCoy .49 powered speed plane. Articles on Glen Temte and Bob Thor also appeared in *Model Craftsman.* They were big fans of some of the nationally known Texas speed fliers and replicated some of their models. The scrapbook contained pictures of Tex Russel's unusual speed jobs. *Courtesy of Bob Maschi.* $2-5.

Helper's pass from the 1948 Nationals in Olathe, Kansas. The Ski-Hi Model Airplane Club of Kansas City helped with the Nationals. *Courtesy of Bob Maschi.* $2-5.

Contestant and helper ribbons from the 1947 Nationals. *Courtesy of Bob Maschi.* $5-10.

"Dragon" stunter, by J.C. "Madman" Yates, placed second in Open Stunt, Junior Champion. David Slagel went on to win the Walker Cup at the 1947 Nationals. The "Dragon" is featured in *Air World*, November 1947. *Courtesy of Bob Maschi.* $5-10.

Radio control at the 1947 Nationals. *Courtesy of Bob Maschi.* $5-10.

Early stunt plane at the 1947 Nationals. *Courtesy of Bob Maschi.* $2-5.

Front of the large radio control plane. The turn out at the 1947 Nationals in the Radio Control event was poor and I don't believe this plane flew. *Courtesy of Bob Maschi.* $3-5.

Leon Shulman and his stunt plane, shown wearing his Brooklyn Skyscrapers MAC t-shirt, 1947 Nationals. The Brooklyn Skyscrapers Model Airplane Club was founded in 1936. *Courtesy of Bob Maschi.* $5-10.

Leon Shulman and his stunt plane at the 1947 Nationals. *Courtesy of Bob Maschi.* $2-5.

Original news clipping of the 1947 National Champion, Frank Cummings Jr. and his wife. *Courtesy of Bob Maschi.* $5-10.

Free flight plane being launched at the 1947 Nationals. One picture shows Red standing in the free flight processing line and the caption under the photo reads "two hours to get one flight, some fun!" *Courtesy of Bob Maschi.* $2-5.

MODERN CRAFT BUILDERS IN JET AGE, TOO

Little Planes, But Big Business

JECTOR, VANE, pulse and thrust have become familiar words in the vocabulary of the model plane builder.

In combination with a few ounces of gasoline, they can send a 25-ounce package of balsa wood and metal hurtling through space at 150 miles an hour.

The age of jet propulsion—and new speed records—is as much of a challenge to the model plane builder as cracking the supersonic barrier is to airforce pilots.

One of the experts in the model jet field is Robert Thor, 22, of 3633 Garfield avenue, himself an air force veteran.

A year ago his jet ship took first place in the speed division of the International Model Airplane contest at Detroit and won for him a $100 cash prize, a permanent trophy and one year's possession of a $10,000 revolving trophy.

When Plymouth Motors sponsors its state model airplane meet at Southport airport at Rosemount, Minn., Aug. 7, Thor will put his model plane know-how to work in the role of co-director with Paul Ring.

Preliminary district contests to decide qualifiers for the state meet have been scheduled this month

BOB THOR SHOWS JET (above) AND CONVENTIONAL PLANES
Model champion will be co-director of state meet Aug. 7.

an air intake valve, and when air is forced through from a tire

and forces the vane open.

After the fuel mixture gets past

Bob Thor in an original news clipping describing the up coming state Plymouth meet, which he co-directed along with 1947 Nationals director Paul Ring, c. 1948. *Courtesy of Bob Maschi.* $2-5.

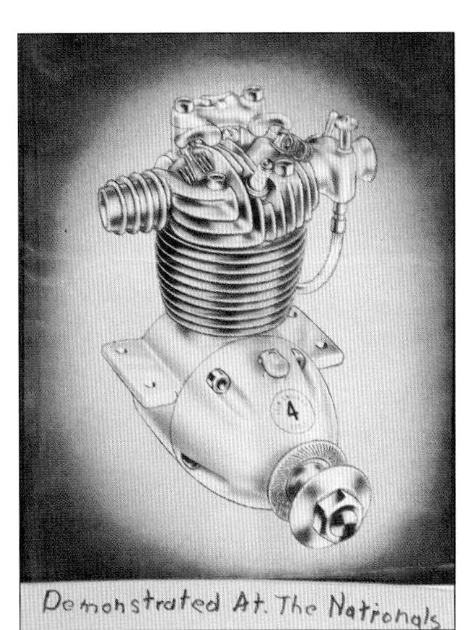

Photo from a brochure on the 1947 Leja .994 four cycle engine, this rare engine was demonstrated at the 1947 Nationals. *Courtesy of Bob Maschi.* $5-10.

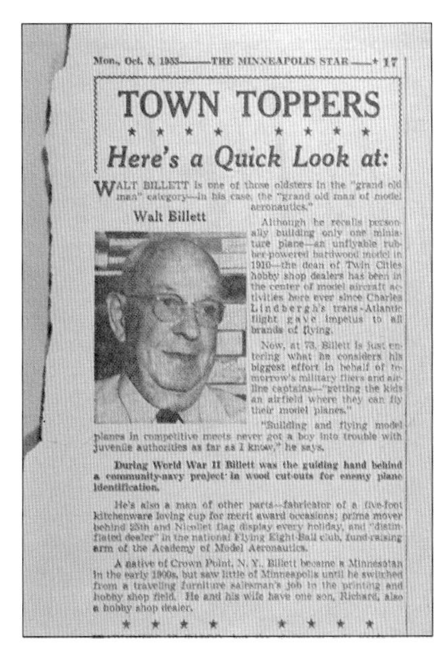

Mon., Oct. 5, 1953——THE MINNEAPOLIS STAR——17

TOWN TOPPERS

★ ★ ★ ★ ★ ★ ★ ★

Here's a Quick Look at:

WALT BILLETT is one of those oldsters in the "grand old man" category—in his case, the "grand old man of model aeronautics."

Walt Billett

Although he recalls personally building only one miniature plane—an unflyable rubber-powered hardwood model in 1910—the dean of Twin Cities hobby shop dealers has been in the center of model aircraft activities here ever since Charles Lindbergh's trans-Atlantic flight gave impetus to all brands of flying.

Now, at 73, Billett is just entering what he considers his biggest effort in behalf of tomorrow's military fliers and airline captains—"getting the kids an airfield where they can fly their model planes."

"Building and flying model planes in competitive meets never got a boy into trouble with juvenile authorities as far as I know," he says.

During World War II Billett was the guiding hand behind a community-navy project in wood cut-outs for enemy plane identification.

He's also a man of other parts—fabricator of a five-foot kitchenware loving cup for merit award occasions; prime mover behind 25th and Nicollet flag display every holiday, and "distinguished dealer" in the national Flying Eight-Ball club, fund-raising arm of the Academy of Model Aeronautics.

A native of Crown Point, N. Y., Billett became a Minnesotan in the early 1900s, but saw little of Minneapolis until he switched from a traveling furniture salesman's job in the printing and hobby shop field. He and his wife have one son, Richard, also a hobby shop dealer.

★ ★ ★ ★ ★ ★ ★ ★

News clipping on Walt Billet. *Courtesy of Bob Maschi.* $2-3.

Photo of early radio control flyers, 8"x 10" black and white, c. 1950s. *Courtesy of Bob Maschi*. $10-15.

JET MODEL PLANE SPEEDS 137 MPH

City Youth Tops Meet Record

Model Airplane Trophies Awarded

Model Air Show Thrills Audience

Featured by Loops Dives and Crashes

WINNERS NAMED IN AERO EVENT

Model Planes Soar at Old 'U' Airport

STATE MODEL PLANE MEET

Miniature Air Armada to Fill Rosemount Sky

S. D. TOWN OPENS 'BUSINESS' WEEK

Jet Model Plane Contestants Fail to Crack Record

Model Airplane Club Conducts Air Show

Various news clippings from the scrapbook on model airplane contests in the Minneapolis area. *Courtesy of Bob Maschi*. $3-7.

Jet Model Plane Contestants Fail to Crack Record

A national speed record for jet propelled model plans set July 1[1] by Glenn H. Temte, Minneapoli[s] fireman, stood intact today afte[r] numerous attempts were made t[o] better the mark in competitio[n] Sunday.

With a speed of 137.72 miles pe[r] hour, Don Block, 3029 Holmes ave nue, topped all contestants in th[e] jet-propelled class at Sunday's mee[t] at Southport airport. But it fell 4[2] miles an hour short of Temte's rec ord-smashing attainment.

Roger Sorenson, 1379 Osceola avenue, St. Paul, won first place in the stunting planes division.

Class winners in the meet sponsored by Willys Motor Co. and Minneapolis Model Aero club include:

Class D—Bob Green, 307 Dupont avenue N., 127.75 miles per hour; Class C—Ralph Costlow, 1813 Fifteenth avenue S.; Class C junior —Loran Sullivan, 2143 E. Jefferson avenue, St. Paul, and Jim Holmbeck, Duluth, tied at 100 miles an hour; Class B junior—Steve Braun, 4379 Coolidge street, 67.6; Class B senior—Norman Mayeda, 692 Pleasant avenue, St. Paul, 90.45; Class A senior—Bill Chandler, 1225 Juliett avenue, St. Paul, 90.9.

MINNEAPOLIS MORNING TRIBUNE
26 ★ Monday, June 6, 1949

S. D. TOWN OPENS 'BUSINESS' WEEK

Plane Show, Concert Feature First Day

SPECIAL TO MINNEAPOLIS TRIBUNE

MADISON, S. D.—A model airplane demonstration and a concert by a massed choir of 200 voices Sunday opened Madison's "Know Your Own Strength" week to promote the city's retail business concerns.

The merchandising event, run in conjunction with the community's annual "Welcome, Neighbor" celebration, will continue through Saturday.

It is sponsored jointly by the Madison Chamber of Commerce, the Minneapolis Chamber of Commerce, the St. Paul Association of Commerce and Pathfinder magazine.

The Twin Cities groups are interested in promoting the sale of products manufactured by or distributed through firms in the Twin Cities area.

More than 300 witnessed the model airplane show put on by six Twin Cities hobbyists under the sponsorship of the Madison Kiwanis club.

The fliers were Ralph E. Costlow, Robert Green, Melvin Stone, Robert Thor, Donald Block, all of Minneapolis, and Norman Mayeda, St. Paul. Ed Hallenbach of Madison also participated.

Article on Don Block's failed attempt to break the National speed record on July 11, 1949 and a Model Airplane Show in Red's hometown on June 6, 1949. Don Block is still alive and flying occasionally in the Minneapolis area. *Courtesy of Bob Maschi*. $2-3.

10—THE MINNEAPOLIS STAR—Tues., July 20, 1954

RAY LAGERMEIER SHOWS MODEL PLANE

He's shooting for world title

★ ★ ★ ★ ★ ★ ★ ★

St. Louis Park Man to Try for World Model Air Title

"World's champion model aeronaut."

Ray Lagermeier, 27, 6820 Excelsior boulevard, St. Louis Park, will be shooting for no less a prize than that when he competes in the World Model Air Olympics at Long Island, N. Y., Saturday through Monday.

Winner of Minnesota and central states regional competition held earlier this summer, Lagermeier will be one of four United States contestants in the world meet sponsored by the Academy of Model Aeronautics. The others are from California, Missouri and Washington.

Lagermeier will go to the international contest equipped with a victory habit and a free flight gas model plane which has made a flight of 11 minutes and 38 seconds.

The score of winner cups in his trophy case includes one for third place in the 1947 Plymouth international meet.

Lagermeier will be competing at Long Island backed by moral support from the newly reorganized Minneapolis Model Aero club. President is Roland Dexter, 4343 NE. Monroe street, Upper Midwest grand champion in model aeronautics competition for 1953.

Both Lagermeier and Dexter will be among competitors in the sixth annual PAA load meet at Monticello, Minn., Sept. 5. Grand champion trophy will be sponsored by the Minneapolis Star and Tribune.

Quist New Head of Park Board

Walter P. Quist is the new president of the board of park commissioners for the ensuing year.

He succeeds Edwin L. Haislet, who did not seek re-election.

Quist served two one-year terms as board president between 1950 and 1952. He has been a member of the park board since March 8, 1935, and in point of service is now the oldest of the 15 park commissioners.

Elected vice president for the

5 Aboard Raft Day Overdue

AVALON, SANTA CATA-

News clipping of Ray Lagermeir, 1954, getting ready to go to the World Free Flight Championships held at Long Island, New York. He was one of four U.S. contestants chosen to compete. I found out from Red's wife Birdie that they were responsible for getting Ray and his wife together. Glen Temte, Bob Thor, Ray Lagermeir, and Red were the best of friends. Ray is the only one of old gang still living. *Courtesy of Bob Maschi*. $2-5.

TROPHY FOR MODEL PLANE WINNERS—Among prizes offered in the national model airplane contest at Monticello, Minn., Monday through Thursday is this trophy for the class A gas open model winner being polished by Nanette Pommer at the Pommer Co., 400 Gorham building. In addition to a Piper Cub plane, a $1,650 aeronautics scholarship and cash prizes, entrants will compete for 250 trophies. The award dinner is scheduled for Coffman Memorial union on the University of Minnesota campus at 7:30 p.m. next Friday. The meet is sponsored by the American Legion and 40 & 8.

The National Championship Trophy eventually won by Frank Cummings (a Piper Cub was also awarded to Frank). He was elected to the AMA Hall of Fame in 1986. *Courtesy of Bob Maschi*. $2-3.

"HA'R WE GO NOW!"

Well the Plymouth Meet has been here and gone. Some of you are quite pleased with your results and others naturally disappointed with their hard luck.

And then again a great many of you flyers have been disappointed with the 21 year age limit in recent meets.

Here's your chance to get in there and pitch. No age limit and a good prize list with lots of fun in sight in the coming —

PAA LOAD MEET, SUNDAY, AUGUST 13th

And you younger sprouts, here's your opportunity to get in another meet and see how it is really done or better still, show up your elders.

There's been a lot of discussion about this age and ability question lately. The old boys are on the spot.

PAA Load has two engine Classes, A and B with two age classes in each, Combination Jr.-Sr. and Open. $210.00 in Cash with Trophies and Merchandise Prizes.

There will also be Stunt and Team Racing Events with suitable Trophies and Merchandise Prizes.

Team Racing in Class B, open only and the most fun yet in model flying.

The Radio Control boys will also do their stuff, the first time in any meet in this area.

Get going NOW to be ready for this big 3 Ring Circus Meet.

Full information at any Association Hobby Shop or write or phone Walt Billett, 2548 Nicollet Ave., Regent 0337.

Ralph Costlow reports great activity in Team Racing in Council Bluffs, Sioux City, Omaha, Waterloo and other Iowa spots. Has offered to give a chalk talk in Walt Billett's Rumpus Room, 2548 Nicollet Ave., Monday evening, July 31st. Anyone interested in Team Racing is invited. 7-30

Post card announcing the next club meeting at Walt Billet's home, July 26, 1950. *Courtesy of Bob Maschi*. $2-3.

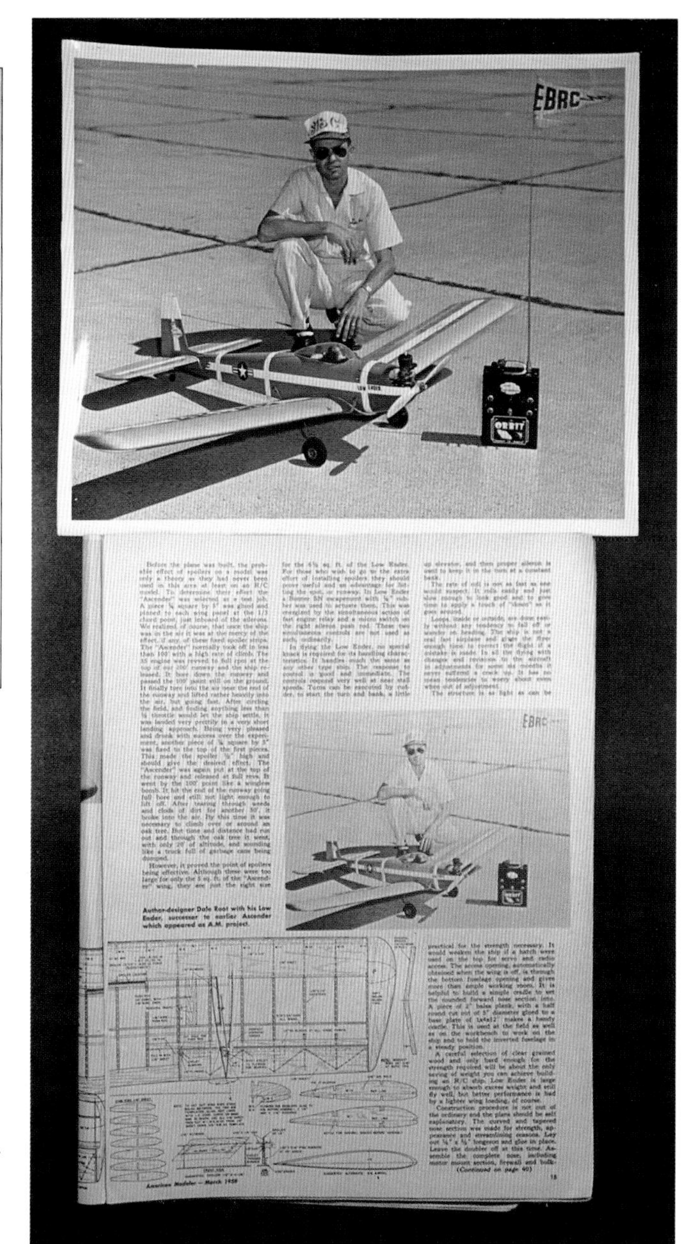

Original photo of Dale Root and article on his famous "Low-Ender" featured in *American Modeler*, March 1959. Another picture of this model at the 1958 nationals is on the cover of *Flying Models*, October 1959. *Courtesy of Bob Maschi*. $15.

Red Costlow with planes from the Ace R.C. product line, 1980, 8" x 10" black and white photo. *Courtesy of Bob Maschi*. $10.

Ralph "Red" Costlow's 1/3 scale Christian Eagle, c. 1979. *Courtesy of Bob Maschi*. $10

Appendix A
Notable eBay Auctions July 2002 to July 2003

"There are no fixed prices for antiques and collectibles. Value floats based on time, place, and individuals involved."

—Harry Rinker
Antiques and Collectibles Magazine
February 2002

Since eBay is used and viewed by collectors worldwide, I believe newly published collector books *should* address this venue. Internet collecting has reshaped regional markets that once stood alone and are now competing globally. It has affected the value of antiques and collectibles at every level of the market place. A greater selection of the more common items is now available and collectors can wait to pick from the best stuff being listed each week. Rare and hard to find items are now easier to find. Over 4000 auctions are listed each week for items related to model airplanes. For the model airplane enthusiast, eBay has become so important that nice collections are being built entirely from these weekly auctions.

The downside to Internet collecting is becoming known as more people use this venue. Trusting sellers seems to be the number one issue facing today's eBay buyers. This issue of trust can be reflected in the final auction values. Sellers with good reputations appear to receive more money for like items. Be aware that even good sellers make mistakes; almost all are willing to rectify the deal and satisfy the buyer. The feedback system used by eBay works to protect both parties when completing a transaction. Leaving feedback should be taken seriously as credibility and reputation play an important role in the exciting world of eBay.

The fear of being cheated or not receiving your purchase is real. Almost every buyer I have talked to has had at least one disappointment. Nothing is more disheartening when the long awaited package arrives and the kit you were told was "complete" is nothing more than left over pieces of balsa wood. Dishonesty can work both ways as I have heard stories of parts being exchanged on engines by the purchaser and then returned to the seller to get his money back. It is hard to buy new and used objects from a two sentence item descriptions and a couple of pictures. Another thing to watch out for are unreasonably high shipping and handling costs. Communication before bidding can solve many unnecessary misunderstandings. The sad fact is that a lot of just plain junk is being unloaded in today's antique and collectibles market and as long as people are willing to keep buying broken and incomplete goods, they will continue to be sold.

If you truly desire collector quality items, buying from established sellers with good reputations is the way to go. For the most part, most sellers are honest. Notable eBay auctions are a record of items that were actually sold and list the exact price paid. The quality of these items is the best to be found during this past year. All are new, new in the box or like new, and rare, or hard to find items. While there are bargains to be found on eBay, they are the exception rather than the rule. Be prepared to pay for the good stuff, but be watchful and knowledgeable when an item exceeds a realistic price. I have watched many items go for extraordinary prices. Recently a 1960s Wen-Mac P-38 Lightning, mint in the box went for $2,600. This exciting auction was fun to follow the week it was listed!

Another downfall is being outbid by twenty-five cents or a dollar, especially if you were the only bidder all week long. I have been "sniped" quite a few times on some nice auctions before action was taken. It is particularly hard to aviod being sniped if you don't have access to a computer or need to be away from your computer at the time an auction is scheduled to end.

There are three ways to win an auction. The first is to bid your best offer and hope no one outbids you in the final moments. If you bid more than the object is worth, a jealous collector can make you pay. There seems to be a bit of competitiveness and sometimes a degree of frustration on eBay trying to compete against bidders whose desire for an item exceeds the real value. The second way to win is to sit in front of your computer and submit a bid or up your bid in the final moments. This can be inconvenient at times, for auctions can end at any hour during a twenty-four hour period. The third way to win is use an automated bidding service. I have used Auction Sniper™ with great success. The beauty of this service is it will bid for you without you being there; your computer does not even have to be turned on. Only someone willing to pay more than you can outbid you using this method. Your high bid remains a secret until the auction ends. It is easy to find the top price bid on eBay's automated system, and then decide if you want to pay more.

On a more exciting note, eBay has enabled collectors to find items they have never seen before. Aside from rare disappointments, many pleasant surprises await potential buyers. As a seller at numerous shows, I have found the common answer to "What are you looking for?" is "When I see it, I'll know what it is!" The Internet and eBay have become a giant swap meet at the tip of your fingers and right in your home. Most collectors of flying model collectibles enjoy eBay. All will readily give their opinion and experiences about using this marvelous new market place. You probably didn't know you wanted it until you saw it on eBay.

There are three important reasons for including this list of notable eBay auctions. The first reason is so that readers can see the wide variety and quality of flying models collectibles that can be found at on-line auctions. The second reason is so that potential buyers can get an idea of the terminology and descriptions used by sellers to describe and rate their collectibles for sale. The third reason for including the list in this book is its value in watching market place trends. Some collector books will never be updated, rendering them useless for determining trends. In a year or two, you will still be able to use this section as a guide to the trends that have taken place since they were recorded. Like an old catalog, price trends can be documented and having a good idea of market trends can be an excellent way to find a starting point for pricing. Trends will identify those collectibles that increase in value and those that do not.

This list **should not** be used as a price guide for assigning value. Sometimes a collector will pay anything to add that missing link in their collection. The prices paid do not always reflect true value or worth.

Often, over three hundred potential buyers view eBay items of extreme interest with great regularity in a seven-day period. An analysis of trends featuring collector quality items shows steady price increases for objects in new condition. Interest in flying models and their history should remain steady for several years to come with some marvelous collections being created. This venue should continue to shape pricing of these collectibles for a while. Today, the market remains strong with competitive bidding on highly sought after items.

Condition and desirability affect value in all collectible markets. The condition of boxes and packaging can sometimes affect the price of an object dramatically. Engines with boxes are more desired but will not keep those without from being sold. One collector related that he listed an Arden .19 model airplane engine with a reserve price of $90; the top bid was $82. A week later, he re-listed the same engine with an original box. Seven days later, it sold for $180. Does this mean someone paid a hundred dollars for a box? Older model airplane kits with excellent boxes simply command higher prices because most are purchased to be displayed. Colorful graphics on packaging is often a reflection of how the products were marketed to young modelers. It is hard not to get excited about an old Cleveland kit or bubble pack Cox engine in pristine condition.

Glossary of Terms used in Notable eBay Auctions

Here is a list of terms used to describe the condition of sold items included in this section. I have tried to give an accurate idea of condition by using the way the seller described the item, as well as from the pictures of the actual listing. Also, it is important to note that good pictures can really make a difference in the price received.

Average. Used with some wear and tear but still very usable.
Good condition. Very usable, complete, sometimes used (especially if the contents were not shown in the auction pictures). Some items are only found in this condition.
Tatty. Shop worn, a little beat up, stained, torn, split; many items on eBay are being offered in this condition. A term used by sellers in the United Kingdom.
Shop worn. This occurs over time usually from being stored openly and shuffled about the shop.
Above average. Item is in really good condition, may have been used (in the case of engines and books). Well cared for or even new but seller did not want to mislead anyone. Stored well over time.
Used but in excellent condition. A very well cared for item, may have been used very little. This is good example of an honest seller (especially when an item is new, but they aren't quite sure).
OK condition. Usable but not really collector quality unless the item is hard to find.
Excellent condition. Well cared for item, may even be new but some sellers know nothing about the things they are selling, they trust the buyer to know what they are buying.
Started. Applies to kits; some assembly may have occurred, parts are punched out, can still be an excellent buy for someone wanting to build the kit.
Complete. Appears to be all there, some assembly may have taken place; applies to items with multiple parts, (you may have to trust the seller on this one). I have viewed many items listed and from experience, they looked complete.
L.N. Like new, same as in excellent condition; could be new but seller is being honest.
N.I.B. New in box, this term can mean many things as far as the box condition goes but the object in the box has never been used.
N.I.P. New in pack, used to describe bubble pack items; the condition of the packaging can vary but the item is new and unused. Cox used two packages that are referred to as bubble pack, one had a red plastic base and the other came on a card enabling it to be hung on a hook. The bubble pack on the card was used on OK Cubs, K&B, Testors, Gilbert, and Wen-Mac small engines.
M.I.B. Mint in box, the condition of the box is also near perfect or new.
Mint. A high quality item near perfect and in new condition.
New sealed in box. Item has never seen the light of day; it is very rare to find stuff like this, but it does occur.
Perfect. The best of the best.
Pristine. Just like perfect, a real nice item.
Beautiful. In near perfect condition.
Hobby Shop new. Just like you would have purchased the item from a hobby shop or distributor.

Other Terminology:
Jewel box. Cox engines that were sold in a clear plastic box in the 1960s and 1970s are described by collectors this way. Jim Walker's Firecracker .065 engine came in a square plastic box around 1956.
NVA. Needle valve assembly.
R.C. Radio control or radio controlled.
R.T.F. Ready to fly.
U/C. U-control, a control line version.

Engines

Aero .35 in-line control line engine from 1963, N.I.B. $450
Al-Ko 726 Czechoslovakian 1941-43 ignition engine, four bolt head, "appears to be brand new." $202.50
Apex Skylark '56' 1936, "appears new," a real nice example. $406
Arden .099 N.I.B. $316
Aristo Pulse Jet engine, made in Germany, box was shop worn, the engine was mint. $250
Atom .098 Super from 1941, in great condition. $178.15
Atom .09 Super from 1941, a virgin engine with an perfect box, copied instructions. $312.77
Atom .09 MK II, 1942, N.I.B. $260
Atwood .049 Shriek 1956 Free Flight version, N.I.B. $114.50
Avion Mercury 1.61 ignition engine, from 1947 with black case, # 1251, an amazing example, N.I.B. with original brochure. $651
Baby Cyclone .36 spark ignition engine from 1938, like new condition. $465.01
Bantam .19, 1947, no spark plug, new condition. $134.07
Bantam .19, 1946 strapcase in new condition. $125
Bond BRL 1946 ignition engine, model A, "rare," used in above average condition. $261.55
Boxer glow engine, in average condition. $158.38
Brown Model B engine, 1938, used but in excellent condition. $200
Brown .29 reproduction of the 1931 ignition engine, this engine was featured on the cover of the 1st edition of *Anderson's Blue Book*. Only 10-12 were made, this example was in mint condition. $630
Brown .60 model B, like new in original box. $285
Brown .60 model D, 1941 in used condition no parts missing, needed cleaning, a runner. $173.70
Brownie .29 1941 complete with the original box and instructions, used lightly and in real nice condition, L.N. $400
Brown Junior .60, Ignition engine, nice engine. $432
Brown Junior Campus Bee 2 cylinder CO2 engine, new. $75.50
Bunch 451 Aero Tiger from 1941, in excellent condition and complete. $196.51
BWM 250 D diesel engine, "nice." $258.89
Cannon 1946 .358 complete and appearing in new condition no box. $135
Comet .35, ignition engine, #1021, complete and in excellent condition did not meet the reserve price, high bid was $202.50
Cox .010, Jewel Box N.I.B. $103.50
Cox .049 Black Widow, first version in a jewel box, has a black widow on the box, N.I.B. $122
Cox .049 Golden Bee, 1959, bubble pack, perfect. $158.71
Cox .049 Tee Dee, new in bubble pack. $183.50
Cox .049 QRC, early Jewel Box version, N.I.B. $112.50
Cox .049 Space Bug, 1953, N.I.B. Perfect. $266
Cox .049 Space Bug Jr. 1959, red tank, in red and yellow bubble pack. Mint. $160.27
Cox .049 Space Hopper in the bubble pack, mint. $168.5
Cox .049 Space Hopper, 1959, N.I.P. from 1-20-2003. $166, one in the same condition sold for $187.73.
Cox .049 Spook, in bubble pack, N.I.P. Perfect. $114.19
Cox .049 Strato Bug 1956, no box but in new condition. $213.50
Cox .049 Thermal Hopper, 1953 Red Box, no instructions, no insert but has decal, nice engine, N.I.B. $166.74
Cox .049 Thermal Hopper, used but in excellent condition. $81
Cox .049 Venom, 1995 N.I.B. $203.50; another one sold for $270; another example sold with "buy it now" for $180. The *Engine Collectors Journal* states this was one of the smallest runs of Cox engines with only 1000 made.
Cox .15 Special MK II, perfect N.I.B. $262
Cox Conquest .15 Diesel, rare, "maybe 20 were made," N.I.B. $473
Cox Conquest .15, glow engine, L.N. $82
Cox Medallion .15 R.C. N.I.B. $90
Cox Olympic .15, new with no box. $144; another sold new in bubble pack for $167.
Cox Pee Wee .020 1970s blister pack, N.I.P. $58 and $52.5
Cox Pee Wee .020 early bubble or blister pack, perfect. $125.50
Cox RR-1 1957 second- version, bubble pack. $256, and another for $262
Cox Schroeder .020 Twin, rare and in new condition. $170.50
Cox Space Bug .049 L.N. $156 N.I.P; bubble pack $131
Cox Stoneway 2002 Black Shadow .049 Custom Stunt engine, new, someone paid $99 for this engine but I have never seen them listed again, there were other people wondering about this engine. The seven- day auction had 322 hits and was talked about on the Stuka Stunt Works website.
Cox Tee Dee .010 Black version N.I.B. $89
Cox Tee Dee .020 in Jewel Box, N.I.B. $72.20
Cox Tee Dee .09 Jewel Box, N.I.B. Mint. $78
Cox Tee Dee .15, 1962, new in a bubble pack, mint. $169.50
David Anderson, MK-2 2.5 diesel engine, from 1954, made in Norway. New condition. $127.50
Delong .30 spark ignition engine, second owner in excellent condition. $149.50
Delta Diesel, rare, good condition. $763
Dennymite 1940s in great condition with the box. $177.50
Dennymite 1940 Airstream Deluxe with no exhaust and short intake, dirty, good condition. $205
Dennymite .604 ignition engine, in good condition. $249
Dooling .38 "Baby" diesel commemorative, 1947-1997, N.I.B. perfect. $158.05
Dooling .29 in excellent condition. $202.50
Dooling .29, no box, but "new" condition. $345
Dooling .61, in like new condition. $565
Dreadnaught .19, 1941, N.I.B. Nice example. $480
Drone Diesel .29, 1948 Gold Crown, ball bearing engine, excellent condition. $140
Dyna Jet, distributed by Citizenship, run 20 minutes, comes with two combustion tubes, flyers, and instruction manual, almost new condition. $371.66
Edco Skydevil, ignition engine, L.N. $316
Edco Skydevil .649 ignition engine in hobby shop new condition, N.I.B. $455
ED-MK 4 Diesel in used good condition. $125
Elf Four Cylinder .38, Arne Hende reproduction, in new condition. $1525, add $80 for the plugs if you want them.
Elf Twin .195, from 1940, pipe intake and rear hanging tank, with box, instructions, brochure, no plugs, N.I.B. $750
Elfin BB 1.49cc diesel, overall in excellent condition, non original NVA. $231.39
Enya .049, control line or free flight engine from 1965, like new condition. $67
Enya .08 control line or free flight engine from 1965, N.I.B. $104.25
Enya .45 # 6001 control line engine, Frank Bowman venturi and ST NVA, used in excellent condition. $136.39
Enya .45 #6002 R.C. engine in never mounted and new condition, $142
Enya .60 from 1960 with a tear drop exhaust in new condition. $132.50
Enya .63 Typhoon C/L engine from the early 1960s, box OK. $120.50; another sold with no box in L.N. condition $102.50
Forster .99 ignition engine, N.I.B. $182.45
Foster .99 ignition engine, 1947, excellent condition. $255
Fox .29x 1962 version, in purple and black box, box in average shape, engine was new. $108.50
Fox .59 Long shaft stunt engine with rear intake, 1951, new condition. $480
Fox .59 R.C. 1962 N.I.B. $147.50
Fox .59 R.C. 1964 N.I.B. $191.50
Fox .59 Stunt engine from 1962-63, M.I.B. as nice an example as you can find. $283.09
Fox .59 U/C Stunt from 1962, with copies of the original paper work N.I.B. $104.27
Frog 100 diesel engine from the late 1940s, listed as like new. $223
Frog 175 Spark Ignition engine, N.I.B. A real nice engine with all accessories, the best you can get. $586.51
Fuji .099 U/C from the 1950s, has red anodized tank built on, head marked up a little, N.I.B. $114.50
Fuji .19 U/C from the early 1950s, has an Arden glow plug. $139.53
Fuji .29 U/C from the 1950s in excellent condition. $129.50
GHQ .51 Aero ignition engine from 1940, in new condition with a stand. $135
G-Mark 5 Cylinder .30 Radial engine, engine needs to be retimed, N.I.B. $276.79
Hayward Connelly .60 racing engine from 1948, dual plug head, very few were made due to a fire at the factory. About 40 were made, #56, mint. $635
Hiness .44 Twin cylinder engine, rare, new condition. $307
Hiness Arrow inline .60 R.C. engine, mint, did not meet the reserve price, the high bid was $510
Holland Hornet .049, N.I.B. $127.55
Hope .29 B (OS .29) N.I.B. $310
Hornet .19 rear intake glow engine assembled for new and used parts. Seller stated that only 200 engines were ever made in 1950. A real nice engine in excellent condition. $280.99

Hornet .60 ignition engine from 1946, excellent condition. $356.99
Jaguar 0.8 ccm diesel engine, in like new condition. $123.72
Jetex 50 power unit, new in a shop worn box. $22.50
Jetex Scorpion 600 engine, mint, N.I.B. $57
Johnson .35 Combat Special, 1960, N.I.B. $207.50
Johnson .35 Combat Special, used with a newer K&B NVA. In good condition. $88
Johnson .35 Combat Special Crankcase and back plate, new. $41
Johnson .35 small case sport engine, almost new condition. $87
Johnson .35 Super Stunt, no paper work but N.I.B. $135
Johnson .36 BB JRC, 1962, N.I.B. $152.50
K&B 3.25 Free Flight engine, N.I.B. $178.57
K&B .35 series 75 control line engine, no needle, new condition. $75
K&B 6.5 pylon engine N.I.B. $93
K&B Green Head .09 control line engine, used, a nice runner. $41.09
K&B Green Head .15 two speed glow engine, hobby shop new condition. $96
K&B Green Head .19 R.C. in hobby shop new condition. $121.38
K&B Green Head .201 control line engine in near new condition. $91.99
K&B Green Head .29R control line racing engine from 1955, new condition. $112.55
K&B Green Head .35 Combat engine, N.I.B. $132.57
K&B Green Head .35 reworked by George Aldrich, chromed liner and fitted piston used but in nice condition. $70
K&B Green Head Torpedo .35, real nice, N.I.B. $147.57
K&B Green Head Torpedo .45 Stunt, 1959 in excellent condition. $307
K&B Infant .020 Large box with all paper work, decal, and aluminum prop. Box a bit "ratty." $114.50
K&B Infant .020 Torpedo, a real nice example, M.I.B. $197.50
K&B Infant .020, L.N. no box. $102.50
K&B .29R 1955 popular rate race engine in like new condition. $123.50
K&B .29 spark ignition, Shilen Aero reproduction, #45, N.I.B. $173.50
K&B .32 Glo Torp engine from 1948 #3511C in excellent condition. $125
K&B Sea Fury .06 outboard engine, though not airplane engine these are still collected by engine collectors. This one was from 1955 and in M.I.B. A beautiful example. $675
K&B .15 Sky Fury Twin 1955, in excellent L.N. condition, this auction was viewed 499 times. $179.50
K&B Stallion .049, New but no box. $53
K&B Torpedo .15R Series 61, mint N.I.B. $215
K&B Torpedo .15R Series 64, FAI speed engine, mint N.I.B. $307
K&B Torpedo Jr. 035 N.I.B. missing the inner sleeve, nice. $135
K&B Torpedo .40 RR, Series 64 control line racing engine, new condition. $129.40
Kavan FK50 MK 1 3.0 cubic inch, with stand and paper work, M.I.B. $1,026
Keil Kraft Keil 6cc or K-6, rare British ignition engine with a decal #1696 in new condition. $286
Ken .60 supercharged ignition engine, #1545, 1946-47, in above average condition. $360
Madewell .147 Wasp from 1939, was listed as a vintage model engine, some one figured out the manufacturer, appeared to be in average condition in one poor picture. $346
McCoy .19 Rear Rotor, used $112.50 another in L.N. condition. $145
McCoy 40 Lighting Bolt Red Head Stunt engine in L.N. condition. $70.97; this engine in new condition can go as high as $140.
McCoy .49 black case Red Head with MUF-LET muffler, 3 venturis, #9434, used in good condition. $152
McCoy .60 1948, near new. $431.26
McCoy .60, Racing engine in L.N. condition. $406
McCoy .60, Series 20, a real nice engine. $871.10
McCoy .60, Series 20, tin box with all paper work, N.I.B. $461
McCoy 60 first model engine, new. $556
McCoy 60 tin box with the cardboard cover, new. $482
Mechanair British 5.9cc ignition engine, 1947, "as new," this engine didn't sell well due to the Arden glow plug being marketed and the introduction of glow engines. $170.74
Merco 61 R.C. diesel, with muffler, N.I.B, beautiful engine. $227.26
Mills 1.3 cc diesel in used but excellent condition, tank may not be original. $114.74
Morton M 5 Second Series, # 0032, N.I.B. $1651.90
Ohlsson .60 custom from 1940, missing plastic fuel tank, other wise complete, good condition. $227.50
OK CO2 engine from 1947, N.I.B. $110
OK .35 Twin Stack .35 from 1955, box is soiled with no insert or directions, new condition. $137.50
OK .29 B-29 1946 spark ignition engine with black Bakelite tank, nice example, L.N. $280
OK .49 "pre-war" #3040, excellent condition. $200
OK .49 1940 ignition engine with motor mounts, coil, and instructions, N.I.B. $315
OK Cub .024 in original plastic wrap on card. $89
OK Cub .049 B M.I.B. $69
OK Cub diesel .074 used in good condition. $52.55
OK Super 60, used in good condition. $133.00 L.N. $167.50 New $127.69
OK Twin 1.2 cubic inch ignition engine from 1945, mint condition $537; another in mint condition went for $860.
Oliver Tiger MK III Diesel, used but in nice condition. $255
O&R .049 Midjet, used but in excellent condition from 1954, with Arden glow plug. $91
O&R .19 from the early 1940s, small head fins, #1768 "super nice" condition. $113.50
O&R .23 FSR spark ignition engine, dull finish on case, in new condition. $154.50
O&R .29 glow engine, has blue anodized head from 1950-51 good condition. $82.01
O&R .60 custom spark engine from 1940, ¼" crankshaft, appeared in excellent condition. $330.99
ORR Tornado .647 ignition engine from 1948, #1286, mint condition. $416.93
Orwick .64 ignition engine from 1946, with a small bit of the green paint missing, excellent, L.N. $273
OS FP 20 R.C. run a couple of times, looks new and complete. $132.50 was paid. Interesting?
OSK6 Replica .60 ignition engine, complete with stand, box and directions, M.I.B. $266
OS Graupner Wankel .30 rotary engine, early version, good condition. $175; another in excellent condition sold for $177.47, and one bought new in 1988 that was N.I.B; $213.60
OS NSU Wankel .30 rotary engine Type 1-49, no instructions, N.I.B. $188.50
OS Max 1cc engine, .06 in the original box with all instructions, from 1966, M.I.B. $154.39
OS Max 15 R.C. 1970s engine complete and N.I.B sold to the same person who bought the FP 20. $113.61
OS Max FP 40 R.C. complete and new in the box. $102.50, the interest in this engine remains high since being discontinued, another sold for $57.50 in the same condition; you never know on eBay.
OS Max .35 Custom X Series, early 1960s, N. I. B. $134.50
OS Max III .35 R.C. L.N. $104.50
OS Max .49 R.C. engine in absolute mint condition, offered from around 1957 through the 1960s. This example was purchased in 1969 and brought back from Japan. $157.50
OS Max H60F R.C. GP series engine from 1972, Gold Head in N.I.B. condition. $165.50
OS Super Jet engine, complete and unused in the original box. $255
OS Twin Stack .29 center had a broken fin, L.N. condition. $75
RAF .40? rear intake, rear exhaust glow engine, this appears to be a pylon racing engine with a black crankcase body, could also be a speed engine, in above average condition. $205.05
REA .29 from the 1950s glow engine, in above average condition. $177.50
Rocket .46 spark ignition engine in new condition, a nice engine! $154.50; another engine in excellent condition went for $203.50
Ross .60 Twin with silencers in good general condition, no box. $170.50
Ross .60 Twin with red anodized heads, no box or instructions, new condition. $232.50
Rossi .15 rear exhaust competition glow engine used for free flight, excellent in the box. $167.50
Sky Chief .526 ignition engine from 1941, in above average condition, appeared to be almost new but had never been cleaned, aged from sitting in a drawer. $180
Super Cyclone 1946 .60 sparker in hobby shop new condition, you would be hard pressed to find an engine better than this or even equal, complete with the box and directions. $275
Super Cyclone .60 spark ignition engine in outstanding condition #GR 19528. $213.50
Super Cyclone .60 1982 re-issue by Tom Morrison, complete M.I.B. $305
Super Tigre .049 Diesel engine from 1955, no box but in good condition. $230
Super Tigre G .15 R.V. glow engine, new. $306
Super Tigre G-28 .05 diesel engine, a nice little engine in excellent condition. $149
Super Tigre G 30 2.5cc C/L diesel engine, rear intake, most likely used for team race, in good condition. $124.74; another was bought with "Buy it Now" in the early orange and horizontal white and black lines box, M.I.B. $125.50
Super Tigre .35 control line engine, in early red box in fair shape, engine was mint. $103.50
Super Tigre G40 R.C. ABC model airplane engine, rear intake, N.I.B. $79.25
Super Tiger .40X control line engine, rear intake and exhaust, N.I.B. $127.50
Super Tigre G-46 R.C. glow engine, the later version with muffler. This auction was ended with "Buy it Now" and was an excellent buy for a N.I.B. example. $130
Super Tigre .60 BB ABC Blue Head from 1974, N.I.B. $156.38
Super Tigre G65R, rear intake speed engine, with S.T. speed spinner, "super nice shape," has been mounted and run. $128
Super Tiger X-29 speed engine in perfect and complete condition. $200
Talisman .60 ignition racing engine from 1946, rare, complete and "new," faint mounting marks. $547.99
Thunderbird .60 by Scott Motors of Phoniex, AZ, #1102, large C/L tank, from 1947, new condition. $475
Veco .19 BB U/C, N.I.B. $77
Veco .19 BB R.C. Lee custom engine # 230, stock and Perry carbs, high compression and standard heads, letter from Clarence Lee, Lee Custom Decals, N.I.B. $72.55
Veco .19 Series 100 C/L engine, Beautiful, N.I.B. $102.50
Veco .35 "Nice sport C/L engine." $80.99
Veco GP .35 A C/L Stunt engine, perfect condition N.I.B. $202.50
Veco 50 custom C/L Stunt engine, chromed and timed by George Aldrich, special muffler adapted, bench run one hour, L.N. condition nice engine! $201.03
Viking .65 twin cylinder engine, red enamel case, like new. $250
Viking .65 Wizard twin cylinder engine, no name on case, long needle valve and blue anodized rear timing cover and spinner, some of these engines were assembled in 1964 from parts. This one was said to be from 1947-48, #1777 in L.N. condition. $258
Vivell Twin .60 ignition engine in good condition. $1,125
Walh-Brown Jr. custom with box, made 2-1-77. These engines were made for about a year and a half. It came with all paper work, twin exhaust stack, new coil, and condenser. Serial #42. Mint condition. $275.24
Webra 2.5 R diesel control line engine, green anodized head, excellent condition. $128.50
Webra Piccolo .049 diesel engine, missing needle on the assembly, auction stated the piston was gone also, but I doubt it as this engine looked nice, N.I.B. $255
Webra Record .09 diesel engine from the early 1970s in N.I.B. condition. $55.95
Webra T4 four cycle engine, from the early 1980s, hobby shop new. $327
Yellow Jacket .061 engine, miniature Dooling model B replica by Bruce Underwood, yellow anodized case, new condition. $205

Radio Control Sets and Related Items

Ace R.C. designed Kraft R.C. 10 radio kit less antenna with five control switches. $113.50
Aristocraft 1960 2AP Rangemaster transmitter, M.I.B. $53
Aristocraft 1960 TRR receiver, M.I.B. $45
Aristocraft Rangemaster 1AP transmitter and CR-1 receiver from the early 1960s in new condition, N.I.B. $102.50
Aristocraft tone transmitter and receiver, good condition. $80
Babcock 1958 BCR-18 receiver M.I.B. $193.52
Babcock 1958 BTR-12 receiver, M.I.B. $193.52
Babcock 1958 Magic Wand transmitter, hobby shop new, M.I.B. $66
Babcock 1958 Selectone R.C. transmitter, M.I.B. $86
Babcock BCC-6 Electrostick transmitter, N.I.B. $100
Babcock BCR-10K Magic Carpet receiver, excellent condition. $56
Babcock BCT-2 transmitter with Otarion receiver #0-21, this example was perfect in every way, no better to be found, M.I.B. $305
Babcock radio set, 1965 BCT-21 transmitter new in original shipping box, with receiver and escapement, complete unit in nice condition. $60
Berkeley 1952 R.C. receiver kit, mint condition. $87.58
Berkeley 1955 R.C. tone Aerotrol transmitter, N.I.B. $157.50
Berkeley 50s Aerotrol R.C. kit N.I.B. $146.50
Bonner Digimite 4 channel R.C. system from 1958, well cared for and in original foam box. $326
Bonner Digimite 4-RS proportional system with four servos, not complete but in good condition. $201.75
Carl Goldberg Models transmitter, used by the military for drones, new condition. $100
Citizen-Ship AR receiver from the early 1950s on 456 MC, to be used with the CC-1 transmitter, new in a slightly worn box. $53
Citizen-Ship 1959 MST-8 transmitter new in a sealed box, this item was just like buying new from the manufacture. $274.17
Citizen-Ship "27" transmitter with homemade receiver, 1954, 27.255 mc, excellent. $97.59
Citizen-Ship BT-6 transmitter with BR-6 receiver in excellent condition. $116.49
Citizen-Ship CC-1 from the 1950s on 456 megacycles, N.I.B. $89.17
Citizen-Ship MSR-8 receiver in a fair box operating on 225 MCs, in new condition. $103
Citizen-Ship Proportional R.C. set with APT transmitter, APR receiver, and three APM servos, with no antenna, in excellent condition. $255
Citizen-Ship SS-MSR8 receiver, 8 channels tuned to 27.045, hobby shop new with a little shelf wear to the box, originally sold for $149.95. $130.67
Citizen-Ship TTX with SE-2 escapement, has the small coil antenna, N.I.B. with an only fair box. $163.49
Controlaire 1966 MK 11 Mule transmitter, good condition. $99
Controlaire Deluxe Galloping Ghost system with OS sticks and SH-112 receiver, with copies of all instructions in working order, a nice radio, excellent. $181.50
Dee Bee Quadruplex CL5 R.C. System, from 1965, 5 channel single stick, like new condition. $291
Ecktronics 1962 Pacesetter Plane Promter, tone single channel R.C. system in pristine condition N.I.B. $172.51
Ecktronics Pacesetter Kraft Tone transmitter with 41" antenna, excellent condition. $46
Futaba F-66 single channel transmitter, this set comes in light blue and black. fair condition. $51; Futaba- MRC F-66 single channel radio set from the 1960s, complete, N.I.B. $86
GA-LIN vintage 10-channel reed system with 5 Bonner Duramite servos and original paper work, no antenna, single tube reed receiver. $120.67
Good Brothers 1949 radio set, manufactured by Beacon Electronics, complete and L.N. in the original box. $264
Kraft Ecktronics 10 channel transmitter in good condition. $125
MacGregor British designed single channel tone MR-200 transmitter and MR-60 receiver in original foam packaging, this system was sold through 1970, no escapement, in working order, excellent condition. $339.11
OS Minitron R.C. transmitter, like new. $284
Robbe transmitter with three receivers, used in great condition. $192.50
Sampey Command Control R.C. servo, N.I.B. $68
Skyleader Courier 4 channel R.C. set on 27 MHz, a complete set the original box, L.N. condition. $130.33
Sterling Command Master R.C. system, model R-T, N.I.B. with above average box. $125
Testors 1960s single channel transmitter, good condition. $56; this set was light blue in color but came in black also.

World Engines Digit Migit R.C. system from the early 1970s, perfect in unused condition from hobby shop stock, N.I.B. $202.50

Model Airplane Kits and Ready to Fly Airplanes

Ace Nomad R.C. glider, 48" wing span, nice condition. $52
Airtronics Aquila standard class 99" wing span sailplane, missing the body, N.I.B. $118.49
Airtronics Olympic 99 R.C. glider. $78; another sold for $110.10. These kits are not being collected as they are excellent kits and fliers, all will most likely be built but are highly sought after.
Airtronics Sagitta 900 Sailplane Glider kit, second version, N.I.B. $157.50
Ambriod early 60s, Ares control line stunt kit, one small stain on the box, N.I.B. $280.50
Ambriod early 60s Stuka Stunt kit, CS-1, tape on box, no decals, complete. $250
American Junior Fireball kit, "98 % is untouched," $157.50
Andrews 1966 Aeromaster II R.C. 48" wing span biplane in mint condition. $135.25
Aurora B-25 R.T.F. type aircraft, called a screwdriver kit with a 25" wingspan. No engines but has firewall marks for the screws, engine can be installed, in excellent condition. $510
Berkeley 1950s Sea-Cat flying boat in excellent condition. $191.49; flying boat kits are highly sought after and should continue to climb in value.
Berkeley 1953 Super Cloud Wakefield competition kit, like new and complete. $78.77
Berkeley Aeronca C-3, fair condition complete. $78.77
Berkeley B-17G Flying Fortress with 52" wing span, faded box, some of the contents less than perfect, good condition. $232.49
Berkeley B-25 Mitchell, Tokyo Raider from 1956, near mint condition. $275
Berkeley Cessna 195 from 1948, plans never opened, spotting on the box, N.I.B. $255
Berkeley Colonial Skimmer 1/2 A, R.C. flying boat, good condition. $143.26; another in excellent condition sold for $144.50.
Berkeley Curtiss SBC-3 Helldiver, good condition. $96.90
Berkeley Custom Privateer Flying Boat, 114" wing span designed for either R.C. or free flight. "Box, plans, and kit are in excellent condition, appears complete." $334.62
Berkeley P-40 Warhawk, C/L, no plans, cracked decals, good box, "appears" to be complete. $272.09; another with a fair box sold for $227.50
Berkeley Pitts Special, 1950, most of the balsa missing, good decals, box in fair condition. $111.11
Berkeley T-28 in above average condition. $104.05
Berkeley Skyray, small control line or free flight kit with a 25" wingspan, water damage on the box, contents in new condition. $83.28
Bridi UFO R.C. pattern kit, N.I.B. $102
Capitol Model Aircraft Co. Staggerwing Beachcraft, complete in a shop worn box, the plans in this kit are works of art, from the late 1940s, a rare example. $205
Carl Goldberg R.C. Skylark, box in only fair condition. $137.50
Carl Goldberg 1/2 A Skylane, mint. $122.50
Carl Goldberg 1949 Glo-Bug control line kit, a nice kit from America Hobby Specialties. $61
Carl Goldberg F.A.I. Viking free flight kit, mint. $51.50
Carl Goldberg Jr. Falcon 1/2 A R.C. kit in mint condition. $81
Carl Goldberg Jr. Satan, 1/2 A, 18" wing span C/L combat kit, average condition. $45.23
Carl Goldberg Li'l Wizard, 1/2 A C/L trainer. Excellent. $38.50
Carl Goldberg R.C. Shoestring Goodyear Racer, both examples were in L.N. condition and complete. $179.50; $152.50
Carl Goldberg Ranger 28, rubber powered kit in excellent condition. $36
Carl Goldberg Ranger 30 in excellent condition. $66.99
Carl Goldberg Ranger 42, R.T.F from the 70s, both examples were in L.N. condition. This was a nice flying little R.C. airplane with the TD .049. $102.; $103.50,
Carl Goldberg Sr. Falcon R.C. kit, very popular kit used to teach many enthusiasts to fly, N.I.B. $187.50
Cleveland 1944 Giant B-17, with a fair box, #SF-100, complete. $256
Cleveland 1946 P-40 Warhawk, flight engineered, complete, and in excellent condition. $73
Cleveland Boeing F4B4 master kit, #SF-29, post war kit. According to this auction, the kit designations were MF and changed to SF after the war; this seller is very knowledgeable and I have personally bought items from him, kit was in L.N. condition. $104.02
Cleveland Douglas A-20 Bomber, #SF-115, M.I.B. $202.50
Cleveland F4F Wildcat 3/4" scale kit, #SF-83, rated a 9 on a scale of 10, nice kit. $140.50
Cleveland F4U Corsair, 3/4" scale kit, #SF-79, museum quality, M.I.B. $118.50
Cleveland Martin B-26 Marauder, #SF-135, wing span 48 3/3" in good condition complete with paints. $97.88
Cleveland P-35 Serversky fighter, #SF-61 3/4" scale with 24" wing span, box is a bit shop worn but the contents were mint. $162.50
Cleveland P-38 Lightning, #SF-85, almost perfect condition. $143.50
Cleveland P-51 Mustang, # SF-91, in excellent condition. $131.50
Cleveland P-6E Hawk, #SF-21, no paints, good condition. $104.49
Cleveland Stuka, #SF-84, box in only fair condition. $80
Comet Clodhopper 11 from 1938, Jim Cahill's winning Wakefield, in real nice condition. $76
Comet Grumman Cougar F9F-6 19 3/4" wing span, N.I.B. $88.91
Comet Saber 44 plastic R.T.F. N.I.B. $175; another sold for $130.27
Comet Tri-Pacer plastic R.T.F. used in the box, above average condition. $76
Cox ME-109 R.T.F. in L.N. condition. $62.99
Cox Miss America P-51, .049 R.T.F. The real airplane campaigned in the early 1970s and displayed at Transpo 72 at Dulles International in the Washington D.C. area. Mint. $199
Cox P-40 .049 R.T.F. original 1964 box, tan camouflage later version was dark green, N.I.B. $113.01
Cox Red Baron Fokker Tri-plane, .049 hobby shop display item, no box, new condition. $100.01
Cox Sopwith Camel WW I bi-plane R.T.F. # 8000 dogfighter series, 1970s, M.I.B. $115.50
Cox Sportavaria, .049 R.C. plane, with Cadet 2CH radio, box fair. $102
Cox Stuka R.T.F. 049 control line R.T.F. absolutely mint in original yellow box. First version from the middle 1960s, stunning example. $377.99
Cox Super Saber F-100 plastic R.T.F. Real nice, M.I.B. $200
COX TD4 R.T.F. with Baby Bee and spare blue wing in mint condition. $275
deBolt Custom Livewire R.C. kit, N.I.B. $267.50
deBolt Livewire Ercoupe 1/2 A single channel R.C. kit, 36" wing span, L.N. $82.17
deBolt Perigee R.C.; pattern kit in excellent condition, appears complete. $122.50
Dodgson Designs Windsong r/c sailplane, competition kit, N.I.B. $203.50
DYO-X1000, 1957 all aluminum control line R.T.F. with K&B Sky Fury .049 engine in absolute mint condition from Collect-Air of Santa Barbara, CA. $275
Ecktronics Nomad R.C. glider for .020 engines, mint. $104.39. This model was later kitted by Ace RC, around 1962 and the House of Balsa.
4K's Models Ed Lamb's "Climber" 1941 design reproduction for rubber power, N.I.B. $44.44
Graupner Hi-Fly R.C. glider from the late 1970s, complete and N.I.B. $186.48
Graupner 1957 Kapistan free flight bi-plane, box a bit "tatty" but intact, otherwise new, this kit was sold into the mid 1960s. $184.50.
Hi-Flight Model Products Mirage glider kit, 112.5" wingspan, N.I.B. $102.75
Ideal Grumman TBM Avenger, rare kit in L.N. condition. $116.23
Jack Armstrong Tru-Flite paper airplanes, 12 total in the original mailing envelope and near museum quality. $129.01
Jetco 1/2 A Cessna 170, free flight or lightweight R.C. kit. $92
Jetco 1958 PT-19 Trainer R.C. kit, 72" wingspan, parts punched out but in good condition, two are listed. $153; $124.83
Jetco Cessna 170, in new condition. $105
Jetco F-51H Mustang, McCroskey scale model, excellent and complete. $150.49
Jetco Imperial R.C. glider with 100" wing-span, an impressive kit, N.I.B. $232.50
Jetco Krackerjac, single channel vintage R.C. kit, designed by Bill Winter; kit was incomplete and box was shop worn with tape around one end, average condition. $132.50
Jetco Lightning Bug .010 single channel R.C. kit, 27" wing span, M.I.B. $94.50
Jetco Navigator 1/2 A, flying boat in N.I.B. condition. $138.78. This kit seems to be one of the more desirable small R.C. kits now being collected.
Jetco Piper Super Cruiser, #S-6 good condition. $152.50
Jetco Rearwin Speedster, has been started. $64
Jetco Saber Stunt kit, in complete and good condition. $90.90
Jetco Shark 15, C/L stunt kit, like new with an excellent box. $81
Jetco Shark 45 stunter complete and N.I.B. $202.50
Jetco Talon A-2 Nordic glider kit, 1965 National Champion, excellent condition. $50
Jetco Thermic B, hand launch glider N.I.B. $29
Jetco Thermic 36 tow-line glider, Superflite, in average condition. $48.51; another M.I.B. $47
Jetco Thermic 50 R.C. slightly faded box but new. $86.50
Jetco Top Kick A-1 Nordic Glider, excellent. $64.99
Jetex R.T.F. Twin "50" Jetex motor Helicopter, good condition. Neat! $158.15
Kenhi Civy Boy 61 free flight competition kit, M.I.B. $127.84
Keil Kraft. The Firebird, control line kit for 2.5cc engines, N.I.B. $245.57
Kiel Kraft Kits "Gypsy" 40" wing-span rubber Wakefield model, M.I.B. $61.36
Kiel Kraft R.T.F. Hurricane fighter, with shop worn box, used very little, nice condition. $112.90
Kyosho Shrike Commander R.C. kit for twin .10 engines, from about 1985, M.I.B. $153.50
Mattel 1970s Super Star electric R.T.F. Mint example complete. $177.50
Megow 1946 Competitor C/L ignition kit, real nice condition. $150
Megow Aeronca A-2 3/4" scale kit from 1936, fair condition. $75
Mercury 1976 Galahad R.C. low winger, 54" wingspan, hobby shop new. $204.02
Midi Pearl free flight kit from the 70s, new condition. $67
Midway Denny Jr. Old Timer Kit, 73" wing-span, N.I.B. $82.32
Midwest Esquire R.C. 15 to .19 size, in fairly good shape and complete. $152.50
Midwest Li'l Esquire 1/2A R.C. kit with 40" wing-span, good condition. $52
Midwest Rat Racer, control line kit, RR-208, N.I.B. $61
Monogram Speedee Panther Kit from the 1950s, mint condition. $100
Pica Duellist twin engine R.C. kit N.I.B. B. $114
Pierce Aero Paramount R.C. Sailplane, 13" wing-span, tape around box but otherwise new. $191.50
Pierce Aero Paragon glider with 118" wing-span, N.I.B. $103.50
Proctor Antic Bipe, from the 1970s in like new condition. $210.48
Satellite City, Satellite 450 free flight kit from 1974, excellent condition. $62.55; this kit could go either way as a builder or a collector, popular nice kit.
Scientific "The Flea" from 1937, some parts cut out still in pristine condition. $82.99
Scientific Piper Cub #8-395, 18" wingspan in excellent condition. $66.56; thousands of these entry level kits were made of over 50 different models but all were basically the same in size and style of kit. Two page advertisements had all kids wishing for one of these kits.
Scientific Super Sonic Guided Missile, above average condition, complete. $35
Sig "Berkeley" P-47N Thunderbolt C/L scale kit, N.I.B. $102.6
Sig ABC Scrambler free flight competition kit, new condition. $51.05
Sig Privateer Super 15 from the 1960s, like new. $107.51
Sig Stratus Class 111 R.C. Pattern kit, M.I.B. $76
Sig Samauri, discontinued slope glider sailplane, N.I.B. $192.50
Sig Witchdoctor 800 free flight kit from the early 1970s, appears new in the box. $67.66
Sterling Flying Fool C/L kit, 2nd version. $70.75
Sterling Fokker D-7 C/L scale kit in the white box, N.I.B. $70.99
Sterling Fokker D-7 R.C. scale kit, 58 1/2" wing span, box and kit in excellent shape, N.I.B. $123.07
Sterling Great Lakes Trainer, C/L scale from the 1970s, N.I.B. $74.99
Sterling Mighty Mambo R.C. kits in nice condition two listed. $253.50 $235.50
Sterling Ringmaster Junior, 1970s version in mint condition. $128, astounding! This kit sold for $2.95 in 1970 at the hobby shop on Ream Field in Imperial Beach, CA. when I was a teenager. The price paid is three times what this kit is really worth.
Sterling Ringmaster Imperial stunt kit, above average condition. $147.49
Sterling Ruffy stunt kit, 1st version, tape around box, complete and in good condition. $159.50
Sterling Ruffy stunt kit, 2nd version in white box, excellent condition. $112
Sterling Southwick Skylark Stunter, N.I.B. $169.59; with the passing of Ed Southwick in 2002 this kit was sought after for sentimental reasons and should remain this way for a while.
Sterling Southwick Skylark, some of the ribs were punched out, other wise in great condition. $222.50
Sterling Spad WW1 C/L scale kit, N.I.B. $79.02
Sterling Super Ringmaster, in the red and white box, mint. $90.55
Streling Schweizer SGS1-34 Sailplane kit 99" wingspan, N.I.B. $104.07
Sterling Tri-Pacer introduced in 1954, 58.75" wing span, in complete excellent condition, M.I.B. $225.55
Sterling Tri-Pacer from the 1970-80s, #FS-37, 44" wing span, in N.I.B. condition. $123.50
Sterling Wizard early R.C. biplane from the 50s, N.I.B. $86.50
Tiger Pulse Jet engine and Starfire F-94C model kit, museum quality. $631.21
Top Flite Cumulus free flight kit from the early 50s, fair condition. $102.50
Top Flite Kwik Fli 111 R.C. pattern kit, N.I.B. $197.50
Top Flite Orion Pattern Kit, two examples both N.I.B. $182.50; $230.39
Top Flite P-47 C/L scale, super form construction with 27" wing span in excellent condition. $58.01
Top Flite Rascal 1/4 A, R.C. kit, 27" WS, mint condition. $105.39; another sold for $104.19
Top Flite Schoolgirl Ken Willard's 1/2A biplane R.C. kit N.I.B. $66
Top Flite Schoolgirl, complete with the parts punched out, excellent. $76.01
Top Flite Super Combat Streak C/L model kit, no plans in overall good condition. $113.05
Veco Chief, early version, excellent condition. $169.16
Veco Redskin C/L, excellent condition. $177.50; another that was fair condition, $96.22
Veco Smoothie C-8, in red and white checkered box, mint condition. $153.59
Veco Squaw C/L, Henry Engineering, N.I.B. $180.66
Veco Taylor Cub, free flight # F-10, fair but complete. $36
Veco Thunderbird stunt kit, Henry Engineering in near mint condition. $192.49
Veco Tom Tom, 1950s 2nd version, large stain on the box. $181.28;Veco kits were great kits and continue to be highly prized by their owners. Another in almost mint condition sold for $231; these are the yellow, red, and blue Henry Engineering kits.
Veco-Dumas Brave C/L kit, excellent condition. $63
Veco-Dumas Chief stunt kit, excellent condition. $169.52; another N.I.B. sold for $155.27
Veco-Dumas Thunderbird stunt kit, in excellent condition, tape on box and a bit shop worn $326. This auction was a good example of some one paying way too much for something. This is why eBay is a poor way to assign value on some items. For less than half this final auction price, this kit can be bought new for building; this kit was not collector quality.
Veco-Dumas Warrior C/L stunt kit, N.I.B. $105
Waneford Feather Airplane from the 20s or 30s original in a box with much wear. $78 (reserve was not met)
Windspiel Cobra 17 Sailplane Kit with 121.5" wing span, from about 1970, complete N.I.B. $152.50
Wen-Mac Dauntless Dive Bomber #170, in original shipping box, mint condition. $639.99
Wen-Mac Dauntless Dive Bomber, blue from 1958, new with no box, just directions. $848
Wen-Mac F4-U Corsair from the early 1960s, in original box and in new condition. $255
Wen-Mac P-38 Lightning, in "played with condition," complete and crack free, excellent. $357.91
Early in 2003, a Wen-Mac P-38 Lightning plastic R.T.F. sold for $2600 in near perfect shape, complete in the box; another in great condition, only missing the guns on the front of the plane, it

sold for $360. The importance of having the box in good condition can be the difference as noted by these two auctions. Later, Testors took over Wen-Mac and produced a chrome version; one of these planes in near mint condition with no box sold for $800.

Wen-Mac P-39, from around 1960, complete and new in the box, excellent example, box cover say it fires 2 rockets, M.I.B. $260.

Zenith Carbon F3J Sailplane RTF, with servos in the plan brand new condition. $910.

Books, Magazines, Catalogs, Art, and Accessories

Air Age Gas Models, 144 page paperback, by Air Age, 1943, excellent. $36.99

A Pictorial A to Z of Vintage and Classic Model Airplane Engines. Mike Clanford. Most examples are in L.N. condition and this book always generates interest At least two dozen copies have been up for auction the past year. $60 (lowest); $159.50 (highest); on June 22, 2003, a copy went for $265

Air Trails, January 1931, excellent condition. $103.01

AMA Kit Plan Book Volume #1, good condition. $42.95

American Legion model meet Bendix air race trophy from the 1940s, huge and beautiful, 33" tall, in excellent condition. $400

Anderson's Blue Book #2. $80.60; I have seen other copies sell in the $50-60 range, some were even signed.

Berkeley Catalog from 1942 in great condition. $52

Blue Blazer 1/2 pint fuel can in above average condition. $33; $38.07; and $45

Boy's Life, Orville Wright issue, September 1914, vol. IV, no. 7 in above average condition. $116.49; collected by everyone interested in the Wright Brothers

Building and Flying Model Aircraft, Paul Garber, 1928. $36.65 (excellent condition with no dust cover); $76 (fair with dust cover)

Comet 1941 catalog in O.K. condition. $21

Comet 1958 catalog #810 in excellent condition. $31

Control Line Manual, 1973, R.G. Moulton, in good condition. $86

Cox TRC glow fuel gallon can in mint condition. $54

Cyclopedia of Hobby Kits, 1959 catalog/book in good condition. $103.50

Flying Aces, nine issues from 1935, with Feb. missing a cover, March, May, June, August, December, in above average condition. $99.99

Dynamic Auto Pitch Prop, perfect condition. $43.51

Estes 1964 Rocket catalog, copyright 1963, in average condition. $76.50

Flying Models, May 1954, comic book issue in average condition. $42

Flying Models; Favorites of the Fifties, Vic Smeed, in good condition. $42

Franciscan Powermist Hornet 1/2 pint fuel can in above average condition. $43

Handbook for Model Builders, 1950, Fawcett Books, in good condition. $46.75

Harper's Aircraft Book, 1913, in excellent condition. $90

Jim Walker red U-Reely, on a blue bubble pack hanging card; the U-Reely most of us know is black. New but shop worn. $48

Jo Kotula 1960s original cover art of an F-3 Demon, mint. $300

Megow 1940 #8 catalog, 96 pages in good condition. $34.33

Model Aero Engine Encyclopedia, R.G. Moulton, 1966 reprint with a nice dust cover. $78.54

Model Aircraft Engineer, November 1934 in average condition. $12.50

Model Airplane Engines, Donald Foote, 1952 with dust cover. $44.89

Model Airplane News, 4 issues, October 1929, February 1930, March 1930, January 1931 with artist Jean Oldham covers, all in above average condition. $135

Model Airplane News, July 1929, first issue in excellent condition. $162.88

Model Airplane News, August 1929, above average condition. $45

Model Airplane News, complete set 1942 in excellent condition. $100.99

Model Airplane News, February 1940 in mint condition. $26.26

Model Airplane News, October 1940 in mint condition. $26

Model Airplane News, January 1950 in excellent condition. $31

Model Airplanes How to Build and Fly Them, Elmer L. Allen, 3rd printing from 1929, average condition. $42.60

Motor Manual by Garami & McEntee, published by Air Age Inc. 1947, excellent condition. $62

Perfect model wheel display case, from the 1950s in nice condition, complete with all the wheels on the display and many other complete sets of wheels inside. $152.72

Propellers, 7 old props, and one Tatone insta-pitch, 2 Rite-Pitch, 1 X-Cell, 1 Tornado, I O&R, 1 Air-O, all in new condition. $86

Speed plane powered by a Dyna Jet pulse jet engine; the airplane a 1950s control line jet in good condition, with take off dolly, a nice example from history. $503.99

Spitzy Nitromic 1/2 A glow, 1/2 pint fuel can, excellent condition. $48.58

Stunt, Control Line Flying, 1949, R.H. Warring, tatty dust cover, in average condition. $30.30

Sonny Schug. Model Aviation box art from 1992, Boeing P-26 Fighter for Hobbycraft Models, 23" x 18". Listed at $550 but received no bids.

Trophy from Model Aircraft Exposition at the New York World's Fair, 1939, sponsored by the baker's of Wonder Bread, belonging to famous modeler Henry Nelson, 11.5" tall and reading "Sky Blazer's Award," excellent condition. $331

The Boys Book of Model Aeroplanes, Francis Collins. This was the first book about model airplanes printed in the United States. Several copies have come up for auction in various conditions. $30 (average); $45 (fair); $55 (excellent). I have also seen it listed on the ABE Books web site for $90.

The Glow Plug Model Engine, 1950-1965, 84 page book with copies of old ads, new condition. $61

Zaic's Model Aeronautic Encyclopedias, Volume 1 and 2, published 1947, excellent condition. $65

Astro Hog from the 1958 Nationals. This design placed 1st, 2nd, and 3rd in the premiere radio event. Fred Dunn designed the Astro Hog in 1957. He was a member of the L.A.R.K.S. Club in Los Angeles. This plane may be Howard Bonner's; on the cover of *Flying Models*, October 1959, four Astro Hogs are pictured at the 1958 Nationals in Glenview, Illinois. Bob Dunham also championed this design and was the winner that year. There is a nice picture of him in the scrapbook, launching a plane. *Courtesy of Bob Maschi*. $10.

Appendix B
Academy of Model Aeronautics Hall of Fame

The creation of a "Modeler's Hall of Fame" first appeared in the March/April 1966 issue of *American Modeler.* Model aviation had grown to include many flying heroes, innovators, and designers; time had come to honor these contributors. The voting for the top ten was done by the modelers of America by mail-in ballot. This was the foundation that lead to the permanent formation of the AMA Hall of Fame.

The Model Aviation Hall of Fame was created in 1969 to recognized those modelers who had made significant contributions to the art and science of model aviation. Later, leaders in the industry would be included to the list of noteworthy contributors. In 1968, Richard Carson and members of the Spokane Barons Model Club organized the selection process and on May 31, 1969, the first seven recipients were inducted. The Washington State Academy of Aerospace Science, in affiliation with the Academy of Model Aeronautics, sponsored the ceremony.

The names of the inductees are included in this book for the sake of history and permanent record for the reader; no other list exists in print. The Model Aviation Hall of Fame elects new members each year from nominations made by AMA members. The AMA consolidates all the applications it receives during the year and sends them to the selection committee each April. It picks from the list of candidates those individuals who have contributed the most to model aviation. Being nominated and elected remains the most prestigious award a modeler can receive. (Jerry Neuberger, *Model Aviation*, September 2002, 74-78).

Model Aviation Hall of Fame Inductees

1969
Walter Billett (deceased)
Carl Goldberg (deceased)
Charles H. Grant (deceased)
Willis C. Brown (deceased) - AMA President 01
Walter A. Good, FL - AMA President 11
N. E. "Jim" Walker (deceased)
Frank Zaic, CA

1970
Dick Korda (deceased)
Al Lewis (deceased) - AMA President 02
Bill Winter (deceased)

1971
None

1972
Howard McEntee (deceased)

1973
Ocie Randall (deceased)

1974
William L. Brown, PA
William R. Enyart (deceased)
Irwin S. Polk (deceased)
Nathan Polk (deceased)
Sal Taibi, CA

1975
Irwin Ohlsson (deceased) - AMA President 04
C.O. Wright (deceased) - AMA President 06
Walt Schroder (deceased)
Jim Kirkland (deceased)
Lieut. Harold W. "John" Alden (deceased)

1976
Harold deBolt, FL
Frank Ehling (deceased)
Merrill C. Hamburg (deceased)
Chester Lanzo (deceased)
Henry Struck (deceased)

1977
John E. Brodbeck, AZ
Maynard L. Hill, VA - AMA President 14
Bert Pond (deceased)
Peter J. Sotich (deceased) - AMA President 12
Ken Willard (deceased)

1978
Duke Fox (deceased)
Phil Kraft, CA
E. T. Packard (deceased)
Leon Shulman, FL
John Worth VA - AMA President 13

1979
John E. Clemens (deceased)
Claude McCullough, IA - AMA President 10
L. Glen Sigafoose (deceased)
Matthew A. (Matty) Sullivan (deceased)
Bill Wisniewski, AZ

1980
Sidney Axelrod (deceased)
Kenneth G. Held (deceased) - AMA President 07
Edward J. Lorenz, FL
Fred W. Megow (deceased)
Ben Shershaw, PA

1981
Mel Anderson
Leroy M. Cox (deceased)
Robert L. Palmer, CA
Louis J. Andrews (deceased)
Edward J. Lidgard, GA

1982
William E. Atwood (deceased)
James Dale Kirn
Joseph S. Ott (deceased)
Edward L. Rockwood
Wally Simmers (deceased)
Stephen Calhoun "Cal" Smith

1983
Maxwell B. (Max) Bassett, CT
Clarence F. Lee
Joseph John Lucas
Dick McCoy
Lee Renaud (deceased)

1984
George M. Aldrich (deceased)
Myrtle Robbers-Coad
George Perryman, GA
Granger Williams and Lawrence Williams (deceased)

1985
Walt Caddell (deceased)
Owen Kampen
Frank Nekimken
Dick Sarpolus
Victor and Joe Stanzel (deceased)

1986
Bill Effinger (deceased)
Dick Everett (deceased)
Paul Guillow (deceased)
Gordon Light
Dan Pruss (deceased)

1987
Frank L. Cummings, Jr.
William C. Hannan
Robert Hatschek
Robert Holland
Walter Musciano
William "Bill" Northrop, CA
William Hewitt Phillips, VA
John Pond (deceased)
Louis Proctor (deceased)
Joseph Raspante (deceased)

1988
Donald Clark (deceased)
Bill Gough
Jim Richmond, FL
Dale Root
Hazel Sig-Hester, IA
Henry A. Thomas, KS
Frank Tlush PA and Charles Tlush (deceased)
Elbert J. (Joe) Weathers
Dolly Wischer, WI

1989
Joseph Bilgri (deceased)
W. L. (Woody) Blanchard, VA
Frank Garcher (deceased)
Earl F. Stahl, VA
Cliff Weirick (deceased) - AMA President 16

1990
Joe Beshar, NY
Paul Boyer, FL
James "Jim" Cahill (deceased)
Carl Fries (deceased)
Milton Huguelet (deceased)

1991
William "Bill" Bishop
Howard Bonner (deceased)
Joseph W. Foster
Don Lowe, FL - AMA President 21
John Tatone

1992
Hurst G. Bowers, VA
Charles Tracy
Earl Witt (deceased) - AMA President 19

1993
Merrick S. "Pete" Andrews (deceased)
Robert A. Champine, VA
Bud Romak, CA
Norman Rosenstock, FL
William Austin Wylam

1994
None

1995
Robert Boucher, CA
Dr. Ralph C. Brooke (deceased)
Vic Cunnyngham
Ed Izzo (deceased)
Frank Hoover

1996
Joseph Bridi, CA
William "Bill" Cannon Jr.
Art Laneau, FL
Dave Platt, FL
Bob Violett, FL

1997
Roy Mayes
Francis McElwee (deceased)
John C. Patton VA - AMA President 17
Robert Underwood, MO
Robert Wischer (deceased)
Neil Armstrong, OH

1998
Bob Aberle, NY
Jack Albrecht, CA
Everet Angus (deceased) - AMA President 05
George Buso, NY
John Grigg (deceased) - AMA President 20
Maxey Hester, IA
Howard E. Johnson (deceased) - AMA President 15
Joe Kovel
Vernon Krehbiel (deceased)
Austin Leftwich
Gerald "Jerry" Nelson, OR
William Netzeband
Frank Parmenter, TX
Len Purdy, GA
Edward Roberts (deceased) - AMA President 03
Art Schroeder, FL
George Steiner, CA
Keith Storey (deceased) - AMA President 09

1999
Arthur Adamisin, MI
Edward Beshar
Roy L Clough Jr.
Robert Dunham (deceased)
John Frisoli (deceased)
C. Leslie Hard, MI
Ronald Morgan, PA
Harold Parenti, IL
Robert Sifleet, PA
Wayne Yeager, MI
Nick Ziroli Sr., NY

2000
Robert Bienenstein, MI
Roland Boucher, CA
Edward Daniel Calkin
Joseph Elgin
Robert Gialdini, WI
Ed Henry, MO
Robin Hunt, PA
George A. Reich, OH
Robert W. Rich (deceased)
Richard J. Sherman, NH
Joe Wagner, AL
LeRoy Weber, CA
Jon Zaic (deceased)

2001
Oba St. Clair (deceased)
Joel Bunch, CA
George Brown, Jr., NY
Fred Reese (deceased)
Stuart Richmond, FL
J. C . Yates, CA
Fred Marks, MD
Francis Reynolds, WA
Peter Waters, MI
Herb Kothe, CO
Jim Alaback, CA

2002
Abram Van Dover, VA
Bob Stalick, OR
Bryant Thompson, CA
Charlie Bauer, IL
Dave Gierke, NY
Howard Johnson, CA (deceased)
Jack Sheeks, IN
John Hunton, VA
Keith Shaw, MI
Mickey Walker, GA
Randy Randolph, TX
Riley Wooten, TX

Appendix C
List of Model Airplane Magazines

Aero Digest, contained model airplane articles starting 1924 through 1932.
Aeromodeller, British magazine with wonderful content, began November 1935 to February 2001.
Air Age, a wartime magazine, the first issue was February 1943, eventually became *Aircraft Age.*
Aircraft Age, c. 1944, *Flying Aces*, *Air Age*, and *Air World* all would be combined by 1948. *Flying Models* absorbed *Air World* in 1945-1948, including *Air Age* in April 1948.
Aircraft Modelworld, scale model plane beginning around 1985.
Air Progress, not much on modeling, some nice covers, edited by C. B. Colby with Bill Winter as associate editor in the 1940s. Harold Stevenson and Cal Smith did covers in the late 1950s and early 1960s.
Air Trails, October 1928-1975 with some years missing. First cover was by Frank Tinsley. In the fall of 1976 to the summer 1979, Challenge Publications put out quarterly issues using reprints from the old issues.
Air Trails, Hobbies for Young Men, began in April 1954 eventually becoming *American Modeler,* around 1957.
American Modeler, see *Air Trails, Hobbies for Young Men.*
American Aircraft Modeler, began around 1957 as *American Modeler*, and went to August 1975. From 1965 to 1975, the AMA used it for their membership publication.
The American Boy began publishing model airplane designs and articles by Merrill Hamberg from January 1927 to 1934. It included news on the AMLA and the first five national contests.
Australian Model Hobbies, Bill Evans started this magazine in the early 1950s.
Aviation Collectors News, middle 1960s bi-monthly publication containing collector news on model engines.
Canadian Boys and Model News, started January 1934.
Cleveland Model Making News and Practical Hobbies, published seven issues, 1933-1934.
Engine Collectors Journal, Tim Dannels started it in 1963; collectors love this magazine.
Flying Aces, October 1928 to April 1944 (no April 1934 issue), due to a printer's error the first issue is identified as Vol.1, No.2.
Flying Age, May 1944 to August 1946.
Flying Age Traveler, one issue in December 1946.
Fly Paper, a bulletin put out by the Metropolitan Model League in August 1936 in the New York City and northern New Jersey area. Registration fee was seventy-five cents.
Flypaper, came out in the early 1950s. I believe this evolved into *Grid Leaks* magazine. It contained articles by John Worth and Paul Runge.
Flying Models, June 1947-present; another of the many faces of *Flying Aces.*
Grid Leaks, Ace R.C. publication October 1957-1966, put out by Paul Runge; edited by Bill Winter in the early to middle 1960s. Paul Runge took over in July 1966, the magazine name changed to *Radio Control World.*
High Flight, official IMAA publication since 1980.
Jr. American Aircraft Modeler, began in 1971 as a companion magazine to AAM.
Mechanix Illustrated included many articles on model airplanes, helicopters, autogyros, boats, and cars by Roy L. Clough Jr., Cal Smith, Bill Winter, and others. Jo Kotula did cover art for this magazine during the war to the late 1940s.
Model Aircraft Engineer, a short-lived magazine, first printed in April 1934; eight issues were printed. Issues are missing from some months.
Model Aircraft World, started in the early 1960s by World Engine distributors.
Model Aircraft, British competitor to *Aeromodeller*, started January 1946 to December 1965, bought by *Aeromodeller.*
Model Aircraft Magazine, March 1942-June 1942, only four issues. Combined with *Model Craftsman* beginning with the July 1942 issue; editor/publisher Charles A. Penn.
Model Airplane News, June 1929-present, no July 1933 issue.
Model Aviation, June 1936-1965, in July 1975 resumed with the bankruptcy of *American Aircraft Modeler.* This is the official publication of the Academy of Model Aeronautics.
Model Aviation Canada, official publication for M.A.A.C.
Model Builder, four issues, from May to August, 1936.
Model Builder, September/October 1971-1995.
Model Craftsman, March 1933, first issue featured a Curtiss Military Helldiver bi-plane. Eventually in 1948-1949 it went full time as a railroad magazine.
Model Engine World, UK publication still being published.
Model News, Australian and New Zealand modeling started by Russ Hammond from 1957-1965.
Model News, an official publication for the Western Associated Modelers; these are hard to find.
Modelers Monthly, Australian, early 1950s to early 1960s.
Monster News, Quarter Scale Association of America, first issue came out in January 1978.
National Free Flight Digest, first issues were circulated at the 1966 Nationals, cover art was done by Ken Johnson. Official publication for the National Free Flight Society.
Popular Aviation, Paul Lindberg was Model editor from February 1934 to December 1940. He is credited with 44 rubber and 14 gas scale model designs in eight short years. Before him, Bertram Pond and Joe Ott were model department heads and are members of the AMA Hall of Fame.
Popular Electronics, Bill Winter was the radio control editor for the first year and a half (October 1954-December 1955).
Popular Mechanics, a long running magazine that included articles on models and a few Jo Kotula covers.
Radio Control Modeller and Electronics, British magazine launched in May 1960 and is still going today.
Radio Modeller, British magazine started January 1966 to February 1998.
RC Report, August 1986 to present
RC Scale Modeler, came out in 1975 and lasted until the mid 1990s.
RC Soaring Digest, 1980s.
RC Sportsman, 1975 to 1980.
Radio Control Modeler, October 1962 to present.
Scale Models, British publication, first issue October 1969; early issues contained radio control models, but it is mostly dedicated to plastic models.
Sig Air Modeler, started in July 1966, Larry Conover was the editor.
Sport Modeler, edited by Bill Winter, 1970s.
Stunt News, 1974 to present, official publication for PAMPA.
The Model Engineer, a weekly British magazine that included engine designs from time to time.
Young Men, 1956, was *Air Trails for Young Men*, and then shortened the name briefly before turning into *American Modeler.* This was just one of many faces of the *Air Trails* magazine.

Resources

Organizations

Academy of Model Aeronautics
5161 East Memorial Drive, Muncie, IN. 47302
www.modelaircraft.org

Federation Aeronautique Internationale
Avenue Mon Repos 24
CH-1005 Lausanne, Switzerland
Email, info@fai.org
www.fai.org

Flying Aces Club
Lin Reiche
3301 Cindy Ln. Erie, PA. 16506
National Contest held in Geneseo, NY.
www.flyingacesclub.net

Frank V. Ehling National Model Aviation Museum
Michael Smith, Curator
765-287-1256, ext 500
michaels@modelaircraft.org
5151 E. Memorial Drive, Muncie, IN. 47302
Rich LaGrange, Librarian
765-287-1256, ext.506 or 800-I-FLY-AMA
www.modelaircraft.org

The Evergreen Aviation Museum
3685 N.E. Three Mile Lane
McMinnville, OR. 97128
503-434-4180, store, 888-9SPRUCE
www.sprucegoose.org

The Internet Craftsman Museum
The Joe Martin Foundation
3235 Executive Ridge, Vista CA. 92083
800-541-0735
Contact, craig@craftsmanshipmuseum.com
www.craftsmanshipmuseum.com
A very nice website featuring model engine designers, tax deductible donations.

Model Engine Collector's Association (MECA)
Woody Bartelt, president
3706 N. 33rd St., Galesburg, MI 49053
Bob McClelland Sec/Tres,
3007 Travis St. Westlake, LA. 70669
337-436-3732, email: mccleb337@aol.com
www.modelengine.org
Dues $25/year, bi-monthly swap sheet

National Free Flight Society, membership office
3317 Pine Timbers Dr.
Johnson City, TN. 37604-1404
Email txtimer@att.net
Bob Stalick, president
5066 NW Picadilly Circle, Albany, OR 97321
541-928-8101
www.freeflight.org

Model Museum in McMinnville, Oregon
Frank Macy, Director and Curator
3182 N.E. Rivergate St., McMinnville, OR 97128
503-435-1916
American Junior Classics, Jim Walker history

Society of Antique Modelers, (SAM)
Tom Mc Coy, President
203 N. Brockfield Drive, Sun City Center, FL 33573
813-634-7749
www.antiquemodeler.org
Dues are $25 for U.S. and $40 for international per year

Western Associated Modelers, (W.A.M.)
Gary Buffon, current secretary
6467 Conlon Ave. El Cerrito, CA. 94530-1612
510-236-7106, Phil Brown's website has a link to their site.

Precision Aerobatics Model Pilots Association, (PAMPA)
Frank McMillan, President
12106 Gunter Grove, San Antonio, TX. 78231
210-492-0243

Shareen Fancher Secretary/Treasurer, (PAMPA)
158 Flying Cloud Isle, Foster City CA. 94404
650-345-0130
www.zianet.com/pampaeditor
Dues, $35 with a nice bi-monthly magazine

Vintage Radio Control Society
Terry Terrenoire
101 Smithfield Dr. Endicott, NY. 13760
www.vintagercsociety.org
Forum, http://groups.yahoo.com/group/VRCS
Dues, $20/year with bi-monthly 20 page newsletter.

Kits and Plans Antiquitous
Morris Leventhal
1788 Niobe Ave., Anaheim, CA 92804
Histories of model airplane companies, trade sheet, dues are $10/year
This organization dedicated kit collecting and model airplane history.

Model Aircraft Museum
311 Baumgarten St.
Schulenburg, TX. 78956
1-979-743-6559
stanzel@fais.net
www.stanzelmuseum.org

Publications

Frank H. Anderson
753 Hunan St. N.E. Palm Bay, FL. 32907-1604
Anderson's Blue Book and *The Golden Age of Model Airplanes, Volumes 1, 2, 3.*
These four wonderful books can be purchased from Frank.

Tim Dannels, Editor
Engine Collector's Journal
P.O. Box 243, Buena Vista, CO. 81211-0243
719-395-8421
ecj@chaffee.net

Jim Dunkin
Model Airplane Engines, Reference Book (.15/2.5cc)
P.O. Box 695
Grain Valley, MO. 64029
816-229-9671
dunkin@discoverynet.com

Flying Models magazine
Carstens Publications
P.O. Box 700, Newton, NJ. 07860
1-800-474-6995
www.flying.models.com

Model Airplane News
P.O. Box 428, Mt Morris, IL. 61054
800-887-5160
www.modelairplanenews.com

Model Aviation, AMA publication
Bob Hunt, aeromodeling editor
5151 E. Memorial Dr. Muncie, IN. 47302.
bobhunt@mapisp.com
610-614-1747
www.modelaircraft.org.

R/C Modeler Magazine
P.O. Box 487, Sierra Madre, CA. 91025
800-523-1736
www.rcmmagazine.com
Most issues are catalogs for everything an R.C. flyer wants.

Stunt News
Tom Morris, editor
327 Pueblo Pass, Anniston, AL. 36206
ctmorris@cableone.net

Collectors and Model Airplane Links

ABE Books
www.abebooks.com
One of the largest websites for books of every kind.

Aeroindex, Mark Fineman
P.O. Box 185124
Hamden, CT. 06518
aeroindex@cox.net
Mark mostly sells on eBay, books, magazines, Aviation related items. However, he will consider requests for items.

Woody Bartelt
3706 N. 33rd Street, Galesburg, MI 49053
616- 665-9693
E-mail: aeroelectric@chartermi.net
Collector, engine builder and parts supplier.

Blackburn Aero Engineering
P.O. Box 15143, Los Altos, CA. 94024
806-622-1657
Engine restoration and rework, hard chrome plating, ignition systems. SASE for catalog

Janet Blair
2105 Boundary St., SE
Olympia, WA 98501
janeteblair@hotmail.com
360-786-5712
Writing, editing, historical research, collecting, and conservation.

Bob Boumstein
10970 Marcy Plaza, Omaha, NE. 68154
402-334-0122
bbhwc@mitec.net
Used engines, buy, sell, and trade.

John J. Brown
13362 Fairmont Way, Santa Ana, CA. 92705
Author of *Model Aviation Bibliography*
Specialist in model aircraft literature, collector.

Brown Only, Jack Van Dusen
189 Centenary Lane, Warminster, PA. 18974
215-672-0608
Brown Jr. engine parts, repair, and rebuild services.

Phil Brown,
Email, philbrown3664155@worldnet.att.net
Largest website on control line to be found anywhere!

Bruan's Antiques and Collectibles
Wayne and Donna Buren
405 Cottonwood Court, Avon Lake, OH. 47150
216-933-5399
LMTWJB@aol.com
Model airplane collectibles, primitive Americana, hobby supplies.
S.A.S.E. and .75 cents for catalog

Collectair, Steve Remington
1324 De La Vina Street, Santa Barbara, CA. 93101
805-560-1323
www.commercemarketplace.com, a nice website
Vintage model and full- scale collectibles, appraisals.

Gil Coughlin
5825 S. Fife St. Tacoma, WA. 98409
253-471-1291
Retired model maker for Boeing, collector, and historian extraordinaire! Gil is the foremost collector of Elf engines in the world.

Dave Day
Email, dd@iroquois.free-online.co.uk
Website, www.iroquois.free.online.co.uk
Aeromodeling website to the world from long time British Modeler.
Large list of control line planes.

Captain Perry R. and Donna M. Eichor, USAF (Ret.)
703 N. Almond Dr. Simpsonville, SC. 29681
864-967-8770
Email, kpmflyn@earthlink.net
Antique aircraft memorabilia, toys, literature and appraisals.

Classic Aircraft Model Engines
http://classicmodelengines.homestead.com
Website showing how to restore model airplane engines
David Lloyd-Jones
www.magazinesandbooks.co.uk
Old British model airplane magazines and books.

Jim Johnson
2105 Boundary St., SE
Olympia, WA 98501
360-786-5712
Email: horsehead@telisphere.com
Collector, builder, and flyer.

Frank Klenk
519-842-8242
Email, fklenk@sympatico.ca
Member of SAM, MAAC, MECA.
Collector and appraiser.

Robert S. Munson
Pathways-Chapter 1- History
www.mindspring.com/~thayer5/pathways/chapter1.html
This website is a treasure trove of information, a good website for kids and adults, many hours of web browsing. Outstanding!

Göran Olsson
Gyllenstiernas vag 20
S-183 56, Taby, Sweden
Email, goran.olsson@alfvenlab
Website, www.plasma.kth.se/~olsson/cl.html
Wonderful control line website, connecting the world.

Gabi Schuhaibar
P.O. Box 1732, Walnut, CA. 91788
Email, toy.tophobby@verison.net
Collector and dealer of model airplane engines, radio gear, RTF planes and other memorabilia.

Bernie Ray - Parts is Parts
6027 W. Ken Caryl Place, Littleton, CO 80128.
Email, burnisr@aol.com
Collector, antique engine parts.

R.C. Web Directory
www.towerhobbies.com
Large website with many links.

Stuka Stunt Works
226 S. 6th Street, Vincennes, IN. 47591
812-895-1476
www.clstunt.com
Control line forum, plans, engines, advice.

Suppliers

Aero Dyne
17244 Darwin Ave. Unit H, Hesperia, CA. 92345
760-948-6334
Ignition engine supplies and repair parts, fuel. Catalog $2.

Aero Electric
3706 North 33rd St. Galesburg, MI. 49053
616-665-9693
Email, aero-electric@worldnet.att.net
Reproduction engines, parts, repairs, engines bought, sold and traded.

Brodak Manufacturing and Distributing Company
100 Park Ave. Carmichaels, PA. 15320
724-966-2726
www.brodak.com
The largest control line model company today!

Campbell Custom Kits, Lee Campbell
P.O. Box 3104, Muncie, IN. 47307
765-289-7753
Email souper30@gte.net
Free flight and modeling supplies, Cox engine parts.

Caswell Inc.
5688 Tellier Rd. Newark NY 14513
315-331-5141
www.caswellplating.com
Engine restoration supplies and electro-plating at home.

Cleveland Model and Supply Company, Inc
P.O. Box 55962
Indianapolis, IN. 46205
317-257-7878
www.clevelandairline.com
Old Time Cleveland Kit Plans Only.

Data Village
#234, 5149 Country Hills Blvd. N.W.
Suite 103
Calgary, Alberta T3A 5K8
Canada
www.DataVillage.com
Collecting software.

Larry Davidson
1 Salisbury Dr. N., East Northport, NY. 11731
631-261-1265
Email, Samffchamp@aol.com
Old time engine supplies, Super Cyclone engines by Apollo.

Davis Model Products
P.O. Box 141, Milford, CT. 06460
203-877-1670
DMPDDD@aol.com
Diesel fuel and conversions, Jet-X.

Tom Dixon
P.O. Box 67166, Marietta, GA. 30066.
(770) 592-3279.
To access his website I go through google and type in his name.
Control line plans, kits, stunt engines, and advice.

EasyBuilt Models
P.O. Box 681744, Prattville, AL. 36068-1744
334-358-5184
Website, www.easybuiltmodels.com

Estes/Cox Industries
Dept. MA, 1295 H Street
Penrose, CO. 81240
www.estesrocket.com
Cox engines and parts.

F.A.I. Model Supply
P.O. Box 366, Sayre, PA. 18840-0366
570-882-9873, $3.00 for catalog
www.faimodelsupply.com
Indoor and outdoor free flight supplies.

Golden Age Reproductions
P.O. Box 1685, Andover, MA. 01810
Nice rubber powered kits (42); $3.00 for their catalog.

Bill Hannan
Hannan's Runway
Email, runway@hrunway.com
Website, www.hrunway.com
Model airplane history and great publications.
Bob Holman Plans
P.O. Box 741, San Bernardino, CA. 92402
Jimmie Allen partial kits and plans.

K&B Model Products
P.O. Box 98, Serria Madre, CA. 91025
www.modelengine.com
MECOA now owns K&B.

A. A. Lidberg Model Plan Service
Al Lidberg
1030 E. Baseline, Suite 105-1074
Tempe, AZ. 85383
480-839-8154
Model designer, old time plans.

Mike McGraw
GCBM R.C. Models, Inc.
5009 Fairdale, Pasadena, TX. 77505
800-609-7951
www.gcbmrc.com
Large old time model airplane kits; Ben Buckle kits.

Model Engine Company of America, (MECOA)
P.O. Box 98, Serria Madre, CA. 91025
www.mecoa.com
Modern old time engines and parts.

Midwest Products Company
400 S. Indiana St. P.O. Box 564
Hobart, IN. 46342
Kits and supplies.

Bill Northrop's Plan Service
2019 Doral Court, Henderson, NV. 89014
702-896-2162
Model Builder magazine plans from 1971-1995.

Penn Valley Hobby Center
837 W. Main St. Lansdale, PA.
www.pennvalleyhobbycenter.com
Authentic reproductions of pre WWII models.

Bill Schmidt
4647 Krueger, Wichita, KS 67220
316-744-0378
Old Time and Classic C/L and FF model airplane plans.

Charles F. Schultz,
910 Broadfields Dr. Louisville, KY. 40207
Earl Stahl Plans, SASE, and $1.00 for a list of plans.

Shilen Aerosports
P.O. Box 1300, Ennis, TX. 75120
972-875-1442
Reproduction antique engines, SAM legal.

Sig Manufacturing Company
Montezuma, Iowa 50171
www.sigmfg.com

Kits and modeling supplies.

Bibliography

Books

Anderson, Frank H. *An Encyclopedia of the Golden Age of Model Airplanes, Volumes 1, 3.* Palm Bay, Florida: Anderson Productions, 1998.
Anderson, Frank H. *Anderson's Blue Book, For This New Millennium*, Palm Bay, Florida: Anderson Productions, 2002.
Brown, John Joseph, *Model Aviation Bibliography*, Anaheim, California: self-published, 2000.
Cooke, David C. and Jesse Davidson. *The Model Airplane Annual 1943*, New York, New York: Robert M. McBride and Company, 1943.
Cuhaj, George, *Standard Price Guide to U.S. Scouting Collectibles*, Iola, Wisconsin: Krause Publishing, 2001.
Grimm, Tom, *The Basic Book of Photography*, New York, New York: Nal Penguin Inc. 1985.
Hubbard, Elbert, *Elbert Hubbard's Scrapbook*, New York, New York: William H. Wise and Company, 1923.
Mackey, Charles, *Pioneers of Control Line Flying.* Anniston, Alabama: Precision Aerobatic Model Pilots' Association, 1995.
Marion, John, and Christopher Andersen. *The Best of Everything: The Insider's Guide to Collecting-For Every Taste and Budget*, New York, New York: Simon and Schuster, 1989.
Marks, Fred M. and William J. Winter. *Radio Control For Model Builders*, Rochelle Park, New Jersey: Hayden Book Company, 1972.
Mathiews, Franklin K. *Flying High*, New York, New York: Grosset and Dunlap Publishers, 1930.
Smeed, Vic, *Model Flying-The First Fifty Years*, London, United Kingdom: Argus Books LTD, 1987.
Smeed, Vic, *The Encyclopedia of Model Aircraft*, London, United Kingdom: Octopus Books Ltd., 1979
Smith, Steven Calhoun, *Cal Smith on Model Building*, Greenwich, Conneticut: Fawcett Publications, 1952.
Shipman, Carl, *Canon SLR Cameras*, H.P. Books, Tucson, Arizona, 1978.
Upton, Barbara and John, *Photography*, Boston, Massachusetts: Little, Brown and Company 1976.
Williams, Guy R. *The World of Model Aircraft*, London, United Kingdom: Chartwell Books Inc. 1973.
Zaic, Frank, *Model Aeronautic Year Book, 1957-58*, Northridge, California: Model Aeronautic Publications, 1958.
Zaic, Frank, *Model Aeronautic Year Book, 1959-61*, Northridge, California: Model Aeronautic Publications, 1961.

Periodicals

Air Trails, "Analyses of High Point Winners, 1949," January 1950, 53-52, 73-75.
Air Trails, " Two Decades of Progress," October, 1948, 28, 102-104.
Air Trails, "2nd International Model Plane Contest," December 1948, 40-43, 97-98.
Air Trails, "5th Internationals," December 1951, 38-41.
Air Trails, "Plymouth's 6th, Internationals," December 1952, 48-52.
Air Trails Model Annual for 1954, "Analyses of Top Place Winners," 52-59.
Alaback, Jim, "Old Timer Topics," *Flying Models*, September 2000, 34-35.
Alaback, Jim, "Old Timer Topics," *Flying Models*, June 2001, 76-77.
Alaback, Jim, "Old Timer Topics," *Flying Models*, July 2001, 44-45.
Alaback, Jim, "O.T. Spark Ignition Engines," *Flying Models*, December 2001, 44-49.
American Modeler, "Berkeley, Where did those kits come from," January 1957, 20, 43).
Boss, Bill, "Control Line Scale" *Model Aviation*, October 2002, 126-127.
Chinn, Peter G.F. *American Aircraft Modeler 1963 Annual*, "Global Engine Review," 36-47, 72-79.
Chinn, Peter G.F. *American Aircraft Modeler 1964 Annual*, "Global Engine Review," 47-55, 58-60.
Chinn, Peter G.F. *American Aircraft Modeler 1966 Annual*, "Global Engine Review," 57-72.
Chinn, Peter G.F. *American Aircraft Modeler 1968 Annual*, "Global Engine Survey-1968," 62-71, 94-95.
Chinn, Peter G.F. "Made in Japan," *Model Airplane News*, November 1956, 28-31.
Chinn, Peter G.F. "Model Motor Museums," *American Modeler*, November 1959, 20-21, 58-59.
Chinn, Peter G.F. "Milestones of Progress, Spark-Ignition Era," *Model Airplane News*, August 1974, 14-16, 50, 52-53.
Chinn, Peter G.F. "Milestones of Progress, Spark-Ignition Era," *Model Airplane News*, September 1974, 14-17, 64-65
Fanelli, Frank, "Left Seat," editorial *Flying Models*, August 2001, 4.
Flying Models, February 1954, 28
Fries, Carl and Black, Dick, "The National Free Flight Society Story," *Model Airplane News*, June 1967, 11, 34.
Gardner, George, "Model Aircraft with a Mission," *Air Trails Hobbies for Young Men*, August 1955, 20-23, 81, 85l
Good, Dr. Walter A., "Walt Good's New Wag," *Air Trails*, April 1954, 42-45l
Hannan, William, "Model Books," *Model Aviation*, April 1982, 33-36, 103-104l
Hannan, William, "Model Books," *Model Aviation*, May 1982, 37-40, 97-98l
Lewis, Al, "Nationals 1947," *Model Airplane News*, August 1947, 12, 66-67l
Maxwell, Hugh, "When Model Airplanes First Went to War," *Model Aviation*, July 1992, 33-36.
Mc Entee, Howard G., "Radio Control Round-up," *Air Trails Annual for 1952*, 68-70.
Mc Entee, Howard G., " Build Your Own Receiver-Transmitter," *Air Trails Annual for 1952*, 71-73, 78. 86-87.
McMullen, Bob, "With Model Builders," *Flying Models*, December 1953, 28, 41.
Model Air Plane News, "Club News, Minnesota" May 1946, 83.
Model Airplane News, " Club News, Oregon" October 1947, 65.
Model Airplane News, "1st International Model Plane Contest," November 1947, 62-63.
Model Airplane News, "1947 Nationals," November 1947, 9-11, 70-72.
Neuberger, Jerry, "Model Aviation Hall of Fame," *Model Aviation*, September 2002, 74-78.
Noll, Bob, "Vintage R.C. Society Reunion," *Model Aviation*, Sept. 2001, 85-88, 93-94.
Norman, Dennis O. "Our Stuff" *Model Aviation*, August 2003, 83-86.
Pond, John, "Plug Sparks," *Model Builder*, December 1989, 104, 106.
Plymouth Motor Corporation, *Plymouth Dealer's Guide Book*, January 1949, 1-22.
Plymouth Motor Corporation, *Plymouth Model Plane News*, Detroit, Michigan, November 15, 1950, 24 pages.
Rinker, Harry, "Rinker on Collectibles," *Antiques and Collectibles Magazine*, February 2002, 26-27.
Root, Dale, "Little Freak 27," *Air Trails Model Annual 1954*, 34-35.
Root, Dale, "Low Ender," *American Aircraft Modeler*, March 1959, 12-14, 40.
Ross, Don, "Jet-X Returns," *Flying Models,* May 2000, 62-65.
Sarpolus, Dick, "75 Years of Model Magazines," *Flying Models*, June 2002, 74-77.
Trumbull, Randall and Haught, Jim, "Simply the Best," *Model Aviation*, May 1999, 10-15.
Temte, Glen and Thor, Bob, "World's Fastest Jet," *Air Trails*, December 1948, 45-47, 99-101.
Wagner, Joe, "The Engine Shop," *Model Aviation*, Sept. 2001, 81-81.
Walters, Bob, "28 to 56, The History of the Nationals," *Flying Models*, November 1956, 8-9, 38.
Wells, George, "AMA Through the Years," *Model Airplane News*, December 1963, 14-15, 34, 37-38.
Winter, William, "Were These The Greatest," *Model Airplane News*, August 1961, 14-15, 43-44, 46.
Winter, William, "Were These The Greatest, Part Two," *Model Airplane News*, September 1961, 20-21, 38-40.
America's Hobby Center catalogs from 1942, 1950, 1954, 1958, 1960, 1962, 1966, and 1969 were used to determine manufacture dates of kits, radio equipment, and accessories.

Index